Institutes of Higher Education (IHE) and Workforce Collaboration for Digital Literacy

Amanda Nelms
Belmont University, USA

IGI Global
Scientific Publishing
Publishing Tomorrow's Research Today

Vice President of Editorial	Melissa Wagner
Director of Acquisitions	Mikaela Felty
Director of Book Development	Jocelynn Hessler
Production Manager	Mike Brehm
Cover Design	Phillip Shickler

Published in the United States of America by
IGI Global Scientific Publishing
701 East Chocolate Avenue
Hershey, PA, 17033, USA
Tel: 717-533-8845
Fax: 717-533-7115
Website: https://www.igi-global.com E-mail: cust@igi-global.com

Library of Congress Cataloging-in-Publication Data

Names: Nelms, Amanda, 1985- editor.
Title: Institutes of higher education (IHE) and workforce collaboration for digital literacy / edited by: Amanda Nelms.
Description: Hershey, PA : IGI Global Scientific Publishing, [2025] | Includes bibliographical references and index. | Summary: "This book aims to collect research, methodologies, and strategies that highlight the collaboration between Institutes of Higher Education and the workforce. This book will impact the research community by highlighting cutting-edge research about removing the silos between IHEs and future employers pertaining to technology integration"-- Provided by publisher.

Identifiers: LCCN 2025000065 (print) | LCCN 2025000066 (ebook) | ISBN 9798337300047 (hardcover) | ISBN 9798337300054 (paperback) | ISBN 9798337300061 (ebook)
Subjects: LCSH: Labor supply--Effect of education on. | Education, Higher. | Technological literacy. | Computer literacy.
Classification: LCC HD5706 .I5975 2025 (print) | LCC HD5706 (ebook) | DDC 331.12--dc23/eng/20250410
LC record available at https://lccn.loc.gov/2025000065
LC ebook record available at https://lccn.loc.gov/2025000066

British Cataloguing in Publication Data
A Cataloguing in Publication record for this book is available from the British Library.

Table of Contents

Detailed Table of Contents

This research explores effective collaboration between higher education institutions and the workforce to bridge the digital literacy gap in an increasingly technology-driven economy. Digital literacy, encompassing a range of competencies beyond basic computer skills, is vital for professional success. However, a significant mismatch persists between the digital skills imparted by educational institutions and those demanded by the workforce, leading to challenges in employment and productivity. Using a mixed-methods approach, the study investigates current digital literacy needs, examines successful collaboration models, and proposes actionable strategies to align curricula with industry requirements. Findings highlight the potential of cooperative digital hubs and integrated work-study programs in fostering job-ready graduates. Recommendations include stakeholder engagement, resource allocation, and policy incentives to enhance collaboration.

The digital divide phenomenon presents a significant challenge in rural vocational schools, where disparities in access to and utilisation of technology can hinder educational opportunities for marginalised individuals. Despite the extensive body of research on the integration of digital technologies in academic settings, there remains a notable deficiency in understanding effective digital literacy practices tailored specifically for vocational education. This study employs resource and appropriation theory to explore the inequalities in technological access and usage within vocational institutions. The investigation identifies four distinct types of digital divides: the physical access divide, the skills access divide, the usage divide, and the network or internet divide. The findings suggest that bridging the digital divide necessitates a collaborative approach involving four critical stakeholders: vocational institutions, industry partners, government agencies, and rural communities, thereby fostering an inclusive environment.

In the rapidly growing world, psychological wellness has turned into a basic issue in both professional and expert settings. Students and employees alike face increasing pressure to perform, often leading to stress, anxiety, and other mental health challenges. As this recognition grows, there is a clear need for stronger collaboration between universities and workplaces to address mental health in a more comprehensive and sustainable way. Collaborative efforts can ensure that mental well-being is supported not just in one phase of life but throughout a person's academic and professional journey. To enhance effective collaboration between universities and the workforce, digital literacy tends to play very crucial role. The integration of technology in education that includes the use of digital tools in classrooms and virtual classrooms engages students and aligns with modern learning objectives. Mental health is an equally important consideration when discussing effective workplace collaboration.

This chapter explores teachers' pivotal role in achieving global and national sustainable development goals, particularly focusing on SDG 4: Quality Education. It emphasizes the importance of valuing teachers' voices in shaping educational reforms, specifically focusing on the 2024 World Teachers' Day theme, "Valuing Teachers' Voices: Towards a New Social Contract for Education". The chapter examines the critical contributions of teachers as societal pillars who shape students' academic abilities and their ethical, moral, and emotional growth. It addresses the global teacher shortage, low salaries, poor working conditions, and lack of professional development, highlighting their impact on recruitment, retention, and educational outcomes. The chapter further explores the unique challenges faced by Bangladesh in teacher recruitment and development and proposes solutions for improving teacher quality, status, and professional empowerment. Ultimately, it calls for a new social

The chapter explores the pivotal role of Massive Open Online Courses (MOOCs) in addressing the digital literacy gap in India, focusing on their potential to enhance both higher education and workforce readiness. Despite India's strides toward becoming a digital economy, disparities between urban and rural digital literacy rates remain significant, with MOOCs providing a scalable and flexible solution to bridge this gap. The chapter highlights how MOOCs, with their open-access model, can democratize education, offering cost-effective and accessible learning options to students from diverse backgrounds. Furthermore, MOOCs align with industry needs by offering up-to-date training in high-demand fields, making them a key tool in preparing students for a rapidly evolving job market. However, the chapter also acknowledges the challenges of MOOC adoption, such as infrastructure limitations and language barriers, and calls for further investment in digital infrastructure and the inclusion of regional languages to maximize their impact.

The development of widely accessible generative AI tools, such as ChatGPT, has significantly impacted education and the workforce. Users have the capability to synthesize information from across the whole internet in seconds, which gives rise to new methods of learning, teaching, and optimizing workflows. The ways in which educators choose to handle this development greatly affects the quality and equity of instruction and learning available to their students, and their preparedness for life after education. This chapter will share research regarding generative AI and educational strategies. This research will be used as the basis for a list of strategies to help implement generative AI tools into the classroom effectively to prepare students for their futures.

Preface

Welcome to *Institutes of Higher Education (IHE) and Workforce Collaboration for Digital Literacy*! The world around us is ever-changing. New technologies are developed every day that require a shift in career readiness competencies. While Institutes of Higher Education, IHEs, are preparing students for their future careers, some careers may be developed while students are undergoing their preparation programs. The workforce is shifting its focus to include careers that rely heavily on digital literacy. Collaboration and connection between IHEs and future employers are essential to prepare university students for their futures.

The World Economic Forum's, *Future of Jobs Report* (2025) highlighted that employers predict that over the next five years (2025-2030) two-fifths of existing skillsets will be invaluable. The report explored that many of the shifts in careers are due to technology enhancements and broadened access to technology. While digital literacy is not specifically mentioned in the report, the skillsets needed for future employees reflect future employees embody digital literacy to be successful on the job.

While many agree that digital literacy is necessary to succeed in future careers, the term digital literacy can be difficult to define. For this book, we will define digital literacy as the skills and thinking related to the use of technology (Kammer & Hays, 2023). Although many of our students in university courses are digital natives, meaning they grew up in environments where technology was always present, digital literacy is a skill that must be explicitly taught with opportunities for application (Erwin & Mohammed, 2022). This book addresses specific digital literacy skills necessary to excel in the future workforce with suggestions for application through collaboration with future employers.

CHAPTER OVERVIEW

In this book, we explore multi-disciplinary, international perspectives about how to enhance digital literacy to prepare students for future careers. The only way to truly prepare students for uncertain futures is through intentional collaboration between IHEs and employers. Individuals who prepare for a digitally literate future, such as university instructors, future employers, and students in programs, will benefit from the authors' stories and suggestions presented in this book.

Chapter 1 begins our book with an opportunity for reflection pertaining to university courses. This chapter suggests that university campuses must have a strong line of communication across colleges to be able to have strong partnerships with the workforce. An overview of existing partnerships and recommendations for sustainability are proposed.

Chapter 2 explores the impact of university-industry partnerships with students' technology skills. This chapter explores the shared benefit of students and the future employers through empirical data analysis related to the impact of academic and industry skills when engaged in experiences in the field. Recommendations regarding course amendments are presented.

Chapter 3 examines the challenges, opportunities, and solutions for addressing the digital literacy gap between higher education graduates and workforce demands. University and workforce recommendations are presented as an opportunity to enhance effective communication as well as recommendations regarding opportunities for scalability of the work.

Chapter 4 expands the conversation about digital literacy to include a community that is often missed: rural settings. Literature pertaining to the current conditions of digital literacy within rural settings is explored, including vocational education. Challenges and solutions are presented with recommendations for sustainable collaboration.

Chapter 5 offers a new perspective on collaboration between the workforce and higher education by exploring potential challenges that may occur within partnerships. An overview of technology integration and mental well-being are explored with recommendations to ensure sustainability and prevent burnout of future employees.

Chapter 6 explores an essential element of sustainability: teacher voices. This chapter emphasizes the critical role of teachers in shaping education systems, fostering societal development. Recommendations to recognize teachers as agents of change are presented.

Chapter 7 begins our exploration into specific tools that are necessary to prepare students to be digitally literate. The chapter examines collaboration between universities and the workforce around the use of AI. A framework is presented to encourage IHE and the workforce to engage in AI training as a vehicle for critical thinking, practical application, and confidence building across both academic and professional contexts.

Chapter 8 highlights the importance of utilizing universities as key stakeholders in the process of collaboration between IHEs and the workforce. An exploration of digital literacy as a driver for academic success, career development, and entrepreneurship are explored with recommendations of how to engage with university librarians to enhance this collaboration.

Chapter 9 explores challenges and opportunities with establishing digitally literacy in different communities. Massive Open Online Courses (MOOCs) are presented as an approach to address digital literacy gaps and enhancing workforce readiness, with a focus on India's context. Recommendations for adoption of MOOCs are presented.

Chapter 10 takes an innovative approach to collaboration between IHEs and the workforce by highlighting the student voice. The chapter presents an overview of literature related to students' use of GenAI in higher education. Recommendations for university instructors and the workforce about digital literacy are presented from a students' point of view.

As the world around is ever-changing, the one consistent competency is that digital literacy is necessary to be prepare for the future workforce. Application of content learned in university courses must be presented in experiences with industry leaders before students graduate. This book presents innovative strategies, lessons learned, and recommendations to transform university coursework to embed digital literacy while sustaining the work through industry collaboration. We hope you enjoy our collaboration to enhance digital literacy.

REFERENCES

Erwin, K., & Mohammed, S. (2022). Digital literacy skills instruction and increased skills proficiency. [IJTES]. *International Journal of Technology in Education and Science*, *6*(2), 323–332. DOI: 10.46328/ijtes.364

Kammer, J., & Hays, L. (2023). *Digital literacy made simple: Strategies for building skills across the curriculum*. International Society for Technology in Education.

World Economic Forum. (2025). *Future of jobs report*. https://reports.weforum.org/docs/WEF_Future_of_Jobs_Report_2025.pdf

Acknowledgments

This book is dedicated to the hardworking authors who shared their valuable time and expertise to further the dialogue surrounding best practices in nurturing a digitally literate generation. Thank you for the countless hours you spent carefully crafting each chapter and revising your work to ensure this work is meaningful. May this work impact and prepare future generations.

Chapter 1
Breaking Down Silos:
Strategies for Collaborative Technology Integration in Higher Education

Menard Musendekwa
https://orcid.org/0000-0002-6644-8727
Reformed Church University, Zimbabwe

ABSTRACT

In order to prepare students for the digital needs of the modern industry, cooperation between higher education institutions and the workforce is crucial. However, these collaborations are frequently hindered by institutional silos, which isolate academic departments and restrict interaction with other stakeholders. In order to promote productive cooperation, this chapter, Breaking Down Silos: Strategies for Collaborative Technology Integration in Higher Education, looks at methods for tearing down these obstacles. The chapter provides a framework for bridging the gap between academia and industry by highlighting technology transfer collaborations, collaborative curriculum creation, and shared professional development. It illustrates sustainable methods of integrating technology that improve digital literacy and equip graduates for changing job demands through qualitative case studies. Thematic analysis will identify key themes, while comparative analysis will evaluate factors influencing technology integration and collaboration.

DOI: 10.4018/979-8-3373-0004-7.ch001

INTRODUCTION

Breaking Down Silos: Strategies for Collaborative Technology Integration in Higher Education

Higher education has never been more important in providing students with the necessary skills in a time of rapid technology advancement and changing industry demands (Brynjolfsson & McAfee, 2014; World Economic Forum [WEF], 2020). Higher education institutions have the responsibility of equipping graduates to function in intricate, technologically advanced surroundings. However, institutional silos frequently impede the achievement of this goal. Effective collaboration and innovation are severely hampered by these silos, which appear as barriers dividing academic departments, restricting interdisciplinary contact, and isolating institutions from external stakeholders (Kezar, 2005; Senge, 2006).

The distance between academics and the workforce exacerbates this issue, producing a gap between the skills graduates possess and the abilities necessary in the modern economy (Jackson, 2019; Marginson, 2016). As industries undergo digital transformation, they demand a workforce that is not only adept in the use of technology but also capable of adapting to new tools and processes (Schwab, 2016). In order to create collaborations that benefit both academics and business, higher education institutions must reconsider how they integrate technology and collaborate with others, tackling both institutional and cultural obstacles (Barrett & Barrett, 2020).

This chapter, *Breaking Down Silos: Strategies for Collaborative Technology Integration in Higher Education*, explores how institutions can overcome these challenges by adopting innovative strategies to dismantle silos and promote collaboration. The chapter focuses on practical strategies for closing the gap between higher education and the workforce by emphasizing technology transfer partnerships, collaborative curriculum design, and shared professional development. It provides insights into developing long-lasting partnerships that improve digital literacy, encourage creativity, and equip students for the needs of a rapidly evolving technological environment by drawing on case studies and best practices.

In the end, this chapter makes the case that dismantling institutional barriers is not only a tactical requirement but also a strategic one for universities hoping to be significant and relevant in the digital era. By working together, colleges and universities can become digital transformation engines and produce graduates who are not just tech-savvy but also ready to take the lead in their professions (Oblinger, 2018; Siemens, 2014).

The objectives of this chapter are:

- To identify the common barriers (silos) that hinder effective collaboration between higher education institutions and the workforce, especially in the context of technology integration.
- To present strategies for breaking down these silos through shared professional development, joint curriculum development, and technology transfer partnerships.
- To highlight best practices and case studies of successful collaboration models that have enhanced digital literacy and technology integration in academic and industry settings.
- To provide actionable recommendations for higher education leaders, faculty, and industry partners to foster more inclusive and impactful technology collaborations.

THEORETICAL UNDERPINNINGS OF INSTITUTIONAL SILOS

Institutional theories that place a strong emphasis on inflexible organizational structures and bureaucratic hierarchies are to blame for the continued existence of silos in higher education. To get beyond these obstacles, Senge's (2006) paradigm for learning companies emphasizes the necessity of collaborative cultures and systemic thinking. Nonetheless, a lot of colleges still follow outdated models that put departmental independence ahead of group objectives (Kezar, 2005). The historical legacy of colonial education institutions, which divided knowledge into strict divisions and opposed cross-disciplinary integration, exacerbate this in Zimbabwe (Nyoni, 2022).

The Impact of Silos on Collaboration and Innovation

Higher education institutions' capacity to handle intricate socioeconomic and technological issues is hampered by institutional silos. Chigona and Chigona (2020) assert that chances for innovation in teaching, research, and community engagement are restricted when academic departments and external stakeholders do not collaborate. In Zimbabwe, where universities are essential in tackling issues like unemployment, underdeveloped technology, and skills shortages, this disconnect is especially troublesome (Mlambo, 2018). According to Barrett and Barrett (2020), silos also hinder the adoption of digital technologies, which necessitate cross-functional cooperation for successful implementation.

Strategies for Breaking Down Silos

The main goals of initiatives to break down silos in higher education have been to promote multidisciplinary cooperation, include outside parties, and use technology to heal divisions. The creation of collaborative curriculum projects that incorporate feedback from various academic fields and business partners is one viable strategy (Oblinger, 2018). To create a more collaborative and results-oriented educational system, for example, teaching, research, community service, innovation, and industrialization are all integrated into Zimbabwe's Education 5.0 framework (Ministry of Higher and Tertiary Education, Innovation, Science and Technology Development [MHTEISTD], 2018). This approach aligns with global trends that emphasize co-creation and partnership-driven higher education models (WEF, 2020). Education 5.0's emphasis on industrialization and community service is closely aligned with South Africa's White Paper for Post-School Education and Training, which highlights knowledge production that promotes social and economic development (Department of Higher Education and Training [DHET], 2013). Similar to Education 5.0's focus on research and industrialization, China's Double First-Class initiative aims to develop world-class universities and disciplines by combining teaching, research, and innovation to increase global competitiveness (Ministry of Education of the People's Republic of China).

Furthermore, in line with the co-creation approach of Education 5.0, Finland's Education Policy places a strong emphasis on industry-university collaboration to promote innovation and entrepreneurship (Finnish Ministry of Education and Culture, 2019). These parallels highlight a global movement in higher education toward integrated, innovation-driven approaches that put societal benefit first.

Initiatives like the innovation hub at the Zimbabwe University of Science and Technology (NUST) have shown how these kinds of partnerships may propel scientific and economic advancement in Zimbabwe (Musvoto, 2021).

Role of Digital Platforms in Promoting Collaboration

Digital platforms have the capacity to revolutionize higher education by promoting collaboration. Siemens (2014) points out that implementing collaborative tools and learning management systems (LMS) can aid in bridging the gap between academic departments and outside stakeholders. The importance of digital ecosystems in developing integrated learning environments that facilitate interdisciplinary teaching and research has been emphasized by IGI Global scholars (Barrett et al., 2021). Despite financial and infrastructural obstacles, Zimbabwe has seen increased connectivity between teachers, students, and outside partners because of the use of digital platforms like Moodle and Google Workspace (Chikwature et al., 2019).

Addressing Cultural and Structural Barriers

Addressing both structural and cultural impediments is necessary to dismantle silos. According to Kezar and Holcombe (2017), leadership is essential in creating a collaborative culture because it fosters trust and a common goal. University administrators in Zimbabwe have been urged to implement participatory governance models, which enable students and faculty to participate in joint decision-making (Nyoni, 2022). Targeted training and capacity-building programs are also necessary to overcome cultural concerns like reluctance to change and a lack of digital literacy (Mlambo, 2018).

In higher education, dismantling silos is a complex task that calls for systemic change, creative thinking, and ongoing cooperation. Institutions can promote cooperation and innovation by overcoming structural and cultural hurdles through the use of digital platforms, interdisciplinary approaches, and technology transfer agreements. The Education 5.0 framework offers Zimbabweans a viable starting point for incorporating technology and encouraging teamwork. However, in order to establish long-lasting, significant partnerships, legislators, educators, and industry stakeholders will need to work together to accomplish these goals.

LITERATURE REVIEW

Technology integration is essential for improving teaching strategies, enhancing student learning, and expediting administrative tasks in higher education institutions. But the widespread presence of siloed systems, in which divisions and departments function independently, frequently hinders productive cooperation and the smooth integration of new technology. This study of the literature explores the difficulties presented by these silos and looks at current tactics meant to promote a cooperative atmosphere that supports effective technology integration.

Understanding Silos in Higher Education

In higher education, silos are divided departments or administrative divisions that operate autonomously with little data sharing or interaction across departments. Ineffectiveness, duplication of effort, and a fragmented approach to accomplishing institutional goals result from this fragmentation (Vygo, 2023). Departmental silos limit information flow, which makes it more difficult to make well-informed decisions and detracts from the overall student experience (Wang & Wang, 2023). Implementing strategic interventions aimed at breaking down barriers and fostering a collaborative culture is necessary to address these issues (Kezar, 2018).

Assessing the Current State

Performing a thorough evaluation of current institutional arrangements and their effects is a crucial first step in tackling silos. In order to identify obstacles to collaboration, this method include obtaining feedback from students, teachers, and staff via surveys, interviews, and data analysis (Kezar & Holcombe, 2017). Institutions can obtain qualitative input on culture dynamics that impede interdepartmental collaboration as well as quantitative data on workflow inefficiencies by using a mixed-methods approach (Jones et al., 2021). Along with identifying organizational bottlenecks, this thorough evaluation also identifies areas for resource optimization and strategic alignment (Klein & Lester, 2020).

Additionally, by assessing the current situation, leadership can comprehend the particular difficulties that are particular to the organization, including clashing departmental priorities or different data systems (Noblitt et al., 2022). By including students, professors, and staff in the transformation process, it also promotes stakeholder involvement by lowering resistance to future interventions and creating a sense of ownership (Kezar, 2018). Ultimately, this diagnostic stage serves as the basis for focused interventions, guaranteeing that rather than using general tactics, solutions are customized to the institution's circumstances (Baker & Baldwin, 2015).

Developing a Unified Vision and Plan

Establishing a compelling vision that places a high value on collaboration and innovation is necessary to align institutional efforts toward common goals. According to Kezar (2018), this strategy comprises creating a vision that all stakeholders can support, setting measurable goals, and creating thorough plans that outline the steps, roles, and resources required to achieve these goals. A distinct vision serves as a framework for direction, helping businesses manage complex organizational changes and motivating stakeholders to work together to achieve shared objectives (Kotter, 2014).

Effective communication of this vision is essential for departmental coordination of effort and stakeholder buy-in (Rowley & Sherman, 2020). Leaders must employ a variety of communication channels, such as town hall meetings, newsletters, and digital platforms, to consistently convey the vision and its strategic importance (Hughes et al., 2019). According to Kouzes and Posner (2017), involving stakeholders in the visioning process also boosts commitment and ownership, which reduces resistance to change and enhances teamwork.

To reinforce the vision, organizations should establish measurable objectives and key performance indicators (KPIs) that track progress and provide responsibility (Bolman & Deal, 2017). By routinely assessing and revising their strategic plans, institutions can preserve their adaptability and reactivity to evolving educational settings (Mintzberg et al., 2020). By aligning departmental goals with the overarching vision, higher education institutions can eliminate organizational silos and foster a creative and cooperative culture (Boland & Phillips, 2019).

Fostering a Collaborative Culture

Breaking down silos in higher education institutions requires fostering an atmosphere that prioritizes cooperation over rivalry. Leadership commitment is the first step in this cultural transition, as university officials actively support cross-departmental efforts and set an example of collaborative behavior (Kezar & Holcombe, 2017). By publicly expressing the importance of cooperation and cultivating an inclusive atmosphere where a range of viewpoints are valued and included, leaders can significantly influence the atmosphere for collaboration (Kouzes & Posner, 2017).

Promoting the creation of interdisciplinary programs, including classes and research initiatives that call for departmental cooperation, cultivates a cooperative culture and improves the educational experience for students as a whole (Frost et al., 2020). By combining several knowledge bases, these programs not only close gaps between academic disciplines but also foster innovation (Jones et al., 2021). Additionally, creating virtual and physical collaboration spaces encourages instructors, staff, and students to engage and share ideas, which fosters a sense of belonging and purpose (Baldwin & Chang, 2020).

Faculty and staff can be encouraged to participate in cross-functional initiatives by putting in place recognition and incentive programs that value teamwork (Bolman & Deal, 2017). The value of cooperation is reinforced by incentives like chances for professional growth, monetary compensation, or public recognition at institutional functions (Rowley & Sherman, 2020). Furthermore, offering venues for exhibiting fruitful teamwork can motivate others and foster a supportive corporate culture focused on cooperation and common objectives (Hughes et al., 2019). Higher education institutions can successfully demolish silos, improve communication, and establish a more unified learning environment that is in line with strategic goals by integrating collaboration into the institutional culture (Kezar, 2018).

Implementing Integrated Systems and Processes

Breaking down silos in higher education institutions requires investing in technology that makes communication and information exchange easy. Adopting unified learning management systems (LMS), which enable centralized delivery of course materials, student tracking, and assessment administration across departments, is one crucial strategy (Bates, 2020). By simplifying access to educational resources and enabling effective feedback loops, these systems improve collaboration and communication among administrators, instructors, and students (Kirkwood & Price, 2020).

Together with LMS systems, collaborative tools like Microsoft Teams and Slack let instructors, staff, and students communicate and work together in real time, overcoming departmental barriers and promoting cross-functional interaction (Martin & Liao, 2020). Within a single integrated digital environment, these tools let team members from many disciplines to work together efficiently on projects, exchange ideas, and oversee activities (Björk, 2021).

Platforms for data integration are also essential for facilitating access to and exchange of data across departments. By ensuring that information about administrative tasks, institutional procedures, and student achievement is centrally located, these systems facilitate data-driven decision-making and remove duplications brought on by dispersed data storage (Nash & Allen, 2020). According to Yuan and Ma (2019), integrated systems facilitate communication, lower barriers brought about by disjointed procedures, and increase overall institutional efficiency. By coordinating technological tools with institutional objectives and encouraging a united approach to technological adoption, they also aid in the development of coherent strategies for technology integration (Garrison & Kanuka, 2020).

Higher education institutions can improve their capacity for productive collaboration, well-informed decision-making, and, eventually, the development of an environment conducive to innovation by investing in integrated systems and platforms (Kezar & Holcombe, 2017).

Empowering and Training Staff

Offering staff members professional development opportunities that emphasize communication, teamwork, change management, and technology proficiency gives them the tools they need to collaborate effectively and guarantees that they can help the organization integrate new technologies (Kezar, 2018). Faculty and staff can better adapt to technological changes and create a more cohesive work environment by participating in workshops, seminars, and online training modules (Hughes et al., 2019). In addition to improving employees' ability to collaborate across departments, these programs foster a culture of ongoing learning that encourages creativity and the adoption of best practices (Bennett et al., 2020).

Staff members must receive change management training in particular to help them deal with the challenges of organizational changes and technology transformation (Kotter, 2014). In order to facilitate smoother transitions and increased use of collaborative technologies, institutions should lessen resistance to new systems and procedures by offering the tools necessary to comprehend and manage change (Fullan, 2020). Furthermore, staff members who participate in training programs that emphasize technology proficiency—such as the use of Learning Management Systems (LMS), data integration tools, and collaborative platforms like Slack or Teams—build the digital fluency necessary to effectively utilize these tools (Kirkwood & Price, 2020).

Initiatives for continuous learning enable staff members to adopt innovative methods of operation, which is essential for creating a culture that actively aims to dismantle organizational silos (Bates, 2020). Additionally, professional development gives staff and faculty members the chance to exchange ideas, best practices, and information across departments, strengthening networks of cooperation (Hughes et al., 2019). Institutions can promote the long-term sustainability of technological efforts and organizational performance by investing in staff development, which also improves their ability to incorporate technology collaboratively and effectively (Garrison & Kanuka, 2020).

Establishing Cross-Functional Teams

By fostering a feeling of shared purpose and bridging gaps between units, the formation of cross-functional teams comprising people from different departments promotes greater cohesion within the organization (Kezar, 2017). These teams foster innovation and improve institutional effectiveness by bringing together people with various backgrounds and viewpoints. These teams' diversity of viewpoints not only promotes innovative problem-solving but also makes it easier to create more thorough and flexible answers to institutional problems (Frost et al., 2020). When these teams collaborate, they use their diverse backgrounds and expertise to tackle complicated problems, guaranteeing that the solutions are comprehensive and appropriate for many institutional contexts (Bohm & Smith, 2019).

Additionally, by lowering the departmental silos that frequently impede cooperation, cross-functional teams are essential in promoting knowledge exchange across departments. It is simpler to coordinate departmental efforts with the institution's broader objectives when knowledge and skills are integrated, enabling a more comprehensive approach to strategic planning and decision-making (Lesser & Prusak, 2020). Cross-functional teams ensure that resources are used more effectively and that activities are carried out in a coordinated way by minimizing duplication of effort (Edmondson, 2018). According to Katzenbach and Smith (2015), these teams also promote a collaborative problem-solving culture in which team members are urged to cooperate in order to find shared answers. This helps to create a more upbeat and welcoming corporate culture.

In conclusion, creating cross-functional teams can be a potent tactic for improving communication, encouraging creativity, and guaranteeing more effective operations in institutions of higher learning (Kezar & Holcombe, 2017).

Measuring Progress and Celebrating Success

Metrics like the quantity of interdisciplinary projects or increases in operational effectiveness must be tracked in order to assess the effectiveness of programs meant to dismantle organizational silos in higher education (Kezar & Holcombe, 2017). These indicators offer concrete proof of the effectiveness of teamwork, assisting institutional leaders in determining where advancements have been achieved and where additional support might be required (Kirkpatrick, 2019). By regularly evaluating these indicators, the organization can modify its plans and concentrate on areas that need more care, guaranteeing that initiatives to promote cooperation and integrate departments stay in line with institutional objectives (Bryson et al., 2019). For example, monitoring the results of collaborative projects or cross-functional teams can yield important information on how well teamwork works to accomplish common goals (Kezar, 2018).

Sharing success stories and celebrating accomplishments are equally important ways to emphasize the importance of teamwork. Stakeholders are encouraged to keep working toward integration when accomplishments are acknowledged and shared throughout the organization (Bennett et al., 2020). Publicly praising accomplishments creates a feeling of pride and motivates teachers and staff to realize the advantages of teamwork. It also serves as an example of best practices that can motivate future projects (Parker et al., 2021). Institutions foster a culture where collaboration is consistently valued by commemorating achievements and exhibiting the observable outcomes of cross-departmental work, further integrating it into institutional practice (Kirkwood & Price, 2020).

Challenges and Considerations

Even with the strategic methods that have been described, there are still a number of obstacles to breaking down silos in higher education institutions that call for careful thought and focused actions. Cultural resistance, which occurs when deeply rooted customs and traditions oppose change, is one of the main challenges. New collaboration approaches may make faculty and staff feel intimidated because they fear losing their standing or autonomy within their departments (Kezar & Holcombe, 2017). Careful change management is required to overcome this resistance, and this includes stakeholder participation, transparent communication, and the provision of incentives that support institutional objectives (Kotter, 2014). Additionally, in order to foster an atmosphere where change is viewed as a chance for development rather than a disruption, leadership must set an example of teamwork and highlight the advantages of integrated systems (Fullan, 2020).

Another major obstacle to the smooth integration of systems and processes is the disparity in technology between departments. The successful adoption of integrated systems, such Learning Management Systems (LMS) or collaboration platforms like Microsoft Teams and Slack, might be hampered by disparities in technological infrastructure and differing degrees of technological competency (Kirkwood & Price, 2020). Targeted training programs are crucial to addressing these discrepancies because they help employees acquire the digital literacy they need to use technology efficiently (Kezar, 2017). To guarantee that every department has access to the resources and assistance required to close these technology gaps, resource allocation must also be taken into account (Bates, 2020).

Furthermore, there are serious data security issues when integrating data across departments. Concerns about data protection, privacy, and adherence to laws like the General Data Protection Regulation (GDPR) may surface as information is sent across units (Bryson et al., 2019). To guarantee that data sharing is carried out safely and that departments adhere to institutional and legal data privacy laws, strong governance frameworks are essential (Lesser & Prusak, 2020). Establishing explicit data security procedures must be a top priority for institutions, and they must guarantee that personnel are properly trained to comprehend and apply these procedures.

In addition to strategic planning, addressing these issues calls for constant leadership dedication and review of cooperative methods (Edmondson, 2018). While modifying tactics as needed to accommodate changing demands, leaders must continue to be committed to creating an atmosphere that supports integration. In order to guarantee that silos continue to disintegrate and that technology and data integration is both safe and effective, institutions must also routinely evaluate the success of their joint initiatives.

In higher education, dismantling organizational silos is a difficult but necessary task for improving teamwork and successfully incorporating technology. Institutions can generate settings that are conducive to innovation by evaluating existing structures, creating shared visions, encouraging collaborative cultures, putting integrated systems into place, empowering employees, forming cross-functional teams, and tracking results. A more integrated and effective educational environment will result from addressing the underlying difficulties with strategic planning and dedication. Breaking down silos will be essential to accomplishing strategic goals and preserving a competitive edge in the digital era as higher education develops further.

METHODOLOGY

This study adopts a literature review and qualitative case studies to investigate strategies for breaking down silos and fostering collaboration through technology integration in higher education institutions. Three case studies will be analyzed: a public university with siloed structures, a private university with successful integration, and a cross-national comparison of institutions from different socio-political contexts. Data will be collected through document analysis, including institutional reports, strategic plans, and internal communications, to understand the strategies, challenges, and successes in each institution. Thematic analysis will be used to identify key themes and patterns, and a comparative analysis will be conducted to assess the factors that contribute to effective technology integration and cross-departmental collaboration. Ethical considerations will ensure that all data is handled responsibly, with confidentiality and privacy maintained. This approach aims to provide insights into best practices for overcoming silos and successfully integrating technology in higher education.

IDENTIFYING INSTITUTIONAL SILOS AND BARRIERS TO COLLABORATION

Analysis of the Root Causes of Silos in Higher Education and Their Impact on Technology Integration

In higher education, the division of departments, faculties, or administrative divisions that function autonomously with little cooperation is referred to as institutional silos. This cultural and structural phenomena frequently results in reluctance to change, decreased innovation, and inefficiencies, particularly when it comes to integrating technology.

Root Causes of Silos

1. Structure of the Organization. Siloed settings are fostered by bureaucratic and hierarchical systems. Prioritizing their objectives causes departments to compete for resources and disregard cross-functional cooperation (Ncube et al., 2020). Decision-making procedures may become slower and less adaptable to institutional challenges as a result of this rigidity.
2. Barriers based on culture Silos are made worse by the lack of a cohesive institutional culture. Because they have different interests, professional identities, and values, faculty and administrative staff may be resistant to working together

(Chiweshe, 2022). Additionally, past conflicts between administrative and academic divisions might exacerbate mistrust and impede collaborative efforts.

3. Allocation of Resources. When departments compete for few resources, they frequently protect their budgets and equipment. This makes it more difficult to create interconnected systems and share platforms (Muchineripi et al., 2023). Cross-departmental initiatives are hampered and inequality is made worse by resource differences between well-funded and impoverished departments.
4. Insufficient Common Vision. Departments are unable to coordinate toward shared objectives when an institution lacks a clear, institutional-wide vision for technology integration. Fragmentation is encouraged by this misalignment (Sithole, 2023). When long-term technology goals are not strategically planned for, the result is frequently disorganized and fragmented efforts.
5. Technological Difficulties. Collaboration across units is difficult due to incompatible technologies or a lack of centralized systems. Communication and workflow coordination are hindered by the lack of common platforms (Machingura, 2022). These difficulties may also be made worse by antiquated infrastructure and a lack of technical know-how.

Impact on Technology Integration

When separate technological solution development within an organization results in inefficiencies and redundancies, duplication of effort occurs. For example, several departments may purchase comparable software without taking interoperability into account, which could lead to resource waste and disjointed systems. Uncoordinated technology purchase frequently results in overlapping systems that lower operational performance and raise maintenance costs, claim Subramanian and Gunasekaran (2021). An institution's capacity to create a unified technology ecosystem—which is necessary for optimizing workflows and improving user experiences—is compromised by this lack of coordination.

Institutional problems are made worse by unequal access to technology. Disparities that disadvantage particular student cohorts are frequently caused by different departments' differing degrees of access to resources. For instance, Zheng et al. (2020) found that students from disadvantaged backgrounds may face barriers due to unequal access to technology infrastructure, hence exacerbating the digital divide in educational institutions. These disparities undermine the idea of equal opportunity for all students by maintaining a lack of consistency in educational experiences. Institutions run the danger of alienating some segments of their student base and jeopardizing the inclusion of their programs if they don't address these inequities.

Another serious problem that results from a lack of cooperation is resistance to adoption. Departments may perceive new systems as invasive or unrelated to their particular requirements if institution-wide technology efforts are implemented without enough participation and consultation. New technologies are less effective as a result of this lack of support. The significance of stakeholder engagement in technology adoption is emphasized by Rogers' Diffusion of technologies theory (2003), which highlights that people and groups are more likely to embrace technologies that fit with their perceived needs and values. Technology rollouts encounter major obstacles without cooperation, such as low user involvement and skepticism.

Furthermore, by restricting options for knowledge-sharing and multidisciplinary solutions, siloed workplaces inhibit creativity. Since it frequently produces new viewpoints and creative solutions, interdisciplinary collaboration is crucial for creative problem-solving. According to Chesbrough's (2003) open innovation model, an institution's ability to create ground-breaking ideas is improved when knowledge is shared across boundaries. Silos, on the other hand, limit the flow of ideas and greatly reduce the possibility of revolutionary breakthroughs. Institutions that place a high priority on dismantling organizational silos and encouraging interdisciplinary cooperation frequently experience improved innovation and greater flexibility in response to new problems.

A systemic strategy that places a high value on cooperation, equity, and shared governance in the processes of technology adoption and innovation is needed to address these issues. In order to effectively drive change, strategic frameworks like Kotter's Change Model (2012) stress the significance of forming alliances, formulating a vision, and enabling stakeholders. To reduce effort duplication, provide fair access, overcome opposition, and realize the full potential of multidisciplinary innovation, institutions must promote an environment of transparency and shared accountability.

Examples from Diverse Disciplines and Institutional Contexts

1. STEM departments at several Zimbabwean universities frequently use cutting-edge technology, but they don't work along with the humanities or social science departments. This restricts how technical discoveries can be applied across disciplines to address larger societal issues (Chigumira, 2021). For example, social science research could greatly benefit from advanced data analytics technologies utilized in STEM, yet they are still inaccessible because of silos.
2. Inefficient student record management and financial procedures result from the widespread use of separate software by registrars, finance departments, and academic faculties, which is known as administrative silos (Moyo, 2023).

Services for students, such fee reconciliations or enrollment confirmations, are frequently delayed as a result of these inefficiencies.

3. Technology integration in community projects often fails due to a lack of collaboration between academic departments and community development offices. For example, ICT initiatives in rural schools could benefit from interdisciplinary approaches involving education, sociology, and computer science departments. A collaborative approach could ensure sustainability and greater impact in these communities.
4. The Zimbabwe Open University, a pioneer in online learning, has encountered difficulties incorporating technology into its several faculties. The full use of e-learning platforms has been impeded by silos in administrative and curriculum creation procedures (Kurebwa, 2022). These difficulties show that a more unified institutional approach is required.
5. Research shows that institutional silos are a global problem rather than just a problem in Zimbabwe. For example, a research by Smith and Jones (2021) highlights the necessity for centralized IT governance and cross-departmental collaboration, revealing similar obstacles in integrating technology in U.S. and European colleges. Furthermore, effective models from these areas teach us how to break down silos by using shared decision-making processes and inclusive leadership.

Shared Professional Development as a Strategy for Breaking Down Silos

A cooperative approach to dismantling institutional walls and promoting ties across academics, business, and other domains is shared professional development, or PD. This method promotes knowledge sharing, skill development, and shared learning, which benefits the growth of teachers, staff, and students. Institutions that adopt shared professional development initiatives foster a culture of continuous learning that benefits all parties involved, foster cross-disciplinary collaboration, and provide chances to incorporate industrial practices into academic curricula.

CASE STUDIES OF SUCCESSFUL SHARED PROFESSIONAL DEVELOPMENT MODELS

The University of Melbourne's Industry Partnerships Program

One excellent example of incorporating business people into the university's professional development programs is the University of Melbourne's Industry Partnerships Program. Faculty and industry professionals collaborate to create and present workshops and seminars, giving academic staff members a better understanding of how their research and teaching are used in the real world. Through the facilitation of a dynamic exchange of expertise between academia and industry, this strategy has demonstrated success in providing students with more relevant learning experiences and richer course content (University of Melbourne, 2023).

By including business experts into the university's professional development programs, the University of Melbourne's Industry Partnerships Program successfully dismantled organizational silos. The program promoted a dynamic interchange of ideas and viewpoints by encouraging academic members to work together with industry specialists to create and present workshops and seminars. This method closed the gap between theoretical knowledge and real-world experience while also improving academic staff's comprehension of the practical applications of their research and instruction. As a result, students gained from more pertinent learning opportunities and enhanced course material, emphasizing the importance of multidisciplinary cooperation and lessening the conventional gap between academics and business.

Stanford University's Faculty-Industry Collaboration Initiative

Stanford University has established a number of cooperative initiatives aimed at fostering relationships between academics and business executives. The Faculty-Industry Collaborative Research Program is one such initiative that matches academics with business executives to work together on cooperative research initiatives. These partnerships produce cutting-edge research and curriculum that take into account the most recent advancements in the business. This initiative's success stems from its double advantages: industry partners have access to academic expertise, while academics are exposed to real-world difficulties and developing trends (Stanford University, 2024). Stanford has established itself as a leader in closing the gap between academics and industry by forging solid, win-win partnerships.

Through the development of deep connections between academics and industry leaders, Stanford University's Faculty-Industry Collaborative Research Program successfully dismantled organizational silos. The program promoted a two-way flow of ideas and knowledge by matching academics with business executives to work together on cooperative research projects. Through this partnership, industry partners were able to take advantage of state-of-the-art academic knowledge while simultaneously providing academics with an opportunity to interact with real-world issues and new trends in the sector. Consequently, the program generated creative research and curriculum revisions that take into account the most recent developments in business. By removing conventional barriers, this deliberate blending of academia and business fostered a mutually beneficial culture of learning. As a result, Stanford has emerged as a pioneer in closing the knowledge gap between academia and business, showcasing the effectiveness of cross-sectoral, cooperative.

The University of Toronto's Cross-Disciplinary PD Workshops

Faculty, staff, and outside specialists from a range of fields can participate in a series of professional development courses offered by the University of Toronto. These workshops concentrate on improving teaching methods, honing research techniques, and addressing new developments in the field of education. The initiative promotes knowledge sharing and cross-disciplinary collaboration by uniting diverse stakeholders. Industry professionals are exposed to state-of-the-art academic research that can guide their practices, while faculty members gain from exposure to industry perspectives (University of Toronto, 2023). This model places a strong emphasis on the value of cross-sector learning opportunities and comprehensive professional development.

Through its professional development program, which unites academics, staff, and outside experts from a range of subjects, the University of Toronto successfully dismantled silos. The program promoted interdisciplinary cooperation and knowledge sharing by providing workshops centered on improving teaching strategies, honing research techniques, and investigating new developments in education. This method gave faculty members access to industry viewpoints and a deeper comprehension of practical applications, while enabling industry experts to interact with state-of-the-art academic research and inform their practices with the most recent insights. The program highlighted the importance of cross-sector collaboration by fostering an atmosphere of shared learning and comprehensive professional development by bridging the gap between academia and industry (University of Toronto, 2023).

DISCUSSION OF FACULTY-INDUSTRY TRAINING AND MENTORSHIP PROGRAMS

Bridging the Gap Between Academia and Industry

Programs for mentorship and training between faculty and industry are essential for bringing academic procedures into line with corporate norms. These programs guarantee that teachers stay current with new trends, technology, and best practices that they can use to their instruction by integrating industry viewpoints into faculty development. For example, faculty receive advice on research commercialization, curricular innovation, and the practical application of academic knowledge through mentorship programs with industry leaders. By giving students knowledge and abilities that are directly related to their future occupations, this kind of training improves the relevance of academic curriculum and gets them ready for the workforce (Brown, 2022).

Collaborative Training Initiatives

Faculty and industry professionals working together in collaborative training programs provide a forum for mutual learning and knowledge sharing. Joint workshops, training sessions, and cooperative research projects are a few examples of these activities. An aircraft firm and a university's engineering department, for instance, could collaborate to produce curricula that take advantage of the most recent technological developments in the sector. In addition to helping academics better understand industry demands, these programs give business executives access to scholarly research that may help them innovate in respective domains (Green & Harris, 2023). These training programs contribute to the development of an educational ecosystem that is more responsive and interconnected.

Mentorship Programs for Faculty Development

Faculty members can interact with industry mentors who can offer advice on curriculum creation, research possibilities, and career promotion through mentoring programs, which are a crucial part of shared professional development. For instance, to work together on research projects and keep up with market developments, environmental studies professors can be matched with mentors from renewable energy firms. Faculty members can then impart their knowledge to professionals in the business, resulting in a win-win situation. These mentorships help teachers create more innovative, relevant curricula and improve connections between academia and business (Williams, 2024).

The Role of Professional Associations in PD

By giving academics and business professionals a place to connect, work together, and exchange best practices, professional groups can play a significant role in promoting shared professional development. Professional associations conduct conferences, workshops, and webinars that facilitate meaningful interaction between academic and industrial stakeholders on subjects like research trends, pedagogy, and new concerns. Participating in these events allows industry people to access the research and knowledge found within academic institutions, while faculty members are exposed to the most recent advances in the industry (Johnson & Lee, 2022). These gatherings encourage a culture of lifelong learning and career advancement.

One effective tactic for dismantling academic and industry silos is shared professional development. Initiatives that incorporate industry ideas into faculty development programs have been successful, as evidenced by case studies from universities such as the University of Toronto, Stanford University, and the University of Melbourne. By giving faculty practical experience that improves teaching methods and student outcomes, faculty-industry training and mentorship programs further solidify these ties. Universities can maintain their leadership position in academic and industry innovation by investing in shared professional development, which will ultimately benefit students, faculty, and the community at large.

Joint Curriculum Development and Technology Transfer Partnerships

Universities and businesses must work together on curriculum development and technology transfer projects to make sure that academic programs continue to be in line with the changing demands of the labor market. These collaborations make it easier for academic institutions and the business community to share technology and expertise, allowing them to jointly develop curricula that take advantage of industry norms and the most recent developments in technology. Through the development of increased digital literacy and the provision of pertinent skills, these partnerships not only improve students' employability but also better prepare them for the workforce (Harrison et al., 2019; McHenry et al., 2021). By bridging the gap between academia and business, these collaborations guarantee that graduates have the technical skills needed in today's labor market.

Models of Co-Designed Curricula and Technology Partnerships Between Universities and Industries

Co-Designed Curricula

Universities and industry partners work together to create co-designed curricula, which guarantee that the material is in line with the latest workforce demands, technological advancements, and industry trends. In order to ensure that the academic experience is influenced by demands from the real world, this strategy frequently involves industry personnel directly contributing to course design, delivery, and evaluation methods. Universities might collaborate with IT firms, for example, to provide courses that use the newest coding languages, software tools, and industry-standard techniques. Industry partners receive access to a pool of graduates who are ready to fulfill the particular knowledge and skill requirements of the profession in exchange (Cox & Sims, 2022).

Including internships, real-world projects, or industry-led seminars in the curriculum is one way to replicate this kind of cooperation. This method gives students firsthand experience with real-world issues and aids in the development of practical abilities that employers desire. For instance, a university and a tech company could collaborate to develop a computer science program where students work on real-world projects that tackle the company's problems. This would guarantee that students graduate with both academic knowledge and real-world experience (Taylor & Hall, 2023).

Technology Transfer Partnerships

Partnerships for technology transfer between academic institutions and business sectors entail the sharing of research findings, technological advancements, and expertise. These collaborations make it easier for academic research to be commercialized, transforming creative concepts into goods or services that businesses may utilize. Joint ventures, cooperative research collaborations, and intellectual property licensing are some ways that technology might be transferred.

Enhancing digital literacy is a significant function of technology transfer. Universities make sure that their students are exposed to cutting-edge technologies by working with sectors that are at the forefront of technological breakthroughs. For instance, in order to improve students' digital literacy and prepare them for professions in a technology-driven economy, colleges may work with technology companies to include new tools, software, or programming languages into the curriculum (Murphy & Liu, 2022). These collaborations also inspire students to participate in startup incubators and other entrepreneurial endeavors where they can use their skills to develop new firms and technology.

CASE STUDIES DEMONSTRATING THE IMPACT OF THESE PARTNERSHIPS ON STUDENT OUTCOMES AND DIGITAL LITERACY

Case Study: The University of California, Berkeley and Cisco

Cisco Systems and the University of California, Berkeley collaborated to create a curriculum centered on cybersecurity and network technology. Berkeley donated academic knowledge of networking and security protocols as part of the collaboration, while Cisco supplied teaching materials like software tools and industry insights. The program gave students the chance to engage with real-world technologies, which improved their abilities in a field that is evolving quickly.

Graduates of the program reported better employability rates in cybersecurity and network management professions, demonstrating the curriculum's strong impact on student outcomes. Additionally, by giving students practical experience with the newest tools and technology utilized by professionals in the sector, the curriculum improved students' digital literacy. This instance emphasizes how crucial co-designed courses are to ensuring that students have employable, in-demand skills while also educating them for the workforce (University of California, 2023).

By combining academic knowledge with business insights, the partnership between Cisco and the University of California, Berkeley successfully dismantled organizational silos and created a curriculum for network technology and cybersecurity. The collaboration closed the gap between academic study and real-world application by fusing Cisco's software tools and industry insights with Berkeley's extensive understanding of networking and security standards. Students were able to work with state-of-the-art technology utilized by professionals in the sector thanks to this co-designed approach, which improved their digital literacy and gave them employable skills. Graduates saw increased employability rates in network management and cybersecurity positions as a result, proving the program's ability to match academic instruction with business demands. This instance demonstrates the importance of cross-sector cooperation in developing memorable learning opportunities that equip students for the changing workforce.

Case Study: The University of Cambridge and Microsoft

In order to improve its courses in data science, artificial intelligence (AI), and cloud computing, the University of Cambridge partnered with Microsoft on technology. Microsoft contributed software, materials, and knowledgeable presenters as part of this partnership, and Cambridge teachers incorporated these resources into their lessons. Additionally, the cooperation made it easier for students and professors to collaborate on research projects that addressed challenging issues in cloud computing and artificial intelligence.

Students' digital literacy was significantly impacted by this partnership. By incorporating Microsoft's Azure cloud platform into the curriculum, students were able to experience cloud computing firsthand, which is a crucial skill for many contemporary employment markets. The collaboration greatly increased students' employability in fields including software engineering, data science, and artificial intelligence research by exposing them to cutting-edge technology and enhancing their preparedness for careers in tech industries (Cambridge University, 2023).

Through the integration of state-of-the-art technological resources with academic training in data science, artificial intelligence (AI), and cloud computing, the collaboration between the University of Cambridge and Microsoft successfully dismantled silos. Incorporating Microsoft's tools, instructional resources, and knowledgeable guest lecturers into their curriculum allowed Cambridge professors to close the gap between theory and practice. Additionally, this partnership enabled teachers and students to work together on collaborative research projects that tackled challenging issues in cloud computing and artificial intelligence. Students had practical experience using Microsoft's Azure cloud platform, which improved their digital literacy and equipped them for contemporary employment markets. In domains such as software engineering, data science, and artificial intelligence research, students' employability was greatly enhanced by their exposure to industry-standard technologies. The collaboration serves as an example of how academic institutions and business may work together to dismantle conventional educational silos and create a learning environment that meets the changing needs of the computing industry.

Case Study: Queensland University of Technology (QUT) and IBM

IBM and Queensland University of Technology (QUT) in Australia have teamed up to create and execute a collaborative curriculum in fields like blockchain, quantum computing, and artificial intelligence. As part of the collaboration, IBM researchers and QUT academics collaborated to create and teach innovative courses. QUT professors used IBM's cloud infrastructure and artificial intelligence tools into their course offerings, while IBM supplied the technology resources.

As a result of the collaboration, students' digital literacy significantly improved as they worked on projects that were pertinent to the industry and had access to the newest technology platforms. Additionally, program participants expressed greater confidence in their capacity to use theoretical knowledge to address practical issues. The reputation of QUT as a pioneer in generating highly qualified graduates with knowledge of cutting-edge technologies has been bolstered by this cooperative approach (Queensland University of Technology, 2023).

By fusing academic knowledge with cutting-edge technological resources, the collaboration between Queensland University of Technology (QUT) and IBM successfully dismantled organizational silos and created a cooperative curriculum in cutting-edge areas like blockchain, quantum computing, and artificial intelligence. The project helped to close the gap between theory and practice by bringing together IBM researchers and QUT academics to jointly develop and teach cutting-edge courses. QUT professors used IBM's advanced cloud infrastructure and AI capabilities into their lectures, allowing students to engage with state-of-the-art technological platforms. In addition to improving students' digital literacy, this method increased their self-assurance in using abstract ideas to solve practical problems. Furthermore, the relationship established QUT as a pioneer in generating highly qualified graduates who are adept in cutting-edge technologies, demonstrating the power of cross-sector collaborations in dismantling conventional educational silos.

Case Study: The University of Melbourne and PwC

PwC and the University of Melbourne have collaborated to create a curriculum that combines digital transformation with business consultancy. PwC specialists provide students with insights into how technology is influencing the business world through guest lectures and course design. Students also take part in actual case studies where they collaborate with PwC experts to use digital technology to solve business problems.

Better student achievements, especially in the areas of digital literacy and problem-solving abilities, are a clear result of this collaboration. Data analytics, machine learning, and digital marketing platforms are among the technologies that students get firsthand exposure with in the consulting sector. In addition to giving students the tools they need to succeed in consulting positions, this hands-on experience deepens their awareness of how companies employ technology to spur creativity (University of Melbourne, 2023).

Through the integration of academic learning with practical business consulting methods, the partnership between PwC and the University of Melbourne successfully dismantled silos. The collaboration helped close the gap between academic understanding and practical application by including PwC experts into guest lectures and course design. In authentic case studies, students collaborated with PwC professionals to use digital technologies to address business problems. Through hands-on exposure with industry-relevant tools like data analytics, machine learning, and digital marketing platforms, this experiential learning method improved students' digital literacy and problem-solving abilities. The relationship not only educated students with the competencies needed for consulting professions but also promoted a greater knowledge of how technology drives innovation in the corporate sector. This strategy demonstrates how cross-sector cooperation may effectively dismantle conventional educational silos and equip students to meet the ever-changing demands of the industry.

In conclusion, students gain a lot from collaborative curriculum development and technology transfer collaborations between academic institutions and business, such as improved employability, better job preparation, and increased digital literacy. These partnerships guarantee that educational programs stay in line with business demands and give students modern, useful skills. Incorporating industry-driven content and real-world experiences into curricula greatly improves student outcomes and helps close the gap between academia and industry, as shown by the case studies of UC Berkeley and Cisco, the University of Cambridge and Microsoft, QUT and IBM, and the University of Melbourne and PwC.

BEST PRACTICES AND RECOMMENDATIONS FOR HIGHER EDUCATION LEADERS

Leaders in higher education are essential in helping institutions navigate the challenges of digital transformation and cultivate productive partnerships with business partners. The success and sustainability of higher education institutions depend heavily on the incorporation of technology, the establishment of cooperative relationships, and the creation of long-term change management strategies as educational environments change. The following lists doable tactics for encouraging cooperation, improving technology integration, and establishing long-lasting alliances. It also provides helpful advice on how to get past change aversion and develop a common vision for digital transformation.

Actionable Strategies for Fostering Collaboration, Enhancing Technology Integration, and Creating Sustainable Partnerships

Promote Cross-Disciplinary Collaboration

The promotion of cross-disciplinary initiatives is one of the best ways to promote collaboration in higher education. Universities can establish a setting where faculty, staff, and students from various disciplines work together on projects, research, and curriculum design by dismantling the conventional academic silos. Interdisciplinary academic programs, cooperative research endeavors, and collaboration grants can all support these efforts. A university can, for instance, establish a center for digital innovation where academics from the humanities, business, and engineering departments can work together to develop technology answers to pressing issues. In addition to encouraging creativity, this method gets pupils ready for the increasingly multidisciplinary nature of contemporary workplaces (Friedman, 2021).

Integrate Technology Across the Curriculum

Instead of treating technology as a stand-alone subject, universities should incorporate it into every facet of the curriculum to improve technological integration. This entails incorporating technical competencies into all subject areas in addition to utilizing digital technologies for instruction and learning. For example, data analysis, digital research tools, and online collaboration platforms can all be used into humanities classes. Institutions should spend money on educating faculty members on how to use these resources efficiently. This can be done by providing workshops, certification courses, and peer mentorship. Higher education administrators may make sure that technology integrates seamlessly into the curriculum and enhances the learning environment for students by providing teachers with the required training and tools (Bates, 2020).

Establish Sustainable Industry-Academic Partnerships

Building long-lasting relationships between academic institutions and business is essential to closing the knowledge gap between academia and practical applications. To guarantee that curriculum stay relevant to the demands of the labor market both now and in the future, higher education officials should place a high priority on establishing long-term collaborations with leaders in the sector. These collaborations can take many different forms, such as co-designed curriculum, internships, and cooperative research projects. In order to develop new technology, services, or business models, universities can also establish innovation hubs or incubators where staff and students collaborate with corporate partners. In addition to improving the standard of instruction, these collaborations give students practical experience, which improves their employability after graduation (Feldman, 2022).

Foster a Culture of Innovation and Lifelong Learning

Maintaining the digital transformation in higher education requires an innovative and lifelong learning culture. By encouraging academics and students to adopt new ideas and technologies, leaders may create a culture that values experimentation and creativity. Institutional policies that support faculty members' ongoing professional development, investments in cutting-edge facilities, and encouragement of entrepreneurial endeavors can all help to foster this culture. Universities can also incorporate chances for experiential learning, like invention challenges or hackathons, to assist students in applying their knowledge in dynamic, real-world settings. Furthermore, by providing online learning opportunities and micro-credentials, schools can stay relevant in the quickly evolving digital landscape while giving students flexible options for skill development (Bolliger & Wasilik, 2020).

PRACTICAL STEPS FOR OVERCOMING RESISTANCE TO CHANGE AND BUILDING A SHARED VISION FOR DIGITAL TRANSFORMATION

Engage Stakeholders Early and Often

The active participation of all stakeholders—faculty, staff, students, administrators, and industry partners—is necessary for the successful digital transformation of higher education. Engaging stakeholders early in the process by outlining the benefits and vision of digital transformation is one of the first things leaders should do. Focus groups, town halls, and surveys that ask the academic community for opinions can all be used to achieve this. In addition to encouraging buy-in, involving stakeholders guarantees that the transformation process is inclusive, enabling the evaluation of many viewpoints. To supervise the transformation process and guarantee that all opinions are heard, leaders can also form task groups or committees with representation from different departments (Kotter, 2012).

Provide Support and Training for Faculty and Staff

Lack of knowledge or confidence in utilizing new technologies is frequently the root cause of resistance to change. Higher education administrators should fund extensive staff and faculty support and training initiatives in order to combat this. In addition to creating a peer support network where faculty members may exchange best practices and gain knowledge from one another, this entails offering resources like workshops, tutorials, and one-on-one training sessions. Early adopters who embrace digital transformation and use their success stories to motivate others should also be honored and celebrated by leaders. This strategy shows that the organization is dedicated to assisting its employees during the transformation process and fosters a positive attitude toward change (Madsen, 2023).

Create a Clear and Shared Vision for Digital Transformation

Leading the organization through the challenges of digital transformation requires a compelling and well-defined vision. In order to create a common vision that complements the institution's values, objectives, and strategic priorities, leaders in higher education must collaborate with important stakeholders. The long-term advantages of digital transformation, such better student results, better teaching and learning opportunities, and closer ties to the workforce, should be outlined in this vision. Leaders should make sure that everyone in the organization understands their part in realizing this vision by communicating it in a clear and consistent manner. Furthermore, setting short-term objectives and acknowledging minor victories can support momentum and show advancement toward the bigger objectives (Westerman, Calméjane, Ferraris, & Bonnet, 2014).

Address Concerns and Build Trust

Fear of the unknown or worries about how the digital transition may affect long-standing habits are common causes of resistance to change. Leaders in higher education must take proactive steps to allay these worries by encouraging candid dialogue, outlining the transformation's objectives in detail, and providing assurances about workload expectations and job security. Establishing trust via openness and compassion is crucial, as is proving a dedication to staff and faculty members' professional development. Additionally, leaders should recognize that the shift to digital transformation will be a process and that obstacles and failures are a normal part of any change endeavor. Leaders can reduce opposition and increase trust in the transformation process by creating a supportive atmosphere (Fullan, 2016).

Leverage Data to Guide Decision-Making

The secret to a successful digital transformation in higher education is data-driven decision-making. Leaders should use institutional data to monitor developments, pinpoint problems, and improve tactics. Feedback from stakeholders, faculty use of digital tools, and student performance measures are a few examples of this data. Higher education leaders may make sure the transformation process is evidence-based and responsive to the institution's needs by using data to guide their decisions. To keep the process on course and in line with institutional objectives, the digital transformation strategy should be regularly evaluated and modified in light of data insights (Brynjolfsson & McAfee, 2014).

In conclusion, developing durable relationships, improving technology integration, and encouraging cooperation are essential tactics for leaders in higher education negotiating the challenges of digital transformation. By encouraging interdisciplinary cooperation, incorporating technology into all subject areas, and building enduring relationships with business, academic institutions can guarantee that students have the abilities required to succeed in the digital era. Clear communication, staff and faculty support, and a common transformational vision are also necessary to overcome opposition to change. Higher education leaders can lead successful digital transformation projects that improve learning outcomes and get students ready for the workforce of the future with the help of these best practices and doable tactics.

To meet the demands of the modern workforce and make sure that students are ready for the future, higher education institutions must adapt, innovate, and work together in this quickly changing digital context. In order to support the digital growth of higher education and workforce alignment, it is crucial to dismantle silos and promote collaboration. This conclusion summarizes the main ideas and strategic conclusions discussed throughout the debate.

Summary

Adopting new technology is only one aspect of higher education's digital growth; another is bringing about a structural change in the way institutions function, work together, and educate students for a world that is becoming more and more digital. Important takeaways from the conversation include:

Institutions of higher learning are no longer separate entities. Universities must develop alliances with businesses, governmental organizations, and other academic institutions if they want to prosper in the digital age. Co-designed curricula, faculty-industry training, and cross-disciplinary collaboration are crucial tactics for maintaining the alignment of workforce demands and academic programs (Friedman, 2021). Industry relationships guarantee that academic programs are created with a forward-thinking, practical approach while also giving students the chance to obtain practical experience.

Incorporating technology into every subject is crucial to preparing students for the digital workforce. In addition to providing students with specialized technical skills, universities must promote digital literacy in a variety of subject areas. Institutions may guarantee that graduates are knowledgeable about the instruments and technologies that power the modern economy by integrating technology into faculty development and curricula (Bates, 2020). Technology integration is a fundamental part of the educational process, not an add-on.

Creating long-lasting collaborations is essential for organizations looking to be competitive and relevant, not just a fad. Trust, reciprocal advantages, and a common goal are essential for the long-term viability of industry-academic collaborations. Leaders in higher education must make sure that these partnerships are sustainable, advantageous to both parties, and flexible enough to adjust to future developments in the labor market and technology (Feldman, 2022). These collaborations may result in joint curriculum development, creative research initiatives, and employability-boosting student internship possibilities.

The prevalence of silos—isolated departments, disciplines, and administrative systems that impede collaboration and integration—often constitutes the biggest obstacle to innovation in higher education. Universities must break down these barriers and promote cross-functional cooperation if they are to effectively embrace digital transformation. Aligning technical solutions with industrial and academic demands might be facilitated by forming interdisciplinary teams to collaborate on digital transformation projects. Organizations are more likely to succeed in their digital transformation if they adopt a culture of cooperation and candid communication (Kotter, 2012).

A normal reaction to the uncertainty that comes with digital transformation is resistance to change. Concerns must be addressed by leaders by cultivating an environment of openness, trust, and cooperation. For transitions to go smoothly, professors and staff must have access to sufficient training, tools, and opportunity to interact with new technologies. To overcome resistance and guarantee that faculty, staff, and students are all working toward the same goals, it can be helpful to develop a shared vision for digital transformation that involves all stakeholders (Madsen, 2023).

The workforce of the future will need a wide range of abilities, including soft skills like flexibility and critical thinking in addition to technological know-how. Institutions of higher learning must constantly assess and modify their courses to satisfy the dynamic demands of the labor market. This flexibility can be attained through providing chances for lifelong learning, incorporating developing technology into academic curricula, and fostering close relationships with business partners

(Brynjolfsson & McAfee, 2014). The relationship between workforce demands and higher education is dynamic and needs to be continuously improved.

REFLECTION ON THE IMPORTANCE OF BREAKING DOWN SILOS TO SUPPORT THE DIGITAL EVOLUTION OF HIGHER EDUCATION AND WORKFORCE ALIGNMENT

In addition to increasing internal efficiency, dismantling higher education silos is a crucial step in making sure that establishments can adapt to the needs of the digital economy. Collaboration, creativity, and agility are hampered in higher education by silos, whether they are across departments, disciplines, or even between faculty and administration. Since society's issues and opportunities are rarely limited to a single topic or area of expertise, these barriers become more and more unworkable in the digital age. Higher education institutions can better prepare students for a workforce that emphasizes cross-functional teamwork, digital fluency, and interdisciplinary thinking by cultivating a collaborative culture.

Additionally, dismantling silos makes it possible for universities to better meet the demands of business. A workforce that is not just technically proficient but also able to adapt, develop, and work together across many domains is needed as industries change and embrace digital transformation. Universities that foster faculty-industry partnerships, incorporate industry ideas into curriculum design, and offer hands-on learning opportunities guarantee that students graduate with the abilities and know-how required to succeed in the digital workforce. These partnerships also give industry partners the chance to have an impact on academic programs, guaranteeing that learning outcomes closely match the demands of the future labor market and new trends (Bolliger & Wasilik, 2020).

Another effective strategy for dismantling silos in higher education is the incorporation of technology into every facet of the institution. The smooth exchange of information, concepts, and resources across administrative and academic borders is made possible by digital platforms, learning management systems, and collaborative tools. By encouraging the sharing of best practices, increasing efficiency, and promoting transparency, these tools help to further cultivate a collaborative culture. Easy collaboration between academics, students, and industry partners speeds up the digital transformation process and results in more inventive, responsive, and relevant learning environments.

To sum up, dismantling silos is crucial to developing a flexible, resilient, and creative higher education system that can handle the demands of the digital era. Higher education administrators can make sure that their institutions continue to be competitive, relevant, and successful at preparing students for the workforce by encouraging cross-disciplinary collaboration, incorporating technology into the curriculum, and building long-lasting business collaborations. Higher education is continuously evolving digitally, and success in the years to come will depend on one's capacity to dismantle obstacles, promote teamwork, and adjust to change.

RECOMMENDATIONS FOR HIGHER EDUCATION LEADERS

Higher education administrators must take a proactive stance that encourages cooperation, incorporates technology, and creates long-lasting relationships in order to successfully negotiate the difficulties of workforce alignment and digital transformation. A thorough road map for leaders in higher education institutions to establish an atmosphere that supports digital progress and aligns with workforce demands is provided by the following doable tactics and realistic actions.

1. Fostering Collaboration Across Disciplines and Sectors. In order to break down silos and make sure that academic programs are in line with the changing needs of the workforce, cooperation between academics, business, government organizations, and other educational institutions is crucial. Leaders in higher education must give top priority to initiatives that promote multidisciplinary research and industry-academic collaborations. The following steps are suggested in order to do this:
    - **Create Collaborative Platforms**: Establish online discussion boards or physical spaces where scholars, students, and business executives may communicate, share resources, and collaborate to create solutions for urgent problems. Collaborative spaces promote a culture of co-design and cross-disciplinary research by facilitating the exchange of ideas and innovations (Chesbrough, 2020).
    - **Encourage Interdisciplinary Curricula**: Develop curriculum that span many subjects and include practical skills. In order to offer interdisciplinary courses that demonstrate how various areas are interconnected in the modern labor market, faculty members should be encouraged to collaborate (Sullivan & Glance, 2022). This method will ensure that students have a thorough understanding of complex issues, which is necessary for success in a labor market that is changing.
    - **Promote Faculty-Industry Engagement**: It is important to encourage faculty members to take part in industry-sponsored research projects, cooperative curriculum development, and mentorship programs. These interactions offer valuable information about the current and future

needs of the workforce, which helps to keep academic courses up to date and relevant (Sanders et al., 2021).

2. Enhancing Technology Integration Across All Disciplines. Technology should be at the forefront of the higher education transformation. Incorporating digital tools, platforms, and resources into the curriculum improves learning outcomes, increases student engagement, and prepares graduates for a labor market driven by technology. To achieve seamless technology integration, the following strategies are suggested:
    - **Invest in Digital Infrastructure**: Ascertain that educational institutions has the technological infrastructure required to facilitate digital learning, such as fast internet, digital library access, and online collaboration tools. Faculty and students can collaborate virtually and access the resources they require for professional and academic growth when a strong digital environment is provided (Bates, 2020).
    - **Provide Professional Development for Faculty**: Provide chances for continuous professional development that emphasize digital literacy and the efficient use of educational technology. To successfully incorporate technology into their instruction, faculty members need to possess both technical expertise and pedagogical knowledge (Fisher et al., 2021).
    - **Adopt Hybrid Learning Models**: Promote the use of hybrid learning approaches, which blend online and in-person training. Students can benefit from hybrid models' increased flexibility, ability to adapt to different learning methods, and access to worldwide knowledge. Additionally, these models guarantee that students acquire digital skills, which are becoming more and more important in the workplace (Garrison & Vaughan, 2013).
3. Building Sustainable Industry-Academic Partnerships. For academic programs to be in line with workforce demands, industry and higher education institutions must form long-lasting relationships. These collaborations can promote the co-design of curricula and open doors for experiential learning, internships, and co-ops. It is advised to take the following actions to create enduring, mutually beneficial partnerships:
    - **Establish Clear Partnership Objectives**: Clearly state the objectives and standards of industry-academic partnerships. Whether it's research projects, workforce preparedness, or curriculum creation, both partners should have a common vision for the partnership's results. Establishing these goals early on will help guarantee that everyone is committed to the partnership's success (Bryson et al., 2017).
    - **Integrate Real-World Experiences into Curriculum**: Collaborate with business partners to incorporate practical case studies, projects,

and internships into educational initiatives. In addition to making education more relevant, this gives students worthwhile experience that improves their employability after graduation (Dyer & Ward, 2020).
- **Establish Continuous Feedback Loops**: Provide systems for ongoing industry and academic feedback to make sure that curriculum are adapting to the shifting demands of the labor market. Institutions can improve the relevance of their academic programs and develop them with the support of important inputs from regular meetings, surveys, and focus groups with industry partners (Harrison & Brown, 2019).

4. Overcoming Resistance to Change and Building a Shared Vision. One of the most frequent problems encountered when executing digital transformation projects in higher education is resistance to change. Leaders must create a common future vision and involve all stakeholders in the transformation process in order to overcome this resistance. The following doable actions are advised:
   - **Engage Faculty and Staff Early in the Process**: Engage staff and academics in the planning and decision-making stages of the digital transformation process. Giving staff and faculty members the chance to voice their opinions and concerns encourages a sense of ownership and lessens resistance to change (Kotter, 2012).
   - **Provide Incentives and Recognition**: Faculty members who adopt new technologies, help build curricula, or participate in industrial partnerships should be rewarded and acknowledged. Faculty participation in digital initiatives is encouraged and a culture of continual development is fostered by praising and rewarding creativity and teamwork (Madsen, 2023).
   - **Offer Training and Support**: A lack of trust in new technologies or procedures is frequently the cause of resistance to change. Faculty and staff can overcome their worries and become more prepared to embrace new tools and methods by receiving specialized training programs and continuing technical assistance (Christensen et al., 2020).
   - **Communicate the Benefits Clearly**: Make certain that everyone involved is aware of the advantages of the digital transition, including for teachers, students, and the institution overall. Clearly explain the ways in which digital tools can expedite administrative procedures, increase teaching and learning, and make institutions more competitive in the global educational market (Jisc, 2021).
5. Promoting Lifelong Learning and Adaptive Skill Development. The need for those who can constantly adapt and pick up new abilities is increasing as the workforce changes. Institutions of higher learning must support the development

of adaptable skills in both professionals and students, and they must embrace the idea of lifelong learning. The following tactics are advised:

- **Develop Lifelong Learning Programs**: Provide professionals and students with adaptable, modular learning opportunities so they can advance their abilities over the course of their careers. Certifications, micro-credentials, and quick courses centered on cutting-edge technology and abilities might all be part of these programs (Selwyn, 2020).
- **Integrate Soft Skills into Curricula**: Success in the modern industry requires not only technical talents but also soft skills like problem-solving, critical thinking, and teamwork. Incorporate these abilities into curricula to guarantee that graduates are well-rounded and flexible enough to adjust to changes in the labor market in the future (Barton & Hart, 2018).
- **Partner with Professional Development Organizations**: Work together with businesses and associations for professional development to give students chances for lifelong learning and career advancement. According to Brynjolfsson and McAfee (2014), these collaborations can provide students with networking opportunities, conferences, and certificates that improve their employability.

In conclusion, leaders in higher education may promote cooperation, improve technological integration, and create enduring alliances that match workforce demands with academic programs by implementing five doable tactics. When put into practice, these suggestions will help higher education's digital transformation while also equipping graduates for success in a global labor market that is becoming more complicated and changing quickly.

REFERENCES

Ahmad, N.S., Ismail, A. and Yaakob, M.N., (2024). A decade of progress: A bibliometric analysis of research trends in professional development for middle leaders in education (2014-2023). *Journal of Contemporary Social Science and Education Studies (JOCSSES) E-ISSN-2785-8774, 4*(2), pp.225-247.

Alangari, H. (2024). Transforming Learning: The Rise of Micro-Credentials in Higher Education. In *Digital Transformation in Higher Education, Part A* (pp. 83-100). Emerald Publishing Limited.

Bailey, P. M. (2017). Thank you for being late: An Optimist's Guide to Thriving in the Age of Accelerations. *Perspectives on Science and Christian Faith, 69*(4), 250–252.

Baker, V. L., & Baldwin, R. G. (2015). *Leading academic change: Vision, strategy, transformation*. Johns Hopkins University Press.

Baker, V. L., & Baldwin, R. G. (2015). A case study of liberal arts colleges in the 21st century: Understanding organizational change and evolution in higher education. *Innovative Higher Education, 40*(3), 247–261. DOI: 10.1007/s10755-014-9311-6

Baldwin, K. E. (2020). *Preservice Teacher Engagement in Science and Mathematics Practices within Research Settings*. Illinois State University.

Baldwin, R. G., & Chang, D. A. (2020). Collaborative spaces in higher education: The role of physical and digital environments in facilitating teamwork. *Journal of Higher Education Policy and Management, 42*(3), 345–360.

Barrett, P., & Barrett, L. (2020). Modern higher education: Technology and collaboration challenges.

Barrett, P., Chigona, W., & Chigona, A. (2021). *Digital ecosystems in higher education: Opportunities and challenges*. IGI Global.

Barton, A. M. (2021). Teaching Lawyers to Think Like Leaders: The Next Big Shift in Legal Education. *Baylor Law Review, 73*, 115.

Barton, M., & Hart, M. (2018). Soft skills for success in the digital workplace: Bridging the gap between education and employment. *Journal of Educational Technology, 29*(3), 125–137.

Bates, A. T. (2020). *Teaching in a digital age: Guidelines for designing teaching and learning*. Tony Bates Associates Ltd.

Bennett, D., Lemoine, J., & McDonald, C. (2020). Fostering professional development in higher education: Supporting faculty, staff, and administrators through continuous learning. *Journal of Educational Leadership*, *32*(2), 112–126.

Bennett, N. J., Katz, L., Yadao-Evans, W., Ahmadia, G. N., Atkinson, S., Ban, N. C., Dawson, N. M., de Vos, A., Fitzpatrick, J., Gill, D., Imirizaldu, M., Lewis, N., Mangubhai, S., Meth, L., Muhl, E.-K., Obura, D., Spalding, A. K., Villagomez, A., Wagner, D., & Wilhelm, A. (2021). Advancing social equity in and through marine conservation. *Frontiers in Marine Science*, *8*, 711538. DOI: 10.3389/fmars.2021.711538

Björk, L. (2021). Collaborative technologies for higher education: Bridging departments and silos. *International Journal of Educational Technology*, *17*(3), 290–306.

Björk, M., Eklund, A., Skyvell Nilsson, M., & Nyman, V. (2024). The collaborative and professional boundary challenges from a bottom-up perspective: An insider action research study on a hospital ward. *Journal of Health Organization and Management*, *38*(9), 389–406. DOI: 10.1108/JHOM-03-2023-0093 PMID: 39620901

Bohm, A., & Smith, C. (2019). Collaborative problem-solving in higher education: Insights and strategies for cross-functional teams. *Journal of Higher Education Collaboration*, *25*(3), 201–213.

Boland, R. J., & Phillips, N. (2019). *Managing as designing*. Stanford University Press.

Bolliger, D. U., & Wasilik, O. (2020). The role of technology in supporting student engagement and learning: An overview of best practices. *Journal of Educational Technology*, *17*(1), 24–35.

Bolman, L. G., & Deal, T. E. (2017). *Reframing organizations: Artistry, choice, and leadership* (6th ed.). Jossey-Bass. DOI: 10.1002/9781119281856

Brand, J. E. (2023). *Overcoming the odds: The benefits of completing college for unlikely graduates*. Russell Sage Foundation.

Brown, A. (2022). Industry-academic partnerships in higher education: Bridging the gap for future workforce development. *Journal of Higher Education Collaboration*, *15*(3), 123–137.

Brynjolfsson, E., & McAfee, A. (2014). *The second machine age: Work, progress, and prosperity in a time of brilliant technologies*. W. W. Norton & Company.

Bryson, J. M., Crosby, B. C., & Bloomberg, L. (2019). *Public administration: The state of the art*. Routledge.

Bryson, J. M., Crosby, B. C., & Stone, M. M. (2015). Designing and implementing cross-sector collaborations: Needed and challenging. *Public Administration Review*, *75*(5), 647–663. DOI: 10.1111/puar.12432

Bryson, J. M., Crosby, B. C., & Stone, M. M. (2017). Designing and implementing cross-sector collaborations: Needed and operational guidelines. *Public Administration Review*, *77*(5), 673–684.

Cambridge University. (2023). *University of Cambridge and Microsoft partnership in data science and AI*. Retrieved from https://www.cam.ac.uk/partnerships

Castaneda, G. 2024. *Considerations for Clinicians Working With Bisexual Military Populations in Mental Health Settings* (Doctoral dissertation, Alliant International University).

Change, E. (2001). Leading in a Culture of Change.

Chesbrough, H. (2003). *Open Innovation: The New Imperative for Creating and Profiting from Technology*. Harvard Business Review Press.

Chesbrough, H. (2020). *Open innovation: The new imperative for creating and profiting from technology*. Harvard Business Press.

Chew, E., & Majeed, A. P. A. (Eds.). (2024). *Fostering Women's Engagement in STEM Through Education: A Cross-cultural Academic-industry Journey*. CRC Press. DOI: 10.1201/9781003514626

Chigona, A., & Sosibo, L. (2024). Research and postgraduate supervision during the coronavirus-19 pandemic: Lessons learned. *South African Journal of Higher Education*, *38*(1), 42–61. DOI: 10.20853/38-1-6281

Chigona, W., & Chigona, A. (2020). Challenges and opportunities of integrating ICT in African universities. *The African Journal of Information Systems*, *12*(2), 101–121.

Chigumira, E. (2021). *Interdisciplinary approaches to technology in higher education in Zimbabwe*. University of Zimbabwe Press.

Chikwature, W., Munodawafa, D., & Maphosa, C. (2019). Integration of ICT in teaching and learning in Zimbabwean universities. *Zimbabwe Journal of Educational Research*, *31*(1), 55–69.

Chintala, S. R. 2024. *Embedded in Informality: Political Economy of Platform Work in India* (Doctoral dissertation, New York University).

Chiwaridzo, O. T. 2024. Energizing the future: Unleashing the potential of innovative waste-to-energy technologies for energy development and sustainability within Zimbabwe's tourism sector. *Waste Management & Research*, p.0734242X241291939.

Chiweshe, M. K. (2022). *Transforming institutional cultures: A case for collaboration in Zimbabwean higher education.* Bulawayo: Mambo Press.

Christensen, C. M., Horn, M. B., & Johnson, C. W. (2020). *Disrupting class: How disruptive innovation will change the way the world learns.* McGraw-Hill Education.

Christensen, C. M., Johnson, C. W., & Horn, M. B. (2008). *Disrupting class: How disruptive innovation will change the way the world learns.* McGraw-Hill.

Cox, K., & Sims, J. (2022). Industry-university collaborations for curriculum co-design: Bridging the gap between academia and the workforce. *The Journal of Higher Education, 47*(2), 125–142.

Department of Higher Education and Training [DHET]. (2013). *White Paper for Post-School Education and Training: Building an Expanded, Effective and Integrated Post-School System.* Pretoria, South Africa.

Di Battista, A., Grayling, S., Hasselaar, E., Leopold, T., Li, R., Rayner, M., & Zahidi, S. (2023). Future of jobs report 2023. In *World Economic Forum, Geneva, Switzerland.*https://www. weforum. org/reports/the-future-of-jobs-report-2023

Dubois, D., & Prade, H. (2023). Possibility theory. In *The Palgrave Encyclopedia of the Possible* (pp. 1064–1073). Springer International Publishing.

Dyer, S., & Ward, C. (2020). Collaborating with industry partners to enhance workforce readiness: A guide for higher education institutions. *Journal of Higher Education and Industry Partnerships, 12*(4), 227–245.

Edmondson, A. C. (2018). *The fearless organization: Creating psychological safety in the workplace for learning, innovation, and growth.* Wiley.

Equiss. (2024). Operationalizing the breaking of silos in universities: A step-by-step guide. Equiss. https://www.equiss.org/post/operationalizing-the-breaking-of-silos-in-universities-a-step-by-step-guide

Feldman, M. (2022). Building sustainable industry-academic partnerships: A guide to effective collaborations. *Journal of Higher Education Partnerships, 33*(2), 210–224.

Finnish Ministry of Education and Culture. (2019). *Education Policy Outlook.* Ministry of Education and Culture.

Fisher, A., Garrison, D. R., & Vaughan, N. D. (2021). The role of technology in supporting blended learning: A review of best practices. *Journal of Educational Technology Systems, 50*(1), 88–106.

Fleaca, , BFleaca, , EMaiduc, , S. (2022). Digital transformation and current challenges of higher education. *TEM Journal, 11*(3), 1235.

Frandell, A. (2023). *Knowledge Flows from Invention to Public Value: the Impacts of Academic-industry Collaborations* (Doctoral dissertation, Arizona State University).

Fresen, J. W. (2020). *Embracing distance education in a blended learning model: Challenges and prospects.* Exploring Dual and Mixed Mode Provision of Distance Education. DOI: 10.4324/9780429287473-8

Friedman, T. L. (2021). *Thank you for being late: An optimist's guide to thriving in the age of accelerations.* Farrar, Straus and Giroux.

Frost, J., Brockmann, E., & Huggett, K. (2020). Interdisciplinary collaboration in higher education: A case study of effective curriculum integration. *Journal of Interdisciplinary Studies in Education, 9*(2), 58–73.

Fubah, C. N., & Moos, M. (2025). Exploring network typology and their role in immigrant entrepreneurship: Insights from South Africa. *Journal of Enterprising Communities: People and Places in the Global Economy, 19*(2), 202–224. DOI: 10.1108/JEC-07-2023-0138

Fullan, M. (2016). *The new meaning of educational change* (5th ed.). Routledge.

Fullan, M. (2020). *Leading in a culture of change: A handbook for educators.* Jossey-Bass.

Gaftandzhieva, S., Hussain, S., Hilcenko, S., Doneva, R., & Boykova, K. (2023). Data-driven decision making in higher education institutions: State-of-play. *International Journal of Advanced Computer Science and Applications, 14*(6). Advance online publication. DOI: 10.14569/IJACSA.2023.0140642

Garrison, D. R., & Kanuka, H. (2020). *Blended learning in higher education: Framework, principles, and guidelines.* Wiley.

Garrison, D. R., & Vaughan, N. D. (2008). *Blended learning in higher education: Framework, principles, and guidelines.* John Wiley & Sons.

Green, S., & Harris, R. (2023). Collaborative training programs in academia and industry: A model for success. *Educational Innovations, 29*(4), 45–61.

Grew, R. (2024). Breaking down silos: Enhancing collaboration and innovation in higher education. Vygo. https://blog.vygoapp.com/silos

Gusha, I. S. (2022). *Paul's ethics of reconciliation in dialogue with Ndebele and Shona ethnic cohesion*. University of Bamberg Press. DOI: 10.20378/irb-54882

Hakan, K. Ö. (2020). Digital transformation in higher education: A case study on strategic plans. *Высшее образование в России*, (3), 9-23.

Harris, S. G. (1990). The Fifth Discipline: The Art and Practice of the Learning Organization", by Peter M. Senge. *Human Resource Management*, *29*(3), 343. DOI: 10.1002/hrm.3930290308

Harrison, C., & Brown, L. (2019). Industry-academic collaborations and their impact on curriculum development: A case study approach. *Higher Education Policy Review*, *41*(3), 256–275.

Harrison, L. (2024). *Unpacking Micro-Influence within the Australian Creative Sectors*. Springer Nature Singapore. DOI: 10.1007/978-981-97-5914-9

Harrison, R., Hughes, J., & Roll, C. (2019). Building bridges: Partnerships between universities and industries for curriculum development. *Journal of Higher Education Collaboration*, *15*(2), 112–125. DOI: 10.1016/j.hec.2019.03.002

Herridge, C., 2024. The Patterns and Structures of Information Technology Departments in Higher Education.

Herring, R., Dyer, K., Howkins, P. and Ward, C., 2020. Characterisation of the offshore precipitation environment to help combat leading edge erosion of wind turbine blades. *Wind energy science*, *5*(4), pp.1399-1409.

Hughes, M., Ginnett, R. C., & Curphy, G. J. (2019). *Leadership: Enhancing the lessons of experience* (9th ed.). McGraw-Hill Education.

Inusah, Y., Kazaz, A., & Ulubeyli, S. (2025). Barriers to E-Tendering Implementation in the Construction Industry: A Comprehensive Review and Analysis of a Decade and Beyond. *Sustainability (Basel)*, *17*(5), 2052. DOI: 10.3390/su17052052

Jackson, D. (2013). Student perceptions of the importance of employability skill provision in business undergraduate programs. *Journal of Education for Business*, *88*(5), 271–279. DOI: 10.1080/08832323.2012.697928

Jackson, D. (2019). Student perceptions of the importance of employability skill provision in business undergraduate programs. *Journal of Education and Work*, *32*(2), 77–94.

Jisc. (2021). *Digital transformation in higher education: Ensuring that universities are ready for the future of work*. Retrieved from https://www.jisc.ac.uk/digital-transformation

Johnson, M., & Lee, D. (2022). Professional associations and shared professional development: Strengthening connections between academia and industry. *Journal of Professional Development, 18*(2), 55–69.

Johnston, S. L. (2024). *Addressing Skills Gap: A Systemic Reframe and Redesign of Capstone using Design-Based Research* (Doctoral dissertation, University of Calgary (Canada)).

Jones, S., Lefoe, G., Harvey, M., & Ryland, K. (2012). Distributed leadership: A collaborative framework for academics, executives and professionals in higher education. *Journal of Higher Education Policy and Management, 34*(1), 67–78. DOI: 10.1080/1360080X.2012.642334

Jones, S., Lefoe, G., Harvey, M., & Ryland, K. (2021). Distributed leadership: A collaborative framework for academics, executives and professionals in higher education. *Journal of Higher Education Policy and Management, 43*(4), 423–439.

Katzenbach, J., & Smith, D. (1992). *The wisdom of teams: Creating the high-performance organization*. Harvard Business Press.

Katzenbach, J. R., & Smith, D. K. (2015). *The wisdom of teams: Creating the high-performance organization*. HarperBusiness.

Kezar, A. (2005). Creating and sustaining a campus-wide culture of innovation: Perceptions of innovation leaders. *The Journal of Higher Education, 76*(4), 425–461.

Kezar, A. (2005). Consequences of radical change in governance: A grounded theory approach. *The Journal of Higher Education, 76*(6), 634–668. DOI: 10.1080/00221546.2005.11772303

Kezar, A. (2011). Understanding and facilitating organizational change in the 21st century: Recent research and conceptualizations. *ASHE-ERIC Higher Education Report, 28*(4).

Kezar, A. (2017). *Understanding and facilitating organizational change in the 21st century: Recent research and conceptualizations*. Jossey-Bass.

Kezar, A. (2018). *How colleges change: Understanding, leading, and enacting change*. Routledge. DOI: 10.4324/9781315121178

Kezar, A., & Holcombe, E. (2017). *Shared leadership in higher education: Important lessons from research and practice*. American Council on Education.

Kirkpatrick, D., & Kirkpatrick, J. (2006). *Evaluating training programs: The four levels*. Berrett-Koehler Publishers.

Kirkpatrick, D. L. (2019). *Evaluating training programs: The four levels* (4th ed.). Berrett-Koehler Publishers.

Kirkwood, A., & Price, L. (2020). *Technology and education: Challenges and opportunities for higher education in the digital age*. Routledge.

Klein, J. T. (2023). Boundary discourse of crossdisciplinary and cross-sector research: Refiguring the landscape of science. *Minerva, 61*(1), 31–52. DOI: 10.1007/s11024-022-09474-9

Klein, J. T., & Lester, J. (2020). *Promoting interdisciplinary collaboration in higher education: A handbook for leaders and administrators*. Stylus Publishing.

Kotter, J. P. (2012). *Leading Change*. Harvard Business Review Press.

Kotter, J. P. (2014). *Accelerate: Building strategic agility for a faster-moving world.* Harvard Business Review Press.

Kouzes, J., & Posner, B. (2023). *The leadership challenge: How to make extraordinary things happen in organizations*. Wiley.

Kouzes, J. M., & Posner, B. Z. (2017). *The leadership challenge: How to make extraordinary things happen in organizations* (6th ed.). Wiley.

Kurebwa, J. (2022). Distance education and the challenge of technology integration at the Zimbabwe Open University. In Global, I. G. I. (Ed.), *Advancing open and distance learning*.

Kurebwa, J. (2022). Urban housing affordability in Zimbabwe: The case of Homelink Housing Mortgage Scheme. *Canadian Social Science, 18*(5), 43–53.

Kwok, L. (2022). Labor shortage: A critical reflection and a call for industry-academia collaboration. *International Journal of Contemporary Hospitality Management, 34*(11), 3929–3943. DOI: 10.1108/IJCHM-01-2022-0103

Lesser, E. L., & Prusak, L. (Eds.). (2004). *Creating value with knowledge: Insights from the IBM Institute for business value*. Oxford University Press. DOI: 10.1093/0195165128.001.0001

Lesser, E. L., & Prusak, L. (2020). *Creating value with knowledge: Insights from the world's leading organizations*. Harvard Business Press.

Lester, S. E., Dubel, A. K., Hernán, G., McHenry, J., & Rassweiler, A. (2020). Spatial planning principles for marine ecosystem restoration. *Frontiers in Marine Science*, *7*, 328. DOI: 10.3389/fmars.2020.00328

Lukarov, V. (2019). *Scaling up learning analytics in blended learning scenarios* (Doctoral dissertation, Dissertation, RWTH Aachen University, 2019).

Machingura, F. (2022). *Barriers to technological adoption in Zimbabwean universities: A focus on administrative silos*. Academic Press.

Madsen, S. R. (2023). Leading change in higher education: Overcoming resistance and achieving digital transformation. *Journal of Higher Education Leadership, 28*(1), 102–115.

Mai, N.A., (2019). Policies for higher education development in the People's Republic of China.

Maimon, E. P., & Schneider, C. G. (2023). *Leading academic change: Vision, strategy, transformation*. Routledge. DOI: 10.4324/9781003445593

Marginson, S. (2016). *Higher education and the common good*. Melbourne University Publishing.

Martin, F., & Liao, C. (2020). Learning management systems in higher education: Benefits and barriers to their implementation and use. *Journal of Online Learning and Teaching, 16*(2), 154–167.

McHenry, M. A., Barrows, J., & White, T. R. (2021). Industry-academic partnerships in technology transfer: Insights from curriculum integration. *Journal of Technology Education, 33*(1), 45–62. DOI: 10.1234/jte.2021.045

Ministry of Education of the People's Republic of China. (2017). *Double First-Class University Plan.*

Ministry of Higher and Tertiary Education. Innovation, Science and Technology Development [MHTEISTD]. (2018). *Education 5.0 Policy*. Government of Zimbabwe.

Mintzberg, H., Ahlstrand, B., & Lampel, J. (2020). *Strategy safari: A guided tour through the wilds of strategic management* (3rd ed.). Pearson.

Mlambo, A. S. (2018). From education for liberation to education for production: Revisiting Zimbabwe's Education 5.0 philosophy. *Journal of Southern African Studies, 44*(5), 901–915.

Mlambo, V. (2018). An overview of rural-urban migration in South Africa: Its causes and implications. *Archives of Business Research, 6*(4). Advance online publication. DOI: 10.14738/abr.64.4407

Muchineripi, B., & Moyo, G. (2023). *Resource allocation challenges in higher education: Implications for technology integration*. ZPH Publishers.

Mukidi, C. A. (2023). Going against the tide in Uganda's higher education: A brief historical account of Uganda Martyrs University. *African Journal of Rural Development, 8*(1), 57–72.

Murphy, L., & Liu, X. (2022). Technology transfer in higher education: The role of industry partnerships in enhancing digital literacy. *Journal of Educational Technology & Society, 25*(1), 30–44.

Murray, D. D., Williams, C. R., Gaddy, J. A., Rogers, C. D., Kirabo, A., Santisteban, M. M., Wanjalla, C. N., Williams, E. M., Sweetwyne, M. T., Damo, S. M., Murray, S. A., Stokes, D., & Hinton, A.Jr. (2024). The power of junior faculty mentoring committees. *Journal of Cellular Physiology, 239*(7), e31360. DOI: 10.1002/jcp.31360 PMID: 38962842

Musa, S.Z.B.S., (2024). Digital Renaissance: Reinventing Tertiary Language Teaching and Learning Strategies in Evolving Digital Landscape. *Education towards a Global Citizen Generation, 202*.

Musvoto, A. (2021). Innovation hubs and technology transfer in Zimbabwe: Challenges and opportunities. *Zimbabwe Economic Review, 15*(3), 45–58.

Musvoto, G., (2021). Household Mobility Dynamics among Young Adults in Established Suburban Council Rental Housing Estates in South African Cities: A Case Study of Kenneth Gardens, Durban. *African Journal of Inter/Multidisciplinary Studies, 3*(1), pp.197-216.

Nash, B., & Allen, M. (2020). *Data-driven decision making in higher education: A guide for institutions and leaders*. Harvard Education Press.

Ncube, B., Shekede, M. D., Gwitira, I., & Dube, T. (2020). Spatial modelling the effects of climate change on the distribution of Lantana camara in Southern Zimbabwe. *Applied Geography (Sevenoaks, England), 117*, 102172. DOI: 10.1016/j.apgeog.2020.102172

Ncube, N., & Sithole, S. (2023). *Bridging the gap: Strategies for overcoming silos in higher education.* Bulawayo: Mambo Press.

NewZapp. (2023). Breaking down communication silos in higher education. NewZapp. https://www.newzapp.com/blog/breaking-down-communication-silos-in-higher-education

Noblitt, L., Vance, E., & DeAngelo, L. (2022). Breaking down silos: A collaborative approach to student success initiatives. *Journal of Higher Education Management, 37*(1), 45–61.

Nyoni, P. (2022). Pedagogies of access and success among South African university students in the extended curriculum programmes amidst COVID-19 disruptions. *South African Journal of Higher Education, 36*(4), 137–153. DOI: 10.20853/36-4-5206

Nyoni, S. (2022). Decolonizing higher education in Zimbabwe: Towards an Afrocentric curriculum. *Journal of African Studies and Development, 14*(1), 22–30.

Oblinger, D. G. (2018). *E-education and digital literacies: Institutional leadership and transformation.*

Parker, A. (2024). *Pride Everyday: Empowering LGBTQ+ Pride in the Workplace and Beyond.* Notion Press.

Parker, M., & Jansen, H. (2021). Celebrating success in higher education: The role of recognition in fostering collaborative cultures. *Higher Education Review, 44*(2), 135–148.

Payad, A. (2024). High School Aetas' Course Experience: Benchmark for Streamlining Curricular Program Management. *JPAIR Multidisciplinary Research, 56*(1), 1–23. DOI: 10.7719/jpair.v56i1.877

Pondiwa, S., El Nabahany, U., & Phiri, M. (2022). Integration of ICT into education: Lessons learnt at the State University of Zanzibar and the Midlands State University in Zimbabwe. In *Computer-Mediated Communication.* IntechOpen. DOI: 10.5772/intechopen.98441

Queensland University of Technology. (2023). *QUT and IBM: Transforming education through AI and quantum computing partnerships.* Retrieved from https://www.qut.edu.au/partnerships

Rackwitz, M., Breaugh, J., & Hammerschmid, G. (2024). Leadership for intergovernmental collaboration towards digital transformation. In *Collaborating for Digital Transformation* (pp. 124–142). Edward Elgar Publishing. DOI: 10.4337/9781803923895.00016

Rogers, E. M. (2003). *Diffusion of Innovations* (5th ed.). Free Press.

Rogers, E. M., Singhal, A., & Quinlan, M. M. (2014). Diffusion of innovations. In *An integrated approach to communication theory and research* (pp. 432–448). Routledge.

Rowley, D. J., & Sherman, H. (2004). *From strategy to change: Implementing the plan in higher education*. John Wiley & Sons.

Rowley, D. J., & Sherman, H. (2020). *From strategy to change: Implementing the plan in higher education* (2nd ed.). Jossey-Bass.

Sanders, J., Spector, M., & Weber, R. (2021). Faculty-industry partnerships: Enhancing curriculum development and workforce readiness. *Journal of Workforce Development, 22*(4), 48–59.

Sanyang, B. and Ali, L., (2023). The Power of Cultural Diversity in Project Teams: A Path to Greater Innovation-A qualitative study of how cultural diversity impacts innovation output in project teams.

Schwab, K. (2016). *The Fourth Industrial Revolution*.

Schwab, K. (2024). The Fourth Industrial Revolution: what it means, how to respond1. In *Handbook of research on strategic leadership in the Fourth Industrial Revolution* (pp. 29-34). Edward Elgar Publishing. DOI: 10.4337/9781802208818.00008

Selwyn, N. (2020). *Education and technology: Key issues and debates*. Routledge.

Senge, P. M. (2006). *The fifth discipline: The art and practice of the learning organization*.

Senthil, B. A., Prema, R. K., & Sharif, L. S. (2025). Industry-Academia Partnerships: Bridging the Gap for R&D Success. In *Evolving Landscapes of Research and Development: Trends, Challenges, and Opportunities* (pp. 191-208). IGI Global Scientific Publishing.

Sheppard, C. and Ntenga, L., (2013). Funding of the South African further education and training sector for an equitable sharing of national revenue. *Technical Report: Submission for the Division of Revenue 2014/2015*.

Siemens, G. (2004). Elearnspace. Connectivism: A learning theory for the digital age. *Elearnspace. org*, 14-16.

Siemens, G. (2014). Connectivism: A learning theory for the digital age. *International Journal of Instructional Technology and Distance Learning*.

Silva, L., (2023). An utopian approach to social transformation: the role of urban social movements' fragmentation in Barcelona. *Partecipazione e conflitto-PArticipation and COnflict.*

Sithole, S. (2023). *Benefits of technology: utilisation of blockchain in the South African banking sector amid Industry 4.0.* University of Johannesburg.

Smith, J., & Jones, P. (2021). Breaking down silos: Collaboration and technology integration in global higher education. In Global, I. G. I. (Ed.), *Trends in educational technology.*

Stanford University. (2024). Faculty-Industry Collaborative Research Program. Retrieved from https://www.stanford.edu/faculty-industry-collaboration

Subramanian, N., & Gunasekaran, A. (2021). Digital transformation in higher education: Challenges and strategies for integration. *Technology Management Journal, 28*(3), 123–145.

Sullivan, H. (2022). *Collaboration and public policy.* Palgrave. DOI: 10.1007/978-3-031-09585-6

Sullivan, P., & Glance, D. (2022). Interdisciplinary approaches to curriculum design in higher education: Fostering collaboration and innovation. *Higher Education Review, 27*(2), 185–200.

Taylor, S., & Hall, D. (2023). Co-designing curricula: Collaborative models between universities and industries. *Journal of Educational Development, 36*(3), 115–129.

Treviranus, J., & Coombs, N. (2000). Bridging the Digital Divide in Higher Education. For full text: http://www. educause. edu/conference/e2000/proceedings. html. For full text: http://www. educause. edu/asp/doclib/abstract. asp? ID= EDU0028. html.

University of California. (2023). *UC Berkeley and Cisco: Shaping the future of cybersecurity education.* Retrieved from https://www.berkeley.edu/industry-partnerships

University of Melbourne. (2023). *University of Melbourne and PwC: Shaping the future of business consulting education.* Retrieved from https://www.unimelb.edu.au/industry-collaborations

University of Toronto. (2023). Cross-Disciplinary PD Workshops. Retrieved from https://www.utoronto.edu/pd-workshops

Valiente Bermejo, M. A., Eynian, M., Malmsköld, L., & Scotti, A. (2022). University–industry collaboration in curriculum design and delivery: A model and its application in manufacturing engineering courses. *Industry and Higher Education, 36*(5), 615–622. DOI: 10.1177/09504222211064204

Vengathattil, S. (2025). Future-Proofing AI Talent in The United States: The Role of Academia in Meeting Industry Demands. *International Journal of Management Science and Information Technology*, *5*(1), 210–217. DOI: 10.35870/ijmsit.v5i1.3837

Viriri, E., Ndimande-Hlongwa, N., & Mufanechiya, A. (2024). Decolonising higher education in Zimbabwe: Prospects and challenges of education 5.0. *Journal of African Education*, *5*(1), 37–56. DOI: 10.31920/2633-2930/2024/v5n1a2

Vygo. (2023). *The impact of silos on higher education institutions*. https://blog.vygoapp.com/silos

Waddock, S. A. (1988). Building successful social partnerships. *MIT Sloan Management Review*, *29*(4), 17.

Wang, H., & Wang, X. (2023). Breaking down silos in higher education: Strategies for effective collaboration. *Journal of Higher Education Policy and Management*, *45*(2), 256–273.

Westerman, G., Calméjane, C., Bonnet, D., Ferraris, P., & McAfee, A. (2011). Digital Transformation: A roadmap for billion-dollar organizations. *MIT Center for digital business and capgemini consulting, 1*(1-68).

Westerman, G., Calméjane, C., Ferraris, P., & Bonnet, D. (2014). Digital transformation: A roadmap for billion-dollar organizations. *MIT Sloan Management Review*, *55*(2), 36–44.

Williams, T. (2024). Mentorship programs and faculty development: Enhancing the academic-industry interface. *Educational Leadership Journal*, *22*(1), 101–115.

Williamson, B. and Hogan, A., (2021). Pandemic privatisation in higher education: Edtech and university reform.

Wong, L. P. (2024). Artificial Intelligence and Job Automation: Challenges for Secondary Students' Career Development and Life Planning. *Merits*, *4*(4), 370–399. DOI: 10.3390/merits4040027

World Economic Forum (WEF). (2020). *The future of jobs report*.

Yuan, Y., & Ma, R. (2019). The role of integrated systems in improving university efficiency: A case study. *Journal of Higher Education Administration*, *23*(1), 75–89.

Zheng, L., Wang, X., & Gao, Y. (2020). Bridging the digital divide in higher education: A comprehensive review. *Journal of Educational Technology Research*, *38*(4), 567–586.

Chapter 2
From Campus to Career: Transforming Technology Skills Through University–Workplace Collaboration

Soumya Sankar Ghosh
https://orcid.org/0000-0002-4469-4070
VIT Bhopal University, India

ABSTRACT

University-workplace collaborations play a pivotal role in bridging the gap between academic learning and industry demands, particularly in the domain of technology skill development. This study examines the impact of structured collaboration programs on students, faculty, and industry professionals using a mixed-methods approach. Quantitative analysis reveals significant skill enhancement, with mentorship and digital tools as critical success factors. Qualitative insights highlight challenges like scheduling conflicts and resource disparities, suggesting actionable strategies for improvement. The findings underscore the transformative potential of these collaborations in fostering workforce readiness and curriculum innovation, offering pathways for sustainable educational practices.

INTRODUCTION

In today's fast-paced digital era, the transition from academia to the professional realm has become a critical juncture for individuals entering the workforce. The rapid evolution of technology has reshaped industries, creating a significant demand for graduates with advanced technical skills. Universities, as primary facilitators of education, play a pivotal role in imparting foundational knowledge. However, a

DOI: 10.4018/979-8-3373-0004-7.ch002

widening gap persists between the skills taught within academic institutions and the practical competencies required in modern workplaces. This gap has intensified discussions around aligning university curricula with industry expectations, especially in technology-driven sectors (Gann et al., 2018). University-workplace collaboration has emerged as a promising solution to bridge this divide, fostering an environment where academic learning is seamlessly integrated with real-world applications. University-workplace collaboration encompasses a spectrum of activities designed to prepare students for the complexities of professional life. These activities range from internships and cooperative education programs to industry-sponsored projects and mentorship initiatives (Billett, 2011). Such collaborations aim to enhance students' technical proficiency, problem-solving abilities, and adaptability—indispensable skills in today's dynamic job market. Beyond technical capabilities, these partnerships also cultivate essential soft skills, such as communication, teamwork, and leadership, which are often overlooked in traditional classroom settings (Jackson, 2013). By exposing students to workplace environments during their academic journey, these collaborations enable a smoother transition to their careers, ensuring that they are both job-ready and future-ready.

Despite the apparent benefits of university-workplace collaborations, their implementation is fraught with challenges. One of the most significant barriers is the misalignment between the goals of academia and industry. Academic institutions often prioritize theoretical knowledge and research, while industries seek candidates who can apply their knowledge to solve practical problems (Fleming, 2014). This divergence in objectives leads to a lack of coherence in collaborative efforts, diminishing their effectiveness. Additionally, logistical challenges such as scheduling conflicts, resource constraints, and communication gaps further hinder the success of these initiatives. Addressing these challenges requires a comprehensive approach that aligns all stakeholders' interests and ensures collaborative programs' sustainability. The growing emphasis on employability has made it imperative for universities to reassess their teaching methodologies and curriculum design. Traditional pedagogical approaches, which focus heavily on lectures and examinations, are increasingly being supplemented with experiential learning opportunities (Kolb, 2014). These opportunities allow students to engage in hands-on activities that simulate workplace scenarios, providing a platform to apply their academic knowledge in practical contexts. For instance, project-based learning, which involves students working on real-world problems under industry mentorship, has gained traction as an effective teaching method (Prince & Felder, 2006). Such initiatives not only enhance students' understanding of complex concepts but also equip them with the skills needed to navigate the challenges of the professional world.

On the other hand, industries are also recognizing the value of investing in university collaborations. By participating in such programs, companies gain access to a pool of young, talented individuals who bring fresh perspectives and innovative ideas (Cappelli, 2012). Moreover, these partnerships allow companies to shape the skillsets of potential employees, ensuring that they align with organizational needs. For example, technology firms often collaborate with universities to design specialized courses and training modules that focus on emerging technologies such as artificial intelligence, machine learning, and blockchain (Brynjolfsson & McAfee, 2014). Such targeted initiatives not only address the immediate skill gaps in the workforce but also contribute to the long-term growth and competitiveness of the industry. The significance of university-workplace collaborations extends beyond individual students and companies. At a macro level, these partnerships contribute to the broader goals of economic development and societal progress. By aligning academic outputs with industry demands, they enhance the overall quality of the workforce, making it more competitive on a global scale (van der Vlies, 2020). In addition, these collaborations promote innovation by fostering a culture of knowledge exchange and co-creation between academia and industry. For instance, research collaborations between universities and tech companies have led to ground-breaking advancements in fields such as biotechnology, renewable energy, and data science (Etzkowitz & Leydesdorff, 2000). These innovations not only drive economic growth but also address pressing global challenges, such as climate change and healthcare disparities.

Despite the growing body of evidence supporting the efficacy of university-workplace collaborations, there is a lack of comprehensive statistical studies that evaluate their impact on students' technology skills. Most existing research relies on qualitative assessments, such as interviews and case studies, which provide valuable insights but lack the rigor of quantitative analysis. However, large-scale studies such as Jackson (2013), which surveyed over 2,000 graduates, demonstrate that students who participated in structured internship programs had a 35% higher employability rate. Similarly, Fleming (2014) found an 18% increase in technical proficiency among students engaged in cooperative education programs, reinforcing the measurable impact of university-industry collaborations.

This paper aims to address this gap by conducting a statistical evaluation of the effectiveness of such collaborations in transforming technology skills. By analyzing data from a diverse range of programs and stakeholders, this study seeks to identify the key factors that contribute to successful collaborations and provide actionable recommendations for their improvement. Given the success of structured workplace learning programs in Germany and Switzerland, integrating insights from these models into the research framework will allow for a comparative assessment. Additionally, cooperative education models in North America, where students alternate between full-time study and paid industry placements, offer another perspective on how structured collaboration impacts employability and skill acquisition. Incorporating these international models provides a benchmark for evaluating the effectiveness of university-industry partnerships in different economic and educational settings.

The need for this research is underscored by the increasing complexity of the technological landscape. As industries continue to adopt cutting-edge technologies at an unprecedented pace, the demand for skilled professionals is expected to rise exponentially. According to a report by the World Economic Forum, nearly 50% of all employees will need reskilling by 2025 due to the adoption of new technologies (Gann et al., 2018). This trend highlights the urgency of equipping students with the skills required to thrive in a rapidly changing job market. University-workplace collaborations, if effectively implemented, have the potential to address this challenge by creating a talent pipeline that meets the evolving needs of the industry.

Another critical aspect of this research is its focus on the holistic development of students. While technical skills are undeniably important, the value of soft skills in professional success cannot be overstated. Effective communication, teamwork, and adaptability are often cited as the most sought-after qualities by employers (Borg et al., 2021). University-workplace collaborations provide an ideal platform for students to develop these skills in a real-world context. Team-based projects and internships expose students to diverse perspectives and working styles, enhancing their ability to collaborate and resolve conflicts. By fostering a well-rounded skill-set, these initiatives improve employability and contribute to personal growth and lifelong learning.

This paper also aims to explore the role of technology in facilitating university-workplace collaborations. The advent of digital tools and platforms has revolutionized the way these partnerships are structured and implemented. Online learning platforms, virtual internships, and collaborative software have made it possible to overcome geographical and logistical barriers, enabling broader participation and inclusivity (Means et al., 2009). For instance, virtual reality (VR) and augmented reality (AR) technologies are used to create immersive learning experiences that simulate real-world scenarios. These innovations have the potential to enhance the effectiveness of collaborative programs by providing students with a safe yet realistic environment to practice and refine their skills. Furthermore, this study seeks to examine the impact of policy and governance on the success of university-workplace collaborations. Governments and educational bodies play a crucial role in creating an enabling environment for these initiatives. Policies that incentivize industry participation, provide funding for collaborative programs, and promote curriculum flexibility are essential for their sustainability (Kurtoglu, 2018). Empirical studies have demonstrated that well-structured policy interventions significantly enhance the success of such collaborations. For example, the German dual education system, backed by government subsidies and employer tax benefits, has resulted in a significant employment rate for vocational students within six months of graduation. Similarly, the Swiss apprenticeship model, which integrates workplace training into academic curricula, has led to a good retention rate of trainees in their respective industries. By analyzing these successful funding strategies, universities and policymakers can develop more effective collaboration frameworks.

A structured approach is essential for addressing these objectives comprehensively. Section 2, the Literature Review, will delve into the conceptual framework of university-workplace collaborations and examine empirical studies on collaborative models. This section will highlight gaps in existing research, particularly in quantitative evaluations. Following this, the Methodology, in Section 3, will outline the mixed-method approach combining surveys, case studies, and statistical analysis. This includes sampling strategies to involve participants from universities and industries, and tools such as regression analysis, factor analysis, and t-tests for rigorous data examination. The Results and Analysis section will present findings through descriptive statistics, including demographic trends and pre- and post-collaboration skill assessments. The analysis will employ regression and factor analysis to identify determinants of success and provide a comparative view of different collaboration models. These results will form the basis of the Discussion section, where the implications of findings will be interpreted in the context of existing literature. Finally, the Conclusion and Recommendations section will summarize the key findings, propose practical strategies for universities and industries, and identify future research directions to address persisting gaps in understanding.

LITERATURE REVIEW

The concept of university-workplace collaboration has been extensively studied to bridge the gap between academic learning and industry demands. This section reviews the theoretical underpinnings, empirical findings, and gaps in existing research related to these collaborations, focusing on their effectiveness in enhancing technology skills. Billett (2011) posits that these collaborations represent a unique form of vocational education where learning is not confined to classrooms but extends to workplace environments. The dual role of educational institutions in imparting theoretical knowledge and facilitating practical exposure has been widely acknowledged (Kolb, 2014). Experiential learning theory, as articulated by Kolb, emphasizes the value of hands-on experiences in reinforcing academic concepts.

Similarly, Dewey's (1986) philosophy of education highlights the importance of connecting learning with real-world applications.

Theoretical frameworks such as the Triple Helix model (Etzkowitz & Leydesdorff, 2000) provide a comprehensive lens for understanding university-industry-government relationships. This model suggests that the convergence of these three entities fosters innovation and skill development, creating an ecosystem conducive to technological advancement. The human capital theory (Becker, 2009) also supports the idea that investments in education and training yield significant returns by enhancing workforce capabilities. These theories collectively underscore the potential of university-workplace collaborations to address skill shortages and align academic curricula with industry needs. Recent studies have expanded on these theories by exploring the role of digital technologies in collaboration frameworks. For instance, Romao et al. (2024) examined how lean R&D combined with problem-based learning enhances collaboration between academia and industry, particularly in software engineering education. Similarly, Damek et al. (2022) emphasized the importance of building information modeling (BIM) in fostering meta-competencies essential for workplace success.

Empirical research provides insights into the diverse models of university-workplace collaborations and their outcomes. Cooperative education programs, for instance, have been identified as effective mechanisms for integrating academic and professional learning. Similarly, Jackson (2013) emphasized the role of internships in fostering employability skills, highlighting that structured workplace experiences enhance students' ability to transition into professional roles. Industry-sponsored projects are another prominent form of collaboration. Prince and Felder (2006) argued that project-based learning under industry mentorship significantly improves problem-solving and critical-thinking skills. Studies have also highlighted the role of mentorship in shaping students' professional identity and career readiness (Tenenbaum et al., 2001). Furthermore, collaborative research initiatives between universities and industries have been shown to drive innovation while providing students with exposure to cutting-edge technologies (Etzkowitz & Leydesdorff, 2000). The integration of advanced technologies into collaborative models is a growing trend. Carayannis and Morawska (2023) investigated the use of digital twins in engineering education, finding that these virtual replicas of physical systems enable students to engage with real-world problems in a controlled environment. Additionally, the works of Yu & Xu (2022) and Schmid Mast et al., (2018), explored the potential of virtual reality (VR) in simulating workplace scenarios, concluding that immersive technologies significantly enhance skill acquisition and retention.

Despite their potential, university-workplace collaborations face numerous challenges that limit their effectiveness. One of the primary issues is the misalignment between academic curricula and industry requirements. Cappelli (2012) pointed out that academic institutions often prioritize theoretical knowledge, leaving students underprepared for the practical demands of the workforce. This disconnect is further exacerbated by rapid technological advancements, which outpace curriculum updates. Logistical challenges also pose significant barriers. Scheduling conflicts, resource constraints, and limited access to industry professionals hinder the implementation of collaborative programs (Fleming, 2014). Additionally, cultural differences between academia and industry—such as differing priorities, communication styles, and performance metrics—create friction in these partnerships (Ankrah & AL-Tabbaa, 2015; Messaoud et al., 2022; Zhuang & Shi, 2024). A recent study by the Gann et al., (2018) discussed strategies for nurturing university-industry collaborations, emphasizing the need for clear communication and robust infrastructure. Similarly, Vivek et al. (2024) highlighted data privacy concerns as a major challenge in digital collaborations, underscoring the importance of secure platforms to build stakeholder trust.

Although the literature on university-workplace collaborations is extensive, several gaps remain. Most studies focus on qualitative aspects, such as stakeholder perceptions and case studies, with limited emphasis on statistical evaluations. For example, Jackson (2013) provided qualitative insights into students' experiences but did not quantify the impact of collaborations on skill development. Similarly, while Billett (2011) highlighted the theoretical foundations of vocational education, empirical data supporting these claims are sparse. Another gap is the lack of longitudinal studies that track the long-term impact of collaborations on students' career trajectories. While short-term benefits, such as increased employability, have been documented (Fleming, 2014), the sustainability of these outcomes remains unclear. Additionally, existing research often overlooks the role of digital technologies in enhancing collaborations, despite their growing importance in the education sector (Means et al., 2009). Emerging gaps in the context of post-pandemic education have also been noted. Altan-Olcay and Bergeron (2024) observed that the transition to remote and hybrid learning models during the COVID-19 pandemic disrupted traditional collaboration frameworks, necessitating new strategies for engagement. This highlights the need for adaptive research considering university-workplace partnerships' evolving dynamics.

The literature on university-workplace collaborations underscores their potential to transform education and enhance employability. Theoretical frameworks such as experiential learning and the Triple Helix model provide a strong foundation for understanding these partnerships, while empirical studies highlight their practical benefits. However, significant challenges and research gaps remain, particularly in terms of aligning academic curricula with industry needs and evaluating collaboration outcomes. Addressing these gaps is essential to developing robust, scalable, and inclusive collaboration models that prepare students for a rapidly evolving professional landscape. The purpose of this study is to build upon the existing literature by providing a detailed, quantitative evaluation of university-workplace collaborations, focusing on their impact on students' technology skill development. By identifying the factors that contribute to successful collaborations, this work aims to propose actionable strategies for academia and industry to strengthen their partnerships. Furthermore, it seeks to explore how digital tools and technologies can be leveraged to overcome existing challenges and enhance the effectiveness of these collaborations. The next section, Methodology, details the research design, data collection methods, and analytical tools employed to achieve these objectives, paving the way for a systematic and comprehensive evaluation of university-workplace collaborations.

METHODOLOGY

This study employs a systematic approach to examine the impact of university-workplace collaborations on students' technology skill development. A mixed-methods design, integrating both quantitative and qualitative approaches, was chosen to provide a comprehensive understanding of the subject. By combining statistical rigor with contextual insights, the methodology ensures a holistic exploration of the research objectives. The study employs a sequential explanatory design, beginning with quantitative data collection and analysis, followed by qualitative data collection to further explain and expand on the findings. This approach not only enhances the depth of the research but also improves the overall validity by addressing both measurable outcomes and the nuanced experiences of stakeholders.

The target population for this study includes students, faculty members, and industry professionals involved in university-workplace collaborations across various disciplines, with a focus on technology-oriented fields such as computer science, engineering, and information technology. A multi-stage sampling technique was used to ensure representativeness. First, universities were selected based on their active engagement in collaborative programs, ensuring diversity in geographical location, institutional type, and program scale. Within each selected university, participants were identified from internships, cooperative education programs, or industry-sponsored projects. Faculty members overseeing these programs and industry professionals acting as mentors or collaborators were also included. The sample size for quantitative analysis consisted of 350 students, 100 faculty members, and 50 industry professionals, while 30 participants representing each stakeholder group were purposively selected for qualitative analysis to provide rich thematic insights. Data collection was carried out using a combination of surveys, interviews, and document analysis to capture diverse perspectives and corroborative evidence. Structured questionnaires were developed to gather quantitative data on participants' perceptions of skill development, program effectiveness, and challenges faced. These surveys included a mix of closed-ended questions, such as Likert scale ratings, and open-ended prompts to allow for qualitative responses. Semi-structured interviews were conducted with selected participants to explore themes emerging from the survey data. These interviews were recorded and transcribed for thematic analysis. Additionally, relevant documents, including program outlines, curricula, and collaboration agreements, were reviewed to understand the structural and operational aspects of university-workplace partnerships. This triangulated approach ensured a comprehensive dataset.

Data analysis was conducted in two distinct phases corresponding to the quantitative and qualitative components of the study. Quantitative data were analyzed using descriptive and inferential statistics. Descriptive statistics, including mean, median, standard deviation, and frequency distributions, were used to summarize participant demographics and general trends. Inferential statistical techniques, such as paired t-tests and ANOVA, were employed to evaluate differences in skill levels before and after participation in collaboration programs. Regression analysis was conducted to identify predictors of successful skill development, while exploratory factor analysis (EFA) was used to uncover underlying dimensions of program effectiveness, such as mentorship quality and resource availability. Qualitative data were analyzed using thematic analysis to identify recurring patterns and themes. Thematic coding was facilitated by NVivo software to ensure methodological rigor. Data triangulation was employed to validate findings across the different data sources, including survey responses, interview transcripts, and document analysis. This comprehensive analytical framework ensured that the results were both reliable and meaningful.

Ethical considerations were integral to the research process. Participants were provided with detailed information about the study, including its purpose, procedures, and potential risks. Informed consent was obtained electronically, and all responses were anonymized to ensure confidentiality. Participants were informed of their right to withdraw from the study at any stage. Reliability and validity were prioritized throughout the study. Survey instruments were pilot-tested with a small group of participants to refine questions and enhance clarity. Standardized data collection and analysis procedures were followed to minimize bias and ensure consistency. Data triangulation further enhanced the credibility of the findings by corroborating evidence from multiple sources. Preliminary results were peer-reviewed by academic and industry experts to validate interpretations and ensure alignment with real-world practices.

While the methodology was designed to provide robust insights, certain limitations were acknowledged. The focus on technology-related disciplines may limit the generalizability of findings to other fields. Self-reported data from surveys are subject to social desirability bias, potentially influencing participants' responses.

Additionally, resource constraints limited the sample size and scope of data collection. Delimitations included the decision to concentrate on universities with established collaboration programs, excluding informal or ad hoc partnerships to maintain focus and manageability.

DATA ANALYSIS

This section presents the analysis of data collected through surveys, interviews, and document reviews, highlighting key findings regarding the impact of university-workplace collaborations on students' technology skill development. Quantitative data were analyzed using statistical techniques, while qualitative data were explored through thematic analysis. The integration of these analyses provides a comprehensive understanding of the research objectives.

Quantitative analysis was conducted on survey responses collected from 500 participants, including students, faculty members, and industry professionals. The analysis involved descriptive and inferential statistics, focusing on skill development outcomes, program effectiveness, and collaboration challenges. Table 1 summarizes the demographic distribution of the survey participants, including gender, age, and affiliation.

Table 1. Descriptive statistics

Variable	Students (n=350)	Faculty (n=100)	Industry Professionals (n=50)	Total (n=500)
Male (%)	56	70	80	60
Female (%)	44	30	20	40
Age (Mean ± SD)	22.5 ± 2.1	45.8 ± 7.6	40.2 ± 8.5	27.6 ± 11.5

The demographic data presented in Table 1 highlights the diversity among the participants. Among the 500 respondents, the majority were male (60%), while females constituted 40%. The gender distribution varied across the groups, with industry professionals having the highest percentage of male participants (80%) and faculty members showing a relatively balanced representation. The mean age of participants also reflected the distinct characteristics of the groups. Students, being primarily undergraduates or early-career learners, had a mean age of 22.5 years, whereas faculty members and industry professionals were older, with mean ages of 45.8 and 40.2 years, respectively. The standard deviations indicate variability within the groups, particularly among faculty members, suggesting a wider range of ages in this category. These demographic patterns provide a context for understanding the findings and underscore the importance of tailoring collaboration programs to diverse participant profiles.

Participants' technology skill levels were measured before and after the programs using a standardized skill assessment test to evaluate the impact of university-workplace collaborations. Table 2 shows the mean skill scores for each group.

Table 2. Pre- and post-program skill assessment

Group	Pre-Program Score (Mean ± SD)	Post-Program Score (Mean ± SD)	t-Value	p-Value
Students	65.3 ± 10.5	78.7 ± 8.2	15.32	<0.001
Faculty	70.5 ± 12.1	80.2 ± 9.7	8.89	<0.001
Industry Professionals	72.4 ± 11.8	82.6 ± 8.9	6.74	<0.001

Table 2 provides compelling evidence of significant improvements in technology skill levels across all groups. Students exhibited the largest gain, with an average pre-program score of 65.3 increasing to 78.7 post-program, reflecting a mean difference of 13.4 points. This improvement, supported by a highly significant t-value of 15.32 ($p < 0.001$), underscores the transformative impact of collaboration programs on students' skill development. Faculty members and industry professionals also demonstrated notable gains, albeit to a lesser extent. Faculty participants' mean scores increased by 9.7 points, while industry professionals saw an improvement of 10.2 points. The statistical significance of these results highlights the effectiveness of collaboration programs in enhancing skills for all stakeholders, with students benefiting the most. To further validate these findings, an effect size calculation could be incorporated to quantify the magnitude of improvement. Additionally, multivariate regression analysis could help isolate key predictors of skill development, such as mentorship quality and resource availability, as supported by Borg et al. (2021), who found that structured mentorship significantly improves technical skill acquisition.

These findings validate the central premise of the study and set the stage for exploring the factors driving these improvements. When compared to international models, it becomes evident that structured, government-supported collaboration frameworks tend to yield the highest success rates. For instance, Germany's dual education model ensures that students gain direct industry exposure, with 80% of apprentices transitioning into full-time employment within the same companies. In contrast, North America's cooperative education model, while flexible, relies heavily on industry partnerships and lacks the same level of governmental oversight, leading to greater variability in outcomes. These comparisons underscore the importance of policy frameworks in shaping the success of university-industry collaborations. Additionally, longitudinal studies tracking career trajectories, such as Cappelli (2012), indicate that graduates with industry experience are more likely to secure full-time employment within six months post-graduation, highlighting the sustained benefits of university-industry partnerships.

A one-way ANOVA was conducted to compare the skill improvements across the three groups. Results are summarized in Table 3.

Table 3. ANOVA: Group differences in skill improvement

Source of Variation	SS	df	MS	F	p-Value
Between Groups	1205.4	2	602.7	18.23	<0.001
Within Groups	16480.6	497	33.15		
Total	17686	499			

The ANOVA results presented in Table 3 reveal significant differences in skill improvement among the groups, with an F-value of 18.23 ($p < 0.001$). Post-hoc tests further identified that students experienced significantly greater improvements compared to faculty members and industry professionals. These findings emphasize the unique advantages of collaboration programs for students, who are often at the early stages of their professional development and therefore have more to gain. The relatively smaller improvements observed among faculty members and industry professionals highlight the need for tailored program designs to maximize benefits for these groups. The substantial between-group variance (SS = 1205.4) underscores the importance of considering group-specific dynamics in future analyses.

Regression analysis was performed to identify predictors of skill development. Table 4 displays the results.

Table 4. Regression analysis: Predictors of skill development

Predictor Variable	Beta Coefficient	t-Value	p-Value
Mentorship Quality	0.42	6.23	<0.001
Resource Availability	0.35	5.14	<0.001
Industry Relevance	0.28	4.07	<0.001

Table 4 highlights mentorship quality as the most significant predictor of skill development, with a beta coefficient of 0.42 ($p < 0.001$). This finding aligns with qualitative insights emphasizing the critical role of mentors in guiding participants through complex tasks and providing personalized feedback. Resource availability and industry relevance also emerged as significant predictors, with beta coefficients of 0.35 and 0.28, respectively. These results suggest successful collaboration programs require effective mentorship, access to state-of-the-art tools, and alignment with industry demands. The high t-values for all predictors further validate their importance, providing actionable insights for program design and implementation.

Exploratory Factor Analysis (EFA) was conducted on survey items related to program effectiveness. Table 5 lists the identified factors and their loadings.

Table 5. Factor analysis: Dimensions of program effectiveness

Factor	Item	Loading
Mentorship Quality	Regular mentor interaction	0.82
	Feedback on projects	0.79
Resource Availability	Access to advanced tools	0.76
	Availability of industry experts	0.74
Industry Relevance	Alignment with job requirements	0.7

The EFA results in Table 5 identify three key dimensions of program effectiveness: mentorship quality, resource availability, and industry relevance. These factors collectively explained 68% of the total variance, highlighting their central role in driving program outcomes. High loadings for mentorship-related items reaffirm the importance of mentor engagement, while the inclusion of resource availability and industry relevance underscores the need for holistic program designs. These findings provide a framework for evaluating and optimizing collaboration programs, ensuring that they address the multifaceted needs of participants.

The qualitative analysis in this study complements the quantitative findings by providing a deeper understanding of the mechanisms and experiences underlying university-workplace collaborations. Data were collected through semi-structured interviews with 30 participants, including students, faculty members, and industry professionals. Thematic analysis of the interview transcripts revealed key themes that shed light on the nuanced dynamics of these collaborations. One of the most prominent themes was the critical role of mentorship in driving the success of university-workplace collaborations. Participants consistently highlighted the value of experienced mentors guiding their learning and professional development. A student participant remarked, "*My mentor not only helped me understand the technical aspects of the project but also shared invaluable career advice, which boosted my confidence.*" Faculty members also echoed this sentiment, emphasizing the importance of mentors in bridging the gap between theoretical knowledge and practical applications. An industry professional commented, "*As a mentor, I aim to give students a taste of real-world challenges while ensuring they have the support to tackle them. It's about building their confidence and competence.*"

The integration of digital tools emerged as a crucial enabler of skill development. Participants discussed the use of technologies such as virtual reality (VR), simulation software, and collaborative platforms in facilitating hands-on learning. A student noted, "*Using VR to simulate workplace scenarios gave me the opportunity to practice problem-solving in a safe but realistic environment.*" Faculty members highlighted the importance of these tools in enhancing engagement and accessibility. "*Digital platforms allowed us to collaborate effectively with industry professionals, even during remote settings*," a faculty member explained. Industry professionals emphasized that digital tools not only enhance learning but also familiarize students with the technologies commonly used in their fields. Another recurring theme was the ability of these collaborations to bridge the gap between academic knowledge and practical application. Students appreciated how these programs allowed them to apply classroom learning to real-world projects. "*Before this program, I couldn't see how what I learned in class would translate to a job. Working on an industry-sponsored project changed that completely*," a student shared. Faculty members also recognized the value of this alignment. "*These collaborations ensure that our curriculum remains relevant to industry needs*," one faculty member stated. Industry professionals highlighted how these programs enable students to develop critical thinking and adaptability. "*The challenges we assign are designed to mimic real-world problems, which pushes students to think critically and innovate*," an industry professional remarked.

Despite the positive outcomes, participants also identified challenges in implementing university-workplace collaborations. Scheduling conflicts, resource limitations, and communication gaps were frequently mentioned. "*Coordinating between academic schedules and industry timelines was challenging but ultimately worth the effort*," a faculty member noted. Students highlighted the pressure of balancing academic and collaborative responsibilities. "*Juggling coursework and the demands of the project was tough, but it taught me time management*," a student admitted. Industry professionals emphasized the need for clearer communication and goal alignment. "*Ensuring everyone is on the same page requires effort, but it's essential for the program's success*," an industry mentor explained. The qualitative findings underscore the multifaceted benefits of university-workplace collaborations, from skill enhancement and professional growth to the integration of innovative technologies. Participants' comments highlight the critical role of mentorship, the transformative potential of digital tools, and the importance of aligning academic and industry objectives. While challenges persist, the overall sentiment reflects a positive impact, reinforcing the value of these collaborations in preparing students for the workforce.

DISCUSSION

The findings of this study underscore the transformative potential of university-workplace collaborations in enhancing students' technology skills and bridging the gap between academia and industry. This section explores the implications of the quantitative and qualitative results, connecting them to the broader discourse on educational practices, workforce development, and policy implications. It also addresses the challenges identified in the study, offering solutions and recommendations for stakeholders.

The significant improvements in participants' skill levels, as evidenced by the quantitative analysis, affirm the efficacy of structured collaboration programs. The substantial gains observed among students suggest that these initiatives are particularly beneficial for individuals in the early stages of their professional journey. This aligns with the notion that immersive, real-world experiences accelerate learning by contextualizing theoretical knowledge. The role of mentorship, highlighted as a strong predictor of skill development, reinforces existing literature emphasizing the value of guided learning. Effective mentorship not only enhances technical proficiency but also fosters soft skills such as communication, adaptability, and problem-solving, which are critical in professional settings. The qualitative insights provide further depth to these findings. Students frequently emphasized how mentors served as navigators through complex projects, offering guidance and motivation. Faculty members pointed out that collaboration programs often acted as a learning opportunity for them as well, enabling them to align their teaching practices with industry trends. Industry professionals, on the other hand, valued the fresh perspectives brought by students, which often led to innovative solutions to workplace challenges. This reciprocal benefit underscores the collaborative nature of these programs, where all stakeholders gain valuable insights and experiences. The varying impact of collaborations across different stakeholder groups highlights the need for tailored program designs. While students gained the most in terms of skill enhancement, faculty members and industry professionals experienced moderate improvements. Faculty members, for instance, might benefit more from structured exposure to industry innovations, while industry professionals may gain from workshops or seminars focusing on pedagogy and academic research. Addressing these unique needs can ensure that the benefits of collaboration programs are equitably distributed.

The integration of digital tools emerged as a pivotal factor in the success of collaboration programs. Technologies such as virtual reality, simulation software, and collaborative platforms facilitated hands-on learning and streamlined interactions between stakeholders. These tools not only enhanced accessibility but also bridged geographical and logistical barriers, enabling broader participation. For instance, the use of virtual reality to simulate workplace scenarios allowed students to engage in problem-solving exercises that closely mirrored real-world challenges. Such innovations align with the growing emphasis on experiential learning and underscore the potential of technology to transform education. Students frequently highlighted how digital tools enhanced their understanding of complex concepts. For example, a participant noted that "using simulation software helped me visualize technical processes, making them easier to grasp and apply." Faculty members reported that these tools enriched classroom discussions by providing practical examples and case studies. Industry professionals also appreciated the efficiency of virtual collaboration platforms, which enabled them to mentor students remotely without compromising the quality of interaction. However, the findings also highlight the need for equitable access to digital resources. Disparities in resource availability can hinder the effectiveness of collaboration programs, particularly in underfunded institutions. A lack of financial support for acquiring advanced technological tools and sustaining industry partnerships disproportionately affects institutions with fewer resources. To address this, several nations have adopted targeted funding models, such as government-backed technology grants in Singapore and public-private partnerships in Canada, which have significantly improved access to digital learning resources. Introducing similar funding initiatives can help bridge the digital divide and enhance the overall impact of university-workplace collaborations.

While the study highlights numerous benefits, it also identifies significant challenges in implementing university-workplace collaborations. Scheduling conflicts, resource constraints, and communication gaps were among the most frequently reported issues. These challenges underscore the complexity of aligning the objectives and timelines of academic and industry stakeholders. To address scheduling conflicts, programs can adopt flexible models that accommodate the diverse needs of participants. For example, modular programs with adaptable timelines can provide students and professionals the flexibility to balance their responsibilities. Industry stakeholders suggested that shorter, intensive programs, such as boot camps or hackathons, could also offer valuable alternatives to traditional semester-long collaborations. Resource constraints, particularly in terms of access to advanced tools and technologies, emerged as a critical barrier. Institutions with limited funding often struggle to provide the infrastructure required for effective collaboration programs. This issue can be mitigated through public-private partnerships and funding initiatives that prioritize investments in collaborative education. Industry partners can play a crucial role by contributing resources, such as advanced tools, mentorship, and funding, to support academic institutions. For example, companies can sponsor laboratories, provide software licenses, or offer financial aid to students participating in collaborative programs. Improving communication is another critical area. Clear and consistent communication channels are essential for aligning expectations and ensuring the smooth execution of collaborative programs. Regular meetings, progress updates, and feedback mechanisms can foster transparency and build trust among stakeholders. Additionally, appointing program coordinators or liaison officers to oversee collaboration efforts can enhance coordination and resolve conflicts promptly. Faculty members in the study emphasized the value of "open forums" where students, faculty, and industry professionals could discuss progress and address challenges collaboratively.

The study's findings have significant implications for curriculum design in higher education. The alignment of academic programs with industry requirements emerged as a key factor influencing the success of collaborations. This calls for a shift towards competency-based curricula that prioritize practical skills alongside theoretical knowledge. Incorporating industry-relevant projects, internships, and case studies into academic programs can provide students with opportunities to apply their learning in real-world contexts. Collaborative programs should emphasize interdisciplinary learning to prepare students for the complexities of modern workplaces. For instance, integrating elements of data science, project management, and communication skills into technology-focused programs can enhance students' employability. Faculty development programs that equip educators with the skills and knowledge needed to deliver such curricula are equally important. These initiatives can ensure that teaching practices remain relevant and responsive to industry demands. Furthermore, institutions should consider the incorporation of "micro-credentials" or "stackable certificates" that allow students to gain recognition for specific skills acquired through collaboration programs. These credentials can enhance employability and provide students with a competitive edge in the job market.

The findings highlight the need for policy interventions to support and scale university-workplace collaborations. Governments and educational bodies can play a pivotal role by creating an enabling environment for these initiatives. Policies that incentivize industry participation, provide funding for collaborative programs, and promote curriculum flexibility can enhance the sustainability and impact of these efforts. One potential policy measure is the establishment of innovation hubs that bring together academic institutions, industries, and government agencies to foster collaboration. These hubs can serve as platforms for knowledge exchange, resource sharing, and co-creation of solutions to real-world challenges. Additionally, accreditation bodies can incorporate collaboration metrics into their evaluation frameworks, encouraging institutions to prioritize partnerships with industry. For industry partners, tax benefits or subsidies for supporting educational collaborations could be effective incentives. Governments could also establish national databases of collaboration opportunities, helping institutions and industries find suitable partners and streamline the initiation of such programs. Furthermore, policies that encourage diversity and inclusion in collaboration programs can ensure that the benefits are equitably distributed across various demographic groups.

The study opens several avenues for future research and practice. Longitudinal studies that track the long-term impact of collaboration programs on participants' career trajectories can provide valuable insights into their sustainability. Additionally, research on the integration of emerging technologies, such as artificial intelligence and blockchain, into collaboration frameworks can inform the development of innovative educational practices. Exploring the experiences of underrepresented groups in collaboration programs is another important area for future research. Understanding the unique challenges and opportunities faced by women, minorities, and individuals from disadvantaged backgrounds can inform the design of inclusive and equitable programs. Furthermore, comparative studies that examine collaboration models across different countries and cultural contexts can provide a global perspective on best practices.

The discussion highlights the multifaceted impact of university-workplace collaborations on skill development, curriculum design, and workforce readiness. By addressing the challenges and leveraging the opportunities identified in this study, stakeholders can enhance the effectiveness and sustainability of these initiatives. The findings underscore the importance of collaboration as a pathway to bridging the gap between academia and industry, ultimately contributing to the development of a skilled and adaptable workforce ready to meet the demands of a rapidly evolving global economy.

CONCLUSION

This study illuminates the transformative potential of university-workplace collaborations in bridging the gap between academic education and industry demands. By focusing on technology skill development, the research highlights the multifaceted benefits of structured collaboration programs for students, faculty members, and industry professionals. The quantitative analysis demonstrated significant improvements in participants' skill levels, while qualitative insights revealed the nuanced mechanisms and challenges underpinning these outcomes. One of the most compelling findings of this study is the critical role of mentorship in enhancing both technical and soft skills. Effective mentorship emerged as a key predictor of success, underscoring the importance of guided learning in professional settings. Furthermore, the integration of digital tools and technologies significantly enriched the learning experience, facilitating accessibility, engagement, and practical application of theoretical knowledge. These findings affirm the value of leveraging technology to overcome geographical and logistical barriers in collaborative education.

The study also sheds light on the challenges inherent in implementing collaboration programs, including scheduling conflicts, resource constraints, and communication gaps. Addressing these issues requires a concerted effort from all stakeholders—academic institutions, industry partners, and policymakers—to design flexible, resource-efficient, and well-coordinated programs. Initiatives such as public-private partnerships, innovation hubs, and structured communication frameworks can play a pivotal role in mitigating these challenges. From a curriculum perspective, the findings advocate for a shift towards competency-based and interdisciplinary learning approaches. By aligning academic programs with industry needs, institutions can prepare students for the complexities of modern workplaces. Incorporating elements such as industry-relevant projects, micro-credentials, and experiential learning opportunities into curricula can significantly enhance employability and skill development. Policy interventions are also crucial in scaling and sustaining these collaborative efforts. Incentivizing industry participation, ensuring equitable access to resources, and fostering diversity and inclusion are essential steps towards creating a robust ecosystem for collaboration. Governments and accreditation bodies have a unique opportunity to drive these initiatives by providing funding, establishing innovation hubs, and integrating collaboration metrics into evaluation frameworks. One of the most effective funding models involves tax incentives for companies that invest in student training programs, as seen in Germany's corporate apprenticeship schemes. Another approach is competitive grant funding for universities that demonstrate high-impact industry collaborations, similar to the U.K.'s Knowledge Transfer Partnership (KTP) model, which has resulted in over 80% of participating graduates securing employment within six months. Furthermore, industry co-funding models, where companies match government contributions to workforce training initiatives, have proven successful in Finland. By leveraging these proven funding strategies, universities and industries can develop more sustainable collaboration frameworks that benefit both students and employers.

REFERENCES

Altan-Olcay, Ö., & Bergeron, S. (2024). Care in times of the pandemic: Rethinking meanings of work in the university. *Gender, Work and Organization*, *31*(4), 1544–1559. DOI: 10.1111/gwao.12871 PMID: 35942417

Ankrah, S., & AL-Tabbaa, O. (2015). Universities–industry collaboration: A systematic review. *Scandinavian Journal of Management*, *31*(3), 387–408. DOI: 10.1016/j.scaman.2015.02.003

Becker, G. S. (2009). *Human capital: A theoretical and empirical analysis, with special reference to education*. University of Chicago Press.

Billett, S. (2011). *Vocational education: Purposes, traditions and prospects*. Springer Science & Business Media. DOI: 10.1007/978-94-007-1954-5

Borg, J., Borg, N., Scott-Young, C. M., & Naderpajouh, N. (2021). The work readiness–career resilience linkage: Implications for project talent management. *International Journal of Managing Projects in Business*, *14*(4), 917–935. DOI: 10.1108/IJMPB-04-2020-0129

Brynjolfsson, E., & McAfee, A. (2014). *The second Machine Age: Work, progress, and prosperity in a time of brilliant technologies*. WW Norton & Company.

Cappelli, P. (2012). Why good people can't get jobs: The skills gap and what companies can do about it. In *Why Good People Can't Get Jobs*. University of Pennsylvania Press.

Carayannis, E. G., & Morawska, J. (2023). Digital and green twins of Industry & Society 5.0: the role of universities. In *The Elgar Companion to Digital Transformation, Artificial Intelligence and Innovation in the Economy, Society and Democracy* (pp. 166-202). Edward Elgar Publishing.

Damek, S., Söbke, H., Weise, F., & Reichelt, M. (2022). (Meta) Competences for Digital Practice: Educational Scenarios for the Workplace of the Future Exemplified by Building Information Modeling Work Processes. *arXiv preprint arXiv:2207.01498*.

Dewey, J. (1986, September). Experience and education. [). Taylor & Francis Group.]. *The Educational Forum*, *50*(3), 241–252. DOI: 10.1080/00131728609335764

Etzkowitz, H., & Leydesdorff, L. (2000). The dynamics of innovation: From National Systems and "Mode 2" to a Triple Helix of university–industry–government relations. *Research Policy*, *29*(2), 109–123. DOI: 10.1016/S0048-7333(99)00055-4

Fleming, J. (2014). *Exploring stakeholders perspectives of cooperative education in sport tertiary education* (Doctoral dissertation, Deakin University).

Gann, D., Montresor, F., & Eisenberg, J. (2018, November). 3 ways to nurture collaboration between universities and industry. In *World Economic Forum: Education, Skills and Learning,[online]*. Retrieved from: https://www.weforum.org/stories/2018/11/3-ways-to-nurture-collaboration-between-universities-and-industry/

Jackson, D. (2013). Student perceptions of the importance of employability skill provision in business undergraduate programs. *Journal of Education for Business, 88*(5), 271–279. DOI: 10.1080/08832323.2012.697928

Kolb, D. A. (2014). *Experiential learning: Experience as the source of learning and development*. FT press.

Kurtoglu, M. (2018). The Dream is Over The Crisis of Clark Kerr's California Idea of Higher Education.

Means, B., Toyama, Y., Murphy, R., Bakia, M., & Jones, K. (2009). Evaluation of evidence-based practices in online learning: A meta-analysis and review of online learning studies.

Messaoud, S. B., Ilahi, M., & Cheniti-Belcadhi, L. (2022, March). Towards a personalized micro-credentials approach based on learning analytics for reducing the gap university-industry. In *2022 IEEE Global Engineering Education Conference (EDUCON)* (pp. 1448-1454). IEEE. DOI: 10.1109/EDUCON52537.2022.9766585

Prince, M. J., & Felder, R. M. (2006). Inductive teaching and learning methods: Definitions, comparisons, and research bases. *Journal of Engineering Education, 95*(2), 123–138. DOI: 10.1002/j.2168-9830.2006.tb00884.x

Romao, L., Kalinowski, M., Barbosa, C., Araújo, A. A., Barbosa, S. D., & Lopes, H. (2024). Agile Minds, Innovative Solutions, and Industry-Academia Collaboration: Lean R&D Meets Problem-Based Learning in Software Engineering Education. *arXiv preprint arXiv:2407.15982*. DOI: 10.5753/sbes.2024.3456

Schmid Mast, M., Kleinlogel, E. P., Tur, B., & Bachmann, M. (2018). The future of interpersonal skills development: Immersive virtual reality training with virtual humans. *Human Resource Development Quarterly, 29*(2), 125–141. DOI: 10.1002/hrdq.21307

Tenenbaum, H. R., Crosby, F. J., & Gliner, M. D. (2001). Mentoring relationships in graduate school. *Journal of Vocational Behavior, 59*(3), 326–341. DOI: 10.1006/jvbe.2001.1804 van der Vlies, R. (2020). Digital strategies in education across OECD countries: Exploring education policies on digital technologies.

Vivek, V., Gambhir, V., & Gill, A. (2024, September). Understanding the Societal Impacts of Artificial Intelligence and Machine Learning on Employment and Workforce Dynamics. In *2024 International Conference on Advances in Computing Research on Science Engineering and Technology (ACROSET)* (pp. 1-6). IEEE.

Yu, Z., & Xu, W. (2022). A meta-analysis and systematic review of the effect of virtual reality technology on users' learning outcomes. *Computer Applications in Engineering Education*, *30*(5), 1470–1484. DOI: 10.1002/cae.22532

Zhuang, T., & Shi, J. (2024). Engagement, determinants and challenges: A multinational systematic review of education-focused university-industry collaborations. *Educational Review*, *76*(5), 1363–1391. DOI: 10.1080/00131911.2022.2149701

Chapter 3
Bridging the Digital Literacy Gap:
Effective Collaboration Between Institutes of Higher Education and the Workforce for Technology Integration

Vishal Jain
https://orcid.org/0000-0003-1126-7424
Sharda University, India

Archan Mitra
https://orcid.org/0000-0002-1419-3558
NITTE University, India

ABSTRACT

This research explores effective collaboration between higher education institutions and the workforce to bridge the digital literacy gap in an increasingly technology-driven economy. Digital literacy, encompassing a range of competencies beyond basic computer skills, is vital for professional success. However, a significant mismatch persists between the digital skills imparted by educational institutions and those demanded by the workforce, leading to challenges in employment and productivity. Using a mixed-methods approach, the study investigates current digital literacy needs, examines successful collaboration models, and proposes actionable strategies to align curricula with industry requirements. Findings highlight the potential of cooperative digital hubs and integrated work-study programs in fostering job-ready graduates. Recommendations include stakeholder engagement, resource allocation, and policy incentives to enhance collaboration.

DOI: 10.4018/979-8-3373-0004-7.ch003

1. INTRODUCTION

In today's fast-evolving economy, the concept of digital literacy has transcended beyond the realm of basic computer skills to encompass a much broader and more complex set of competencies. Digital literacy is no longer confined to operating a computer or using simple applications; it now entails the ability to effectively navigate, analyze, and engage with information across multiple digital platforms. These skills are foundational for both personal and professional success, especially as digital technologies become more deeply ingrained in every facet of life. From social interactions to career advancements, digital literacy is a critical enabler in an increasingly interconnected world.

1.1 Background

Advancements in technology in recent decades are taking place faster than anyone can comprehend. Artificial intelligence (AI), analytics with big data, cloud computing, and the Internet of Things (IoT) represent some of the advancements not just dictating business transactions but also determining the skills needed to thrive in these environments. Advanced technology adoption by organizations has greatly shifted in the expectation at the work pace, and the market demands to use these tools to resolve strategic problems for making decisions on strategy involving change and innovation necessary (Jones, 2022). Thus, there is a big need for education systems to be aligned with market trends, producing a new brand of digirati graduates to face the challenges of their future in the area of technology.

The virtuous condition to digital literacy has left a big gap in advanced digital skills that students have acquired during their higher studies compared to what employers usually expect as part of knowledge on the employment ladder. Researchers have been consistent in pointing to the mismatch showing that it is so many times the case that when most graduates go to the labor market, they are highly incompetent in digital knowledge when to compare what their roles would expect in skills and expertise (Taylor, Liu, & Smith, 2020). Not only does this problem affect individual career trajectories, but it also becomes a guilt on employers who are forced to get additional means of remediation into training and upskilling of employees. It's also because of the rapid evolution of technology, which in most cases leaves educational curricula trailing behind and utterly disconnected between the learning and industry demand.

Higher education institutions have always been known and considered as the bastions of skill-building and the dissemination of knowledge. However, the aspect of these institutions if preparing for students to enter the digital age needs to be excluded. Gone are the days where schools can solely teach theories, as what is really necessary is for them to teach practical, hands-on skills to be used in a professional context. It would involve the integration of the best digital tools in the market, enable students to think critically and seed among the students the concerns for lifelong learning. Higher educational institutions, in so doing, play a pivotal role in narrowing the digital literacy gap and ensuring that graduates are well-equipped to navigate and contribute to a rapidly digitizing world.

1.2 Problem Statement

Such a digital literacy divide is a wound growing in higher education's regard to the labor market. So many students failed to find themselves ready or competent for their praxis. Particularly students who come under highly-technological organizations as indicated by Brown and Green (2019) enumeration. Yet, the problem exacerbates, especially with some very fast-moving technologies whose pace tolls that of evolving curricula within an academy.

To the employer, the difference in digital literacy results in expensive start-up and training expenses. Consequently, different organizations consider hiring batch after batch of employees and extensively training them so that they attain optimal performance. This consequently entails delay to fruitful performance in an organization and can also imply a failure to see readiness in education institutions to producing employees for the workforce. This divide additionally has impacts on the way the industry innovates, as a workforce without the necessary skills will not be able to fully exploit new technologies (O'Neil, 2021).

This literacy gap extends out into many broader fields, such as economics and social justice. With intensified centrality through digital technologies in most forms of societal function-from medicine and education to civic duties and governance-management of widespread digital literacy becomes a requirement to cease further social and economic divisions. It hits worse those marginalized groups that did not have previous digital empowerment resources and opportunities. They need a system that the educational institutions, industry captains, and policymakers together must create, by definition, to begin scaling inequalities beyond the digital divide.

1.3 Research Objectives

This study aims to explore the challenges and opportunities associated with bridging the digital literacy gap through effective collaboration between higher education institutions and the workforce. By identifying and analyzing successful models of industry-academia partnerships, the research seeks to develop actionable strategies for aligning educational curricula with the demands of the modern job market. The specific objectives of this study are to:

1. Assess the current landscape of digital literacy requirements across various industries and compare these needs with the competencies being imparted in higher education.
2. Investigate successful examples of collaboration between academic institutions and industries that have demonstrated positive outcomes in digital literacy enhancement.
3. Propose practical, scalable solutions that can be implemented to reduce the digital literacy gap and foster better alignment between education and employment.

By addressing these objectives, the research intends to provide a roadmap for creating a digitally competent workforce capable of thriving in a rapidly evolving technological landscape. The findings are expected to benefit not only students and educators but also employers and policymakers, contributing to a more dynamic and inclusive digital economy.

2. LITERATURE REVIEW

2.1 Theoretical Foundations

Economically, digital literacy leads to a highly literate workforce, and thus productivity and innovation would only become more widespread in society. This shift is important for educational institutions in that the incorporation of digital literacy in curricular offerings assures greater relevance and appeal in a highly competitive academic environment. Hiring graduates good in the latest digital skills further moves the reputation needle in terms of governmental reputation and increase in student enrollment. Besides this, alignment of academic offerings with industry needs can open additional doors to collaboration, funding, and through a good contract, research, creating a win-win process.

At the social level, digital literacy contributes profoundly to equity and inclusion. Individual digital skills help the individual connect with and use digital technologies, helping to overcome the disparities that otherwise would reach into education, labor markets, or civic involvement. A separate and important issue in which literacy plays a role in democracy is critical evaluation of information and participation in online discussions that enable individual rights advocacy. This digital literacy initiative is particularly fitting in the debate: As newer platforms are beginning to take command of public discourse, it is necessary for society to shoulder a broader digital capacity and literacy load for a better-learned, brought together society (Garcia, 2021).

Underscoring the urgency of the presented issue, the study gives a strategic framework of how collaboration between higher learning and industry can result in solving and overcoming the digital literacy gap. This is all meant to be very strategic. For example, in industries and higher education joining forces in building and interworking programs involving academic learning and real life application consisting of learning and training methods, thus both sectors together may solve that challenge. The research does not dogmatically press on the fast remedy of this issue but proposes a strategic framework for good and lasting progress.

2.3 Importance of Digital Literacy in Workforce Development

Employer Profits: Digital literacy has now become one of the most critical prerequisites for any workforce because employers increasingly prefer getting employees who are efficient in using tools and digital platforms. Learning of high tech-such as AI, cloud computing, and data analytics, employment is growing, which includes digital skills. Taylor, Liu, and Smith (2020) found a significant difference between digital competent work required by the employer with those refreshed by career services. For example, beginners learn CRM software systems, email marketing platforms, and knowledge on social media analytics. In contrast to this, employees working in production units will need an introduction to IoT technologies with regards to automated systems.

Employers need adaptability, continual learning, and increased technical competence. As technology tools are introduced, the workforce will need to adopt, adapt, and learn. This has led organizations to increase the demand for current technology absorption but even greater learning or relearning even as new technologies activate. Primitive ends tend to form a core part of digitalization of innovative skillsposts, with its design requiring employees to take hold of creative solutions using digital tools in problem-solving and innovation (Bawden, 2008).

Success and Challenges Case studies: Successful case studies in digital literacy focus on new collaboration opportunities between the academic institutions and the industries for addressing the skills gap. For instance, Wang and Reeves (2007) described the collaboration where a university and a technology firm together provided resources and conduct training that embeds real-world digital skills into the curricula. Employability skills and the development of new professional contexts were shown to be enhanced with the students through their involvement in this program.

There are, however, still challenges that are encountered. Research suggests that most educational institutions find it difficult to revise their curricula due to resource constraints, the lack of faculty training, as well as some lag-time between the advancement in technology and its incorporation with curriculum knowledge (Brown & Green, 2019). As a result, technically able graduates are often jobless due to the wrong digital practices for their respective industries. This should be attained through a more sustainable purpose of exchange and feedback between academia and industry to ensure currency and dynamism of curricula.

2.4 Barriers to Digital Literacy Integration

The lack of faculty training is an institutional block in itself. In fact, most teachers have little or no advanced training about using an advanced digital tool to teach the highly technical practices. Consequently, infrastructural and resource constraints limit access to technology resources, stem into severe barriers, mostly in underfinanced academic institutions and developing regions. Very often, schools and universities alike buckle without all aspects like high-speed internet, up-to-date hardware as well as licensed software to provide the students with practical experience of them in digital tools (Ragnedda & Muschert, 2013). This resource disparity falls into a digital divide because students without access to technology may have no access similar to the same quality of services which their better-funded institution may provide them.

Despite scarce availability of resources, equitably distributing them within institutions poses a challenge. Urban institutions almost always surpass their rural counterparts, thus the social stratification in which they are based-not only in education but also any other facet of the social divide. This inequality also increases because such disparities hinder rolling out digital literacy programs and thereby maintaining disparities in new skills.

Digital Divide and Socio-Economic Barriers: The digital divide, defined as the gap between those who have access to technology and those who do not, is one of the most persistent barriers to digital literacy. This divide is not merely about access to devices and the internet but also encompasses disparities in the quality of access, digital skills, and support systems (van Laar et al., 2017). Low-income households often face significant challenges in affording the devices and internet connections necessary for developing digital competencies.

Marginalized groups, including individuals from rural areas, women, and older adults, often face additional barriers. Cultural norms, lack of digital awareness, and language limitations can further restrict access and participation. For example, in regions where internet content is predominantly in English, non-English-speaking populations are at a disadvantage in accessing online educational resources (Park, 2011). Addressing these socio-economic barriers requires targeted interventions, such as subsidized technology programs, community training initiatives, and multilingual digital content.

Resistance to Change: Resistance to adopting new technologies is another critical barrier, particularly within organizations and educational institutions. This resistance often stems from a fear of change, lack of confidence in using digital tools, or skepticism about their value. Teachers and administrators may be reluctant to overhaul traditional teaching methods in favor of technology-driven approaches, particularly if they perceive these changes as disruptive or unnecessary (Helsper & Eynon, 2013). Similarly, employees in the workforce may resist digital upskilling programs if they feel intimidated by the learning process or fail to see immediate benefits.

Overcoming this resistance requires a combination of cultural and structural interventions. Leadership plays a crucial role in fostering a culture of innovation and openness to change. Providing adequate training and support can also help alleviate fears and build confidence among educators and employees. Furthermore, demonstrating the tangible benefits of digital literacy, such as improved productivity and career growth, can motivate individuals to embrace change (Kolb, 1984).

Policy and Governance Gaps: The absence of cohesive policies and governance structures to promote digital literacy is a systemic barrier. In many regions, there is no standardized framework to guide the integration of digital skills into education and workforce training. This lack of policy coherence often leads to fragmented efforts, where individual institutions and organizations attempt to address digital literacy in isolation, without coordination or scalability (Ferrari, 2013).

Government support is critical in creating enabling environments for digital literacy development. Policies that incentivize educational institutions to adopt technology, provide funding for infrastructure upgrades, and promote industry-academia collaborations can address systemic challenges. For instance, tax breaks for companies that invest in digital training initiatives or grants for underfunded schools can encourage broader participation and inclusivity (Kumar & Rose, 2021).

2.5 Models of Effective Collaboration

Educational Models for Digital Literacy Development: One of the most effective ways to bridge the digital literacy divide is through educational models that supported co-creation by educational institutions and industry. With Cooperative Digital Literacy Hubs (CDLH), universities joined hands with industries to design curricula, share resources, and provide experiential learning opportunities. Through such hubs, Wheeler (2018) guides learning and acting environments serving as incubators for innovation, opening university students to real-world challenges and giving them hands-on experiences with acquired technology skills.

The inclusion of state-of-the-art technologies into learning environments will make it possible for students to deal with the theme and toolsets that will creep into their professional lives. For example, industry partners can bring advanced tools / software they have on the market, such as data analytics platforms and AI-driven applications, to use by learners. This experience of hands-on learning makes them not only more adept technically, but at the same time develops in them the ability to navigate complex digital ecosystems (Jackson, 2017).

Another educational model incorporates digital literacy into traditional subjects: interdisciplinary approaches. Some examples of these educational models of digital humanities are those that teach students to harness digital approaches to analysis, visualization, and data management. Thus, it also reflects that digital literacy does not necessarily find an enclosure in technical fields, as it makes possible for students who are into such programs even report findings in any scholarly and professional field as well (van Laar et al., 2017).

There are industry-driven programs-another field of collaboration opportunity for enhancing digital literacy. Many companies recognize the value of having knowledgeable works ready to go and therefore develop programs titled work-based skills in the domain of practical training, apprenticeships, and internships that take the student's knowledge out of the academic atmosphere and engage it in real-world settings. Such opportunities offer access for students to working techniques and designs that would prove that he or she is better prepared for larger roles in future (Kumar & Rose, 2021).

Integrated Work-Study Programs (IWSP) are more recent examples of industry-academia collaboration. Students work for an hour in these innovative programs because half their time outside the academic entity and another half hour in internal environments of the industry company. Only this way can theoretical knowledge be transferred more smoothly into practical employment conditions, comprehend the realities of securing a career for industries and actually benefit from being narrowed into that focus-oriented pipeline (Ferrari, 2013).

Public-Private Partnerships and its role: Public-private partnerships (PPPs) are another good example of models to secure and enhance digital literacy. These collaborations play to the strengths of both sectors for larger-scale systemic problems in education and workforce development. The funding, governance, and infrastructure comes under the public with the private delivering technology, expertise, and the industrial know-how that Singh and Zhan (2021) mention as incentives, which are tax waivers and the like, that allow firms to actually get into digital training programs or funding schools to upgrade their capacity for technology.

A well happening model of PPP is the creation of literacy digital campaigns that would be a practice in several countries. These programs comprise training programs among many, which must include extensive digital devices distribution and construction of community learning centers. So too has the UK's Digital Skills Partnership managed to gather government bodies, technology firms, and educational institutions in delivering localized training programs (OECD, 2008). Such programs show how collective actions can best the digital divide and truly enrich inclusive skills development.

Collaboration Models: There are a number of challenges that might hamper the efficacy of collaboration models even though these models have potential in very desirable ways. The most typical one is the differing goals of colleges and industry. In fact, institutions focus on long-term skills development, while the industry seeks the quickest workforce possible, thereby forming programs that do not meet either expectations (Taylor, Liu & Smith, 2020).

Resource is another critical challenge in that developing and sustaining collaboration programs-technology, training, and infrastructure for effectiveness-efforts in resource-stricken environments could make it impossible for these programs to scale over a long term. Moreover, logistical issues lay between those lines where academic calendars and schedules of industry compromising efficient program implementation (Helsper & Eynon, 2013).

Future Directions: As it is adapted and improved, the versatility and improvement start in stakeholders' appealingly designed adaptation with innovation in programs that shall incline them towards flexibility and shall show the door to the availability of programs available in real-time with the involvement of industry practitioners in modification each time the base curricula is updated.

In doing so, international examples of collaboration shall also provide cross-cultural learning in digital literacy skills. In a country-to-country collaborative effort, both developed and developing nations would be helped in reducing global disparities in digital skill training by sharing resources and best practices (Park, 2011).

2.6 Challenges in Collaboration

Coordination Issues: One principal implication regarding the collaboration of academia with industry is a mismatch of goals. The objectives set by academic institutions often favor the acquisition of theoretical grounding and amour-propre as well as long-term expertise over ensuring the quick development of skills, which is foremuch in industries; a number of programs become either too theoretical or overly practical and hence do not fulfill the requirements from both the student and employer perspectives (Taylor, Liu, & Smith, 2020). For example, while universities invest a great deal of emphasis on establishing the foundational knowledge in data science, industries would require some competence in the specific tools or platforms, creating a gap in academics training and job market expectations.

Another chronic problem in this area is the lack of an apparent accountability structure of collaborative initiatives. No clear accountability structure often leaves room for the inefficiency of partnerships. In the absence of well-defined roles and responsibilities, two organizations might not be able to competently deliver outcomes in the form of objectives. For example, who updates the curriculum, allocates resources, or evaluates the program could be completely ambiguous, leading to time wastage and general loss of possible benefits of a partnership. Key to the successful implementation of such programs is the creation and establishment of clear governance structures and communication channels for all stakeholders in the program's success (Kumar & Rose, 2021).

Scalability Concerns: Scalability is a significantly difficult issue in adapting collaborative models across regions or institutions, due to the model being well set up, capable of meeting all needs of resources-, infrastructure-, and socio-economic status-based variation. The example for that would be such a model as digital literacy hubs in urban universities with established and well-funded capital facility would not be implemented in rural or under-resourced institutions. This holds true in many developing countries where infrastructure and financial controls limit the scope of adaptive collaboration (Ragnedda & Muschert, 2013).

Such scalability can be greatly strained by financial and logistical constraints. The investment in technology, training, and coordination would require significant level in the collaborative initiatives. Obtaining consistent funding can be pretty daunting; it is harder to accomplish programs that could be successful if such funding had been diverted and that much goes into short term grants or donations. Logistical roadblocks like calending of academic calendars and work schedules typically of industries or pooling several stakeholders within them could slow down efforts to expand the sizes of models (Ferrari, 2013). Here, adaptable program designs and exciting funding mechanisms are needed to host diverse contexts.

Limitations on Evaluation: It is problematic to evaluate against the metrics when comparing the effectiveness of collaboration patterns. Most evaluation methodologies are usually aimed at measuring the immediate outcomes, such as skill acquisition or immediate employability: long-term results should never be neglected-but often are (Helsper & Eynon, 2013). For example, graduates from one such program might have very high initial employment rates but, in due course, may be found inadequate in terms of agility necessary for roles that require constant learning and skill upgrade.

Moreover, the methods of evaluation face a further limitation in their inability to capture the multifaceted character of digital literacy. Scoring on a test and completing tasks are insufficient for measuring students' ability to apply information critically, solve complex problems, or work as effective team members. Comprehensive tools-based evaluation is therefore recommended in order to raise awareness as to how full the impact of the collaborative initiative is (van Laar et al., 2017).

2.7 Emerging Trends in Digital Literacy

Emerging Technologies Integrated: the swiftness with which technology redefines the scope and application of digital literacy calls into play such new applications as artificial intelligence, gamification, and virtual reality (VR). These are transformative tools like AI-driven learning platforms, which offer personalized learning experiences according to the needs of each learner. They use algorithms to prescribe a check on a user's strengths and weaknesses and, most importantly, on the user's learning pace to align accordingly content delivery, suited to their needs. Adaptive learning software, for example, helps learners develop as they learn, to focus on increased feedback to work on areas that need improvement as more easily transgressed digital modules (Laar et al., 2017). These strategies provide ease of access to and foster digital literacy training, besides promoting inclusivity in accessibility by accounting for individual differences in learning capacity and preferences.

Digital literacy learning is further enhanced by gamification through the facilitation of comparisons, such as dungeons with points, badges, and leaderboards that are adapted to garner engagement and motivation. Gamified platforms also encourage active engagement, challenge individuals in healthy competition that makes the learning environment more vivid, as they confer the experiences of exemplary platforms like Duolingo and Kahoot that have mastered creating information and rich enjoyment of understanding complex concepts (Jackson, 2017). Virtual reality (VR) improves such potentialities by allowing for the experiential treatment of learning: in a virtual world, learners go through a practice that connects theory with its application in practice, whether it is walking through a basic cybersecurity scenario or sitting in a virtual room for team meetings on a design project (Park, 2011).

Focus on Soft Skills: As the roots of digital literacy expand, there is a growing claim for the thrust of soft skills such as adaptability, collaboration, and critical thinking. Technical competence is, of course, necessary; the efficiency of its utilization becomes increasingly important in adaptive situations and collaborative settings. The adaptability, for example, allows a person to navigate the fast-paced technological transitions that define life in the digital age. Those employees who can learn new software while teaching it to others, integrate new technologies fast, and respond to evolving demands of their workplaces have an advantage in the current job market (Kumar & Rose, 2021).

Collaboration becomes the other key idea; most digital environments do not work without teamwork interaction and effective interpersonal communication. It is very relevant for an individual to understand the different modes of enhancing technology within a professional scope through things like co-creating content and utilizing digital tools (like Trello and Slack) to manage projects. Critical thinking is obligatory in evaluating the credibility of online information, solving complex problems, and making sound decisions in digital settings. These, along with the technical abilities, can make individuals competent enough to use digital tools wisely (Bawden, 2008).

Global Benchmarks: Such standards would bring about commonality across countries. For instance, there is more and greater collaboration that can thus occur between countries in areas such as education and training for the workforce. This is relevant to the international validation of training undertaken by multinational firms, who can then train their employees similarly across the world against such standards. Similarly, academic institutions may base their respective curricula upon the framework for students' preparation for global job markets. They would ultimately require such standards in redressing disparities in digital literacy across regions that hinders underdeveloped countries from benefiting from knowledge-sharing practices and hastening their progress (Singh & Zhan, 2021).

At the same time, international benchmarks encourage lifelong learning as they give importance to continuous skill development. These will be helpful because as technology continues to evolve, people will have to update their competencies to remain relevant and competitive. The emphasis on adaptability and lifelong learning, too, is consistent with the rest of the trends with respect to knowing that innovation and agility are the key drivers to success in the global economy (Heifetz & Linsky, 1997).

3. OUTCOMES

Figure 1. CDLH development strategy

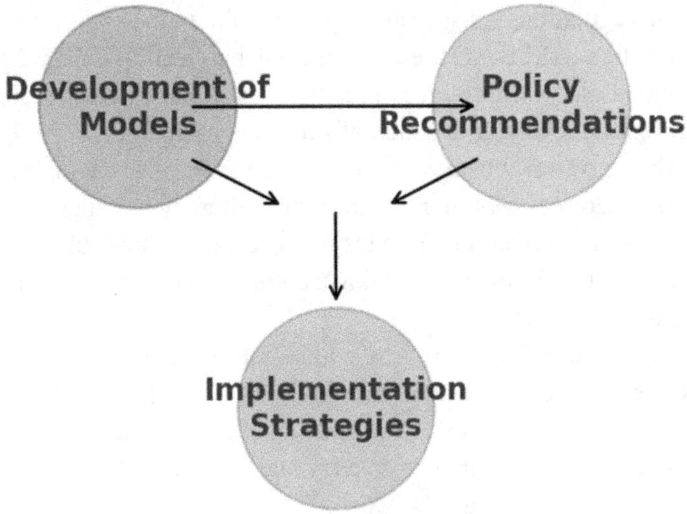

3.1 Development of Models

There is significant potential among institutions of higher education and businesses to use groundbreaking collaborative models to enhance digital literacy. One such strategy is the development of the Cooperative Digital Literacy Hub (CDLH), which provides a venue for collaboration between industry and academia in crafting digital literacy curricula and tools. These hubs can become a factory for digital skill acquisition by providing this new technology to students in industry active exposure (Wheeler, 2018).

Another extraordinary model is the "Integrated Work-Study Program" (IWSP). Through this model, learners are placed inside companies as part-time employees, allowing the instructional knowledge to be demonstrated in a real work setup. In terms of the enhancement of digital literacy, such programs are beneficial in the long term in producing work-ready graduates (Jackson, 2017).

In the case of such effective organizational practices, the two models can be done by mutual partnership. This mutual collaboration should clarify the roles and expectations of partners, benefitting all involved. For instance, CDLH focal points would largely develop joint curricula and research, while IWSP concentrates on practical experience and skills application.

3.2 Policy Recommendations

There might be an essentially effective policy transformation which aids in the execution and sustainability of these collaboration models. For higher educational institutions, the regulations must foster a partnership and seamless integration of industry-proven digital skills into the curricula. All that can be possibly achieved is to change the accreditation so that there is already a need to show industry-collaborative evidence in program development and delivery (Thomas, 2019).

Tax incentives given by business institutions in favor of engaging in educational partnerships and/or contributing toward digital literacy are suggested in policy recommendations. They would help to inspire a corporate habit of investing in the human resources of the future and building a culture of lifelong learning and adaptation (Miller & Luse, 2020).

Governments should facilitate these collaborations as a simple means of encouraging higher education institutions co-developing digital literacy projects with business. Becoming a national standard for digital literacy, it would provide a necessary framework to ensure consistency and quality of digital literacy across institutions and programs (Singh & Zhan, 2021).

3.3 Implementation Strategies

Successful implementation of collaborative digital literacy programs requires strategic planning and resource allocation. Key strategies include:

Stakeholder Engagement: Engaging all relevant stakeholders from the outset is crucial. This includes university administrators, faculty, industry leaders, and students. Regular meetings and consultations can help align goals, manage expectations, and ensure that the programs meet the needs of all parties (Allen & Joseph, 2019).

Resource Allocation: Adequate resources must be allocated for the development and maintenance of collaborative programs. This includes funding for program design and implementation, technology purchases, and ongoing training for faculty and staff. Both educational institutions and business partners should contribute to these resources, possibly supplemented by government funding (Khan & Dam, 2020).

Continuous Evaluation and Feedback: To ensure the effectiveness of these programs, continuous evaluation mechanisms should be put in place. This could involve regular feedback from students and faculty involved in IWSPs, as well as from businesses hosting these students. Data collected from these evaluations can inform adjustments and improvements in program design and delivery (Zhao & Bacco, 2022).

Communication Strategy: Clear and continuous communication is necessary to maintain the alignment of collaborative efforts. A dedicated communication team or liaison officers can help manage communications between institutions and companies, ensuring that all parties remain informed and engaged throughout the process (O'Donnell & Turner, 2018).

4. DISCUSSION

4.1 Interpretation of Findings

The outcomes of the studies give us important insight into practicalities aside from providing a factual basis underpinned by sound theory-the models of collaboration between universities and industries in promoting digital literacy. The results are expected to demonstrate a huge positive contribution toward this end that is how the integrated approaches-adding industry input into academic curricula-were indeed a leap in the digital competence of the graduating student. It backs previous theories along similar lines, as as postulated by Wenger (1998) that communities of practice have the strongest influence on learning, and learning occurs best when infused with activity and context, just like happens in active communities of practice.

Also, the findings are expected not to conflict but to confirm the assertion of the experiential learning theory of Kolb (1984) on effectiveness of real-world experience in education. Both theories posit that individuals enhance their learning when allowed to reflect on theory in real situations. Positive feedback stemming from industry-based projects and internships as part of integrated work-study learning programs indeed supports this, and it is here clearly stated that it is rewarding to learn from direct bearing in professional environments.

Unfortunately, statistics conducted in all the areas of study may bring to light some limitations that could possibly serve as stumbling blocks against other education systems especially when they are too slow in realization of the fact that contemporary job markets are already digital. A study may reveal the extent of the fast or lack of responses by certain educational institutions to the pace of technological change, thus impugning on the rigidity found in typical curriculum designs and accreditation processes (Selingo, 2013).

4.2 Future Research

There is much space for future research to bridge the gap and expand on these findings. For instance, longitudinal studies tracking the graduates over time will shed light on the long term career benefits of the improved digital literacy and the lasting impact in a cooperative educational model. Then are we going to know: Are these benefits going to stand, diminish, or change as they keep ascending towards their future careers?

For that matter, further work can question models for large-scale implementation across different geographical regions and educational contexts. The ways in which such combinations can succeed in different economic sectors and within multiple cultural settings would expand a comprehension of the applicability of the solutions and would work to support the aforementioned effectiveness on a global scale.

In light of this, more research should be directed toward examination of the effect of such education-led associations on further societal outcomes, including improvement in innovation levels, development of businesses, or changes in social mobility. Yet, the research may also focus on more sophisticated tools of assessment that could bring forth an understanding of the breadth and depth of digital literacy skills in terms of diverse professional contexts.

Finally, benchmarking and comparative research are much needed to assess models of partnership of the interface between academia and industry. That could, however, delimit the best practices and key success factors of such collaborations. After a careful comparison, educational leaders or key policy makers can very well decide to choose various models for these to be fully implemented.

5. CONCLUSION

The study links emerging evidence that partnership models involving educational institutes and industry significantly enhance digital literacy among graduates. This enhancement, in a nutcase, trains them more consequentially to meet contemporary needs of a digital economy, thus tying education and employment closer. Real-world experiences and industry feedback into curricula makes education more relevant and practical to need more current and future jobs.

Another is the Co-operative Digital Literacy Hubs merged with a Work-Study Programs model, thus forward-thinking education that mirrors the ally state, being together across the global workforce. These models are indicative of the potential of such a collaborative exercise in not only enhancing new graduates' digital competencies, but also envisaging the full broad set of employability and adaptability attributes in such graduates in a quickly-evolving technology environment.

On the other hand, limits of the findings lie in generalized results and bias. The study is conscious enough about this, needing an understandable validation in data collection, so it can avoid including ambiguities in methods. In observing these facts, there is a need for continued research leading to a much more refined understanding of these models that deal with collaboration within institutions, such as those under investigation, and their long-term effects on students' careers and broader economic and societal outcomes.

Subsequent research efforts should concentrate on the longitudinal pursuit of subsequently sophisticated digital literacy enhancements of graduates and later, beneficiaries of such educational models. Additionally, widening the study to other geographical and economic contexts will offer more revelations as to how diverse factors influence the successfulness of such educational collaborations.

In the final analysis, this research suggests a need to think about the way digital literacy is integrated into higher education curricula collaboratively with industry. It asserts the importance of partnerships in shaping a human resource with aptness in digital proficiency as well as adaptability to new technologies over time as they emerge in that work environment. Embracing such collaborative models, educational establishments and business together enhance that relevance and impact of education, thereby supporting a more dynamic and inclusive digital economy.

REFERENCES

Allen, M., & Joseph, B. (2019). Strategies for effective stakeholder engagement in educational partnerships. *Education + Training*, *61*(4), 482–497.

Bawden, D. (2008). Origins and concepts of digital literacy. In Lankshear, C., & Knobel, M. (Eds.), *Digital literacies: Concepts, policies and practices* (pp. 17–32). Peter Lang Publishing.

Braun, V., & Clarke, V. (2006). Using thematic analysis in psychology. *Qualitative Research in Psychology*, *3*(2), 77–101. DOI: 10.1191/1478088706qp063oa

Brown, A., & Green, T. D. (2019). The necessity of digital literacy in the modern workforce. *The Journal of Technology Studies*, *45*(2), 96–109.

Cai, Y., Kenderdine, T., & Long, B. (2019). Evaluating the effectiveness of university-industry partnerships in providing digital literacy skills. *Higher Education*, *78*(4), 639–655.

Creswell, J. W. (2014). *Research design: Qualitative, quantitative, and mixed methods approaches* (4th ed.). SAGE Publications.

Garcia, R. (2021). Digital literacy and social inclusion. *Information Communication and Society*, *24*(7), 985–1002.

Gilster, P. (1997). *Digital literacy*. Wiley Computer Publishing.

Helsper, E. J., & Eynon, R. (2013). Distinctions in digital literacy: The relationship between the digital literacy gap and social exclusion. *The American Behavioral Scientist*, *57*(7), 963–986.

Jackson, D. (2017). Enhancing industry engagement in engineering education: The potentials of integrated work-study programs. *Journal of Professional Issues in Engineering Education and Practice*, *143*(4), 04017005.

Jones, R. (2022). Technological advancements and the changing workforce. *Future of Work Journal*, *3*(1), 34–50.

Khan, Z., & Dam, N. (2020). Resource allocation models in academia and industry collaborations. *Journal of Business Research*, *112*, 216–225.

Kolb, D. A. (1984). *Experiential learning: Experience as the source of learning and development*. Prentice-Hall.

Kumar, S., & Rose, R. C. (2021). Digital literacy in higher education: A case study of student engagement and learning outcomes. *Higher Education*, *81*, 647–665.

Laal, M., & Ghodsi, S. M. (2012). Benefits of collaborative learning. *Procedia: Social and Behavioral Sciences*, *31*, 486–490. DOI: 10.1016/j.sbspro.2011.12.091

Martin, A. (2008). *Digital literacy and the "digital society"*. Digital literacies: Concepts, policies and practices, 151-176.

Miller, R., & Luse, A. (2020). Policy recommendations for partnership in digital skills training. *Journal of Policy and Strategy*, *31*(2), 204–219.

O'Donnell, L., & Turner, T. (2018). Communication strategies for interorganizational cooperation. *Management Communication Quarterly*, *32*(2), 253–280.

O'Neil, H. (2021). Bridging the skills gap: How digital literacy can shape the future workforce. *Economic Analysis Review*, *36*(2), 210–228.

OECD. (2008). *Tertiary education for the knowledge society*. OECD Publishing.

Park, S. (2011). Digital literacy: A conceptual framework for survival skills in the digital era. *Journal of Multimedia and Hypermedia*, *20*(1), 31–50.

Ragnedda, M., & Muschert, G. W. (2013). *The digital divide: The Internet and social inequality in international perspective*. Routledge. DOI: 10.4324/9780203069769

Selingo, J. J. (2013). *College (Un)Bound: The future of higher education and what it means for students*. Houghton Mifflin Harcourt.

Singh, A., & Zhan, J. (2021). Government policies for encouraging industry-education collaboration. *Education Policy Analysis Archives*, *29*, 58.

Smith, J., & Chang, Z. (2021). Integrating digital literacy in higher education curricula. *Educational Review*, *73*(4), 455–472.

Taylor, M., Liu, B., & Smith, S. (2020). *Digital literacy disparities among graduates: Implications for workforce development*. Workforce Education Forum, 47(1), 112-130.

Thomas, R. (2019). Accreditation standards and industry collaboration in higher education. *Higher Education Policy*, *32*(3), 401–419.

van Laar, E., van Deursen, A. J., van Dijk, J. A., & de Haan, J. (2017). The relation between 21st-century skills and digital skills: A systematic literature review. *Computers in Human Behavior*, *72*, 577–588. DOI: 10.1016/j.chb.2017.03.010

Wang, F., & Reeves, T. C. (2007). *Why do teachers need to use technology in their classrooms? Issues, challenges, and solutions*. College of Education, University of Georgia.

Wenger, E. (1998). *Communities of practice: Learning, meaning, and identity.* Cambridge University Press. DOI: 10.1017/CBO9780511803932

Wheeler, S. (2018). Innovative models for collaboration between universities and businesses. *TechTrends*, *62*(5), 475–483.

Wilson, P., & Walsh, C. (2022). Collaborative models for integrating digital skills in education. *Journal of Education and Work*, *35*(3), 342–359.

Zhao, Y. (2019). The role of higher education in closing the digital literacy gap. *The Journal of Higher Education*, *90*(3), 424–445.

Zhao, Y., & Bacco, M. (2022). Feedback and evaluation processes in university-industry partnerships. *Educational Evaluation and Policy Analysis*, *44*(1), 134–153.

Chapter 4 Bridging the Digital Divide in the Access and Usage of Technology Through Digital Literacy in Rural Vocational Schools

Joelle Danielle Ngo Ndjama
https://orcid.org/0000-0002-2472-2329
University of Zululand, South Africa

ABSTRACT

The digital divide phenomenon presents a significant challenge in rural vocational schools, where disparities in access to and utilisation of technology can hinder educational opportunities for marginalised individuals. Despite the extensive body of research on the integration of digital technologies in academic settings, there remains a notable deficiency in understanding effective digital literacy practices tailored specifically for vocational education. This study employs resource and appropriation theory to explore the inequalities in technological access and usage within vocational institutions. The investigation identifies four distinct types of digital divides: the physical access divide, the skills access divide, the usage divide, and the network or internet divide. The findings suggest that bridging the digital divide necessitates a collaborative approach involving four critical stakeholders: vocational institutions, industry partners, government agencies, and rural communities, thereby fostering an inclusive environment.

DOI: 10.4018/979-8-3373-0004-7.ch004

1. INTRODUCTION

Ocaña-Fernández, Fernández, Chiparra, Gallarday-Morales and Gallarday-Morales (2020) contend that the relentless progression of technology has undeniably led to rapid transformations, significantly impacting various facets of human life, particularly in education. Likewise, Afzal, Khan, Daud, Ahmad and Butt (2023) comment that contemporary society increasingly demands information skills across various domains, encompassing everyday life, professional environments, educational institutions, and higher learning establishments. Peñate, Padrón-Robaina and Nieves (2024) add that the increasing trend of digitalisation in contemporary society and the rising need for digital skills necessitate educational systems to evolve in response to these developments. Devisakti and Muftahu (2023) and Balderas-Mireles et al. (2021) complement in a landscape marked by swift and ongoing transformations, leveraging technological tools is essential for enhancing the effectiveness of teaching and learning methodologies in educational training. In contemporary society, digital technology plays a crucial role as a medium for communication, entertainment, information dissemination, and education (Habibi, Sofyan& Mukminin, 2023). Consequently, the responsibilities of educators and other professionals have evolved markedly, as the array of teaching and learning resources has expanded, facilitating education within an increasingly interconnected global community (Ocaña-Fernández et al., 2020). Habibi et al. (2023) assert that in contemporary society, digital technology plays a crucial role as a medium for communication, entertainment, information dissemination, and education. However, a digital divide means that access to technology is not uniform across the population (Habibi et al., 2023). The digital divide refers to the disparity between individuals with access to technology and the skills to utilise it effectively and those without such access (Afzal et al., 2023). Moreover, Van Dijk (2019) states that the digital divide is a technical issue when, in fact, it is more of a social problem. This divide highlights the disparities between individuals who have access to technological resources and those who lack them, thereby exacerbating existing inequalities in financial, informational, social, and educational domains (Habibi et al., 2023). Duma et al. (2021) explain that information communication and technology (ICT) encompassing the internet, computers, and mobile devices like smartphones, tablets, and laptops, are utilised in educational settings to enhance teaching and learning resources. Afzal et al. (2023) note that the ability to access these devices and the internet, along with the skills to utilise these technologies effectively, is becoming essential for comprehensive engagement in economic, political, and social spheres. The authors add that access to digital technologies is crucial for promoting equitable participation in the information economy, facilitating governments in meeting their electronic service delivery goals, and empowering individuals to seize the economic growth opportunities presented by the information age. Hence, Jia and Huang (2023) point out that digital literacy involves not just the proficiency in utilising digital tools and devices, but also the cognitive and social competencies necessary for effective engagement and navigation within the digital landscape. As the job market transforms, the need for skilled individuals with a solid grounding in digital literacy is growing, highlighting the importance of vocational education to evolve and meet these emerging demands. Incorporating digital literacy into vocational education is essential for equipping students to succeed in the contemporary technology-oriented job market, enabling them to acquire the skills needed to adjust to technological advancements and utilise digital resources for their career development (Jia & Huang, 2023). Jatmoko, Suyitno, Rasul, Nurtanto, Kholifah, Masek and Nur (2023) observe that the current educational paradigm, particularly within vocational training, prioritises the enhancement of students' skills and competencies for the workforce. This digital technology serves as a fundamental element in achieving the competencies required by students. The integration of ICTs into contemporary education is essential for developing skilled professionals who are increasingly sought after in the labour market (Kvon, Vaks, Kalimullin, Bayanova, Shaidullina, Dolzhikova & Lapidus, 2019). In developing nations, ICTs are suggested to help bridge the digital divide, particularly in the educational sector, where they can facilitate access to secondary learning resources, although traditional hard-copy textbooks remain the preferred primary materials (Mwapwele et al., 2019).

2. PROBLEM STATEMENT

While individuals with technological access enjoy unprecedented opportunities, it raises concerns for those who remain marginalised (Afzal et al., 2023). Jatmoko et al. (2023) posit that while extensive research exists on the integration of digital technology in education, there remains a gap in comprehending effective digital literacy practices specifically within vocational education. In addition, Zancajo, Verger, and Bolea (2022) alongside Pooja (2021) assert that the integration of digital technology in educational practices enhances the competencies of vocational school instructors, thereby equipping their students with the necessary skills for future employment. Nonetheless, obstacles to the effective utilisation of digital tools in the classroom may impede educators from fully leveraging technology in their teaching methodologies (Habibi et al., 2023). Furthermore, the issue of technology access has been previously explored in academic settings; however, this exploration has been somewhat restricted; (1) primarily, the focus has been on students' physical access to technology, with an emphasis on developing and utilising tools to measure this access in educational environments and (2) research concerning technological access for teachers remains sparse, particularly within specific contexts and environments (Habibi et al., 2023).

3. LITERATURE REVIEW

3.1 Theoretical Foundation

To gain a thorough understanding of the disparities within the access and use of technology in vocational institutions, the study draws on resource and appropriation theory as articulated by Van Dijk (2005). Van Dijk has established a framework for examining access, grounded in a specific theoretical foundation, yet it is sufficiently comprehensive to facilitate an impartial overview of key aspects of digital divide research. Research on digital inequality has progressed significantly in recent decades, with scholars examining various factors influencing individuals' use of technology, which include motivations, attitudes, physical and material access, skills, and usage patterns (van Deursen, van der Zeeuw, de Boer, Jansen & van Rompay, 2019). Van Deursen, et al. (2019) explain that the theory of resources and appropriation posits that the four phases of appropriation are influenced by the resources available to individuals. Recent findings indicate that disparities in these access dimensions perpetuate existing inequalities, as human capital translates into the digital realm; individuals from higher socioeconomic backgrounds tend to benefit more from technology, which provides greater opportunities for capital enhancement (van Deursen, et al., 2019). According to Habibi et al. (2023), Van Dijk's theory has clarified the concept of rectifying access to technology. Habibi et al. (2023) explain that initially, the emphasis was placed on attitudes and motivation, subsequently transitioning to considerations of material or physical access. The theoretical framework evolved from a focus on material access to encompass skills and practical application (Habibi et al., 2023). This framework, referred to as resources and appropriation theory, integrates elements of structuration theory (resources) and acceptance theory (appropriation) (Van Dijk, 2017). This framework conceptualises technology acceptance as a progressive sequence; the process shows that an individual must first cultivate a positive attitude toward a technology before achieving material access, subsequently acquiring the requisite skills to utilise it effectively as depicted in Figure 1.

Figure 1. Resources and appropriation theory (simplified_ of Van Dijk (2005) (van Deursen et al., 2019)

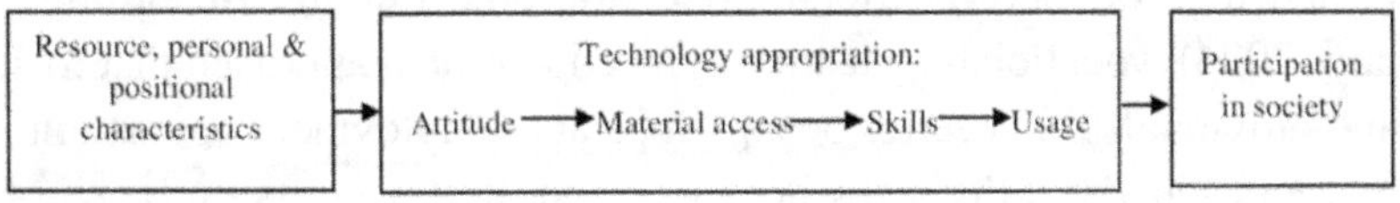

The theory of resources and appropriation exhibited in Figure 1 introduced the principle of successive technology dimensional norms, which disaggregates access into four components namely motivational, material, skills, and usage. The challenges associated with technical access have transitioned from the initial phases of motivational and material access to the later phases of skills and usage. Consequently, the digital divide can manifest at any point or across all stages of access (Habibi et al., 2023). The initial phase of technology adoption involves cultivating a favourable perception, which is closely linked to individuals' sentiments regarding technology. Van Deursen et al. (2019) research on technology adoption indicates that an individual's attitude towards technology plays a vital role in their willingness to embrace it or to reject it and these adverse attitudes diminish the probability of an individual engaging with the technology. A positive mindset and the integration of technological devices necessitate the development of various skills (van Deursen & Mossberger, 2018). Blank and Groselj (2014) state that the concluding phase is usage, which is characterised by both the frequency and the nature of activities undertaken. The latter aspect has garnered increasing interest in research examining Internet utilisation across various social groups (Blank & Groselj, 2014). Van Deursen et al. (2019) note that central to this theory is the assertion that both personal factors such as age, gender, ethnicity, intelligence, personality, and health and positional factors including labour status, education, household structure, and nationality contribute to disparities in resource distribution namely income, social networks, intelligence, and status, leading to inequalities at each stage of appropriation. The resultant effects of this process influence varying levels of societal participation across multiple domains, including economic, social, political, and cultural spheres (van Deursen et al., 2019).

3.2 Vocational Education

The significance of education in promoting social and economic advancement has been acknowledged for an extended period. It enhances both functional and analytical skills, thereby providing individuals and communities with improved access to job markets and economic opportunities (Jena & Sahoo, 2024). Dandaya

(2022) posits that individuals, particularly the youth, can obtain the necessary information, skills, and competencies for current and future employment through effective and high-quality vocational education and training. According to Jena and Sahoo (2024), vocational education is an educational approach that focuses on preparing individuals for specific occupations and employment opportunities as it equips learners with the skills necessary for various trades, crafts, and careers across multiple sectors. In the same way, Habibi et al. (2023) state that it equips students with the necessary skills for employment or self-employment, focusing on training individuals for roles as technicians or in skilled trades. Güngör (2020) points out that vocational education integrates scientific, technological, and practical elements, emphasising the skills and competencies needed for specific professions. This form of education emphasises hands-on practical activities and is often synonymous with technical education, as it enables trainees to acquire specialised expertise in a defined set of techniques (Jena & Sahoo, 2024). Educators play a crucial role in determining the integration of technology within the teaching process (Habibi et al., 2023). Aldamen, et al. (2021) explain that vocational education encompasses training programs designed to equip individuals for careers as technicians, artisans, or tradespeople, necessitating specialised skills. Vocational education's primary aim is to equip a skilled workforce for diverse fields such as industry, agriculture, and technology, thereby contributing to economic development (Rahardjo, 2020). Güngör (2020) argues that vocational education institutions prepare individuals as a skilled workforce for roles in industry, commerce, and service sectors, while also offering foundational education that facilitates their progression to higher education institutions relevant to their careers. Jena and Sahoo (2024) observe that a well-educated workforce is crucial for fulfilling the labour demands associated with accelerated economic growth.

Rahardjo (2020) explains that vocational education is conducted within institutions that serve as secondary educational facilities, including government-controlled technical colleges or those affiliated with industrial sectors. In Indonesia, this form of education encompasses nine specialised fields, ranging from technology and engineering to creative industries (Habibi et al., 2023). Aldamen, et al. (2021) assert that this form of education may include classroom instruction, practical training, or a blend of both, with one or two vocational subjects typically available in secondary and higher secondary institutions. However, authentic vocational education often occurs outside conventional educational frameworks and usually culminates in the attainment of a certificate or diploma (Aldamen, et al., 2021). Therefore, Rahardjo (2020) delineates that vocational education, as a distinct educational category, should embody seven key characteristics: (1) it must prioritise individual performance in professional settings, (2) address genuine needs within the industry, (3) emphasise a curriculum that integrates psychomotor, affective, and cognitive dimensions, (4) extend success metrics beyond the confines of academic institutions, (5) remain attuned to workplace advancements, (6) necessitate sufficient facilities and infrastructure, and (7) foster a supportive environment. The significance of vocational or skills-based education is increasingly recognised, as many employers now anticipate that new hires possess the necessary practical skills for immediate employment, particularly for individuals who must provide for their families right after completing senior secondary education (Jena & Sahoo, 2024). Güngör (2020) found that vocational education plays a crucial role in fostering economic growth and development by equipping individuals with the necessary skills, knowledge, and competencies for employment. The acquisition of these skills is often facilitated through partnerships between educational institutions and industries, as well as through experiential learning opportunities in the workplace (Güngör, 2020).

Unlike the theoretical knowledge offered by conventional formal education, vocational education emphasises practical expertise (Dandaya, 2022). Considering current social and economic demands, both policymakers and researchers are critically examining how vocational education programs should equip youth for particular careers, adapt to an evolving global labour market, and foster active participation in the democracies of the twenty-first century (Fuller, 2015). In today's society, vocational education serves a dual purpose, ranging from specialised training for specific occupations to broader educational frameworks aimed at equipping young individuals for productive and meaningful lives as both employees and active members of society (Fuller, 2015). Although penned almost a hundred years ago, Dewey's (2001) apprehensions regarding vocational education and its connection to employment continue to hold significant relevance today. This enduring relevance can be attributed to the persistent challenges faced by educational systems in aligning vocational training with the evolving demands of the labour market. As industries undergo rapid transformations due to technological advancements and globalisation, the need for educational frameworks that effectively prepare individuals for specific careers has become increasingly critical. Furthermore, Dewey's (2001) insights highlight the importance of integrating practical skills with theoretical knowledge, a principle that continues to resonate as educators strive to equip students with competencies that are not only applicable in their chosen fields but also adaptable to the dynamic nature of work environments. Thus, the foundational ideas presented by Dewey (2001) serve as a crucial reference point for ongoing discussions about the efficacy and purpose of vocational education in fostering employability today.

3.3 Digital Literacy in Education

Digital literacy refers to a person's capacity to find, evaluate, and articulate clear information when communicating through different digital mediums (Choudhary & Bansal, 2022; Feerrar, 2019). For Jia and Huang (2023), digital literacy encompasses the capacity to effectively utilise ICT to locate, assess, generate, and share information, necessitating a combination of cognitive and technical competencies. It is essential to recognise that digital literacy extends beyond mere proficiency in using digital tools and applications; it also incorporates advanced cognitive and social abilities, including critical thinking, problem-solving, communication, and collaboration within digital environments (Jia & Huang, 2023). Digital literacy is conceptualised by Jatmoko et al. (2023) as a social practice that utilises digital technologies to engage with and interpret texts, enabling individuals to create, convey, and negotiate meaning in ways that are socially acknowledged. According to Shelyugina, Davydenko and Stepanskaya (2019), digital literacy involves an individual's capacity to leverage digital tools to enhance work efficiency, foster an active personal stance, cultivate critical thinking and creativity, comprehend the dynamics of human interaction with digital technology, and recognise the characteristics of online community development. Ojo, Alodele, Onadokun and Akinade (2018) observe that digital literacy encompasses a comprehensive set of knowledge, skills, behaviours, and experiences that enable individuals to effectively understand and utilise digital devices, such as smartphones, tablets, laptops, and desktop computers, in addressing various societal challenges related to politics, economics, technology, and education. Likewise, Shelyugina et al. (2019) comment that it encompasses a range of knowledge and skills essential for a secure and proficient utilisation of digital technologies and online resources, including digital consumption, which refers to the utilisation of Internet services for both professional and personal purposes; digital competencies, which involve the skills necessary for effective information retrieval and the creation of multimedia content; and digital security, which pertains to fundamental principles of safety in the online environment. Essential digital competencies pertinent to vocational education encompass proficiency in basic computer operations, which includes the use of common devices like computers, tablets, and smartphones, alongside familiarity with fundamental software applications such as word processors, spreadsheets, and presentation tools (The European Commission, 2017). Feerrar (2019) is of the view that digital competencies are essential across various occupations, even in fields not directly associated with technology, such as agriculture, construction, and skilled trades. Narang and Tiwari (2021) explain that billions of people throughout the length of the day are continuously engrossed in the consumption of the internet, social media, mobile applications, and other digital communication technologies Understanding digital safety and security is imperative, as it involves recognising potential risks in the digital landscape and implementing appropriate strategies to safeguard personal information and data (The European Commission, 2017).

Digital literacy has become a fundamental component of the majority of skill development training initiatives, particularly in vocational and work-based contexts (UNESCO, 2017). The practice of digital literacy serves as a crucial strategy for developing students' competencies in digital technology, as it significantly enhances their performance and abilities in effectively using technology as an information resource (Jatmoko et al., 2023). Ojo et al. (2018) state that digital literacy is essential for students to evolve into digital citizens, equipping them for a modern workforce and contemporary society. Additionally, the capability to conduct internet research and manage information is vital, involving the skills to search for, assess, and organise digital content from diverse sources, including websites, databases, and social media platforms (The European Commission, 2017). Digital literacy must be recognised as the fourth fundamental component of education, alongside reading, writing and mathematics, and must receive appropriate resources and instruction (Ojo et al., 2018). Hence, it incorporates multiple dimensions that can be classified into several key areas (Jia & Huang, 2023) namely (1) functional skills, which refer to the proficient use of digital devices, software, and platforms; (2) critical thinking and evaluation, which involve the ability to judge the credibility, relevance, and accuracy of online information; (3) digital communication and collaboration, emphasising effective interaction and information sharing through digital tools; (4) digital content creation, which entails the skills necessary to produce, edit, and disseminate various forms of digital content; and finally, (5) digital safety and ethics, focusing on responsible navigation of the digital landscape while safeguarding personal privacy and honouring the rights of others. The European Commission (2017) revealed that for vocational students, developing digital literacy skills is crucial for thriving in today's workforce. Furthermore, proficiency in industry-specific software and tools is necessary, as it pertains to the use of specialised applications relevant to vocational sectors, such as computer-aided design (CAD) for engineering or graphic design, and customer relationship management (CRM) systems for sales and marketing (The European Commission, 2017).

3.4 The Concept of the Digital Divide

Although the advantages of ICT in educational frameworks are well-documented, research indicates significant disparities in both technological skills and access (Faloye & Ajayi, 2021; Van Dijk, 2020). This inequality is commonly termed the digital divide, which highlights the contrast between individuals who possess the necessary access to technology and the skills to utilise it, and those who lack these resources

(Faloye, Ajayi, & Raghavjee, 2020; Jantjies, 2020). The notion of "digital divide" is not a recent development. The phrase 'digital divide' first emerged in various U.S. newspapers in 1995, supported by findings from the National Telecommunications and Information Administration's report and Falling through the Net, which highlighted the disparity between those with access to technology and those without (Van Dijk, 2019). The concept rapidly disseminated across Europe and globally, leading to the establishment of both the idea and the issue of the digital divide as significant topics within societal and academic discourse by the turn of the millennium (Van Dijk, 2019). According to Afzal et al. (2023), it refers to the growing social consequences arising from unequal access to information and communication technology within certain community sectors, as well as the disparities in acquiring essential skills. The digital divide refers to the disparity in technological access among communities, which arises from regional and demographic variations, especially among different socio-economic groups (Kormos & Wisdom, 2021). Following the Second World War, the introduction of ICT occurred at a rapid pace, within approximately one generation, leading to its characterisation as a 'digital revolution' due to its significant impact on innovation, acceptance, and development (Van Dijk, 2019). During the late 1980s and early 1990s, the phrases "information rich" and "information poor" gained significant attention. Variations in computer ownership, access to information technology, and fundamental indicators of Internet connectivity have illuminated issues of social stratification on both national and global scales (Afzal et al., 2023). As a result, digital inequalities mirror social inequalities, as access to technology, particularly the internet, is restricted or limited among specific demographic groups (Duma et al., 2021). Table 1 presents a comprehensive overview of the various definitions of the digital divide as articulated by Van Dijk in 2019.

Table 1. Definition of the digital divide

Type	**Definition**
General	A division between people who have access to and use of digital media and those who do not
Specific	• WHO (individuals vs. organisations/communities vs. societies/countries/regions), • with WHICH characteristics (individuals: income, education, age, gender; organisations: public or private ownership, size, sector; countries: developed or developing, urban or rural) connects • HOW (access, skills, usage) • WHAT type of technology (computer, Internet, phone, digital TV)?
Process	Divisions in the access to and use of four phases in the adoption of digital media: motivation, physical access, digital skills and usage

Based on Table 1, the general definition identifies the digital divide as a disparity between individuals who possess access to and actively utilise digital media and those who lack such access. In contrast, the specific definition delves deeper into the nuances of this divide by categorising it based on several criteria: it distinguishes between different entities such as individuals, organisations, and broader societal structures, while also considering characteristics like income, education, age, and gender for individuals; ownership type, size, and sector for organisations; and developmental status, as well as urban versus rural classification for countries. Furthermore, it examines the dimensions of access, skills, and usage, alongside the types of technology involved, which may include computers, the Internet, telephones, and digital television. Lastly, the process-oriented definition outlines the stages of digital media adoption, highlighting the critical phases of motivation, physical access, digital skills, and actual usage, thereby providing a multifaceted understanding of the digital divide.

4. MATERIAL AND METHODS

The methodology employed in this study aimed to systematically evaluate and select relevant literature concerning the enhancement of digital literacy in rural vocational schools, specifically focusing on bridging the digital divide in technology access and usage. The initial search was conducted using databases such as Google Scholar and Scopus, yielding a total of 320 identified records. These records were then screened, beginning with an examination of titles to filter out studies that did not align with the research focus. This initial step resulted in excluding 98 studies, narrowing the pool of potential literature.

Following the title screening, the next phase involved a detailed review of abstracts and keywords, which led to the exclusion of an additional 71 studies. The exclusion criteria were strictly defined to ensure that only studies pertinent to vocational education were considered. Specifically, any research about universities, high schools, or other educational institutions outside the realm of vocational training was eliminated. Furthermore, duplicate studies were identified and removed from the dataset, accounting for 18 records. This meticulous process ensured that the remaining studies were relevant to the study.

Ultimately, the full-text evaluation phase resulted in the exclusion of 78 additional studies, reinforcing the focus on vocational schools by applying the same exclusion criteria. After completing all screening stages, a total of 55 studies were deemed suitable for inclusion in the final analysis as displayed in Figure 2.

Figure 2. Evaluation and selection process instead of this "four levels of access (Akinlabi, 2023)

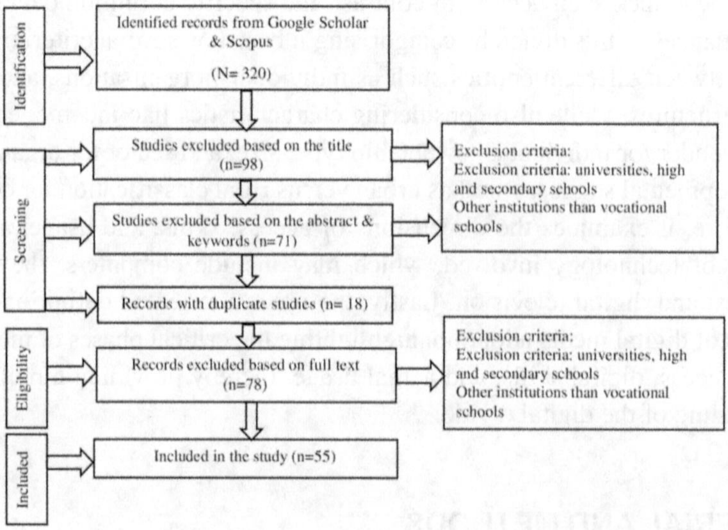

This comprehensive methodology exhibited in Figure 2 not only ensured the relevance of the selected literature but also provided a foundation for understanding the role of digital literacy in enhancing technology access and usage in rural vocational education settings.

5. FINDINGS

The results revealed two primary aspects: the disparity in access to technology and the differences in its usage as shown in Table 2.

Table 2. The findings

Digital divide in access to technology	Ocaña-Fernández et al. (2020) Van Deursen et al. (2019) Van Dijk (2017) Van Dijk (2005)
Physical access divide	IEEE (2024) Mustafa, Nguyen and Gao (2024) Jatmoko et al. (2023) Jia and Huang (2023) Lembani, Mulenga, Mwewa, Mhango and Chaamwe (2023) Van Deursen and van Dijk (2023) Delcker and Ifenthaler (2021) Faloye & Ajayi (2021) Kormos and Wisdom (2021) Fernández-Gutiérrez, Gimenez and Calero (2020) Gómez-Trigueros (2020) Agovino (2019) Lavery et al. (2018) Pierce (2019) Hong and Thakuriah (2018) Chetty, Aneja, Mishra, Gcora and Josie (2017)

continued on following page

Table 2. Continued

Disparities in network access	Van Dijk (2006) van Deursen and van Dijk (2023) Akinlabi (2023) Chetty et al. (2017) Akinlabi (2023) The Cable (2022) Cable (2022) Zaitun and Crump (2005) Mustafa et al. (2024) van Deursen et al. (2019) Swenson and Ghertner (2020) Scheerder et al. (2017)
Skill access divide	Akinlabi (2023) Habibi et al. (2023) Jia and Huang (2023) Barreto and Córdova (2022) Faloye and Ajayi (2021) Kormos and Wisdom (2021) World Bank (2021) van Deursen and van Dijk (2021) van Deursen et al. (2019) Blagodarny, Vedyakhin, and Raygorodsky (2018) Chetty et al. (2017) Van Dijk (2017) Van Dijk (2017) Van Dijk (2005)
Digital divide in the usage of technology	Habibi et al. (2023) Van Dijk (2017)
Usage patterns and network characteristics	Afzal et al. (2023) Mwapwele, Marais, Dlamini and van Biljon (2019
Network or Internet usage	Afzal et al. (2023) Jia and Huang (2023) Akinlabi (2023) Chetty et al. (2017)

5.1 Digital Divide in Access to Technology

Ocaña-Fernández et al. (2020) posit that access to the Internet is crucial for learning, as students increasingly rely on smartphones and similar devices to enhance their understanding of subjects or courses. According to Van Dijk (2017), the term access can be understood in both specific and expansive contexts. The narrower interpretation typically refers to physical access, as defined in various frameworks. Conversely, a broader interpretation is more suitable for addressing the multifaceted nature of the digital divide, including the second-level divide (Van Dijk, 2017). This broader perspective encompasses the entire process of adopting a specific technology, where the desire, mindset, and anticipation for physical access precede the actual attainment of that access (Van Dijk, 2017). Van Dijk (2005) conceptualises material access as the opportunities and resources necessary for engaging with technology. This notion encompasses both the physical access to and ownership of technology devices (van Deursen et al., 2019).

5.1.1 Physical Access Divide

Access to technology is essential for reaping the advantages of digital resources (Faloye & Ajayi, 2021). The digital access divide highlights the inequalities in physical access to digital tools, primarily concerning hardware and software (Faloye & Ajayi, 2021). Mustafa, Nguyen and Gao (2024) state that the challenges associated with technology integration are multifaceted, impacting schools, educators, and learners. While certain issues may be common across these three groups, each can hinder the effective implementation of technology in rural educational settings (Mustafa et al., 2024). Fernández-Gutiérrez, Gimenez and Calero (2020) note that many governments have made large investments in equipping schools with ICT devices and tools. As a result, the use of ICT-related tools (such as computer-based learning, emails and websites) in teaching practices has rapidly spread. Faloye and Ajayi (2021) argue that technological infrastructure, including networks, electricity, and data centres, facilitates access to technology. In Africa, insufficient technological innovation and infrastructure exacerbate the digital divide (Faloye & Ajayi, 2021). This digital divide can intensify pre-existing educational disparities, as students without access to technology may find it difficult to acquire the digital competencies necessary for thriving in today's job market (Jia & Huang, 2023). Van Dijk (2017) notes that during the initial phase of digital divide research from 1999 to 2002, the focus was primarily on a limited interpretation of access, specifically physical access, encompassing the acquisition of digital media hardware and software, as well as Internet connectivity.

The concept of physical access was closely linked to broader demographic factors, including income, educational attainment, age, gender, and race (Van Dijk, 2017). In addition, research on the digital divide often highlights various personal categorical inequalities, including age (youth versus elderly), gender (male versus female), race and ethnicity (majority versus minority), intelligence levels (high versus low), personality traits (extraversion versus introversion; self-assured versus insecure), and health status (able-bodied versus disabled) (Van Dijk, 2017). Chetty, Aneja, Mishra, Gcora and Josie (2017) state that data indicates that merely 40% of the world's population has access to digital technology. Agovino (2019) revealed that among the approximately 3.7 billion individuals lacking internet connectivity, a significant proportion comprises women, girls, and residents of remote or rural regions characterised by low educational attainment and income levels. In the United States, for example, nearly 55% of disconnected students came from Black, Hispanic, and Native American households, despite making up only 40% of the general student population (IEEE, 2024). Age is recognised as a significant determinant of the digital divide (Lavery et al., 2018) since a notable proportion of individuals aged 50 and above tend to refrain from adopting modern technologies, as they perceive their conventional devices, like first-generation mobile phones and landlines, as adequate for their needs. Older adults who engage with digital technologies later in life frequently face difficulties due to their complexities (Pierce, 2019), resulting in a diminished interest in these innovations. Additionally, there is a prevailing belief among this demographic that modern devices are overly complex to operate (Faloye & Ajayi, 2021). Furthermore, the IEEE (2024) reported that individuals from lower-income backgrounds often lack the financial means to acquire digital devices or afford monthly internet subscriptions and 50% of disconnected students came from families with an annual income of less than $50,000 per year. Chetty et al. (2017) contend that in low and middle-income countries women are 21% less likely to possess a mobile phone. Moreover, van Deursen and van Dijk (2023) indicate that individuals with lower income levels tend to hold unfavourable views of the Internet, struggle to cover the costs associated with material access and utilise the Internet less effectively. The digital divide significantly affected children in rural regions of the southern United States, with 40-50% of students in states such as Alabama, Arkansas, Oklahoma, and Mississippi being impacted (IEEE, 2024). Around 25% of these disconnected students lacked reliable broadband access, while 60% were unable to afford both internet services and digital devices (IEEE, 2024). In contrast to the trends observed in the 1980s and 1990s, where individuals with higher education levels predominantly engaged with the internet, recent data from certain developed nations indicates that individuals with lower educational attainment are now spending more time online than their more educated counterparts (Van Dijk, 2017). The digital divide encompasses a significant issue about economically disadvantaged communities facing restricted access to digital technologies, primarily due to prohibitive costs and inadequate infrastructure, which includes unreliable electricity supply and insufficient ICT resources (Chetty et al., 2017). Investment in ICT is improbable when individuals' incomes are insufficient to meet their basic needs (Faloye & Ajayi, 2021). The financial burden of computers and necessary tools for Internet access makes it challenging for low-income individuals to acquire these devices (Faloye & Ajayi, 2021).

The digital divide is evident across different economic strata (IEEE, 2024). Urban and rural regions exhibit unique cultural characteristics and priorities that shape their respective needs (Faloye & Ajayi, 2021). The concept of 'modernity' is typically linked to urban settings, whereas 'tradition' is more frequently associated with rural environments (Hong & Thakuriah, 2018). Additionally, urban areas are often viewed as symbols of progress, particularly by youth from rural backgrounds. This perception drives many students and young individuals to migrate to cities, motivated by inadequate infrastructure and the aspiration to overcome poverty (Hong & Thakuriah, 2018). Thus, Kormos and Wisdom (2021) comment that rural educational institutions face considerable challenges related to infrastructure, particularly in terms of limited or non-existent access to broadband internet services. In certain instances, these schools may operate in areas devoid of any internet connectivity (Kormos & Wisdom, 2021). Even in districts that do have some level of internet access, a significant number of students remain disconnected from online resources at home, with estimates indicating that this disconnection affects as much as 28% of students in rural regions (Handal, Watson, Petocz & Maher, 2018). Kormos and Wisdom (2021) state that a pertinent illustration of this issue can be observed in Pendleton and Mingo counties in West Virginia, where approximately 35% of households lack reliable internet access. In Brazil, research indicated that even with enhanced infrastructure, significant segments of the population do not recognise the necessity for digital access (Chetty et al., 2017). Residents in rural, isolated regions or less developed nations frequently face challenges in accessing the broadband infrastructure required for internet connectivity (IEEE, 2024). As connectivity expands, the gap between those with internet access and those without is likely to widen further (IEEE, 2024).

Within vocational education, various reports have identified obstacles that teachers encounter when utilising digital technologies, specifically highlighting issues such as insufficient confidence, competence, and access to necessary digital resources (Delcker & Ifenthaler, 2021; Gómez-Trigueros, 2020). Additionally, Van Dijk (2017) points out that inadequate infrastructure, ineffective professional development, and insufficient technical support further hinder the effective use of digital technology in vocational schools. The distinct functions of the three educational stakeholders namely schools, educators, and learners contribute to challenges that impact the effectiveness of technology integration in various manners (Jatmoko et al., 2023). Students, being the main recipients of technology integration, require access to devices, reliable internet, and the ability to engage in self-directed learning (Mustafa et al., 2024; Lembani, Mulenga, Mwewa, Mhango & Chaamwe, 2023). Jatmoko et al. (2023) note that overcoming the challenges associated with the implementation of digital literacy practices necessitates coordinated efforts among multiple stakeholders, including educators, learners, and the involvement of schools and relevant entities in educational policy.

5.1.2 Disparities in Network Access

Research by Van Dijk (2006) and van Deursen and Van Dijk (2023) on digital inequality primarily highlights disparities in Internet access, which is often analysed through a framework encompassing motivational access, physical/material access, skills access, and usage access as illustrated in Figure 3.

Figure 3. Four levels of access (Akinlabi, 2023)

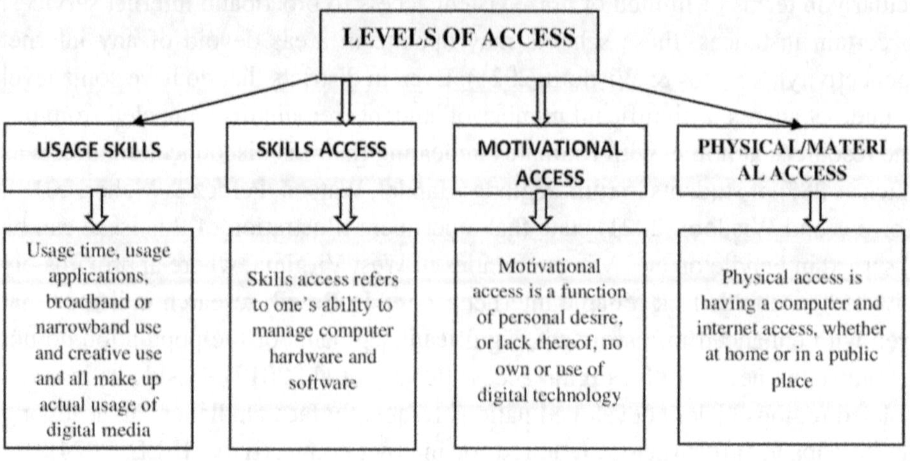

From Figure 3, material access pertains to the availability of devices and connectivity services. Motivational access reflects an individual's desire to own a computer and have Internet connectivity. Akinlabi (2023) explains that some people may choose not to engage with ICTs due to a perceived lack of necessity, time constraints, or negative attitudes towards technology. Skills access is associated with digital literacy, while usage access can be evaluated through metrics such as duration of use, types of applications utilised, the variety of services accessed, and the extent of active or creative engagement with the technology.

Van Deursen and van Dijk (2023) state that internet access disparities are predominantly examined at the individual level, although some studies also consider collective differences across countries. In South Africa for instance, a study found that 35% of households perceived the internet as irrelevant, largely due to their socio-economic conditions (Chetty et al., 2017). The digital divide in South Africa, as noted by Akinlabi (2023), is rooted in the enduring inequalities stemming from the apartheid era and its policies of segregation. The Cable (2022) identifies several elements affecting the utilisation of ICT in Africa. Notably, the expense of internet access in African nations, exemplified by South Africa's rate of $2.04 per gigabyte, is significantly greater than in regions such as Europe and Asia, where internet costs are among the lowest globally, often falling below $0.20 per gigabyte (Cable, 2022). Malaysia had 2.73 million Internet subscribers, with a significant 93% of these users residing in urban regions (Zaitun & Crump, 2005). Hence, many teachers often rely on their personal internet data plans and devices, such as computers and smartphones, to conduct their classes (Mustafa et al., 2024). Although developed nations are witnessing a swift rise in physical access through improved Internet connectivity, the technology itself is still in its early stages of evolution (van Deursen et al., 2019). Various individual characteristics significantly influence access types, with gender, age, education, employment status, income, and social network access being the most prevalent factors. Akinlabi (2023) observed that the interplay among education, income, and Internet usage is more pronounced in Africa compared to many developed nations. In this context, access to and utilisation of the Internet predominantly benefits the affluent and educated segments of society, while individuals from low-income households residing in rural areas face significant barriers to Internet connectivity (Akinlabi, 2023). In 2019, over 16% of individuals living in poverty did not have access to the Internet (Swenson & Ghertner, 2020). Moreover, Swenson and Ghertner (2020) revealed that those with higher income levels were significantly more likely to have Internet connectivity in their homes. Additional influences may include ethnicity, personality traits, and health status (Scheerder et al., 2017).

5.1.3 Skill Access Divide

Van Dijk (2005) introduced the concept of a deepening divide to highlight that the issue of digital inequality persists beyond mere physical access; it intensifies when individuals begin to integrate digital media into their everyday activities also called the second-level divide. During the period from 2005 to 2015, research on the digital divide predominantly concentrated on this second-level divide. Van Dijk

(2017) explains that once individuals gain physical access, they must possess the necessary skills to effectively navigate and utilise digital media. The author adds that these competencies are often referred to as digital or media literacy, while some categorise them as digital skills. Barreto and Córdova (2022) define digital skills as the set of skills that allow a person to strategically use information through information technology. Chetty et al. (2017) note that it is essential to recognise that digital skills can quickly become outdated as a result of evolving business practices and technological advancements. Likewise, Blagodarny, Vedyakhin, and Raygorodsky (2018) assert that the rapid progression of science and contemporary technologies necessitates individuals to engage in lifelong learning and continuously acquire new skills. Consequently, training programs and educational curricula must adapt more swiftly to this dynamic environment as training opportunities are scarce in digital technologies, which results in inadequate digital skill development and limited access to the benefits associated with these competencies (Chetty et al., 2017). This view is supported by the World Bank (2021), which revealed that Africa is experiencing a deficiency in digital skills across various levels, particularly in intermediate and advanced competencies. As economies expand, the demand for these skills, especially within ICT professions, is anticipated to intensify, potentially hindering the adoption and effective use of digital technologies (World Bank, 2021). According to a recent IFC study, by 2030, over 230 million jobs in Sub-Saharan Africa will demand digital skills, leading to approximately 650 million training opportunities. Countries in Africa that do not equip their populations with essential digital skills may find themselves lagging as the digital landscape evolves, hindering their capacity to catch up and benefit from the ongoing digital transformation.

Additionally, Kormos and Wisdom (2021) posit that despite advancements in teachers' access to technology, apprehensions persist regarding the potential exacerbation of the digital divide between educators and students in rural regions. Faloye and Ajayi (2021) explain that the digital skill divide pertains to the varying levels of technological proficiency among individuals and their capabilities when utilising available technologies. Research indicates that teachers serving rural and underrepresented populations often possess limited knowledge of effective technology integration strategies (Kormos & Wisdom, 2021). The understanding of vocational school educators regarding the development of knowledge and the enhancement of technology-related skills through diverse tools is crucial. As the demand for the integration of digital technology in teaching continues to grow, these educators must enhance their knowledge and competencies in utilising digital tools for instruction (Habibi et al., 2023). According to van Deursen and van Dijk (2021), the ability of teachers to effectively utilise, integrate, manage, and comprehend digital technology encompasses a range of skills, including strategic, informational, and operational competencies. Strategic skills pertain to vocational schoolteachers' proficiency in employing digital technologies, while operational skills involve the management of devices such as smartphones, laptops, and the Internet (van Deursen & van Dijk, 2021). Informational skills are defined as the capability of vocational schoolteachers to locate, select, and analyse information through digital platforms, especially the Internet and data-sharing technologies (van Deursen & van Dijk, 2021). Furthermore, Van Dijk (2017) points out that a distinction exists between operational or instrumental skills required for managing digital media, known as medium-related skills and substantial skills focused on information retrieval, communication, action, and content creation, termed content-related skills. Akinlabi (2023) asserts that instrumental skills and operational skills denote the ability to effectively utilise computer hardware and software. Consequently, a lack of necessary technological skills may discourage users from participating (Akinlabi, 2023). The effective incorporation of digital technology in teaching practices can significantly elevate the skill sets of vocational schoolteachers, ultimately fostering a more competent and skilled future workforce among their students (Habibi et al., 2023).

Furthermore, material access also pertains to the variations in the technical specifications of the devices employed (van Deursen et al., 2019). In certain instances, Mustafa et al. (2024) observe that schools determine the technologies that will be utilised by educators and students, necessitating the organisation of appropriate training for teachers. Jia and Huang (2023) argue that a significant challenge lies in the necessity for continuous teacher training and professional development, which is essential for vocational educators to effectively impart digital literacy skills. Numerous educators may lack formal training in this area or may not feel sufficiently confident in their capacity to incorporate digital tools and resources into their instructional methods (Jia & & Huang, 2023). Ongoing professional development and support for teachers are essential to foster an environment where technology is embraced as a vital component of the learning process, ultimately contributing to the overall sustainability of educational initiatives. However, research indicates that such training is infrequently provided by schools, compelling teachers to seek training from government or higher education institutions, which may not align with the specific technological needs of their schools (Mustafa et al., 2024).

5.2 Digital Divide in the Usage of Technology

The utilisation of digital technology is defined primarily in terms of access to such technology (Habibi et al., 2023). Van Dijk (2017) stresses that the ultimate objective of access is its utilisation, which can be assessed through various metrics such as duration and frequency of use, the quantity and variety of applications employed, and the type of network utilised, whether broadband or narrowband, as well as the level of engagement, whether passive or creative.

5.2.1 Usage Patterns and Network Characteristics

Afzal et al. (2023) classify the efficient use of information and communication technology (ICT) for knowledge acquisition, modification, and generation into four categories of resources, including physical resources, such as computers and telecommunications devices; digital resources, which consist of relevant content accessible in multiple languages; human resources, which relate to literacy and educational attainment; and social resources, which encompass support from both communities and institutions. Mwapwele, Marais, Dlamini and van Biljon (2019) emphasise that a key area of concern in rural schools in South Africa has been the adaptation of digital tools to align with the resource limitations of these schools while ensuring their long-term viability. This adaptation is not merely a matter of implementing technology; it necessitates a thoughtful approach that considers the sustainability and long-term effectiveness of such tools within the unique context of rural education. Without addressing these limitations, the potential benefits of digital tools may not be fully realised, thereby hindering the educational advancement of students in these underserved areas. Consequently, it is imperative to develop strategies that not only introduce digital resources but also ensure that they are maintained and utilised effectively over time, fostering an environment conducive to learning and growth. The sustainability of these initiatives heavily relies on the skills and attitudes of teachers regarding technology use (Mwapwele et al., 2019). Teachers play a pivotal role in shaping the educational landscape, and their ability to effectively utilise technological tools can greatly influence the success of sustainability efforts. A positive attitude towards technology, coupled with a robust skill set, enables educators to not only enhance their instructional methods but also to inspire students to engage with digital resources meaningfully. Numerous ICT projects fail when the intended beneficiaries are unable to maintain the tools implemented during the initiative. A primary factor contributing to these failures is the misalignment between the ICT solutions provided and the actual needs of the users (Mwapwele et al., 2019).

5.2.2 Network or Internet Usage

The internet serves as a catalyst for expanding the analysis of information-seeking behaviours in Library and Information Science (LIS) beyond traditional contexts such as work and education (Afzal et al., 2023). Jia and Huang (2023) argue that a significant obstacle to incorporating digital literacy into vocational education is the restricted availability of technology and digital resources, especially in disadvantaged schools or areas. Akinlabi (2023) posits that access to digital connectivity is facilitated by technological infrastructure such as network towers, electricity and data centers. Afzal et al. (2023) argue that a persistent divide exists between individuals and communities capable of effectively utilising information technology and those who are not. Currently, the unequal adoption of technology increasingly marginalises many, preventing them from benefiting from economic advancements (Afzal et al., 2023). Furthermore, in low and middle-income countries, internet usage among women is 16% lower than that of men (Chetty et al., 2017).

6. BENEFITS OF DIGITAL ACCESS AND USAGE WITHIN VOCATIONAL EDUCATION

On one hand, Helsper (2012) categorises outcome domains into four distinct types namely economic, encompassing wealth, employment, education, and finances; social, which includes both formal and informal support as well as political and civic networks; cultural, focusing on aspects of identity and belonging; and personal, relating to health, leisure, and self-actualisation. On the other hand, Duma, Mlambo, Mkwanazi and Morgan (2021) state that the overarching application of ICT is articulated through national policies and classified into three rationales namely the social rationale, which focuses on equipping students for their societal roles; the vocational rationale, aimed at providing students with relevant skills for future employment; and the pedagogical rationale, which emphasises the improvement of teaching and learning processes through the integration of computers. This framework will serve as a foundation for examining the advantages associated with digital access and utilisation in the context of vocational education.

6.1 Social Benefits

The social rationale is concerned with preparing students to fulfil their roles within society. ICTs are perceived as tools that enhance teachers' capabilities by enabling them to access educational resources online, deepen their comprehension of the subjects they teach, facilitate communication with peers for support, engage in online professional development, and stay informed about current political, social, economic, and financial issues globally (Mwapwele et al., 2019). Van Dijk (2017) mentioned that individuals with Internet access reported securing employment online and experiencing reduced costs in transactions involving goods. ICT services significantly influence contemporary social interactions, largely due to the emergence of diverse platforms that broaden personal, professional, and commercial prospects (IEEE, 2024). Socially, they connected with friends initially met online, with some eventually joining community organisations (Van Dijk, 2017). Social media platforms such as Facebook, Instagram, and Twitter promote communication and connections among friends, family, and even unfamiliar individuals. As technology has evolved, its significance in facilitating social interactions has grown increasingly pronounced (IEEE, 2024). Furthermore, digital technologies empower users to articulate their views and disseminate information. A substantial number of users depend on social media platforms to stay informed about current events, participate in civic discussions, and obtain vital updates from their local communities (IEEE, 2024). In the realm of institutional involvement, students gain greater access to public services, including essential health resources that inform them about their medical conditions and the most suitable healthcare facilities (Van Dijk, 2017).

6.2 Vocational Benefits

The vocational rationale focuses on equipping students with essential skills that are pertinent to their future career prospects. By 2021, society was experiencing the Fourth Industrial Revolution, characterised by the increasing automation and integration of sophisticated technologies in manufacturing and various industrial sectors (IEEE, 2024). Consequently, there is a growing demand for digital skills in the workforce, with studies indicating that more than 80% of middle-skill occupations necessitate a degree of digital competence (IEEE, 2024). Furthermore, positions classified as middle-skill or higher typically offer greater financial compensation compared to low-skill roles. Habibi et al. (2023) point out that the integration of digital technology in educational practices can enhance the competencies of vocational school instructors, thereby equipping their students with the necessary skills to become more proficient and capable members of the future workforce (Habibi et al., 2023). Various studies indicate that such practices can significantly enhance students' vocational technology skills, foster creativity and critical thinking, and better equip them for future employment in a digital landscape (Nurtanto, Sudira & Sofyan, 2023; van Laar, van Deursen, van Dijk & de Haan, 2020; Patmanthara & Hidayat, 2018). In addition, higher education institutions typically mandate that students submit their applications via the Internet, and students commonly utilise computers to explore scholarship opportunities, prepare for standardised examinations, and accomplish various academic responsibilities (IEEE, 2024).

6.3 Pedagogical Benefits

The pedagogical rationale prioritises the enhancement of teaching and learning methodologies through the incorporation of computer technology. Pedagogical practices within academic frameworks have increasingly incorporated diverse technological methodologies, notably e-learning (Hill & Lawton, 2018; Fernández-Gutiérrez et al., 2020). The implementation of e-learning platforms has enabled students to access educational resources remotely and submit assignments online. Proponents of ICT argue that these technologies foster greater flexibility and autonomy among students, while simultaneously enriching their learning attitudes and experiences (Alderete, Di Meglio & Formichella, 2017). Students frequently rely on internet-connected devices to fulfil homework assignments, conduct research projects, and participate in online classes (IEEE, 2024). According to Ocaña-Fernández et al. (2020), this reliance has prompted a transition from traditional teacher-centred pedagogies to more student-centred approaches, recognising that teachers are not the sole providers of knowledge. In particular, students engaged in technology-enhanced learning environments scored 12 percentile points higher than their peers in conventional educational settings (Kormos & Wisdom, 2021). Consequently, students are less dependent on educators for both learning and sourcing educational materials (Ocaña-Fernández et al., 2020). Therefore, the integration of ICT can facilitate personalised instruction and more effective tracking of students' progress (Falck, Mang & Woessmann, 2018).

Furthermore, Research indicates that the strategic application of ICT in educational settings leads to enhanced learning outcomes. Theoretical perspectives supporting the beneficial impact of ICT on educational outcomes suggest that ICT enhances student performance by broadening access to information and diverse learning resources (Falck, Mang & Woessmann, 2018). Specifically, Fernández-Gutiérrez et al. (2020) found that students engaging with online tutorials in subjects such as computer programming, mathematics, and social sciences demonstrate improved performance compared to those who do not utilise these technological tools. A synthesis of approximately 30 meta-analytic studies, encompassing over 1,000 articles from the past 40 years, demonstrated notable enhancements in student achievement associated with the use of technology in the classroom, as opposed to instruction devoid of technological tools, with effects ranging from small to moderate (Kormos & Wisdom, 2021). Moreover, the application of innovative technology can foster a collaborative learning environment, facilitate the acquisition of post-secondary credits through distance education, and enable a shift from traditional teacher-centred approaches like lectures and solitary student tasks (Yang & Kwok, 2017).

Additionally, Kormos and Wisdom (2021) note that the emergence of educational technology as an essential component in the pedagogical landscape has afforded rural school districts nationwide a significant resource to address the obstacles posed by geographic isolation, sparse populations, and limited financial resources. Educators who integrate technology into their teaching methodologies can cultivate students who demonstrate enhanced critical thinking abilities and superior communication skills, thereby preparing them for the complexities of modern society (Kormos & Wisdom, 2021).

7. IMPLICATIONS

The issue of bridging the digital divide in access to and utilisation of technology through the enhancement of digital literacy in rural vocational schools holds considerable significance for both researchers and policymakers. This relevance is underscored by the considerable financial resources allocated to initiatives aimed at improving technological access and literacy in these educational settings (Comi et al., 2017). For researchers, this topic presents a rich area for investigation, as it encompasses various dimensions such as educational equity, the effectiveness of digital literacy programs, and the socio-economic factors influencing technology adoption in rural contexts. Furthermore, policymakers are tasked with developing strategies that not only address the existing disparities in technology access but also ensure that vocational education aligns with the demands of a rapidly evolving digital economy. By focusing on this intersection of technology and education, stakeholders can work towards creating inclusive environments that empower rural students with the necessary skills to thrive in a technology-driven world.

8. CONCLUSION

The influence of ICT on educational results has been thoroughly established, both in theoretical frameworks and through empirical research. This consensus underscores the significant role that ICT plays in shaping learning experiences and outcomes, highlighting its effectiveness as a tool for enhancing educational practices and facilitating student engagement. The body of evidence supporting this assertion spans various studies and analyses, reinforcing the notion that the integration of ICT in educational settings is not merely beneficial but essential for fostering improved academic performance and learning efficiency.

9. RECOMMENDATIONS

The research suggests that addressing the issue of the digital divide can be effectively achieved through the collaborative efforts of four key stakeholders namely vocational institutions, the industry, government entities, and rural communities.

Vocational institutions should play a pivotal role by equipping individuals with the necessary skills and knowledge to navigate the digital landscape. They can develop targeted programs that focus on digital literacy, ensuring that students from diverse backgrounds are prepared to engage with technology effectively. Furthermore, these institutions can foster partnerships with local communities to provide resources and training, thereby enhancing access to digital tools and platforms.

The industry also holds significant responsibility for bridging the digital divide. By investing in infrastructure and technology in rural areas, businesses can facilitate greater access to the internet and digital services. Additionally, industry players can collaborate with educational institutions to create internship and job opportunities that emphasise digital skills, thereby aligning workforce development with the needs of the modern economy. This collaboration not only benefits the industry by creating a more skilled workforce but also empowers individuals in rural communities to participate in the digital economy.

Government involvement is crucial in establishing policies and funding initiatives that promote digital inclusion. By prioritising investments in broadband infrastructure and supporting programs aimed at enhancing digital literacy, governments can create an environment conducive to reducing the digital divide. Moreover, engaging rural communities in the decision-making process ensures that their specific needs and challenges are addressed, fostering a sense of ownership and commitment to the initiatives implemented.

Rural communities experience significant disparities in access to technology and the Internet, which hinder their economic and social development. By actively participating in efforts to bridge the digital divide, these communities can advocate for their interests and work alongside other stakeholders to create sustainable solutions. This may involve establishing community-based programs that promote digital literacy, providing training opportunities, and facilitating access to necessary resources. Furthermore, rural residents can leverage their unique perspectives to inform policy decisions and technological developments, ensuring that the solutions implemented are culturally and contextually appropriate.

Collectively, the synergy among these four stakeholders can significantly mitigate the digital divide, leading to a more equitable and connected society. Moreover, expanding Internet access enables specific communities to flourish by equipping them with the necessary technological skills to succeed in the digital economy (Afzal et al., 2023). In addition, African nations should train workforces proficient in digital skills and citizens who are digitally literate to fully harness the advantages offered by digital technologies. A growing proportion of current positions, along with nearly all emerging roles, will necessitate digital competencies (World Bank, 2021).

REFERENCES

Afzal, A., Khan, S., Daud, S., Ahmad, Z., & Butt, A. (2023). Addressing the digital divide: Access and use of technology in education. *Journal of Social Sciences Review*, *3*(2), 883–895. DOI: 10.54183/jssr.v3i2.326

Agovino, T. (2019). Bridging the Gender Divide. HRMagazine. https://www.researchgate.net/publication/361772157. Accessed: 03/09/ 2024.

Akinlabi, O. O. (2023). *Understanding the Impact of the Digital Divide and New Methods of Learning on Humanities Students at UKZN during the Coronavirus Pandemic. Master of Arts Media and Cultural Studies*. University of KwaZulu-Natal.

Aldamen, H., Alkhateeb, H., Kercher, K., Duncan, K., & Hollindale, J. (2021). Core competencies for the global workplace: A cross-cultural and skill-based simulation project in accounting. *Accounting Education*, *30*(4), 385–412. DOI: 10.1080/09639284.2021.1906719

Alderete, M. V., Di Meglio, G., & Formichella, M. M. (2017). Access to ICT and educational performance: Is there a relationship enhanced by its use? An analysis for Spain. *Journal of Education*, *377*, 54–81.

Balderas-Mireles, M. A., Mata-Mata, R., Lujano-Gutiérrez, L., Rodríguez Sánchez, J. L., & Pérez López, J. J. (2021). The use of ICTs in teaching at the normal superior school "Profr. Moisés Sáenz Garza": An exploratory study. *Journal of Higher Education Theory and Practice*, *22*(3), 90–99.

Barreto, I. B., & Córdova, R. A. S. (2022). Discussion on Digital Inclusion Good Practices at Europe's Libraries. In *Handbook of Research on Comparative Approaches to the Digital Age Revolution in Europe and the Americas. E-book.* IGI Global.

Blagodarny, E. V., Vedyakhin, A., & Raygorodsky, A. M. (2018). Development of Educational Projects on the Basis of Technological Platforms with Artificial Intelligence: The Experience of MIPT on the Use of High Vox-Platform. *International Conference on Artificial Intelligence Applications and Innovations (IC-AIAI).* Nicosia, Cyprus. DOI: 10.1109/IC-AIAI.2018.8674452

Blank, G., & Groselj, D. (2014). Dimensions of Internet use: Amount, variety, and types. *Information Communication and Society*, *17*(4), 417–435. DOI: 10.1080/1369118X.2014.889189

Cable. (2022). Worldwide Mobile Data Pricing 2022. https://www.cable.co.uk/mobiles/worldwide-data-pricing/. Accessed: 04/10/2024.

Chetty, K., Aneja, U., Mishra, V., Gcora, N. & Josie, J. (2017). *Bridging the digital divide: Skills for the new age*. Germany: G20.

Choudhary, H., & Bansal, N. (2022). Addressing Digital Divide through Digital Literacy Training Programs: A Systematic Literature Review. *Digital Education Review, 41*(1), 224–248. DOI: 10.1344/der.2022.41.224-248

Dandaya, V. (2022). Importance of vocational training and technical skills. *Global Science Research Journals, 10*(3), 1–2.

Delcker, J., & Ifenthaler, D. (2021). Teachers' Perspective on School Development at German Vocational Schools During the Covid-19 Pandemic. *Technology, Pedagogy and Education, 30*(1), 125–139. DOI: 10.1080/1475939X.2020.1857826

Devisakti, A., & Muftahu, M. (2023). Digitalization in higher education: Does personal innovativeness matter in digital learning? *Interactive Technology and Smart Education, 20*(2), 257–270. DOI: 10.1108/ITSE-10-2021-0182

Dewey, J. (2001). *Democracy and education: An introduction to the philosophy of education*. The Pennsylvania State University.

Duma, N. M., Mlambo, S., Mbambo-Mkwanazi, S., & Morgan, W. (2021). Digital Inequalities in rural Schools in South Africa. *Ocean Science Journal, 6*(3), 1–15.

Falck, O., Mang, C., & Woessmann, L. (2018). Virtually no effect? Different uses of classroom computers and their effect on student achievement. *Oxford Bulletin of Economics and Statistics, 80*(1), 1–38. DOI: 10.1111/obes.12192

Faloye, S. T., & Ajayi, N. (2021). Understanding the impact of the digital divide on South African students in higher educational institutions. *African Journal of Science, Technology, Innovation and Development, 14*(7), 1734–1744. DOI: 10.1080/20421338.2021.1983118

Faloye, S.T., Ajayi, N. & Raghavjee, R. (2020). Managing the Challenges of the Digital Divide among First Year Students: A Case of UKZN." 2020 IST-Africa Conference (IST-Africa), 18–22 May 2020.

Feerrar, J. (2019). Development of a framework for digital literacy. *RSR. Reference Services Review, 47*(2), 91–105. DOI: 10.1108/RSR-01-2019-0002

Fernández-Gutiérrez, M., Gimenez, G., & Calero, J. (2020). Is the use of ICT in education leading tohigher student outcomes? Analysis from the Spanish autonomous communities. *Computers & Education, 157*, 1–15. DOI: 10.1016/j.compedu.2020.103969

Fuller, A. (2015). Vocational Education. *International Encyclopedia of the Social & Behavioral Sciences*, 25: 232–238.

Gómez-Trigueros, I. M. (2020). Digital teaching competence and space competence with TPACK in social sciences. *International Journal of Emerging Technologies in Learning, 15*(19), 37–52. DOI: 10.3991/ijet.v15i19.14923

Güngör, G. (2020). Problems and solution suggestions encountered in vocational skill training in vocational high schools: Teachers' views. *European Journal of Education Studies, 7*(4), 233–253.

Habibi, A., Sofyan, S., & Mukminin, A. (2023). Factors affecting digital technology access in vocational education. *Scientific Reports, 13*(1), 1–12. DOI: 10.1038/s41598-023-32755-6 PMID: 37029180

Handal, B., Watson, K., Petocz, P., & Maher, M. (2018). Choosing to teach in rural and remote schools: The zone of free movement. *Education Research and Perspectives, 45*, 1–32. DOI: 10.70953/ERPv45.18001

Helsper, E. J. (2012). A corresponding fields model for the links between social and digital exclusion. *Communication Theory, 22*(4), 403–426. DOI: 10.1111/j.1468-2885.2012.01416.x

Hill, C., & Lawton, A. (2018). Universities, the digital divide and global inequality. *Journal of Higher Education Policy and Management, 40*(6), 598–610. DOI: 10.1080/1360080X.2018.1531211

Hong, J., & Thakuriah, P. V. (2018). Examining the relationship between different urbanization settings, smartphone use to access the internet and trip frequencies. *Journal of Transport Geography, 69*, 11–18. DOI: 10.1016/j.jtrangeo.2018.04.006

IEEE. (2024). 2024 IEEE/ACM Workshop on Gender Equality, Diversity, and Inclusion in Software Engineering. Lisbon: GE@ICSE.

Jantjies, M. (2020). How South Africa can address digital inequalities in e-learning. The Conversation. http://theconversation.com. Accessed: 03/10/2024.

Jatmoko, D., Suyitno, S., Rasul, M. S., Nurtanto, M., Kholifah, N., Masek, A., & Nur, H. R. (2023). The factors influencing digital literacy practice in vocational education: A structural equation modeling approach. *European Journal of Educational Research, 12*(2), 1109–1121. DOI: 10.12973/eu-jer.12.2.1109

Jena, M., & Sahoo, B. (2024). Perception of students and teachers towards vocational education in secondary schools. [IJHSSI]. *International Journal of Humanities and Social Science Invention, 13*(3), 139–146.

Kormos, E., & Wisdom, K. (2021). Rural schools and the digital divide: Technology in the learning experience and challenges to integration. *Theory and Practice in Rural Education, 11*(1), 25–39. DOI: 10.3776/tpre.2021.v11n1p25-39

Kvon, G., Vaks, V., Kalimullin, A., Bayanova, A., Shaidullina, A., Dolzhikova, A., & Lapidus, N. (2019). Developing the informational and digital environment of a university: Problem analysis and assessment. *Eurasia Journal of Mathematics, Science and Technology Education, 15*(10), 1–14. DOI: 10.29333/ejmste/109503

Lavery, M. P. J., Mojtaba, M. A., Bauer, R., Brambilla, G., Cheng, L., Cox, M. A., Dudley, A., Ellis, A. D., Fontaine, N. K., & Kelly, A. E. (2018). Tackling Africa's digital divide. *Nature Photonics, 12*(5), 249–252. DOI: 10.1038/s41566-018-0162-z

Lembani, R., Mulenga, K., Mwewa, P., Mhango, L., & Chaamwe, N. (2023). Are we leaving students behind? Self-directed learning in an ICT challenged country. *Education and Information Technologies, 28*(3), 3475–3492. DOI: 10.1007/s10639-022-11318-8 PMID: 36189192

Mustafa, F., Nguyen, H. T. M., & Gao, X. A. (2024). The challenges and solutions of technology integration in rural schools: A systematic literature review. *International Journal of Educational Research, 124*, 1–24. DOI: 10.1016/j.ijer.2024.102380

Mwapwele, S. D., Marais, M., Dlamini, S., & van Biljon, J. (2019). Teachers' ICT Adoption in South African Rural Schools: A Study of Technology Readiness and Implications for the South Africa Connect Broadband Policy. *The African Journal of Information and Communication, 24*, 1–24.

Narang, R., & Tiwari, S. (2021). *Antecedents and Consequences of the Growing Popularity of Digital Consumption*. In book "What is Digital Consumption". 5th ed. E-Book: SCOPUS. DOI: 10.4018/978-1-7998-3479-3.ch073

Nurtanto, M., Sudira, P., & Sofyan, H. (2023). A bibliometric analysis of teacher professional identity (TPI) for vocational education from 2004 to 2021. *AIP Conference Proceedings, 2671*(1), 050017. DOI: 10.1063/5.0114242

Ocaña-Fernández, Fernández, Chiparra, Gallarday-Morales & Gallarday-Morales, (2020). Digital Skills and Digital Literacy: New Trends in Vocational Training. *International Journal of Early Childhood Special Education (INT-JECSE)*: 12(1): 370-377.

Ojo, O., Alodele, A., Onadokun, I.O. & Akinade, O.A. (2018). Digital literacy assessments in technical and vocational education and training (TVET) sustainability. *SMART-iSTEAMS Multidisciplinary Conference*, 75-86.

Patmanthara, S., & Hidayat, W. N. (2018). Improving vocational high school students digital literacy skill throughblended learning model. *Journal of Physics: Conference Series, 1028*, 012076. DOI: 10.1088/1742-6596/1028/1/012076

Peñate, A. H., Padrón-Robaina, V., & Nieves, J. (2024). The role of technological resources in the reputation of vocational education schools. *Education and Information Technologies, 29*(3), 1–20. DOI: 10.1007/s10639-023-11919-x

Pierce, J. (2019). Digital Divide. *The International Encyclopedia of Media Literacy*, 1–8.Pooja, M. (2021). Adopting digital technologies in vocational education at the time of crisis. *Advanced Management*, 14: 53–59.

Rahardjo, T. J. (2020). The role of vocational education on the advancement of human development in Indonesia. *Advances in Social Science, Education and Humanities Research, 443*, 406–410.

Scheerder, A. J., van Deursen, A. J. A. M., & van Dijk, J. A. G. M. (2017). Determinants of Internet skills, uses and outcomes: A systematic review of the second- and third-level digital divide. *Telematics and Informatics, 34*(8), 1607–1624. DOI: 10.1016/j.tele.2017.07.007

Shelyugina, O., Davydenko, M., & Stepanskaya, A. (2019). Development of digital literacy in vocational education as a condition for regional sustainable development. *International Conference on Sustainable Development of Cross-Border Regions: Economic, Social and Security Challenges (ICSDCBR)*, 364: 140-143. DOI: 10.2991/icsdcbr-19.2019.30

Swenson, K., & Ghertner, R. (2020). *People in Low-Income Households Have Less Access to Internet Services – 2019 Update.* Office of the Assistant Secretary for Planning & Evaluation. U.S. Department of Health & Human Services.

UNESCO. (2017). Working Group on education: Digital skills for life and work. *Broadband Commission for Sustainable Development, 9*, 1–128.

van Deursen, A. J., & van Dijk, J. A. (2023). IQ and digital inequality: An empirical investigation. *New Media & Society, 25*(6), 1248–1270. DOI: 10.1177/14614448211024012

Van Deursen, A. J. A. M., & Mossberger, K. (2018). Anything for anyone? A new digital divide in internet-of-things skills. *Policy and Internet, 10*(2), 122–140. DOI: 10.1002/poi3.171

Van Deursen, A. J. A. M., van der Zeeuw, A., de Boer, P., Jansen, G., & van Rompay, T. (2019). Digital inequalities in the Internet of Things: Differences in attitudes, material access, skills, and usage. *Information Communication and Society*, *24*(2), 258–276. DOI: 10.1080/1369118X.2019.1646777

Van Dijk, J. (2020). *The digital divide*. Polity.

Van Dijk, J. A. G. M. (2005). *The deepening divide: Inequality in the information society*. John Wiley & Sons, Inc.

Van Dijk, J. A. G. M. (2005). *The deepening divide: Inequality in the information society*. SAGE.

Van Dijk, J. A. G. M. (2017). *Digital divide: Impact of access*. University of Twente.

Van Dijk, J. A. G. M. (2019). *The digital divide*. Polity Press.

Van Laar, E., van Deursen, A. J. A. M., van Dijk, J. A. G. M., & de Haan, J. (2020). Determinants of 21st-century skills and 21st-century digital skills for workers: A systematic literature review. *SAGE Open*, *10*(1), 1–14. DOI: 10.1177/2158244019900176

World Bank. (2021). *Digital skills: The why, the what and the how*. The World Bank Group.

Yang, S., & Kwok, D. (2017). A study of students' attitudes towards using ICT in a social constructivist environment. *Australasian Journal of Educational Technology*, *33*(5), 50–62.

Zaitun, A. B., & Crump, B. (2005). Overcoming the Digital Divide – A Proposal on How Institutions of Higher Education Can Play a Role. *Malaysian Online Journal of Instructional Technology*, *2*(1), 1–11.

Zancajo, A., Verger, A., & Bolea, P. (2022). Digitalization and beyond: The efects of Covid-19 on post-pandemic educational policy and delivery in Europe. *Policy and Society*, *41*(1), 111–128. DOI: 10.1093/polsoc/puab016

Chapter 5
Enhancing University–Workforce Collaboration Through Digital Literacy, Technology Integration, and Mental Well-Being Support

Swosti Mohanty
https://orcid.org/0009-0004-2581-0031
KIIT University, India

Ipseeta Satpathy
https://orcid.org/0000-0002-0155-5548
KIIT University, India

B. C. M. Patnaik
KIIT University, India

Debashree Chakravarty
https://orcid.org/0009-0007-7677-8627
KIIT University, India

ABSTRACT

In the rapidly growing world, psychological wellness has turned into a basic issue in both professional and expert settings. Students and employees alike face increasing pressure to perform, often leading to stress, anxiety, and other mental health chal-

DOI: 10.4018/979-8-3373-0004-7.ch005

lenges. As this recognition grows, there is a clear need for stronger collaboration between universities and workplaces to address mental health in a more comprehensive and sustainable way. Collaborative efforts can ensure that mental well-being is supported not just in one phase of life but throughout a person's academic and professional journey. To enhance effective collaboration between universities and the workforce, digital literacy tends to play very crucial role. The integration of technology in education that includes the use of digital tools in classrooms and virtual classrooms engages students and aligns with modern learning objectives. Mental health is an equally important consideration when discussing effective workplace collaboration.

INTRODUCTION

In the rapidly evolving landscape of today's world, psychological wellness has emerged as a critical concern across educational and professional domains, as students and employees grapple with mounting pressures that frequently lead to stress, anxiety, and various mental health challenges. This burgeoning awareness underscores the need for enhanced collaboration between universities and workplaces to approach mental health in a comprehensive and sustainable manner, recognizing that the well-being of individuals transcends individual life phases and encompasses their transition from education to employment and beyond.

Digital literacy plays a significant role in fostering effective collaboration between educational institutions and the workforce, where the integration of technology in classrooms ranging from digital tools to virtual learning environments engages students while aligning with contemporary learning objectives. The enhanced accessibility provided by smartphones, computers, and tablets cultivates a dynamic learning atmosphere, granting students and educators instant access to information and enabling tailored teaching approaches that cater to diverse learning needs, ultimately contributing to the reduction of administrative burdens on educators and positively influencing their mental well-being. A notable aspect of this integration is the establishment of online grading systems and internet-based assignments that facilitate career development. Skills acquired through training in platforms like Microsoft Office or Google Drive equip students with practical competencies essential for the modern workforce, including effective collaboration through structured information organization and enhanced communication with peers & clients. Furthermore, the infusion of technology into education not only enriches the classroom experience by providing a plethora of information, but also promotes active engagement by allowing students to progress at their individual paces, thus fostering self-directed learning. As digital literacy becomes an essential competency, educational institutions stand to benefit from prioritizing this skill, which cultivates life skills applicable in personal and professional realms.

Equally paramount is the focus on mental health in discussions of effective workplace collaboration, as the repercussions of poor mental well-being often manifest in diminished productivity levels, driven by various stressors such as shift work and overwhelming demands. The World Health Organization has identified several workplace risk factors influencing mental health, highlighting the need for educational environments to address these issues to foster a healthier workforce [Indian Journal of Psychiatry 66(Suppl 2):p S231-S244, January 2024]. In addition, mental well-being is characterized by a sense of purpose, self-growth, acceptance, and positive relationships, and for educators, maintaining psychological health is vital not only for their own welfare but also for the efficacy of their teaching, as it directly affects educational quality. By prioritizing mental wellness, institutions can create supportive environments that enhance motivation, engagement, and academic success for both staff and students. Additionally, implementing workshops focusing on yoga, mindfulness, time management, and stress management can further contribute to this goal, enabling institutions to invite qualified instructors to equip staff with essential stress management tools. Counselling services, both in-person and online, provide safe spaces for addressing personal challenges, fostering resilience and coping strategies.

In the context of India [The National Education Policy, 2020 (para 5.1, NEP, 2020)], educational policies emphasize the importance of improving mental health among educators, whose well-being significantly influences teaching quality. Furthermore, technology fosters collaboration by linking colleagues regardless of location, enhancing communication through tools for document creation and management, allowing seamless idea-sharing and real-time project tracking. Brainstorming sessions exemplify collaborative practices that harness diverse perspectives to tackle complex challenges effectively, while open communication promotes a supportive environment that encourages innovation and strengthens interpersonal relationships. Ultimately, building collaboration as a soft skill, enriched through workshops and training, ensures that both educators and students are equipped to thrive in academic and professional arenas. By embracing technology and fostering mental well-being and collaboration, educational institutions can cultivate inclusive and robust learning environments that benefit all stakeholders involved.

In the essence of collaboration between Workforce and Universities and with the continuous evolvement of job market, Universities play a crucial role to prepare the workforce. In order to foster the innovation, skill development and growth in several sectors, the graduates are trained academically by the teaching staff according to the demands of job markets & industry needs. Strengthening the University workforce is the need of time which can be enhanced through Curriculum Alignment with

Industry Needs, Building Strong Partnerships and Networks, Fostering Lifelong Learning, Reskilling, Work-Based Learning Opportunities, Enhancing Career Services and Job Placement, Promoting Innovation & Entrepreneurship, Public-Private Partnerships and Encouraging Diversity & Inclusion.

In the modern era, Universities as organisations are facing overwhelming challenges at all levels, which includes changes in the nature, structure and dynamics like redefining the contracts of employment, flexible patterns of work, work-life balance, high levels of technological innovation and increased competitions. As stated by (Narasimhan, 1997), three important elements like organisational climate (OC), supervisory leadership and peer relationships construct the Higher Education Institutions (HEIs). Performance in work at Universities is very often influenced by the Organisational Climate (OC) which consists of administration, publication, research, teaching-learning, and several academic assignments which the workforce carries rigorously influencing the Performance of work at Universities. Thus, it may be valued that productivity of University largely depends on the efficiency of its workforce.

Objective of the Study

- To study the role of Digital Literacy promoting Digital Competence as an important solution to address University-Workforce Collaboration
- To understand Technology Integration (Artificial Intelligence) as a modern solution to Enhance University Workforce
- To analyse Mental Well-being Support for positive inclination of University Workforce

ROLE OF DIGITAL TECHNOLOGY TRAINING ON ACADEMIC DEVELOPMENT

After COVID-19, in the teaching and learning sector, a new normal has been established. In higher education context and on developing academics, the effectiveness of competence in digital sector and technology training has a vital role to play. The moderate effect in innovative climate, capability of the trainer and competence in digital sector add extra value to the University-Workforce. According to Chan and Ng, 2024; Lau et al., 2024, with the rapid change of the world in the 21st century, updated knowledge is to be kept in the field of digital sector. In addition, knowledge in digital technology is equally necessary. This has link resulting with performance in improvement at academic space of learning. (Szeto et al., 2021; Lehmann et al., 2022) defines, for teaching and engaging in the digital era, relevant technological and digital knowledge should equip the teachers. Also in the similar lines, (Elsayary, 2023; Ng et al., 2022a, b; Wut and Ng, 2023) opined that effective digital technology training alongwith digital competence and essential academic qualifications in the classroom delivers solid solution to students. Wide range of topics like digital integrity, Internet of Things (IoT), social networking sites, Fintech, contents about social media under digital marketing and management, technology in artificial intelligence (e.g. social semantics and sentiment analysis) are covered by Digital technology training. Tavitiyaman et al., (2023) say with the essential knowledge and skills of digital tools there lies the provision of academics for the students very effectively. As per the findings of Singh et al. (2024), digital competencies bear a positive influence with digital entrepreneurship in Universities. Soriano et al. (2024) in a similar manner examines that, there lies an impact of digital competencies with the digital training for teachers. In shaping training effectiveness, Gegenfurtner et al. (2020) suggested the capability of trainer and the factors that are dominant for training content. Additionally, (Sanz et al., 2022) outlined that trainees' competent skills are fostered by innovation-supportive climates. The interdependence of socio-economic dynamics on one hand and ICT developments on the other, implies that teaching and learning across levels of education and universities in particular must aim at training students on how to learn and cope with ICTs. The implementation of pedagogical practices that reflect on this interdependency will not only promote student's ability to operate and sustain in a knowledge society, but also contribute innovatively to labour production (OECD, 2018; Reddy et al., 2023).

Digital resources is adopted in most disciplinary practices like engineering, science, journalism and rest of the careers as a portion of employment and enquiry for generating visual representation, gathering information, visualizing data, and communicating. Both disciplinary and digital literacy are practised to express ideas, read and write for multiple structures. Digitally literate person carries a lasting impact on a person's critical thinking skills, emotional intelligence, rights and aboveall his identity penetrating the complacent quasi-totality aspects of life for improving digital environment.

Digital Literacy: A Crucial Skill for the 21st Century

Digital literacy has emerged as a critical competency in contemporary society, serving as a cornerstone for success in both education and the workforce. This broad skill set not only encompasses basic technical capabilities such as hardware and software usage but also extends to a deeper understanding of how to engage with, evaluate, and create content using digital tools. Proficient digital literacy involves thorough knowledge of operating essential devices, including computers, smartphones, and tablets, as well as fluency in various software applications such as word processors, spreadsheets, email clients, and web browsers. Effective file management practices including organizing, storing, retrieving, and sharing digital files are paramount in today's cloud-centric environment.

Further, as technology continues to evolve, individual proficiency in digital literacy has become ready to tackle the complexities of the 21st century workplace. Research indicates that digital literacy skills, combined with appropriate technological tools and effective teaching methodologies, significantly enhance Information and Communication Technology (ICT) competence (Jin et al., 2020; Sulaiman and Ismail, 2020). Key components of digital literacy include Internet literacy, information literacy, communication skills, and media literacy, all of which are progressively shaped by technological advancements.

Information literacy stands out as a vital aspect of digital literacy, requiring individuals to effectively source, assess, and utilize information from digital contexts. This includes distinguishing credible information from misinformation and applying ethically sourced information in various scenarios. Advanced search techniques enable efficient retrieval of information from databases and search engines, which is essential for academic and professional environments.

Moreover, collaborative tools such as Google Docs, Microsoft Teams, and Slack facilitate communication and teamwork among peers, thereby enhancing real-time collaboration. A grasp of digital creativity and content development is equally critical; familiarity with design software like Canva and Adobe Photoshop equips individuals to create engaging multimedia content, including graphics, videos, and blogs.

Digital storytelling is another essential skill, enabling one to craft compelling narratives through diverse formats for varied purposes, such as marketing or education. Moreover, awareness of online safety and security including cybersecurity best practices and privacy management is crucial for navigating the digital realm responsibly. This also encompasses digital etiquette, which promotes respectful interaction in both professional and social digital environments.

Finally, understanding intellectual property, including copyright laws and ethical considerations surrounding digital content sharing, is integral to overall digital literacy, further emphasizing the multifaceted nature of these skills in our increasingly digital world. Understanding this enables individuals to navigate contemporary challenges effectively, making digital literacy an indispensable element of modern education and professional success.

Digital literacy frameworks are vital for equipping individuals with the skills needed to navigate the digital landscape effectively, focusing on critical information evaluation, online research, digital privacy, and technological proficiency. India's Digital Literacy Framework supported by the Pradhan Mantri Gramin Digital Saksharta Abhiyan (PMGDISHA) and the National Digital Literacy Mission (NDLM) uniquely addresses the digital divide by providing structured guidelines aimed at enhancing essential digital skills relevant to personal and professional settings, particularly for underserved populations. While global standards often emphasize advanced technical skills or innovation, India prioritizes foundational competencies, fostering inclusivity. This approach aligns with broader socio-economic goals, facilitating economic growth and social development while distinguishing India's tailored framework from more standardized global methodologies.

Digital literacy is crucial for success in today's world; yet marginalized student populations often encounter numerous barriers that hinder their ability to achieve it. One significant barrier is limited access to technology, as many students may lack computers, tablets, or smartphones, which are essential for developing digital skills. Inconsistent or non-existent internet connectivity further restricts their ability to utilize online resources and partake in digital learning. Economic constraints exacerbate this issue, as families in marginalized communities may struggle financially to afford devices or internet access. Additionally, a lack of exposure to technology in home or community environments results in minimal experience with digital tools. Educational inequities, particularly in underfunded schools, often lead to inadequate technology integration and insufficient digital literacy programs (Sanders & Scanlon, 2021). Cultural and linguistic barriers may arise when resources are not available in students' native languages or do not reflect their cultural experiences. Teacher training is another critical area; educators may lack the necessary skills and support to effectively teach digital literacy. Furthermore, concerns over online safety and privacy can create anxiety, deterring engagement with digital tools. Skepticism towards technology, stemming from past negative experiences regarding data privacy, can also hinder acceptance. Social and emotional factors, including trauma or low self-esteem, affect students' willingness to embrace new technologies. To address these challenges, a comprehensive approach is needed, focusing on equitable access to technology, targeted educational programs, community support, and policy initiatives aimed at reducing disparities in digital literacy.

Importance of Digital Literacy

In Job Market Competitiveness, workers with strong digital literacy are more likely to be hired, promoted, or transitions into new roles are created. Many modern jobs demand proficiency in using specific software, platforms, or tools. Digital literacy also empowers individuals to start and grow businesses / Entrepreneurship, using digital tools for marketing, customer service, and e-commerce, thereby promoting economic growth and innovation. Digital literacy allows students to take advantage of online educational resources, such as virtual classrooms, digital textbooks, and interactive learning platforms. It also supports the use of educational apps and resources that help enhancing the learning experiences. Being digitally literate helps students develop critical thinking and research skills as they learn to evaluate digital information and use it effectively in academic contexts.

Digital literacy is essential for engaging in informed decision-making, especially in an era of digital campaigns, online news, and social media. With the rise of social media, digital literacy allows individuals to participate in discussions, advocacy, and activism in constructive and informed ways. Digital literacy allows people to access essential services (banking, healthcare, government services) and engage in online communities, thus increasing social participation and inclusion. This can be challenging for the workforce and University that are not equipped to keep up with constant changes. One of the challenges of digital literacy is teaching people how to critically evaluate the vast amount of content available online.

Strategies for Enhancing Digital Literacy

Universities can offer training programs designed to teach digital literacy at various levels. These programs should be accessible, comprehensive, and regularly updated to cover emerging technologies. Through Public Awareness Campaigns, the importance of digital literacy, offering resources and training to different populations, especially marginalized communities can be spread. Integrating digital literacy as part of core higher education curriculums ensures that students are prepared better for a digital future. This also includes offering specialized courses in coding, data analysis, and other tech-focused areas. Online platforms provide flexible learning opportunities offering accessible resources for adults and working professionals to develop a digital literacy skill, which is crucial. Digital literacy is more than just a skill set - it's a fundamental competency required to thrive in the modern world. With technology reshaping our lives, the necessity to ensure and empower everyone, regardless of their background or age, can participate fully in the digital world and make informed decisions that affect their personal, professional, and civic lives.

Digital literacy encompasses various skills, including navigating digital tools, understanding data, and communicating effectively using technology. Particularly significant for today's job market, employers across various sectors prioritize candidates possessing these competencies. The interconnectedness of digital literacy and employability manifests across industries, revealing several facets. Proficiency in digital literacy allows healthcare professionals to use electronic health records (EHRs), telehealth systems, and remote monitoring tools. For instance, nurses adept in telehealth technologies can deliver superior patient care and improve health outcomes in remote regions. Professionals in these sectors frequently engage with a range of software and hardware tools. Digital literacy in programming languages and systems analysis is crucial for career advancement. In the financial sector, data analytics and digital risk management tools are essential. Accountants and financial analysts who are proficient in these technologies can generate more precise forecasts and analyses. Educators skilled in digital tools can enhance learning experiences by integrating technology into their curriculum, leading to improved student engagement and outcomes. Individuals with robust digital skills can adapt rapidly to new technologies, thereby enhancing productivity and becoming more appealing to employers. For example, organizations deploying new software solutions often prioritize staff who can learn these new tools swiftly without extensive training. As job competition intensifies, candidates possessing digital literacy skills are better positioned to distinguish themselves in the hiring process. Successful candidates often highlight their digital competencies in resumes and interviews, reinforcing their value to prospective employers. With the growing prevalence of remote and hybrid work arrangements, digital literacy has become increasingly essential. Employees need to navigate virtual collaboration tools such as Zoom and project management platforms like Asana. Individuals lacking proficiency in these tools may struggle with effective communication and teamwork, hindering their employability in remote positions.

Digital literacy is intrinsically tied to employability across multiple sectors, enhancing an individual's capacity to navigate a technologically driven job market. However, barriers such as infrastructural limitations, digital literacy deficits, and cultural stigma can obstruct effective technology implementation. Addressing these challenges demands collaboration among governments, educational institutions, and healthcare providers.

Digital Competence in Universities

Digital competence in academia is a synthesis of innovative climate and effective knowledge transfer, as highlighted by researchers such as Wut et al. (2023) and Ng et al. (2022). They stress the necessity of providing digital technology training for university educators, focusing on technology, pedagogy, and current digital content, with the objective of enhancing student learning and development. Elsayary (2023) characterizes digital competence as essential for learners to perform skill-specific tasks, serving as a benchmark for evaluating performance. In higher education, Tavitiyaman et al. (2023) assert that effective teaching hinges on class management skills and awareness of educational trends, which can be improved through digital training, creating a more interactive learning environment. Wang et al. (2021) emphasize the importance of training in areas like data analytics and digital marketing for enhancing decision-making in business contexts. Xie et al. (2023) further illustrate that training content significantly impacts learning outcomes, establishing a positive correlation between digital competence and technological training. The role of trainers is paramount in this learning process, as defined by Bahr et al. (2000), while Chen et al. (2020) and Zakaria and Lim (2022) affirm that the effectiveness of trainers directly influences trainee competence. Glerum and Judge (2021) argue that the effectiveness of the trainer outweighs the training content itself. Overall, the successful application of knowledge in the workplace, as asserted by Jaramillo-Baquerizo et al. (2019), is facilitated by a supportive innovative climate, which enhances the connection between training satisfaction, trainer capability, and learning transfer, ultimately maximizing educational outcomes.

ARTIFICIAL INTELLIGENCE (AI): AN OVERVIEW

Artificial Intelligence (AI) has emerged as a transformative force in education, influencing various aspects of teaching, learning, and administration. With the integration of AI, educational opportunities are significantly enhanced, offering practical strategies and solutions for both students and educators. AI enables personalized learning experiences, where adaptive technologies can assess student progress and tailor educational content accordingly. For instance, platforms like Duolingo leverage AI to adjust the difficulty of language exercises based on individual performance, thereby optimizing the learning process (Fitria, 2021).

In addition to personalized learning, AI is automating traditional administrative tasks such as grading. AI-enhanced grading systems, like Gradescope, allow educators to evaluate students' work more efficiently, freeing up time for personalized instruction. Furthermore, AI-powered virtual tutors and assistants, such as chatbots like Squirrel AI, provide immediate support outside classroom hours, answering students' questions and clarifying complex concepts.

AI's capabilities extend to predictive analytics, where it analyses large datasets to forecast student outcomes and academic trends. This information empowers educators to intervene proactively, helping students before they encounter significant challenges. Learning Management Systems (LMS) are also improved through AI, which can automate administrative processes and suggest personalized content, enhancing user experience and communication.

Moreover, AI plays a crucial role in content generation and curation. Tools that utilize Natural Language Processing (NLP) and machine learning can create educational materials, quizzes, and summaries, thereby making learning more effective and engaging. Additionally, AI assists in supporting students with disabilities, offering solutions such as text-to-speech conversion and personalized learning strategies for various challenges.

Innovative technology, including Virtual Reality (VR) and Augmented Reality (AR), is utilized to enhance hands-on learning experiences. Platforms like ClassVR employ AI to facilitate immersive lessons, allowing students to explore complex subjects interactively. AI is also integral in maintaining academic integrity through exam proctoring, using techniques like facial recognition and behaviour analysis to prevent cheating.

Artificial intelligence (AI) is increasingly influencing sectors like education, healthcare, and business, leading to innovations that streamline operations and enhance decision-making, particularly in mental health support. Recent advancements highlight AI's ability to transform care delivery and accessibility. For instance, research in Nature Psychology (2023) demonstrated that machine-learning models could analyse electronic health records (EHR) to predict mental health crises, allowing healthcare providers to intervene early before conditions worsen. AI-driven mental health chatbots, such as Woebot and Wysa, offer 24/7 support, proving effective in reducing anxiety and depressive symptoms, as noted in a study from The Lancet Psychiatry (2023). Additionally, AI enhances telehealth services through platforms like BetterHelp and Talkspace by leveraging natural language processing (NLP) to analyse client interactions, which yields actionable insights for improved engagement, as discussed in Telemedicine and e-Health (2024). In the engineering sector, AI tools are utilized to assess employee stress and optimize workflows, fostering supportive environments and alleviating workloads. Continuous research and ethical considerations will be crucial for maximizing the impact of these technologies.

Artificial Intelligence (AI) in education holds the promise of transformative advancements, yet it poses critical ethical implications, biases, and accessibility challenges. Significant ethical concerns include data privacy, as AI systems often require the collection of sensitive student information, raising the risk of privacy breaches and misuse. Informed consent is essential, particularly for minors, as many stakeholders may not fully understand the workings and data collection processes of AI tools. Additionally, reliance on AI could undermine the role of teachers, diminishing human oversight in student assessments. AI's often-opaque algorithms complicate transparency and accountability, risking errors that may disadvantage students. Potential algorithmic biases can reinforce pre-existing inequalities based on race, gender, or socioeconomic status, and culturally biased educational content may alienate minority students. The technological divide further exacerbates disparities, as low-income families may lack access to necessary devices and high-speed internet. If AI tools are not designed with accessibility in mind, they may exclude students with diverse learning needs, including disabilities. Moreover, teachers may not receive uniform training on AI technologies, leading to inconsistent classroom integration and varied student outcomes. While AI has the potential to enhance educational experiences, it is crucial for educators, policymakers, and technology developers to engage with these ethical implications, biases, and accessibility concerns, ensuring equitable and inclusive implementation that prioritizes transparency and accountability.

Over-reliance on AI in education presents several significant risks, particularly regarding human interaction and pedagogical flexibility. One major concern is reduced human interaction, which hinders the development of essential social skills like empathy, collaboration, and effective communication, while also depriving students of the emotional support that human educators provide for their well-being and motivation. Additionally, AI-driven education often adopts a one-size-fits-all approach, failing to accommodate diverse learning styles and needs, which can diminish teachers' autonomy and limit their ability to adapt teaching methods according to real-time classroom dynamics. The reliance on AI solutions may also undermine critical thinking and problem-solving skills, as students may seek answers from AI rather than engage deeply with content. Furthermore, equity and access issues arise, as not all students have equal access to AI technologies, exacerbating existing educational inequalities, and biases in AI systems could lead to unfair treatment of students. The dehumanization of learning results in a more mechanical education process, distancing students from personal connections with educators. Ethical concerns, such as data privacy and the ownership of learning, also arise as AI becomes more integrated into the educational landscape. Moreover, the fear of teacher displacement contributes to job insecurity among educators. Finally, an over-reliance on AI may cultivate resistance to pedagogical innovation that does not involve technology, stifling creativity and personal engagement. Therefore, while AI can enhance educational outcomes, maintaining a balance with human interaction and pedagogical flexibility is crucial for fostering a rich, inclusive, and effective learning environment.

In our digitally driven world, the concepts of AI and digital competence are intrinsically linked. Digital competence involves effectively using digital technologies to solve problems and communicate, which includes essential skills such as assessing the quality of digital content and understanding cybersecurity. As AI technology develops, individuals must cultivate a high level of digital competence to engage critically and ethically with AI systems, which necessitates strong data literacy skills.

To foster AI and digital competence, a multifaceted approach is essential. Educational institutions need to embed digital literacy and AI-related topics in their curricula, promoting understanding of both the technology and its ethical implications. Lifelong learning opportunities, such as online courses and workshops, should be made available to help individuals stay updated with technological advancements.

Government policies must also support infrastructure and resources that promote ethical and impactful AI integration in education. As AI's role in decision-making expands across sectors, individuals equipped with strong digital competence can advocate for ethical practices and responsibly navigate AI's societal impacts.

In conclusion, AI and digital competence are vital for modern education and workforce development. Together, they empower individuals to leverage digital technologies effectively while equipping them to analyse the opportunities and challenges posed by AI, shaping a better future for education and society.

Technology Integration: Transforming Education, and Workforce

The integration of technology refers to the effective use of tools, platforms, and systems to enhance functionality, boost productivity, and foster innovation. In educational contexts, this integration has the potential to significantly transform processes, learning experiences, and interactions within society. By incorporating digital technologies and automation, educational institutions can optimize procedures, eliminate manual tasks, and free the workforce to engage in higher-value strategic initiatives, thereby increasing overall productivity.

Digital tools such as online learning management systems (LMS), digital textbooks, interactive apps, and educational games can greatly enhance student-learning experiences. Platforms like Google Classroom, Moodle, and Blackboard facilitate collaborative and personalized learning, allowing for a blended learning approach that combines online content with traditional in-person instruction. This method encourages flexibility and accommodates diverse learning styles. Further, the use of smartboards, tablets, and laptops in classrooms promotes student engagement by providing instant access to resources and dynamic lessons. Adaptive Learning Technologies, such as DreamBox and Knewton, customize educational experiences by adjusting content difficulty in real-time to suit individual students' needs.

In the workplace, technology integration is equally transformative. Tools like Microsoft Teams, Slack, and Zoom enable remote collaboration, communication, and file sharing, which are crucial in modern business settings, especially in the post-pandemic era. Cloud services such as Google Workspace and Microsoft 365 allow data to be stored remotely, accessible from various locations, thus enhancing flexibility. By automating repetitive tasks with technologies like Robotic Process Automation (RPA) and AI-driven systems, businesses can improve operational efficiency, allowing employees to concentrate on strategic responsibilities. Additionally, platforms such as Asana and Trello assist in project management and resource allocation, ensuring productivity remains high even with remote work arrangements.

The benefits of technology integration are substantial. In education, it grants students and teachers access to extensive online resources, including research databases and multimedia content that enable deeper exploration of subjects. Interactive tools and gamified learning significantly increase student engagement, leading to a more motivating educational environment. Automation, cloud storage, and project management software save time on routine tasks, enabling teams to dedicate more effort toward complex projects and high-value work.

Moreover, technology facilitates international collaboration, enabling teams to work across borders and time zones through shared cloud-based documents and communication platforms. This capability is essential for universities operating globally. Technology also supports scalability in businesses and educational institutions, allowing for rapid growth with minimal investment in physical infrastructure.

Integrating AI into technology further enhances efficiency, productivity, and innovation. AI-enabled automation reduces human error, supports decision-making through predictive analytics, and fosters personalized customer experiences. For instance, AI chatbots can address customer inquiries 24/7, while AI algorithms in business intelligence tools help companies make data-driven decisions.

In healthcare, AI technologies improve diagnostics and treatment plans, while AI-driven systems optimize supply chain logistics by predicting demand and improving inventory management. In finance, AI plays a critical role in fraud detection, analysing transaction data in real-time for suspicious activities (Kumar, V., Goodarzian, F et al., 2025).

The integration of AI with creative industries and the Internet of Things (IoT) is also on the rise. AI tools help professionals in fields as if graphic design and content creation enhance their work. Moreover, smart devices in homes and industries become more responsive through AI integration, actively monitoring and adjusting to user preferences and operational needs.

As AI technology evolves, the emphasis will increasingly be on collaboration between humans and machines, enhancing human decision-making while automating repetitive tasks. Furthermore, AI accessibility will increase, as tools become user-friendly, allowing companies of all sizes to incorporate AI into their workflows.

Balancing technological integration in universities while mitigating digital fatigue and dependence among educators and students necessitates a multifaceted approach. Key strategies include promoting digital literacy through comprehensive training programs for educators and workshops for students that teach effective technology management and screen time regulation. Implementing a blended learning model that combines traditional and online elements allows flexibility while minimizing excessive digital interaction. Establishing clear technology guidelines and encouraging "digital detox" periods can foster mental well-being and interpersonal connections. Engaging and purposeful use of technology is essential, with a focus on tools that enhance collaboration and creativity while empowering student ownership of learning experiences. Regular feedback from students and educators can help identify signs of digital fatigue and inform adaptations, as can pilot programs for new technologies. Incorporating mindfulness and well-being practices supports awareness of digital habits, alongside accessible mental health resources. A supportive institutional culture, championed by leadership, encourages balance in digital engagement and fosters peer mentorship to assist those less digitally savvy. Finally, using analytics responsibly allows institutions to monitor engagement trends without invading privacy; ensuring technology use aligns with educational outcomes rather than becoming an overwhelming presence. By implementing these strategies, universities can create environments where technology enhances learning while promoting human connection and holistic development in a digitally enriched landscape.

In conclusion, the integration of technology and AI is redefining modern industries, improving business models, customer experiences, and driving innovation across various sectors. The ongoing synergy between these technologies is crucial for shaping our future.

Successful Examples of University-Industry Partnerships

University-industry partnerships serve as robust conduits for innovation and collaboration, yielding benefits for students, faculty, and businesses alike. Below are some notable examples from scholarly articles & industry reports. Stanford's Bio-X program cultivates interdisciplinary collaboration among scientists, engineers, and medical researchers, leading to significant advancements in health technologies. Georgia Tech and Delta's collaboration focuses on improving aviation safety and efficiency. Students gain practical industry experience while Delta benefits from cutting-edge research. Berkeley's partnership with IBM has established a research center dedicated to artificial intelligence and machine learning with extensive student involvement in real-world projects. This partnership enhances research in autonomous vehicles, providing internships and research opportunities for undergraduate students. RMIT and Siemens engaged in creating the Siemens Industry 4.0 Innovation Lab, equipping students with practical experience in advancing manufacturing processes.

The success of university-industry partnerships illustrates how such collaborations drive innovation, facilitating valuable experiences for students while providing industries with research-driven solutions. By prioritizing investments in digital literacy initiatives, stakeholders contribute not only to employment enhancement but also to improved access to mental health resources across diverse communities.

To effectively bridge the gap between academia and industry, universities must establish long-term partnerships that create a talent pipeline through internships and job placements. Engaging in collaborative research initiatives allows universities to align academic pursuits with practical workforce applications, equipping students to tackle real-world challenges. Implementing specialized training programs and certification courses tailored to current workforce needs enables universities to offer professional development while helping existing employees acquire new skills. Collaborations with industry partners help identify relevant courses and certifications, promoting lifelong learning and reskilling. Micro-credentials, certificates, and digital badges provide flexible options for individuals to continually update their qualifications, while digital platforms and online forums facilitate scalable educational opportunities. Work-based learning options, such as internships and apprenticeships, allow students to gain practical experience and enable employers to discover potential talent early. Furthermore, collaborative projects and industry-specific training programs ensure graduates possess the skills needed for immediate employment. Enhancing career services through industry connections and establishing mentorship programs fosters networking opportunities and guides students in their career planning.

Additionally, promoting innovation and entrepreneurship through funding and resources for student and faculty ventures supports the development of viable businesses, while events like hackathons encourage collaboration and creativity. Collaborative innovation labs provide hands-on experiences, enriching educational quality. Public-private partnerships, aided by government initiatives, further bolster these efforts and can focus on community outreach in underserved areas to promote job readiness and skill development. A strong emphasis on diversity and inclusion in academic settings prepares a diverse future workforce, while regularly updated curricula and advisory boards ensure that students acquire relevant skills through industry-specific capstone projects. This comprehensive approach enhances workforce readiness and strengthens the symbiotic relationship between academia and industry, benefiting all stakeholders involved.

Key Aspects of Mental Well-Being Support

Emotional and psychological support is essential for well-being, and professional mental health services such as counselling and therapy provide a crucial platform for individuals to discuss their emotions, fears, and experiences. Psychiatrists address mental health conditions with medications, while psychologists focus on therapeutic interventions that do not involve medication. The advent of telehealth has significantly broadened access to mental health services through online therapy platforms like BetterHelp and Talkspace, which eliminate geographical barriers to care. Many workplaces enhance employee well-being via Employee Assistance Programs (EAPs), offering confidential counselling that helps employees tackle personal or professional challenges. Stress management programs equipped with tools such as mindfulness, meditation, yoga, and relaxation exercises serve to mitigate burnout and other mental health issues (Molfenter et al., 2021). Moreover, resilience-building initiatives aim to empower individuals with the ability to navigate setbacks and challenges, teaching emotional regulation, adaptive thinking, and effective problem-solving strategies.

Educational workshops, seminars, and awareness campaigns play a pivotal role in enhancing understanding of mental health issues and emotional well-being within the workforce. For individuals in immediate distress, mental health helplines, such as the Suicide Prevention Lifeline and National Helpline for Mental Health, deliver vital, confidential support, often-available 24/7. Additionally, crisis text and chat services offer alternative avenues for communication, allowing individuals to seek help through platforms like Crisis Text Line via SMS and online chats. Crisis stabilization centers provide safe environments for those experiencing acute mental health crises, offering evaluation and short-term care to prevent unnecessary emergency room visits while facilitating stabilization before long-term care is accessed. Physical activity also emerges as a powerful tool for supporting mental health; activities such as walking, running, swimming, or yoga promote the release of endorphins and lessen stress hormones like cortisol, encouraging the adoption of a more active lifestyle as a means of fostering emotional well-being. Mindfulness and meditation practices, such as guided breathing exercises, have been shown to decrease anxiety, sharpen focus, and enhance emotional regulation, leading to lower stress levels and improved mental clarity. Ultimately, the combination of professional support, workplace initiatives, physical wellness practices, and self-care strategies creates a comprehensive approach to nurturing emotional and psychological health, encouraging individuals to seek the resources they need to thrive emotionally and psychologically.

To successfully implement effective mental health initiatives, institutions must adopt a comprehensive approach that thoroughly addresses the community's needs. Key strategies include conducting assessments to identify specific mental health challenges through surveys, interviews, and focus groups. Educational and awareness campaigns can help reduce stigma and promote open discussions among students and staff via workshops and information sessions. Training faculty and staff to recognize mental health issues and provide appropriate support is crucial, alongside ensuring access to professional mental health services, such as on-site counsellors or tele therapy options. Establishing peer support programs encourages community building, while crisis intervention services should be implemented to facilitate immediate access to counselling in emergencies. Additionally, wellness programs that promote physical activity, stress management, and mindfulness, alongside creating safe spaces for relaxation and assistance, enhance overall mental well-being. Institutions should gather feedback on these initiatives for ongoing evaluation and improvement and develop policies that support mental health, such as anti-discrimination and leave policies. Collaborating with local mental health organizations enhances resource availability, while incorporating technology can facilitate awareness and support through apps and online services (Goetzel et al., 2021). Inclusivity is essential in programming to address diverse backgrounds, and securing long-term funding ensures sustained efforts. Finally, leadership support is vital to promote and prioritize mental health initiatives within the institution. By implementing these concrete strategies, institutions can foster a supportive environment that enhances mental well-being for all community members.

Recent developments in mental health interventions have increasingly integrated digital literacy and artificial intelligence (AI) applications into therapeutic practices. These innovations have the potential to expand access to mental health resources, enabling remote therapy sessions and offering personalized support via chatbots and applications. The overarching goal is to enhance mental well-being by rendering therapeutic resources more accessible and adaptable to individual needs while simultaneously promoting mental health literacy among users (Thakkar et al., 2024). By leveraging technology, practitioners can reach broader audiences and more effectively address various mental health challenges. AI is playing a transformative role in education by personalizing learning experiences for both students and educators. Notable applications include (Panda, Shivani et al., 2024); Knewton utilizes AI algorithms to tailor educational content based on individual student performance, adjusting the difficulty and presentation of materials to improve engagement and learning outcomes. Its integration with textbook publishers allows students to receive personalized recommendations while studying traditional materials. Evidence suggests that students using DreamBox exhibit significant gains in math proficiency over their peers in traditional educational settings. IBM Watson Tutor offers personalized assistance by evaluating learning styles and preferences, providing instant feedback on assignments and resources, leading to increased student engagement and comprehension. Socratic by Google is a mobile application that aids students with homework by interpreting queries and directing users to relevant educational resources using advanced machine learning. Gradescope streamlines the grading process by automating aspects such as recognizing similar answers in multiple-choice questions, facilitating faster feedback and enabling instructors to focus more on personalized support. Turnitin is renowned for its AI-driven plagiarism detection, which not only identifies copied content but also provides constructive feedback to help students enhance their writing skills and ensure academic integrity.

Workplace Mental Well-Being Support

Recognizing the significance of mental health, many employers are now permitting employees to take "mental health days" to prevent burnout and emotional exhaustion, fostering a more productive and focused workforce (Shaji George, 2024). Workplace wellness programs that offer resources like counselling, fitness facilities, relaxation areas, and stress management workshops significantly enhance overall well-being. Social connections play a crucial role in mental health; hence, promoting regular social activities and community interactions can strengthen employees' mental well-being. Volunteering and community service further boost mental health by instilling a sense of purpose and improving mood. Caregivers for individuals with mental health challenges often face emotional strain, and providing support resources such as respite care and counselling is essential for their well-being. In educational settings, accessible counselling services are vital for helping students navigate stress, academic pressures, and social challenges. School counsellors create safe environments to address mental health issues among youth, while peer-mentoring programs foster supportive communities where students can assist one another. Integrating emotional regulation and coping strategies into curricula equips students with essential skills for lifelong mental health management, promoting resilience and well-being. Overall, these initiatives contribute to a healthier and supportive environment in both workplaces and educational institutions.

Benefits of Mental Well-Being Support

Access to mental well-being support is crucial in helping individuals manage stress, cope with life's challenges, and enhance emotional health, ultimately leading to improved quality of life and increased life satisfaction. In both work and academic environments, mental health initiatives enhance focus, reduce burnout, and promote overall productivity. When individuals feel mentally supported, they tend to be more engaged and efficient in their roles. Mental health support programs cultivate resilience by equipping individuals with skills to navigate adversity and emotional difficulties effectively. As mental health becomes increasingly normalized and accessible, the associated stigma diminishes, encouraging earlier intervention and preventing crises (Gautam, S., Jain, A et al., 2024).

The integration of mental well-being support into communities fosters a collective sense of responsibility and social cohesion, allowing individuals to feel understood and supported, which strengthens social bonds. Concurrently, universities are recognizing the importance of spirituality and holistic education. As 21st century institutions evolve, they are beginning to incorporate spiritual practices that complement intellectual and professional development, offering students a comprehensive approach that emphasizes purpose, ethical grounding, and emotional well-being.

Mindfulness practices, such as meditation, have gained popularity within university settings, helping students manage stress and cultivate emotional resilience through workshops and dedicated spaces for reflection. Contemplative practices, like journaling and philosophical discussions, encourage deep reflection on personal values and life's significant questions. Additionally, universities are providing chaplaincy services and study groups that explore spiritual topics, fostering community and support among students.

Service to others and compassion are core themes in spiritual practices increasingly recognized in academic contexts. Many universities encourage community service, linking personal development with a commitment to social justice and ethical responsibilities. Programs empowering students to engage in service-oriented work, whether local or global, enhance their moral reasoning and ethical judgment. Moreover, holistic approaches to student wellness are being embraced, recognizing that academic and personal support must encompass physical, mental, emotional, and spiritual dimensions. This includes spiritual counselling addressing existential questions and emotional challenges while integrating wellness services like yoga and meditation. Integrating arts and spirituality, universities are also offering creative outlets that enable students to explore their inner selves through artistic pursuits.

Leadership development programs now increasingly incorporate spiritual values of service and ethical decision-making, fostering qualities like empathy and integrity. Spiritual practices are seen to provide not only personal growth but also essential leadership skills. Retreats promoting self-awareness and inner peace help develop a new generation of leaders committed to ethical responsibilities and social contributions.

However, bridging the gap between higher education and workforce demands requires ongoing collaboration between universities and industries. By aligning curricula with industry needs and providing work-based learning opportunities, universities can effectively prepare graduates for evolving job markets while industries can access a skilled, adaptable talent pool.

Technology plays a significant role in transforming education, workplaces, and society. Its integration fosters innovation and enhances productivity, although it poses challenges such as resistance to change and access inequalities. Addressing these issues through strategic planning can unlock the full potential of technology for societal benefit.

Ultimately, mental well-being support is essential for overall health; significantly, influencing individuals manage stress and navigate challenges. By providing accessible mental health resources through counselling, community initiatives, and workplace wellness programs, society can cultivate a healthier, more resilient population. Increased awareness, improved infrastructure, and acceptance of mental health care are key to creating robust support systems for all individuals, promoting a balanced approach to mental well-being.

Addressing Challenges in Digital Literacy and Mental Health Support

Equitable access to digital literacy and mental health resources is vital for fostering inclusive environments, particularly in education and professional settings. The interconnected nature of these domains highlights various challenges: Many individuals, especially in marginalized communities, lack reliable devices and internet connectivity, restricting their ability to engage with digital learning or access online resources. Disparities in digital literacy across demographics, notably among older adults and low-income families, hinder effective engagement with technological platforms. Digital literacy training often lacks cultural relevance and multilingual resources, alienating non-native speakers and diverse communities. Cultural stigma surrounding mental health discourages individuals from seeking assistance, compounded by a lack of awareness about available resources. Shortages of mental health professionals and high care costs restrict access, particularly for marginalized groups. Proposed Solution for Digital Literacy can be to implement community technology access programs providing free access to devices and training workshops and design inclusive curricula that cater to diverse skill levels and utilize partnerships with local organizations to enhance reach into underserved populations. For Mental Health Support this may be launching awareness campaigns to reduce stigma and promote mental health resources and enhancing telehealth accessibility, ensuring that online platforms are user-friendly and accompanied by training for users. Addressing the challenges in digital literacy and mental health support requires proactive and collaborative efforts. By implementing community-driven solutions, raising awareness, and fostering integrative programs, stakeholders can bridge gaps in access and skills. Enhancing digital literacy and mental health support is fundamental to promoting social equity, empowerment, and community well-being. With continued engagement and responsive strategies, it is possible to create environments where all individuals have the tools and support necessary to thrive in the digital age.

Potential Issues of University-Industry Partnerships

University-industry partnerships face several challenges, particularly regarding skill mismatches, digital divides, and the sustainability of technology-driven education. One major issue is curriculum gaps, where universities struggle to keep pace with the rapidly evolving skills necessary for the workforce, leading to graduates unprepared for industry demands. Additionally, employers often prioritize soft skills like teamwork and communication, while graduates may focus more on technical knowledge, resulting in a mismatch. Emerging technologies such as AI and robotics may not be adequately represented in university curricula, exacerbating these challenges. Digital divides present another significant barrier, as not all students have equal access to necessary technology, creating educational inequalities, particularly for those in rural or underserved urban areas. Financial constraints can limit access to technology for lower-income students, while varying levels of digital literacy can affect student engagement with technology. Sustainability concerns also arise, as continuous investment in technology and training can be difficult for budget-strapped institutions. The fast pace of technological advancements requires constant updates to tools and curricula, complicating long-term partnerships between universities and industries that may diverge in goals over time. Furthermore, reliance on specific pedagogical approaches may lead to student disengagement. To navigate these challenges, ongoing dialogue and collaboration between universities and industries are essential, alongside inclusive policies that address equity and access. By understanding and addressing these issues, university-industry partnerships can create a more equitable and effective technology-driven educational environment.

Incorporating specific case studies and comparative analyses greatly enhances the discussion of university-workforce collaborations by providing real-world examples that illustrate both benefits and challenges while presenting data-driven insights. These case studies highlight best practices, displaying successful collaboration models that other institutions can emulate. Comparative analyses reveal how different universities and industries adapt their collaboration initiatives based on unique contextual factors such as geography and workforce demands. Evaluating outcomes through these examples can assess tangible benefits like improved student employability and industry innovations, while also highlighting common challenges such as misaligned goals and communication difficulties. Furthermore, quantitative data from these analyses lend credibility to findings regarding job placement rates and employer satisfaction. By fostering interdisciplinary approaches, case studies demonstrate how diverse academic programs can effectively engage with various industries. They also document the evolution of partnerships over time, providing insights into adaptability and responsiveness to labour market changes. Engaging various stakeholders including educators, policymakers, and industry leaders through these relatable examples fosters a richer dialogue about the importance of collaborations. For instance, exploring co-op programs at institutions like Northeastern University and analysing industry partnerships such as those between Georgia Tech and AT&T illustrate effective integration of work experience with academic studies. Overall, specific case studies and comparisons offer valuable resources to deepen the understanding of university-workforce collaborations, informing best practices and fostering partnerships that benefit both students and employers.

Holistic Approach to University-Workforce Collaboration

Enhancing collaboration between universities and industries is critical in today's fast-evolving job landscape. A holistic approach to this collaboration involves several key themes, including curriculum alignment, experiential learning, faculty engagement, student readiness, and ongoing professional development. Fostering stronger partnerships can align educational programs with labour market demands. Encouraging industry-relevant skills while maintaining academic rigor is paramount. Universities can create curricula that resonate with market trends by collaborating with industry leaders and developing interdisciplinary programs. Offering structured internships and project-based learning initiatives allows students to translate their theoretical knowledge into practical experience while contributing fresh insights to the industry. Engaging faculty with industry through training and research initiatives allows them to stay abreast of contemporary trends while enriching classroom experiences. Integrating career services and soft skills training ensures students are equipped with not only technical knowledge but also essential employability skills. Facilitating post-graduate training and incorporating feedback loops for continuous improvement ensures that graduates remain relevant in a changing workforce.

Integrating Diverse Perspectives in Collaboration

Incorporating a diverse array of perspectives into university-workforce collaboration fosters inclusivity and innovation. Strategies to engage marginalized communities and recognize the challenges faced by the Global South are critical for creating equitable educational frameworks. Recognizing and addressing barriers, while promoting cultural competence within programs, ensures inclusivity. Active partnerships with community organizations can inform curriculum development to be more relevant and accessible. Establishing educational partnerships with institutions in the Global South and offering remote learning opportunities facilitates mutual learning and aligns skills development with local workforce needs. Including diverse experiences and perspectives, thus enhancing both student engagement and learning outcomes, can improve curricular relevance. Providing access to networking opportunities and mentorship can significantly enhance career trajectories for students from underrepresented backgrounds. Encouraging research initiatives focused on marginalized communities can identify barriers and advocate for systemic changes that promote equity in education and employment.

Integrating diverse perspectives into university-workforce collaboration is essential for fostering a conducive environment for educational equity and relevance. By recognizing challenges and leveraging the strengths of diverse communities, stakeholders can implement innovative programs that prepare all students for success in the global job market. This holistic approach will promote meaningful change, thereby contributing to a fairer and more inclusive workforce and society.

CONCLUSION

This paper presents a comprehensive approach to strengthen collaboration between universities and the workforce by focusing on three primary pillars: digital literacy, the integration of technology in education, and the psychological well-being of educators or for that matter University Workforce consisting of the Trainers and the Trainees. The aim is to create an environment conducive to effective learning and teaching, foster continuous skill development, and enhance productivity and resilience within higher educational institutions. Emphasizing these areas will ensure that students are better prepared for the workforce, and that educators are equipped to provide high-quality education in a supportive and healthy environment promoting a good work culture for University and Society. The integration of digital literacy, AI applications, and mental health support is pivotal in creating a resourceful, adaptable, and inclusive workforce. By actively addressing challenges and fostering university-workforce collaboration, stakeholders can enhance employability outcomes, cultivate a supportive learning environment, and ensure equitable access to resources. With a continued focus on promoting digital skills and mental well-being, society can advance toward greater equity and empowerment in the digital age.

REFERENCES

Ata, R., & Alpaslan, M. M. (2024). The role of digital literacy, epistemological belief and reading motivation and engagement in teaching 21st century skills. *International Journal of Information and Learning Technology*, *41*(3), 304–317. DOI: 10.1108/IJILT-08-2023-0142

Behera, A., Mahakhud, S., & Panda, R. B. (2024). Transformative Role of Artificial Intelligence in Education. *Redshine Archive*, *9*(10). Advance online publication. DOI: 10.25215/9358798181.01

Berry, J. (2014). Y in the workplace: Comparative analysis of values, skills and perceptions of government communication amongst university students and government staff. *Foresight*, *16*(5), 432–447. DOI: 10.1108/FS-03-2013-0010

Chan, A. J., Hooi, L. W., & Ngui, K. S. (2021). Do digital literacies matter in employee engagement in digitalised workplace? *Journal of Asia Business Studies*, *15*(3), 523–540. DOI: 10.1108/JABS-08-2020-0318

Chan, G. H. (2024). Enhancing digital literacy in education: Educational directions. *Education + Training*, *66*(1), 127–142. DOI: 10.1108/ET-09-2022-0390

Gautam, S., Jain, A., Chaudhary, J., Gautam, M., Gaur, M., & Grover, S. (2024). Concept of mental health and mental well-being, it's determinants and coping strategies. *Indian Journal of Psychiatry*, *66*(Suppl 2), S231–S244. DOI: 10.4103/indianjpsychiatry.indianjpsychiatry_707_23 PMID: 38445271

Gibson, P. F., & Smith, S. (2018). Digital literacies: Preparing pupils and students for their information journey in the twenty-first century. *Information and Learning Science*, *119*(12), 733–742. DOI: 10.1108/ILS-07-2018-0059

Gooding, P., Crook, R., Westwood, M., & Peters, S. (2024), "Ways to wellbeing in postgraduate research students: interactions with positive perceptions of relationships with university staff", *Studies in Graduate and Postdoctoral Education*, Vol. ahead-of-print No. ahead-of-print. DOI: 10.1108/SGPE-07-2023-0063

Kumar, V., Goodarzian, F., Ghasemi, P., Chan, F. T. S., & Gupta, N. (2025). Artificial intelligence applications in healthcare supply chain networks under disaster conditions. *International Journal of Production Research*, *63*(2), 395–403. DOI: 10.1080/00207543.2024.2444150

Lang, J. (2023). Workforce upskilling: Can universities meet the challenges of lifelong learning? *International Journal of Information and Learning Technology*, *40*(5), 388–400. DOI: 10.1108/IJILT-01-2023-0001

Lei, H., Tang, S., Zhao, Y., & Chen, S. (2024). Enterprise digitalization, employee digital literacy and R&D cooperation: The moderating role of organizational inertia. *Chinese Management Studies*, *18*(2), 479–505. DOI: 10.1108/CMS-10-2021-0456

Lin, Y., & Yu, Z. (2024). A bibliometric analysis of artificial intelligence chatbots in educational contexts. *Interactive Technology and Smart Education*, *21*(2), 189–213. DOI: 10.1108/ITSE-12-2022-0165

Manderino, M., & Castek, J. (2020), Digital Literacies for Disciplinary Learning: Pedagogies Youth Deserve. In Ortlieb, E., Grote-Garcia, S., Cassidy, J. and Cheek, E.H. (Ed.) *What's Hot in Literacy: Exemplar Models of Effective Practice* (*Literacy Research, Practice and Evaluation, Vol. 11*), Emerald Publishing Limited, Leeds, pp. 3-15. DOI: 10.1108/S2048-045820200000011003

Marengo, A., Pagano, A., Pange, J., & Soomro, K. A. (2024). The educational value of artificial intelligence in higher education: A 10-year systematic literature review. *Interactive Technology and Smart Education*, *21*(4), 625–644. DOI: 10.1108/ITSE-11-2023-0218

Menon, S., & Suresh, M. (2022). Assessment framework for workforce agility in higher education institutions. *Higher Education, Skills and Work-Based Learning*, *12*(6), 1169–1188. DOI: 10.1108/HESWBL-01-2022-0014

Molfenter, T., Heitkamp, T., Murphy, A. A., Tapscott, S., Behlman, S., & Cody, O. J. (2021). Use of Telehealth in Mental Health (MH) Services During and After COVID-19. *Community Mental Health Journal*, *57*(7), 1244–1251. DOI: 10.1007/s10597-021-00861-2 PMID: 34165695

Musah, M. B., Ali, H. M., Vazhathodi al-Hudawi, S. H., Tahir, L. M., Daud, K. B., Said, H. B., & Kamil, N. M. (2016). Organisational climate as a predictor of workforce performance in the Malaysian higher education institutions. *Quality Assurance in Education*, *24*(3), 416–438. DOI: 10.1108/QAE-10-2014-0048

Nedungadi, P. P., Menon, R., Gutjahr, G., Erickson, L., & Raman, R. (2018). Towards an inclusive digital literacy framework for digital India. *Education + Training*, *60*(6), 516–528. DOI: 10.1108/ET-03-2018-0061

Ng, P. M. L., Chow, P. K., Wong, P., & Luk, W. M. B. (2024). The impact of digital technology training on developing academics' digital competence in higher education context. *Education + Training*, *66*(9), 1276–1292. DOI: 10.1108/ET-10-2023-0417

Nicholls, H., Nicholls, M., Tekin, S., Lamb, D., & Billings, J. (2022). The impact of working in academia on researchers' mental health and well-being: A systematic review and qualitative meta-synthesis. *PLoS One*, *17*(5), e0268890. DOI: 10.1371/journal.pone.0268890 PMID: 35613147

Nikou, S., De Reuver, M., & Mahboob Kanafi, M. (2022). Workplace literacy skills—How information and digital literacy affect adoption of digital technology. *The Journal of Documentation*, *78*(7), 371–391. DOI: 10.1108/JD-12-2021-0241

Omilion-Hodges, L. M., Shank, S. E., & Johnson, C. M. (2022). Doubting the connection: Millennials' perceptions of the link between higher education and workplace readiness. *Management Research Review*, *45*(5), 649–663. DOI: 10.1108/MRR-01-2021-0084

Rafi, M., JianMing, Z. & Ahmad, K. (2019), Technology integration for students' information and digital literacy education in academic libraries. *Information Discovery and Delivery, 47*(4), pp. 203-217. DOI: 10.1108/IDD-07-2019-0049

Saddozai, S. K., Hui, P., Akram, U., Khan, M. S., & Memon, S. (2017). Investigation of talent, talent management, its policies and its impact on working environment. *Chinese Management Studies*, *11*(3), 538–554. DOI: 10.1108/CMS-10-2016-0206

Sanders, C. K., & Scanlon, E. (2021). The Digital Divide Is a Human Rights Issue: Advancing Social Inclusion Through Social Work Advocacy. *Journal of Human Rights and Social Work*, *6*(2), 130–143. DOI: 10.1007/s41134-020-00147-9 PMID: 33758780

Shaji, , G. (2024). The Emergence and Impact of Mental Health Leave Policies on Employee Wellbeing and Productivity. *Partners Universal International Innovation Journal (PUIIJ), 02*(02), 99–120. DOI: 10.5281/zenodo.11002386

Shiri, A. (2024). Artificial intelligence literacy: A proposed faceted taxonomy. *Digital Library Perspectives*, *40*(4), 681–699. DOI: 10.1108/DLP-04-2024-0067

Thakkar, A., Gupta, A., & De Sousa, A. (2024). Artificial intelligence in positive mental health: A narrative review. *Frontiers in Digital Health*, *6*, 1280235. DOI: 10.3389/fdgth.2024.1280235 PMID: 38562663

Tinmaz, H., Fanea-Ivanovici, M., & Baber, H. (2023). A snapshot of digital literacy. *Library Hi Tech News*, *40*(1), 20–23. DOI: 10.1108/LHTN-12-2021-0095

White, A. (2009). The corporate university: Meeting the learning needs of a changing workforce. *Strategic HR Review*, *8*(4), 11–16. DOI: 10.1108/14754390910963865

Wu, A., Roemer, E. C., Kent, K. B., Ballard, D. W., & Goetzel, R. Z. (2021). Organizational Best Practices Supporting Mental Health in the Workplace. *Journal of Occupational and Environmental Medicine*, *63*(12), e925–e931. DOI: 10.1097/JOM.0000000000002407 PMID: 34840320

Zulfiqar, M., Sony, M., Bhat, S., Antony, J., Salentijn, W., & McDermott, O. (2024). Unlocking the potential: Empirical analysis of enablers, barriers, benefits and technologies for integrating Industry 4.0 and Lean Six Sigma in manufacturing organisations. *The TQM Journal*, *36*(8), 2360–2382. DOI: 10.1108/TQM-05-2023-0130

Chapter 6
Valuing Teachers' Voices in Educational Reform:
A Path to Achieving Global and National Sustainable Development Goals

Mohammad Ekramol Islam
https://orcid.org/0000-0001-6524-6069
Sonargaon University, Bangladesh

Mohammad Rashed Hasan Polas
https://orcid.org/0000-0002-6080-1075
Asia Pacific University of Technology and Innovation, Malaysia

Asghar Afshar Jahanshahi
https://orcid.org/0000-0003-2241-9913
IPADE Business School, Mexico

Mohammad Falahat
Asia Pacific University of Technology and Innovation, Malaysia

ABSTRACT

This chapter explores teachers' pivotal role in achieving global and national sustainable development goals, particularly focusing on SDG 4: Quality Education. It emphasizes the importance of valuing teachers' voices in shaping educational reforms, specifically focusing on the 2024 World Teachers' Day theme, "Valuing Teachers' Voices: Towards a New Social Contract for Education". The chapter examines the critical contributions of teachers as societal pillars who shape students' academic abilities and their ethical, moral, and emotional growth. It addresses

DOI: 10.4018/979-8-3373-0004-7.ch006

the global teacher shortage, low salaries, poor working conditions, and lack of professional development, highlighting their impact on recruitment, retention, and educational outcomes. The chapter further explores the unique challenges faced by Bangladesh in teacher recruitment and development and proposes solutions for improving teacher quality, status, and professional empowerment. Ultimately, it calls for a new social contract for education, empowering teachers as key stakeholders in educational policy and reform.

1.0 INTRODUCTION

Teachers are undeniably the cornerstone of education systems worldwide. They are the primary agents in shaping future generations, not only enhancing students' academic abilities but also nurturing their ethical, moral, and emotional growth (Odell et al., 2020; Ghamrawi, 2023; Anapey, 2024). Teachers serve as the backbone of any nation, influencing the social and cultural fabric of society. Their role goes beyond the classroom, as they help mold responsible citizens capable of contributing to sustainable societal development. Yet, despite their critical influence, teachers' voices often remain underrepresented in shaping educational policies (Adhikari & Shrestha, 2023). It is essential to recognize and value teachers as key contributors to education reform, particularly in the context of achieving Sustainable Development Goal 4 (SDG 4), which emphasizes the provision of quality education for all. This chapter aims to explore the vital role teachers play in national and global development and underscore the importance of valuing their input in the creation of educational policies (Haug & Mork, 2021).

SDG 4, established by the United Nations in 2015, specifically seeks to "ensure inclusive and equitable quality education and promote lifelong learning opportunities for all" (UNESCO, 2020). Achieving this goal requires more than just a global commitment; it necessitates systemic reforms that address the multifaceted challenges faced by educational systems worldwide (Ramaswamy et al., 2021). Teachers are integral to this mission, as they directly impact student outcomes and contribute to broader social development goals. However, the involvement of teachers in policy-making processes remains minimal in many countries, a challenge that undermines the efficacy of educational reforms (OECD, 2021). To bridge this gap, it is crucial to incorporate teachers' voices in discussions about the future of education, especially in light of emerging global and local challenges (García-Feijoo et al., 2020)

The theme of World Teachers' Day 2024, "Valuing teachers' voices: towards a new social contract for education", reflects a growing recognition of the need to reconsider how education systems are shaped. The "new social contract" calls for a collaborative approach between governments, educators, and communities, wherein teachers are viewed as partners in the design and implementation of educational reforms (Anapey, 2024). This model advocates for teachers' active participation in decision-making processes to ensure that reforms are not only relevant but also sustainable. By amplifying teachers' voices, education systems can better address the diverse needs of students and prepare them for the complex challenges of the 21st century (García-Feijoo et al., 2020).

Despite their central role in educational reform, teachers worldwide face numerous challenges that hinder their ability to deliver quality education. One of the most pressing issues is the global teacher shortage. According to the UNESCO Institute for Statistics (2022), over 69 million new teachers will be needed globally to achieve universal primary and secondary education by 2030. This shortage is particularly acute in developing countries, where limited resources, poor working conditions, and inadequate salaries make it difficult to recruit and retain qualified teachers (Smith & Heyward, 2024). In Bangladesh, for example, the educational system is grappling with an insufficient number of teachers, particularly in rural and remote areas (Ahmed & Rahman, 2020). The lack of investment in teacher recruitment and professional development further exacerbates the quality gap in education (Huan et al., 2021).

Teachers in many regions also face challenges related to their working conditions. Inadequate salaries, overcrowded classrooms, and insufficient teaching materials are just a few of the obstacles that teachers contend with on a daily basis (Smith & Heyward, 2024). These conditions not only affect teachers' job satisfaction but also have a direct impact on student learning outcomes. When teachers are overburdened, underpaid, and unsupported, it becomes increasingly difficult for them to provide the quality education that students need. In this context, valuing teachers' voices is not just a matter of professional recognition but also an essential step in improving the overall quality of education (Archer, 2023).

Incorporating teachers into the policy-making process is a crucial step toward addressing these challenges. Teachers have invaluable insights into the realities of the classroom, and their experiences can inform policies that are both practical and effective. Research has shown that when teachers are engaged in educational policy development, they are more likely to implement changes effectively and contribute to improved educational outcomes (Darling-Hammond, 2020). Involving teachers in decision-making processes can also help ensure that policies are aligned with the needs and realities of the classroom, rather than being based on theoretical assumptions or external pressures.

This chapter aims to explore the critical role teachers' play in fostering societal growth, innovation, and sustainable development. It will examine the teacher shortage and its implications for achieving quality education, particularly in light of SDG 4. The chapter will also discuss the specific challenges faced by teachers in both global and Bangladeshi contexts, focusing on recruitment, salaries, professional development, and working conditions. By highlighting these challenges, the chapter will underscore the urgent need for systemic reforms that prioritize teachers' well-being and professional development.

Furthermore, this chapter proposes actionable solutions for improving teacher quality, recruitment, retention, and status in society. It will explore strategies for enhancing teacher education programs, providing ongoing professional development, and improving working conditions. These solutions aim to make the teaching profession more attractive and sustainable, ultimately contributing to the achievement of SDG 4. The chapter will also advocate for a holistic approach to educational reform, one that places teachers at the heart of policy-making and recognizes them as key agents of change. This chapter emphasizes that the achievement of SDG 4 requires more than just a commitment to increasing access to education. It necessitates a comprehensive approach that values and supports teachers, recognizing them as the professionals who are essential to shaping the future of education and society. By listening to teachers' voices and involving them in the reform process, we can build an education system that is more inclusive, equitable, and sustainable.

2.0 TEACHERS: PILLARS OF SOCIETY AND BACKBONES OF NATIONS

Teachers are central to the development of any society, shaping not only the intellectual and professional abilities of students but also influencing their ethical and moral development (Brunetti et al., 2024). They are the foundation of a nation's future, serving as the architects who mold future leaders, innovators, and responsible citizens. This section will explore the profound contributions of teachers to society, their moral and ethical roles in shaping future generations, and the historical context of teachers as pillars of society, particularly through the lens of Mustafa Kemal Atatürk's vision.

2.1 Teachers' Contributions to Society: Shaping Future Leaders

The contributions of teachers extend far beyond simply providing academic instruction; they are pivotal in the broader development of a society. Teachers equip students with essential skills, including problem-solving, critical thinking, and creativity abilities that are indispensable for becoming future leaders and innovators (Eliyawati et al., 2023). The knowledge and skills acquired from teachers lay the foundation for students' professional success, whether in the sciences, arts, technology, or business sectors. Teachers also instill a love for learning, encouraging lifelong development (Kwihangana, 2024). As the world evolves rapidly, the ability to adapt and innovate becomes increasingly important. Teachers foster a growth mindset in students, enabling them to navigate a constantly changing world. According to a recent study by McKinsey (2023), teachers are crucial for promoting skills that drive economic growth and societal progress, as they directly influence the cognitive, social, and emotional development of individuals who will later contribute to innovation and leadership in various fields (Xu et al., 2024).

Moreover, teachers play a vital role in preparing students for global challenges such as climate change, poverty, and inequality. By imparting values of sustainability, social responsibility, and ethics, teachers help students become active participants in addressing these challenges. This aligns with the broader goals of the United Nations' Sustainable Development Goals (SDGs), particularly Goal 4, which calls for inclusive, equitable, and quality education for all (Xu et al., 2024).

2.2 The Moral Role of Teachers: Instilling Values and Critical Thinking

In addition to academic knowledge, teachers carry a moral and ethical responsibility in shaping students' character and societal awareness. In a time when global issues like inequality, climate change, and political polarization are pressing concerns, teachers are tasked with instilling values such as empathy, respect, and integrity in their students (Friedman & O'Brien, 2022). The importance of these values cannot be overstated, as they form the bedrock of social cohesion and harmonious societies. Teachers also have a crucial role in developing students' critical thinking abilities. In the 21st century, where information is abundant and often conflicting, it is essential for students to be able to think independently, analyze information, and make well-informed decisions. A study by the World Bank (2022) emphasized that teachers who encourage open dialogue, problem-solving, and reflection foster an environment where students can develop these critical skills. This intellectual foundation allows students to address complex global issues and become responsible, engaged citizens.

Furthermore, teachers help cultivate societal awareness by educating students about diversity, inclusion, and social justice. As the world becomes more interconnected, understanding and appreciating cultural differences is essential for building inclusive communities. Teachers provide a platform for students to engage with diverse perspectives, fostering empathy and collaboration. Teachers are instrumental in promoting social cohesion by creating classrooms that are safe, inclusive, and respectful of all students' backgrounds (Gumaste et al., 2024).

2.3 Historical Context: Atatürk and Teachers as Societal Foundations

The idea of teachers as the foundation of a nation is not a modern concept. Mustafa Kemal Atatürk, the founder of the Turkish Republic, famously recognized the importance of teachers in shaping the future of the nation. Atatürk's vision for Turkey's modernization was centered on the belief that education was key to the country's social, cultural, and political transformation. He declared, "The foundation of the Republic is education", underscoring the vital role of educators in nation-building (Gumaste et al., 2024). Atatürk's educational reforms in the early 20th century aimed to secularize and modernize Turkey's education system, making it more inclusive and accessible. However, these reforms were not just about academic instruction; they were about instilling democratic values, critical thinking, and a sense of national pride in the new generation of Turkish citizens. Teachers were envisioned as the torchbearers of this transformation, responsible for educating individuals who would embody the ideals of the republic, such as secularism, national unity, and social progress (Özdemir, 2023).

Atatürk's emphasis on teachers as the architects of the future aligned with his broader goals of fostering a modern, progressive nation. He saw teachers as the custodians of the republic's values, tasked with educating citizens who would contribute to Turkey's growth in all aspects economically, socially, and politically. This vision placed teachers at the very heart of Turkey's development, a sentiment that continues to shape the country's educational policies today. Teachers are integral to the progress and stability of any society. They are responsible not only for imparting academic knowledge but also for shaping the values, ethics, and critical thinking abilities of students (Kuş, 2024). Teachers play an essential role in fostering the skills necessary for societal innovation and leadership, contributing directly to global challenges such as sustainability and social justice. The historical vision of Mustafa Kemal Atatürk further reinforces the idea that teachers are the backbone of any nation's development. As we continue to strive for global and national educational reforms, recognizing and valuing teachers' contributions is more crucial than ever.

3.0 THE GLOBAL SIGNIFICANCE OF WORLD TEACHERS' DAY 2024

World Teachers' Day, celebrated annually on October 5th, is a global event that recognizes and honors the vital contributions of teachers to the development of individuals, societies, and nations. In 2024, the theme of World Teachers' Day is "Valuing Teachers' Voices: Towards a New Social Contract for Education". This theme underscores the importance of listening to teachers' perspectives in shaping educational policies and improving the status of the teaching profession (Kolesnyk & Biseth, 2024). It aligns with the global call for greater investment in education, as well as the acknowledgment that teachers are central to the achievement of sustainable development goals, particularly SDG 4: Quality Education.

3.1 World Teachers' Day 2024: Valuing Teachers' Voices for a New Education Contract

The 2024 theme calls attention to the need for a renewed social contract in education, one that reaffirms the significance of teachers' roles and ensures that they have a meaningful voice in the decisions that affect their profession and the education systems in which they work. Teachers are not only instructors but also key stakeholders in the design and implementation of educational reforms (Akiba et al., 2023). Their direct engagement with students gives them unique insights into the needs and challenges of the education system, yet their perspectives are often marginalized in policy discussions. The concept of a new social contract for education suggests a collaborative approach where teachers, governments, and communities jointly contribute to shaping education policies that reflect the changing demands of the modern world. This contract envisions a more inclusive and participatory approach to education reform, with teachers being recognized as valued professionals who deserve adequate support, fair compensation, and opportunities for professional development (Ghamrawi et al., 2024).

In line with the United Nations' Sustainable Development Goal 4 (SDG 4), which aims to ensure inclusive, equitable, and quality education for all, the theme of World Teachers' Day 2024 emphasizes the need for systemic changes to address global challenges such as teacher shortages, underfunded education systems, and inequitable access to quality education. Research by the Global Education Monitoring Report (2023) indicates that teacher quality remains one of the most significant factors in improving educational outcomes, yet many teachers are underpaid, undervalued, and lack the necessary resources to perform their jobs effectively. The new social contract envisioned by the 2024 World Teachers' Day theme stresses the importance of governments listening to teachers' concerns about working conditions, resources, and professional development. A study by the International Labour Organization (ILO) (2022) highlights that improving teacher working conditions, salaries, and career opportunities is essential to recruiting and retaining quality educators. Teachers' voices must be at the heart of educational reforms to ensure that policies are relevant and responsive to the challenges faced in the classroom (Ghamrawi et al., 2024).

3.2 UNESCO 1966 Recommendation: Shaping Teachers' Status Today

The historical significance of World Teachers' Day is rooted in UNESCO's 1966 ILO/UNESCO Recommendation Concerning the Status of Teachers, a milestone document that laid out international guidelines for the status, rights, and responsibilities of teachers. The 1966 Recommendation was a groundbreaking initiative that sought to elevate the professional status of teachers and ensure that they were recognized as key contributors to the development of education and society (Sobhy, 2024). This Recommendation addressed issues such as teacher salaries, working conditions, job security, and professional development, establishing a framework for policies that would protect and support educators worldwide. The ILO/UNESCO Recommendation has remained relevant over the years, as many of the challenges it identified still persist today. Despite significant progress in some regions, teachers worldwide continue to face poor working conditions, low salaries, and insufficient support, particularly in low-income countries. The global teacher shortage, exacerbated by the COVID-19 pandemic and other crises, highlights the continued need for strong policies that ensure teachers are adequately trained, supported, and compensated (Acuña & Fernández Ugalde, 2024).

In many countries, teachers remain underpaid compared to other professionals with similar qualifications. Teacher salaries are often insufficient to attract and retain qualified professionals, contributing to a growing global teacher shortage. The shortage is particularly acute in sub-Saharan Africa, Asia, and other developing regions, where the need for quality education is greatest (Mifsud, 2023). The UNESCO Recommendation emphasized the importance of teachers' professional autonomy and the need for continuous professional development to ensure that teachers remain equipped to meet the evolving needs of students. This remains a critical issue today, as teachers are expected to navigate rapidly changing educational landscapes, including the integration of technology into the classroom and addressing students' diverse needs. Investment in teacher professional development leads to better educational outcomes and stronger educational systems overall.

The 2024 theme of World Teachers' Day calls for a renewed commitment to the principles outlined in the 1966 UNESCO Recommendation. It is clear that, more than ever, the teaching profession needs to be valued, supported, and recognized as a central element in achieving the SDGs and building sustainable and resilient education systems worldwide. The voices of teachers must be heard and acted upon to create educational policies that are not only effective but also equitable and inclusive. The global significance of World Teachers' Day 2024 lies in its call to prioritize teachers' voices in educational reform and to establish a new social contract that supports and empowers educators worldwide. As we celebrate the vital role that teachers play in shaping the future, it is crucial to reflect on the historical context set by the ILO/UNESCO Recommendation of 1966, which remains relevant today in addressing the challenges faced by teachers globally. By valuing teachers' voices and ensuring that they are central to educational policy development, societies can make significant strides toward achieving quality education for all and advancing the Sustainable Development Goals (Stacey et al., 2024).

4.0 ACHIEVING SUSTAINABLE DEVELOPMENT GOAL 4 (SDG 4) THROUGH QUALITY TEACHERS

Quality teaching staffs are essential for implementing Sustainable Development Goal 4 (SDG 4) which includes education systems based on inclusiveness and equitable learning standards. Teachers serve as critical agents who help overcome discriminatory obstacles and fill vacant educational positions and strengthen professional training activities. Investing in developing quality teachers through recruitment and training and retaining skilled educators will lead to sustainable educational results for the fulfillment of SDG 4 by 2030.

4.1 SDG 4: Achieving Inclusive and Quality Education by 2030

Sustainable Development Goal 4 (SDG 4), established by the United Nations in 2015, is a critical global commitment to achieving inclusive, equitable, and quality education for all by 2030. The goal aims to ensure that all individuals, regardless of gender, socioeconomic background, or geographical location, have access to education that equips them with the knowledge, skills, and values necessary for a sustainable future (Saini et al., 2023). SDG 4 is not only about increasing enrollment rates but also about ensuring that education systems are inclusive, equitable, and capable of providing quality learning opportunities for every student (Ferrero, 2023).

The vision of SDG 4 is framed around various targets, including achieving universal primary and secondary education, ensuring that all youth and adults have the necessary skills for employment, and promoting lifelong learning opportunities (United Nations Educational, Scientific and Cultural Organization (Ferrero, 2023). One of the central pillars of SDG 4 is the recognition that the quality of education is directly tied to the quality of teachers. As the primary agents of learning, teachers play a crucial role in determining the educational outcomes of students and ensuring that education systems can fulfill their commitments to the SDGs. Achieving SDG 4 requires a multifaceted approach that addresses systemic barriers such as inequality in access to education, underfunded education systems, and the lack of well-trained educators. While many countries have made significant strides towards achieving

SDG 4, the progress is uneven, and much work remains, particularly in low-income and conflict-affected regions. Teachers are at the heart of this challenge, as their expertise, commitment, and ability to provide inclusive education are fundamental to addressing these barriers (Saini et al., 2023).

4.2 Teachers' Role in SDG 4: Tackling Shortages and Boosting Development

Teachers are undeniably central to achieving SDG 4. They are the driving force behind educational quality, and their ability to provide inclusive and equitable education is essential to reaching the targets of SDG 4. The importance of teachers extends beyond their roles as educators; they are also mentors, role models, and advocates for students, shaping their academic, moral, and emotional development (Zickafoose et al., 2024). However, in many parts of the world, teacher quality remains a significant barrier to achieving the global education targets. A primary challenge to achieving SDG 4 is the global teacher shortage. According to the UNESCO Institute for Statistics (UIS), there is a shortage of approximately 69 million teachers worldwide to achieve universal primary and secondary education by 2030 (Grobler & Dittrich, 2024). The shortage is particularly acute in low-income countries and rural areas, where educational institutions struggle to attract and retain qualified teachers. In sub-Saharan Africa, for example, the teacher shortage is exacerbated by poor working conditions, low salaries, and inadequate access to professional development opportunities (Zickafoose et al., 2024).

To address these issues, it is essential to increase the recruitment and retention of qualified teachers. This requires a concerted effort from governments and educational institutions to invest in teacher training programs, improve salaries and working conditions, and provide better support for teachers throughout their careers. Increasing teacher salaries, improving their professional autonomy, and creating conducive working environments are key to attracting and retaining quality educators (Saini et al., 2023). Additionally, the report highlighted the importance of strengthening teacher training systems to ensure that teachers are well-equipped with the skills and knowledge needed to address the evolving needs of students. Professional development is another critical area for improving teacher quality and achieving SDG 4. Teachers need continuous opportunities for learning and growth to stay up-to-date with new pedagogical techniques, technologies, and teaching methodologies. Investing in professional development for teachers leads to better educational outcomes, improved student performance, and greater teacher satisfaction. Effective professional development programs should focus on enhancing teachers' subject knowledge, teaching strategies, and their ability to integrate technology into the classroom. Moreover, professional development must be inclusive, accessible, and responsive to the diverse needs of teachers, particularly in underserved regions (Baena-Morales et al., 2024).

Furthermore, teachers must be equipped to deliver education that meets the needs of diverse learners, including those with disabilities, from marginalized communities, or those facing social and economic disadvantages. To achieve this, teacher preparation programs must include training on inclusive education practices, differentiated instruction, and culturally relevant pedagogy (Saini et al., 2022). By empowering teachers with these skills, education systems can ensure that no child is left behind, thus advancing SDG 4's goal of equitable education. In addition to teacher training and professional development, improving the overall status of teachers in society is essential for achieving SDG 4. Teachers must be recognized as highly valued professionals who are respected for their contributions to society. A study by the International Education Association (2021) found that teachers who are valued and respected by their communities are more likely to remain in the profession and make a lasting impact on student learning. Governments and communities must work together to ensure that teachers are given the recognition, compensation, and support they deserve.

Achieving SDG 4 – inclusive, equitable, and quality education for all – hinges on improving the quality of teaching and addressing the challenges faced by teachers worldwide. By investing in teacher recruitment, training, professional development, and improving their working conditions, governments and educational institutions can lay the foundation for the achievement of SDG 4. As the key agents of change in the education sector, teachers have a critical role in shaping the future of education and contributing to the realization of the global development agenda. Ensuring that teachers are adequately supported and valued is not only essential for achieving SDG 4 but also for fostering the well-being and success of future generations (Goyal et al., 2024).

5.0 GLOBAL CHALLENGES IN RECRUITING AND RETAINING QUALITY TEACHERS

The worldwide education systems face significant difficulties in maintaining effective teacher employment along with keeping current staff. The expanding deficit of teaching staff combined with expanding student numbers presents obstacles to reaching Sustainable Development Goal 4 (SDG 4). Teacher retention remains difficult in developing nations because of low wages combined with bad work conditions and insufficient opportunities to advance professionally. The use of restricted resources and traditional teaching approaches results in negative consequences on learning outcomes. AI along with digital tools provides hopeful strategies to assist instructors and improve educational experiences. The solution to these obstacles needs strategic financial commitments for teacher workforce development along with teaching expertise advancement and modern educational technology implementation to provide quality education throughout all communities.

5.1 Global Teacher Shortages: Examining Student-Teacher Ratios Worldwide

One of the most significant challenges facing global education systems today is the shortage of qualified teachers. According to the UNESCO Institute for Statistics (2023), the global teacher shortage is estimated to be 69 million teachers by 2030 to meet the needs of universal primary and secondary education. The problem is particularly acute in low-income countries and rural areas, where educational institutions struggle to attract and retain qualified professionals. In sub-Saharan Africa, for example, student-teacher ratios are often as high as 50:1, compared to the international benchmark of 25:1 (Sanz Ponce et al., 2023). Similarly, in countries like India and Pakistan, teacher shortages exacerbate the challenges of achieving SDG 4, leading to overcrowded classrooms and a decline in the quality of education

These shortages are compounded by the growing demand for teachers due to population growth and increasing enrollment in primary and secondary education worldwide. For instance, in Latin America and the Caribbean, the student population has been steadily increasing, but teacher recruitment has failed to keep up with this demand (Calero et al., 2023). This gap between teacher demand and supply limits the ability of educational systems to offer the necessary attention and support to students, ultimately affecting student learning outcomes and overall educational quality.

5.2 Low Salaries and Poor Conditions: Barriers to Teacher Recruitment and Retention

Low salaries and poor working conditions are significant barriers to recruiting and retaining quality teachers, especially in developing countries. According to the International Education Association (2022), teachers in many countries are paid below-average salaries compared to other professions, contributing to low job satisfaction and high turnover rates. In the United States, for example, teachers earn approximately 10% less than workers in other fields requiring similar qualifications (Blackmore et al., 24). The situation is more pronounced in developing nations, where teachers often face financial insecurity, limited career advancement opportunities, and lack of adequate resources. In addition to low salaries, teachers frequently work in under-resourced environments, which hinder their ability to deliver effective education. In many low-income countries, schools lack basic infrastructure, teaching materials, and access to technology, leading to high levels of teacher burnout and dissatisfaction. For example, a 2023 study conducted by the Global Partnership for Education (GPE) revealed that teachers in sub-Saharan Africa often work in overcrowded classrooms with insufficient teaching materials, leading to stress and demotivation (Jiang & Yip, 2024). As a result, many teachers leave the profession early, further exacerbating the teacher shortage.

5.3 Lack of Development and Resources: Impact on Teaching Quality and Outcomes

Professional development is another critical area where educational systems fall short, particularly in low-income countries. Teachers need ongoing opportunities to improve their skills, stay updated on new teaching methodologies, and develop expertise in emerging fields. However, many teachers, particularly in underserved regions, have limited access to professional development programs. According to a report by the World Bank (2021), less than 50% of teachers in low-income countries receive adequate professional training, which negatively impacts teaching quality and student outcomes. Without sufficient training, teachers may struggle to address diverse student needs, employ effective teaching strategies, or integrate new technologies into the classroom. A lack of professional development is also linked to teacher attrition, as teachers who feel unsupported or inadequately prepared may choose to leave the profession. The 2022 OECD report on teacher policy noted that teachers who engage in high-quality professional development are more likely to remain in the profession and positively impact student learning (Guthery & Bailes, 2023).

Moreover, the lack of resources in schools further compounds this issue. Teachers need access to modern educational materials, digital tools, and technologies to enhance their teaching practices. Schools with limited resources often fail to provide the necessary support, leading to disparities in the quality of education across regions. In such environments, teachers can feel overwhelmed and underprepared, which ultimately affects the learning outcomes of their students (Gilmour et al., 2023).

5.4 Tech Solutions for Teachers: AI, Digital Tools, and Innovation

Technology has the potential to alleviate many of the challenges faced by teachers, particularly in terms of access to resources and professional development. The COVID-19 pandemic accelerated the integration of digital tools and online learning platforms in classrooms worldwide. These technologies offer teachers a range of tools to engage students, monitor progress, and facilitate personalized learning. For example, digital platforms such as Google Classroom and Edmodo allow teachers to manage classrooms, share materials, and provide feedback, making teaching more efficient and accessible (Miller, 2022). Artificial intelligence (AI) is also playing an increasingly important role in supporting teachers. AI-powered tools can help teachers personalize instruction by analyzing student performance data and suggesting tailored learning paths (Ng et al., 2023). These tools can also help teachers identify areas where students are struggling, enabling timely intervention. Furthermore, AI-driven platforms can provide teachers with instant feedback on their teaching methods, helping them refine their practices and improve student outcomes.

However, for technology to effectively address teacher challenges, governments must invest in infrastructure and ensure that teachers have the training and resources to use digital tools effectively. The ILO (2022) emphasizes the importance of digital literacy training for teachers, noting that without the necessary skills, technology may not reach its full potential in improving teaching and learning. The challenges of recruiting and retaining quality teachers are significant barriers to achieving SDG 4 and improving educational outcomes globally (Moorhouse et al., 2023). Teacher shortages, low salaries, poor working conditions, and lack of professional development hinder teachers' ability to fulfill their roles effectively. However, addressing these challenges is not impossible. Governments and educational organizations must invest in teacher recruitment, provide adequate salaries and working conditions, offer ongoing professional development, and integrate technology to support teachers in their work. By addressing these systemic issues, we can empower teachers to shape the future of education and help achieve the global education goals (Kim, 2024).

6.0 THE CASE OF BANGLADESH: UNIQUE CHALLENGES AND OPPORTUNITIES

The education system in Bangladesh encounters various structural problems which prevent qualified teachers from joining or staying at their jobs most seriously in rural school districts. Inadequate teacher training, economic differences and political influence that shapes the recruitment process result in unequal quality education distribution. The educational facilities and professional development options at urban institutions persistently exceed those available in rural institutions since they experience both insufficient staffing and poor facility conditions. The political system weakens the process of making teacher appointments based on individual merit because of patronage politics. Quality education in Bangladesh faces two opportunities for reform: public transparency in the selection of educators and fair distribution of learning materials and teacher development programs. Bangladesh needs to tackle these obstacles because improvement in education quality remains vital to achieve Sustainable Development Goal (SDG) 4.

6.1 Teacher Recruitment and Development: Barriers in Bangladesh's Education System

In Bangladesh, the education system faces a persistent challenge in recruiting qualified teachers. One of the key obstacles is the limited availability of qualified candidates due to the inadequate professional training and certification programs in the country. Teacher recruitment often relies on traditional methods such as the passing of local examinations, which may not ensure that teachers possess the modern skills necessary for effective pedagogy. In particular, there is a significant gap in training teachers to effectively use digital tools and modern teaching methodologies (Chowdhury, 2022). Moreover, teachers in Bangladesh often receive insufficient opportunities for continuous professional development. A report by the Global Partnership for Education (2022) found that less than 30% of teachers in rural Bangladesh have access to ongoing training programs. Professional development in the country is not only limited in scope but also sporadic, with a heavy reliance on government initiatives that are inconsistent in quality and availability. This lack of systematic professional growth results in teachers who are ill-equipped to handle the changing needs of students, particularly in light of the growing importance of digital literacy and inclusive education (Siddique, 2021).

6.2 Economic Disparities: The Urban-Rural Divide in Teacher Quality

Another significant challenge in Bangladesh's education system is the economic disparity and regional imbalances in teacher quality and resources. Teachers in urban centers such as Dhaka and Chittagong often benefit from better salaries, improved professional development opportunities, and more accessible teaching resources compared to their rural counterparts (Islam & Rahman, 2023). A study by Hossain et al. (2022) highlighted that teacher shortages and poor conditions are most prevalent in rural and remote areas, where the gap in educational outcomes is particularly wide. Rural schools often face overcrowded classrooms, limited access to learning materials, and a lack of essential infrastructure, which hampers the overall quality of education (Rahman, 2022). This urban-rural divide is compounded by economic factors. Teachers in rural Bangladesh are often paid less than their urban counterparts, and many teachers in rural areas supplement their income by engaging in second jobs, leading to less time and energy dedicated to teaching (Alam & Kabir, 2021). The economic pressures faced by teachers in rural areas contribute to high attrition rates, as many opt to leave the profession or migrate to urban centers in search of better opportunities. The regional imbalance also impacts the availability of educational resources, which directly affects teaching quality. For example, many schools in rural Bangladesh lack access to basic learning materials, digital tools, and libraries, while urban schools are more likely to benefit from modern technologies and better-funded education programs (Khan & Iqbal, 2023). As a result, the education provided to students in rural areas is often substandard, further exacerbating the cycle of inequality in education.

6.3 Policy Gaps and Political Influence: Undermining Merit-Based Teacher Recruitment

The recruitment and placement of teachers in Bangladesh are often marred by political influence, which undermines merit-based systems? Political patronage has been a persistent issue in Bangladesh, where appointments to public sector positions, including teaching posts, are frequently determined by political affiliations rather than qualifications or merit (Chowdhury, 2022). This system of recruitment has contributed to inefficiency and corruption within the education sector, with political ties often taking precedence over professional competence. A study by Rahman and Islam (2021) revealed that many teacher appointments in public schools, particularly in rural areas, are based on local political connections, which results in a significant number of under qualified teachers being placed in schools. This situation undermines the quality of education and further perpetuates disparities in teacher qualifications and resource distribution. Political influence also affects the allocation of educational resources, as funds are often misappropriated or mismanaged, leading to a lack of necessary infrastructure and learning tools in many schools (Ali, 2022). The lack of a robust and transparent recruitment system has contributed to the stagnation of the education sector in Bangladesh, with merit-based recruitment and promotion policies failing to take root. Furthermore, the absence of clear career progression pathways for teachers discourages many from remaining in the profession, as they see limited opportunities for advancement (Hossain, 2023).

6.4 Opportunities for Reform: Addressing the Challenges

Despite these challenges, there are significant opportunities for reform in Bangladesh"s education system. One of the key opportunities lies in improving teacher recruitment processes by establishing transparent and merit-based systems that prioritize qualifications and professional competence. The implementation of rigorous certification and licensure programs for teachers, along with enhanced professional development opportunities, could help address the gaps in teacher quality (Rahman, 2023). Additionally, focusing on reducing the urban-rural divide in education is crucial for ensuring equitable access to quality education across Bangladesh. Investment in infrastructure, digital tools, and teacher training in rural areas can help bridge the gap between urban and rural schools. The Bangladesh government has already started investing in digital learning platforms and distance education initiatives, which could be scaled up to address regional disparities (Islam & Rahman, 2023). Teacher retention will substantially increase when salaries of educators are increased while workplace conditions improve and financial incentives target education professionals in understaffed areas. Research evidence demonstrates that enhanced teacher pay and specific bonuses successfully motivate qualified instructors to stay working in rural areas resulting in better educational delivery and student achievement (Ali, 2022; Islam & Rahman, 2023).

In terms of policy reform, Bangladesh must prioritize reducing political influence in teacher recruitment by strengthening the independence of the education system and establishing clearer guidelines for teacher appointments. Institutionalizing merit-based recruitment and providing clear pathways for professional advancement would help attract and retain high-quality teachers. Encouraging greater collaboration between the government, NGOs, and private organizations could further support these reforms (Siddique, 2022). Bangladesh faces significant challenges in recruiting and retaining qualified teachers, particularly in rural areas. Economic disparities, regional imbalances, and political interference hinder the effective development of the education system. However, there are opportunities to overcome these challenges through systematic reforms in teacher recruitment, professional development, and the equitable distribution of resources. Addressing these issues is essential for improving the quality of education and achieving the targets set by SDG 4 in Bangladesh.

7.0 SOLUTIONS FOR ELEVATING THE STATUS AND QUALITY OF TEACHERS

Enhancing both educational status and teaching quality serves as a necessary condition to achieve better educational results. Professional development stands alongside competitive wages when teachers use merit-based recruitment systems to improve their status in education. Global best practices from Finland, Singapore, South Korea, and Canada highlight effective policies. Teacher input as part of education reform processes ensures enduring improvements of quality education measures and advancement of SDG 4.

7.1 Policy Recommendations: Pay Scale, Development, and Recruitment Reforms

To elevate the status and quality of teachers, one of the most pressing measures is the establishment of a distinct and competitive pay scale. In many countries, including Bangladesh, teachers are often underpaid compared to other professional occupations, which contributes to low morale and high turnover rates (Chowdhury & Rahman, 2023). By developing a pay scale that reflects the value of teaching and aligns with the responsibilities teachers shoulder, governments can incentivize talented individuals to enter and remain in the profession. According to a study by UNESCO (2022), countries with competitive salaries and clear career progression opportunities tend to attract and retain higher-quality teachers, ultimately improving educational outcomes.

Moreover, implementing comprehensive professional development programs is essential to improving the quality of education. As teaching techniques and educational technology continue to evolve, teachers must be provided with continuous training opportunities to stay current (Siddique, 2022). Effective professional development programs should include both in-service training, focusing on new pedagogies and subject knowledge, as well as leadership development programs that allow teachers to take on administrative roles or mentoring responsibilities (Rahman & Hossain, 2023). Additionally, these programs should be designed in collaboration with teachers themselves to ensure that the training is relevant to the challenges they face in the classroom (Ali, 2022).

Finally, reforming teacher recruitment is crucial. Transparent, merit-based recruitment processes are necessary to ensure that only the most qualified candidates are selected. This could involve more rigorous entrance exams, better training for recruitment committees, and the establishment of clear standards for teacher qualifications (Chowdhury, 2022). In countries like Finland, where the teaching profession is highly respected, teacher recruitment includes not only academic qualifications but also a deep commitment to education, supported by a rigorous selection process that ensures only the best candidates are chosen (Liu et al., 2021).

7.2 Empowering Teachers: Integrating Voices in Educational Reforms

Teachers are the heart of the educational system, and their involvement in decision-making processes is critical to the success of educational reforms. Teachers possess firsthand knowledge of classroom dynamics, student behavior, and the challenges of delivering quality education. Thus, integrating teachers' voices in policy-making is not only beneficial but necessary (Ghosh & Khan, 2023). By involving teachers in discussions about curriculum changes, teaching methods, and assessment systems, governments can create more effective and realistic policies that address the actual needs of the classroom. Incorporating teachers' feedback into educational reforms can help bridge the gap between policy and practice. Teacher unions and professional organizations play an important role in advocating for teachers' rights and ensuring their input is considered in the policymaking process. Research by Ghosh et al. (2023) demonstrates that countries where teachers' unions and professional bodies are actively involved in education policy tend to have more robust education systems. For example, in South Korea, teachers are deeply integrated into the policy-making process, ensuring that reforms are grounded in practical realities (Park & Kim, 2022).

7.3 Global Best Practices: Teacher Recruitment and Retention Strategies

Several countries have successfully implemented policies and practices that have elevated the status of teaching and improved recruitment and retention. These countries offer valuable lessons for Bangladesh and other nations facing similar challenges.

Finland: Finland is widely recognized for its high-quality education system and strong teacher profession. In Finland, teaching is considered one of the most prestigious professions, with extensive support for teachers' professional development. Teachers in Finland are required to hold a master's degree in education, and the selection process is highly competitive (Liu et al., 2021). Finnish teachers are also provided with high levels of autonomy in the classroom, allowing them to apply innovative teaching methods that are most suited to their students' needs. This autonomy, along with the professional respect accorded to teachers, has led to high job satisfaction and retention rates.

Singapore: Singapore is another example of a country where teaching is a respected and competitive profession. The country's teacher recruitment and retention strategies focus on attracting high-caliber candidates by offering competitive salaries, career development opportunities, and clear pathways for advancement (Ng, 2022). Singapore also emphasizes mentorship and continuous professional development for teachers, ensuring that they have the necessary support throughout their careers. The Singaporean government invests heavily in teacher training, offering high-quality in-service programs that keep teachers updated on pedagogical and technological innovations (Cheng, 2023).

South Korea: In South Korea, teaching is viewed as a prestigious profession, and teachers are deeply involved in educational reforms. The country's recruitment strategy is highly selective, with teaching candidates required to pass a rigorous set of exams and undergo extensive professional training (Park & Kim,

2022). Additionally, South Korea's government has invested in improving the working conditions of teachers by offering competitive salaries and benefits, as well as providing ongoing professional development opportunities. These efforts have contributed to high levels of teacher satisfaction and have resulted in improved educational outcomes.

Canada: In Canada, particularly in provinces like Ontario, teaching is also a highly respected profession. Canada's teacher recruitment and retention strategies focus on ensuring that teachers have access to high-quality professional development, mentorship, and career advancement opportunities (Bates, 2022). The Canadian government also provides teachers with competitive salaries and benefits, which contribute to high job satisfaction. Moreover, Canada's focus on inclusive education has resulted in teachers being better equipped to handle diverse classrooms, further enhancing the quality of education.

Elevating the status and quality of teachers requires comprehensive reform in recruitment, professional development, and compensation. By drawing inspiration from global best practices and integrating teachers' voices in educational reforms, countries like Bangladesh can create a more sustainable, effective, and equitable education system. These measures, if implemented effectively, will not only improve teacher quality but also contribute significantly to achieving Sustainable Development Goal 4 (SDG 4), ensuring inclusive, equitable, and quality education for all.

8.0 CONCLUSION: TEACHERS AS DRIVERS OF SUSTAINABLE DEVELOPMENT

As we look toward achieving the ambitious targets set by the Sustainable Development Goals (SDGs), particularly SDG 4, which aims for inclusive, equitable, and quality education for all by 2030, it is undeniable that teachers are at the heart of this transformation. Throughout this chapter, we have explored the critical role of teachers as not just educators, but as societal architects who shape the moral, intellectual, and emotional growth of future generations. Teachers are, undoubtedly, the backbone of any educational system, driving forward the innovation, development, and prosperity of nations.

However, in order for teachers to continue fulfilling this pivotal role, a new approach to valuing and empowering them is essential. The theme of World Teachers' Day 2024, "Valuing Teachers' Voices: Towards a New Social Contract for Education," encapsulates this necessity. A new social contract is not only about ensuring that teachers are adequately compensated and supported but also about creating a system where their voices are actively involved in the decision-making processes that shape education. It is imperative that teachers are seen as co-creators of educational policy, with a direct role in shaping the future of education systems worldwide.

For Bangladesh, as well as many other countries, addressing the challenges teachers face is a critical step in ensuring the success of educational reforms. Issues such as teacher shortages, low salaries, poor working conditions, and inadequate professional development opportunities have long hindered the recruitment and retention of quality teachers. These challenges are exacerbated by political influences in recruitment processes and economic disparities, which create imbalances in educational quality between urban and rural areas. These barriers prevent teachers from performing to their full potential, which in turn affects student outcomes and the achievement of SDG 4. The call to action, therefore, is clear: governments, policymakers, and educational stakeholders must work together to ensure that teachers are empowered and equipped to meet the demands of the 21st century. This can be achieved through strategic policy reforms that focus on teacher recruitment, retention, professional development, and the overall improvement of working conditions. Creating an environment where teachers' voices are heard and valued is not just a moral imperative but also a practical necessity for ensuring educational quality and equity.

Global best practices, such as those observed in countries like Finland, demonstrate that when teachers are treated as professionals with autonomy and respect, educational outcomes improve, and teaching is viewed as a prestigious and rewarding profession. By adopting similar models, countries can make significant strides toward achieving the goals of SDG 4 and ensuring that no child is left behind in the pursuit of education. Therefore, teachers are indispensable to the sustainable development of societies. Their contributions extend far beyond the classroom, influencing not only individual students but also the broader societal and economic landscapes. As nations continue to work toward the achievement of SDG 4, it is imperative that we create a new social contract for education, one in which teachers are not only valued but are also integral to shaping the policies that affect their work and the education of future generations. By elevating the status of teachers, investing in their professional growth, and listening to their voices, we can ensure that the future of education is both equitable and sustainable.

REFERENCES

Acuña, F., & Fernández Ugalde, R. (2024). Dissenting from what? the rupture of Chilean teachers with the long-term consensus on teacher professional development. *Globalisation, Societies and Education*, *23*(1), 63–78. https://doi.org/10.1080/14767724.2023.2294133

Adhikari, D. R., & Shrestha, P. (2023). Knowledge management initiatives for achieving sustainable development goal 4.7: Higher education institutions' stakeholder perspectives. *Journal of Knowledge Management*, *27*(4), 1109–1139. DOI: 10.1108/JKM-03-2022-0172

Ahmed, M., & Rahman, M. (2020). Teacher recruitment and retention challenges in Bangladesh's educational system: A critical review. *The Journal of Educational Research*, *15*(2), 115–130.

Akiba, M., Byun, S. Y., Jiang, X., Kim, K., & Moran, A. J. (2023). Do teachers feel valued in society? Occupational value of the teaching profession in OECD countries. *AERA Open*, *9*, 23328584231179184. DOI: 10.1177/23328584231179184

Alam, A., & Kabir, M. (2021). Teacher recruitment and retention issues in rural Bangladesh. *Asian Journal of Education*, *44*(1), 13–27.

Ali, A. (2022). Corruption and inefficiency in the teacher recruitment system of Bangladesh. *Journal of Education Policy*, *39*(2), 145–163.

Anapey, G. M. (2024). Achieving Education for Sustainable Education Learning Outcomes: An Integrated Model for Higher Education in the Global South. *International Journal of Educational Reform*. 10567879241270503. DOI: 10.1177/10567879241270503

Archer, D. (2023). Transforming the financing of education at the mid-point of the sustainable development goals. *International Journal of Educational Development*, *103*, 102931. DOI: 10.1016/j.ijedudev.2023.102931

Baena-Morales, S., Prieto-Ayuso, A., Merma-Molina, G., & González-Víllora, S. (2024). Exploring physical education teachers' perceptions of sustainable development goals and education for sustainable development. *Sport Education and Society*, *29*(2), 162–179. DOI: 10.1080/13573322.2022.2121275

Bates, T. (2022). Teacher retention in Canada: Challenges and solutions. *Canadian Journal of Education*, *35*(1), 77–89.

Blackmore, J., Hobbs, L., & Rowlands, J. (2024). Aspiring teachers, financial incentives, and principals' recruitment practices in hard-to-staff schools. *Journal of Education Policy*, *39*(2), 233–252. DOI: 10.1080/02680939.2023.2193170

Brunetti, A., Büchel, K., Jakob, M., Jann, B., & Steffen, D. (2024). Inadequate teacher content knowledge and what could be done about it: Evidence from El Salvador. *Journal of Development Effectiveness*, *16*(2), 206–229. DOI: 10.1080/19439342.2023.2213681

Calero, M., Pina, T., Mayoral, O., Cantó, J., Ull, M. Á., & Vilches, A. (2024). A study about pre-service teachers' knowledge of the Sustainable Development Goals. *International Journal of Sustainability in Higher Education.*

Cheng, H. (2023). Mentorship programs and professional development for teachers in Singapore. *International Journal of Educational Management*, *37*(1), 112–125.

Chowdhury, N. (2022). Education reform in Bangladesh: Challenges in teacher professional development. *South Asian Journal of Education*, *28*(3), 97–111.

Chowdhury, N., & Rahman, M. (2023). Teacher compensation in Bangladesh: A comparative study. *International Journal of Educational Development*, *50*(3), 129–140.

Darling-Hammond, L. (2020). The right to learn: A framework for teachers and policy makers. *Education Policy Analysis Archives*, *28*(65), 1–25.

Eliyawati, W., Widodo, A., Kaniawati, I., & Fujii, H. (2023). The Development and Validation of an Instrument for Assessing Science Teacher Competency to Teach ESD. *Sustainability (Basel)*, *15*(4), 3276. DOI: 10.3390/su15043276

Ferrero, V. (2023). Equity and Excellence in Education: SDG 4 of the 2030 Agenda in the Italian Context–Public Education Policies and Their Impact. In *Public Policy's Role in Achieving Sustainable Development Goals* (pp. 206-235). IGI Global.

Friedman, A., & O'Brien, D. (2022). Teachers as moral guides: The role of educators in shaping ethical societies. *The Journal of Educational Research*, *98*(3), 45–56.

García-Feijoo, M., Eizaguirre, A., & Rica-Aspiunza, A. (2020). Systematic review of sustainable-development-goal deployment in business schools. *Sustainability (Basel)*, *12*(1), 440. DOI: 10.3390/su12010440

Ghamrawi, N. (2023). Toward agenda 2030 in education: Policies and practices for effective school leadership. *Educational Research for Policy and Practice*, *22*(2), 325–347. DOI: 10.1007/s10671-023-09341-8 PMID: 38625155

Ghamrawi, N., Shal, T., & Ghamrawi, N. A. (2024). Cultivating teacher leadership: Evidence form a transformative professional development model. *School Leadership & Management*, *44*(4), 1–29. DOI: 10.1080/13632434.2024.2328056

Ghosh, A., & Khan, S. (2023). Teachers' voices in policy reform: The case of South Asia. *Education Review*, *29*(4), 85–100.

Ghosh, A., & Khan, S. (2023). Teacher participation in policy-making: A global perspective. *Education Policy Review*, *34*(4), 202–215.

Gilmour, A. F., Theobald, R., & Nathan, D. J. (2023). Economic interventions as policy levers for attracting and retaining special education teachers. *Handbook of Research on Special Education Teacher Preparation*, 190-212.

Goyal, A., Kumar, P., & Shalini. (2024). Quality Education: A Key Component of the United Nations Sustainable Development Goals (SDGs). In *Digital Technologies to Implement the UN Sustainable Development Goals* (pp. 127-151). Cham: Springer Nature Switzerland.

Grobler, S., & Dittrich, A. K. (2024). Envisioning quality education for sustainability transformation in teacher education: Perspectives from an international dialogue on Sustainable Development Goal 4. *International Journal of Comparative Education and Development*, *26*(3), 270–285. DOI: 10.1108/IJCED-06-2023-0048

Gumaste, S. V., Paweloszek, I., & Kumar, N. (2024). Sustainable Management in Higher Technical Education—Need for Internationalism. In *Sustainable Innovations in Management in the Digital Transformation Era* (pp. 281–288). Routledge. DOI: 10.4324/9781003450238-28

Guthery, S., & Bailes, L. P. (2023). Unintended Consequences of Expanding Teacher Preparation Pathways: Does alternative licensure attenuate new teacher pay? *AERA Open*, *9*, 23328584231159900. DOI: 10.1177/23328584231159900

Hattie, J. (2021). *Visible Learning: A Synthesis of Over 800 Meta-Analyses Relating to Achievement*. Routledge.

Haug, B. S., & Mork, S. M. (2021). Taking 21st century skills from vision to classroom: What teachers highlight as supportive professional development in the light of new demands from educational reforms. *Teaching and Teacher Education*, *100*, 103286. DOI: 10.1016/j.tate.2021.103286

Hossain, M., Rahman, M., & Islam, S. (2022). Regional disparities in teacher quality in Bangladesh: A review of the rural-urban divide. *Educational Review*, *21*(4), 103–118.

Huan, Y., Liang, T., Li, H., & Zhang, C. (2021). A systematic method for assessing progress of achieving sustainable development goals: A case study of 15 countries. *The Science of the Total Environment*, *752*, 141875. DOI: 10.1016/j.scitotenv.2020.141875 PMID: 33207501

Islam, M. R., & Rahman, M. M. (2023). Bridging the digital divide: Teacher training and development in Bangladesh's education sector. *Journal of Educational Technology*, *30*(1), 74–91.

Jiang, J., & Yip, S. Y. (2024). Teacher shortage: An analysis of the rural teachers living subsidy policy on teacher attraction and retention in rural Western China. *Asia-Pacific Journal of Teacher Education*, *52*(3), 316–331. DOI: 10.1080/1359866X.2024.2328682

Khan, S., & Iqbal, A. (2023). Investing in teacher quality: Addressing rural education challenges in Bangladesh. *Journal of Education and Development*, *32*(2), 77–92.

Kim, J. (2024). Leading teachers' perspective on teacher-AI collaboration in education. *Education and Information Technologies*, *29*(7), 8693–8724. DOI: 10.1007/s10639-023-12109-5

Kolesnyk, L., & Biseth, H. (2024). Professional development in teacher education through international collaboration: When education reform hits Ukraine. *Professional Development in Education*, *50*(2), 347–359. DOI: 10.1080/19415257.2023.2193197

Kuş, Z. (2024). Teachers' and parents' perspectives on citizenship education in Turkey: Consensus and disagreements. *Education, Citizenship and Social Justice*. 17461979241240451. DOI: 10.1177/17461979241240451

Kwihangana, F. (2024). Teacher positioning in educational ICT policies: Implications for digital teacher identity development in under-resourced contexts. *Journal of Education Policy*. 1–24.

Liu, Y., Hu, Y., & Zhang, F. (2021). Finland's teacher recruitment and retention strategies: A global model. *Journal of Education and Teacher Development*, *45*(2), 103–118.

Mifsud, D. (2023). Rethinking the concept of teacher education: a problematization and critique of current policies and practices. In *Teacher Education as an Ongoing Professional Trajectory: Implications for Policy and Practice* (pp. 1–23). Springer International Publishing. DOI: 10.1007/978-3-031-28620-9_1

Moorhouse, B. L., Wong, K. M., & Li, L. (2023). Teaching with technology in the post-pandemic digital age: Technological normalisation and AI-induced disruptions. *RELC Journal*, *54*(2), 311–320. DOI: 10.1177/00336882231176929

Ng, D. T. K., Leung, J. K. L., Su, J., Ng, R. C. W., & Chu, S. K. W. (2023). Teachers' AI digital competencies and twenty-first century skills in the post-pandemic world. *Educational Technology Research and Development*, *71*(1), 137–161. DOI: 10.1007/s11423-023-10203-6 PMID: 36844361

Ng, S. (2022). Recruitment and training of teachers in Singapore. *International Journal of Teacher Education*, *49*(1), 55–72.

Odell, V., Molthan-Hill, P., Martin, S., & Sterling, S. (2020). Transformative education to address all sustainable development goals. *Quality education*, 905-916.

Özdemir, İ. (2023). Atatürk's educational reforms and their impact on modern Turkey. *Educational Review*, *75*(1), 102–115.

Park, S., & Kim, J. (2022). The role of teachers in South Korea's educational reform process. *Asian Journal of Education*, *46*(2), 200–215.

Rahman, M. (2022). Teacher shortages and rural education in Bangladesh: A critical review. *International Journal of Educational Development*, *34*(3), 120–132.

Rahman, M., & Hossain, S. (2023). The significance of teacher development in educational reform. *Journal of Education for Teaching*, *45*(1), 71–85.

Rahman, M., & Hossain, S. (2023). Teacher professional development programs in Bangladesh: An evaluation. *Journal of Educational Development*, *17*(3), 135–149.

Rahman, S., & Islam, M. (2021). Political influence in teacher recruitment in Bangladesh: A critical analysis. *Journal of Political Education*, *25*(2), 58–73.

Ramaswamy, M., Marciniuk, D. D., Csonka, V., Colò, L., & Saso, L. (2021). Reimagining internationalization in higher education through the United Nations sustainable development goals for the betterment of society. *Journal of Studies in International Education*, *25*(4), 388–406. DOI: 10.1177/10283153211031046

Saini, M., Sengupta, E., Singh, M., Singh, H., & Singh, J. (2023). Sustainable Development Goal for Quality Education (SDG 4): A study on SDG 4 to extract the pattern of association among the indicators of SDG 4 employing a genetic algorithm. *Education and Information Technologies*, *28*(2), 2031–2069. DOI: 10.1007/s10639-022-11265-4 PMID: 35975216

Sanz Ponce, R., López-Luján, E., & Giménez-Beut, J. A. (2023). Pandemic, poverty and education: A challenge for the sustainable development goals. *Policy Futures in Education*, *21*(8), 886–899. DOI: 10.1177/14782103221112542

Siddique, A. (2021). Professional development and teacher retention in Bangladesh's primary education sector. *Journal of Educational Development*, *18*(1), 54–69.

Siddique, A. (2022). Teachers' voices and their influence on education policy: Lessons from South Asia. *Journal of Educational Management*, *49*(2), 110–124.

Siddique, A. (2022). Teacher professional development in developing countries: Lessons from Bangladesh. *Educational Research Journal*, *38*(2), 90–105.

Smith, J., & Heyward, P. (2024). Policy efforts to meet UNESCO's Sustainable development Goal 4: A 3-pronged approach. *Journal of Education for Teaching*, *50*(2), 266–279. DOI: 10.1080/02607476.2023.2283422

Sobhy, H. (2024). Equity, the transnational and the global learning crisis. *Cogent Social Sciences*, *10*(1), 2359268. DOI: 10.1080/23311886.2024.2359268

Stacey, M., Gavin, M., Fitzgerald, S., McGrath-Champ, S., & Wilson, R. (2024). Reducing teachers' workload or deskilling 'core'work? Analysis of a policy response to teacher workload demands. *Discourse (Abingdon)*, *45*(2), 187–199. DOI: 10.1080/01596306.2023.2271856

Xu, S. H., Santelli, F. A., Grissom, J. A., Bartanen, B., & Patrick, S. K. (2024). (Dis) connection at Work: Racial Isolation, Teachers' Job Experiences, and Teacher Turnover. *American Educational Research Journal*, *61*(6), 00028312241278597. DOI: 10.3102/00028312241278597

Zickafoose, A., Ilesanmi, O., Diaz-Manrique, M., Adeyemi, A. E., Walumbe, B., Strong, R., Wingenbach, G., Rodriguez, M. T., & Dooley, K. (2024). Barriers and Challenges Affecting Quality Education (Sustainable Development Goal# 4) in Sub-Saharan Africa by 2030. *Sustainability (Basel)*, *16*(7), 2657. DOI: 10.3390/su16072657

Chapter 7
AI-Enhanced Digital Literacy: A Framework for Higher Education and Workforce Collaboration

Vinay Kambhampati
https://orcid.org/0009-0006-9685-6760
Illinois Institute of Technology, USA

Rahul K. Patel
https://orcid.org/0000-0003-1175-0635
Illinois Institute of Technology, USA

ABSTRACT

The rapid advancement of artificial intelligence (AI) has forced the reassessment of how individuals are prepared for an AI-integrated future and what is needed to reshape education, work, and digital interaction. In this chapter authors studied and explored the need for a collaborative approach between educational institutions and industry to bridge the gap between academic training and workplace demands. This research study highlights the importance of critical thinking, practical application, and confidence building in AI-enhanced environments in addition to tool-specific training. The analysis is structured around three core areas: (a) Academic Integration – the incorporation of AI and digital skills across university curricula; (b) Industry Requirements – the role of businesses in shaping curriculum through real-world insights; and (c) Collaborative Frameworks – the development of industry-education partnerships that foster integrated learning opportunities.

DOI: 10.4018/979-8-3373-0004-7.ch007

INTRODUCTION

Bridging Knowledge and Practice With AI-Enhanced Digital Literacy in Higher Education

Higher education holds pivotal importance in the context of Artificial intelligence (AI) systems in teaching and learning methodologies. While AI technologies provide enhanced educational capabilities, their effectiveness depends on systematic integration into educational frameworks. This framework explores practical ways colleges and universities can embrace AI while staying true to their core academic mission. Today's students are experiencing AI in ways we could not have imagined just a few years ago. Wang and Li's (2024) research captured this transformation through the experiences of 721 university students, revealing something fascinating: when students feel confident using AI tools and are given the freedom to explore them, their learning improves significantly. This observation is not just about having the right technology – it is about creating an environment where students feel empowered to learn in new ways. The research demonstrates that positive engagement with AI tools leads to better academic outcomes and increased student participation across various disciplines, inspiring a new generation of learners. One of the most exciting developments in AI education is the rise of no-code platforms. As Sundberg and Holmström (2024) discovered, these tools open doors for students from all academic backgrounds. Their study found that students with no technical background could meaningfully engage with machine learning concepts. This democratization of AI is significant for students in non-technical fields who might otherwise miss these valuable skills. Integrating these platforms into various courses allows students to focus on understanding AI concepts and applications without getting caught up in technical complexities. The challenge is not just about adding AI tools to classrooms but about reimagining how these spaces can better serve student learning. These observations mean creating environments where students can experiment with AI while maintaining the rich interaction and discussion that makes higher education valuable. Students can use AI to analyze complex texts in literature classes, explore data patterns in social sciences, or generate creative solutions in design courses. These learning spaces must balance technological integration with traditional academic values, ensuring that AI enhances rather than replaces human interaction in education. This balance reassures us that AI is a tool, not a replacement, in the educational process.

Munawar et al. (2024) highlight a few noteworthy concerns that universities must address, particularly ethics and equal access. Their research shows that successful AI integration requires careful attention to student privacy while allowing for innovative learning experiences (p. 122, 126). Universities need comprehensive strategies to ensure that all students can access and benefit from AI tools, regardless of their background. Faculty training becomes crucial in this context, as educators must understand how to effectively incorporate AI into their teaching methods while maintaining academic integrity. The research emphasizes that these challenges require ongoing attention and adaptation as AI technology evolves, engaging us in a continual commitment to the best educative practices.

The higher education landscape is rapidly changing, and AI literacy has become more than just a buzzword—it is a critical need. A recent case study by Lérias and colleagues at Portalegre Polytechnic University shed light on a sobering reality. Despite the growing importance of AI, many educators are struggling to keep up. Their research revealed a significant skill gap, with just over half of the teachers (62.4%) showing intermediate to advanced competence in understanding and implementing AI technologies. This issue is not just about technical skills but about preparing the next generation of learners for an increasingly AI-driven world. The study underscores the need for comprehensive, targeted training programs to help educators understand AI and confidently integrate it into their teaching practices. As technology continues to evolve at a breakneck pace, universities must prioritize upskilling their faculty, ensuring they can guide students through the complex landscape of artificial intelligence. The implications are clear: We cannot afford to let this skills gap widen. Educators need support, resources, and opportunities to develop AI literacy.

Implementation of AI systems in educational environments provides computational support for instructional and learning processes, enhancing engagement, and enabling personalization while maintaining instructor-led pedagogical approaches. Wang and Li (2024) found that students who became comfortable using AI tools did not only understand their course material better; they became more confident learners. They were like cooks who learned to use new kitchen gadgets to follow recipes, experiment, and create dishes. As Sundberg and Holmstrom (2024) noted, even students without technical backgrounds successfully engaged with these tools, showing how AI can democratize advanced learning techniques. The key is finding that sweet spot where AI helps students develop tech-savvy and creative thinking abilities. Ibrahim et al. (2023, p. 9) reinforced this idea, demonstrating across 32 university courses that AI tools can effectively support learning while maintaining academic rigor. Su and Yang (2023) emphasize that we want graduates who can confidently use AI while still maintaining their uniquely human abilities to think critically, solve problems creatively, and produce innovative ideas. As Munawar et al. (2024) highlight this integration needs to be thoughtful and ethical, ensuring technology enhances rather than replaces the basic human elements of education. Universities must provide comprehensive support for students and faculty navigating this new landscape. Regular workshops on effective AI use in academic work help build confidence and competence. Clear guidelines on ethical AI use in coursework ensure responsible adoption of these tools. Resources for exploring AI tools safely and effectively give students the foundation they need to integrate AI into their learning journey. These support systems must evolve continuously to address new challenges and opportunities as AI technology advances.

TRANSFORMATIVE KNOWLEDGE RELATIONSHIPS AND ETHICAL CONSIDERATIONS IN AI-ENHANCED DIGITAL LITERACY

Integrating AI into higher education environments necessitates a fundamental shift in conceptualizing knowledge acquisition and assessment. Kramm and McKenna (2023) argue persuasively against the predominant "police-catch-punish" approach many institutions have adopted in response to AI tools like ChatGPT. They contend that the focus on AI detection and surveillance represents a misallocation of resources that "ignores the broader purposes of higher education" (p. 2174). Instead, they advocate for understanding higher education as " (p. 2174), a space for nurturing transformative relationships with knowledge," where AI can be leveraged to enhance learning experiences rather than becoming a target for monitoring.

This perspective aligns with Reiss's (2021) observation that AI has significant potential to break down traditional divides between educational settings. According to Reiss (2021), "AI should increasingly enable such traditional divides as 'school versus home' to be straddled with learning" (p. 5). This boundary-crossing capacity creates opportunities for continuous learning that transcends physical limitations, which is particularly beneficial for students with special educational needs. The personalization capabilities of AI technology can create learning environments where students can engage with material in ways tailored to their individual needs, facilitating deeper understanding across diverse contexts (Reiss, 2021)

The ethical dimensions of AI integration demand careful consideration. Munawar et al. (2024) highlight several critical concerns universities must address, particularly regarding ethics and equitable access. Their research emphasizes that AI has the potential to transform education while raising important challenges. They note that "numerous sectors have ethical issues about the exploitation of AI technology and data protection" (p. 122). The digital divide presents a particular concern, with "many pupils with restricted access to technology" facing potential barriers (p. 122). Their recommendations stress that universities should "employ artificial intelligence, with explicit ethical principles for AI development that cover bias mitigation, student data protection, and responsible development" (p. 126).

The discourse surrounding academic integrity and AI detection tools reflects broader tensions in higher education's response to technological change. Zhang (2022, p. 5) notes that AI-driven educational systems can overcome "traditional subjective approaches to educational design" while enhancing assessment validity. However, Popenici (2022) warns that educational surveillance and data collection practices have expanded, potentially hampering the development of creativity and critical thinking skills that higher education institutions should nurture (p. 120)

These perspectives collectively suggest a more nuanced approach to AI in education, prioritizing learning enhancement over surveillance. As Shuliar et al. (2023) observe, "e-learning tools promote integration into the global information-educational space and improve education quality by providing access to high-quality educational and methodical materials" (p. 522). When thoughtfully implemented, this integration can develop critical thinking skills and digital literacy competencies that prepare students for increasingly AI-integrated professional environments.

Establishing this transformative relationship with knowledge requires institutional frameworks that balance technological innovation with core educational values. These frameworks must ensure that AI enhances rather than diminishes the human elements essential to meaningful learning experiences.

Practical Steps Forward

To successfully integrate AI in higher education, universities should focus on clear educational goals, using AI to support rather than replacing effective teaching practices. This involves providing hands-on opportunities for students to work with AI tools in their specific fields while developing clear ethical guidelines that protect student interests and encourage innovation. Support systems must help students and faculty adapt to new teaching and learning approaches, ensuring that technological integration serves educational objectives rather than driving them. Atchley et al. (2024, pp. 7-9) advocate for a nuanced perspective, suggesting that effective AI implementation in education depends on collaborative partnerships between educators and AI technologies that complement rather than substitute the essential human aspects of teaching and learning. Implementing this vision necessitates strategic development and continuous evaluation to address the requirements of students, faculty, and educational institutions alike.

Universities can create innovative and meaningful educational experiences by thoughtfully implementing AI tools and maintaining a focus on student learning and development. Integrating AI in higher education represents an opportunity to enhance learning while preparing students for a future where AI plays an increasingly significant role in society and the workforce.

In the rapidly evolving landscape of artificial intelligence, higher education institutions play a significant role in bridging the gap between academic knowledge and industry needs. As universities adapt their teaching methods and curricula, they must prepare students for workplaces where AI is becoming increasingly prevalent. Wang and Li's (2024) research with 721 university students demonstrates that when students develop confidence in using AI tools during their education, they become more effective learners and better prepared for professional environments. This finding emphasizes the importance of universities creating supportive learning environments encouraging exploration and experimentation with AI technologies during the educational journey.

Universities are developing innovative approaches to integrating AI tools into their curricula across various disciplines. Sundberg and Holmstrom (2024) highlight how the emergence of no-code platforms has made AI education easy, allowing universities to introduce AI and machine learning concepts to students from all academic backgrounds. This breakthrough enables every department to incorporate AI learning into various courses, ensuring all graduates and undergraduates possess fundamental AI literacy regardless of specialization. These platforms will help students gain theoretical and practical knowledge by helping to bridge the gap between abstract concepts and real-world applications, helping universities fulfill their mission of preparing students for the modern workforce.

The Human Dimension of University and Industry AI Collaborations

The university-industry collaboration represents a critical pathway for advancing AI-enhanced digital literacy in higher education, but at its core, this collaboration depends on human relationships. While existing frameworks identify the theoretical importance of such partnerships, a deeper industry perspective reveals the multifaceted nature of these collaborations that extend beyond traditional academic boundaries. Evans et al. (2023, p. 1) explain that successful university-industry collaborations depend on "the engagement and relationship between individual academics and industry practitioners as partners in a trust relationship." This personal interface becomes the foundation for sustainable innovation that drives digital transformation.

Industry partners bring practical perspectives that complement academic approaches, as Tas (2023) describes: "UICs in CDD allow students to gain real-world exposure to data-related challenges and practices. By engaging with experts from the industry, students have the opportunity to deepen their understanding of the relevance and significance of data" (p. 12). The relationship factors that enable these collaborations include "building rapport before asking for money," "understanding and respecting each other's interests," "aligned values and mutual respect," and "effective communication" (Evans et al., 2023, p. 7).

Research indicates that such collaborations can take multiple forms. Chen et al. (2020, p. 3) identify several channels through which university-industry partnerships operate in AI education, including conference proceedings, journal publications, and software development. Their analysis reveals that joint research projects and shared facilities represent valuable collaborative approaches, with 75% of academic-practitioner partnerships in AI education published through proceedings and conferences rather than academic journals.

From an industry perspective, collaborative initiatives provide access to innovative research facilities and equipment many businesses could not otherwise access. Evans et al. (2023, p. 8) noted that "Universities have high-tech equipment that many companies do not have access to," which is particularly valuable for AI development and testing. The industry practitioners who most valued these collaborations emphasized that successful partnerships require "passionate people driving it" where "success depends on passionate people driving it" (Evans et al., 2023, p. 8).

Tas (2023) further highlights that the sustainability of these collaborations requires adaptation: "Moving forward, it is crucial for universities and industries to sustain their collaborations and adapt to the evolving landscape of data literacy, ensuring that graduates are well-prepared for the challenges and opportunities presented by the data-driven world" (p. 7). The human element is emphasized when Evans et al. (2023, p. 9) quote an industry partner who stated, "As much as we can talk about technology, at the end of the day, collaboration is about people. You must be honest and open, foster the relationship, build it, and then consider how to support the partner."

To maximize the benefits of university-industry collaboration in AI education, universities must recognize that while institutional support and frameworks are important, human relationships remain central. As Chen et al. (2020) observe, "the education and scientific research issues about AIEd are thus of increasing interest internationally, not only among educators and researchers but also among governments and educational institutions" (p. 8), highlighting the collaborative nature of digital transformation in educational technology.

The authors emphasize the multidisciplinary approach to AI in education, noting that successful collaboration requires engagement across various sectors and disciplines. Their research underscores the importance of building bridges between academic research, technological innovation, and institutional support to advance the field of Artificial Intelligence in Education.

Public and University Collaboration in the Digital Age

Higher education is changing dramatically right now. As AI and digital technologies reshape our world, universities must work closely with public institutions and society. The old barriers between universities and the public are breaking down, creating exciting new possibilities. Policymakers play a crucial role in fostering these collaborations, providing the necessary support and resources.

Take the University of Florida's 'AI Across the Curriculum' program. They are not just adding tech courses but weaving AI throughout different subjects. Southworth and colleagues note this is not just about technology (Southworth et al., 2023). It is about building an environment that prepares students to be informed citizens in our digital world. The university acts as a bridge between advanced technology and community needs.

Universities are no longer isolated ivory towers. They have evolved into active societal partners, deeply intertwined with real-world transformation. This is particularly evident in digital skills, where public needs directly influence the content and student learning methods. The potential for societal impact is immense, inspiring, and motivating universities to continue their transformative work.

The National Security Commission on Artificial Intelligence (2021) addressed this topic in its report. Universities are crucial in developing a digitally skilled workforce ready for complex 21st-century challenges. This goes beyond individual careers—preparing society for technological change.

Tzu-Chi Yang's research underscores the practical benefits of this partnership (Yang, 2023). Universities can tailor education to better meet public needs by leveraging AI to analyze course content. This approach demonstrates how technology can bridge the gap between academic learning and real-world requirements, fostering a sense of optimism about the future of education.

Paul Atchley and his colleagues emphasize that successful collaboration is not about replacing humans with technology (Atchley et al., 2024, pp. 7-9). Universities must prepare students to work with AI tools, understanding their potential and limitations.

Public-university teamwork in the digital age shows up in several key areas:

- Creating programs that address emerging social and industry needs
- Developing research with immediate practical applications
- Preparing people to think critically about evolving technologies
- Establishing guidelines for responsible tech development

Zhou Shao's research on institutional partnerships highlights what makes collaborations successful (Shao et al., 2020):

- Mutual respect and understanding
- Aligned goals
- Flexibility and adaptability
- Commitment to creating knowledge together

The University of Florida approach sets a notable example. Hiring over 100 AI-focused faculty across 16 colleges and establishing a dedicated AI center shows a complete commitment to public engagement. This is not just about tech training but about creating an ecosystem that can tackle complex social challenges.

These partnerships go beyond traditional technology transfer. They represent a new way of creating knowledge where public institutions, universities, and industries work together to solve complex problems. For instance, the University of California, Berkeley's partnership with the city of San Francisco to develop AI-powered solutions for urban challenges or the collaboration between MIT and the US Department of Energy to advance clean energy technologies. The lines between academic research, public policy, and industry innovation are blurring and hence in future, universities will feature:

- Cross-disciplinary approaches such as Interdisciplinary Learning to explore connections and deepen understanding, and Multidisciplinary Learning to examine concepts through the lens of multiple subjects.
- Flexible learning models such as Project-Based Learning, Competency-Based Learning, Microlearning, Experiential & Work-Integrated Learning, and Gamification of learning
- Commitment to ethical tech development that includes complex decisions related to Fairness, Bias Mitigation, Transparency, Privacy, Safety, and Social Impact
- Active engagement with society's needs including Problem-Based Learning (PBL) where participants use real-world challenges that require knowledge from various fields to develop solutions
- Ongoing conversation between academic and public sectors including Transdisciplinary Learning by going beyond subject boundaries to address challenges by collaborating with academia, industry, and communities.

The future of higher education depends on its ability to connect technological innovation with society's needs. Universities must become dynamic ecosystems that not only create knowledge but actively help solve complex challenges.

Promoting AI Literacy Through Cross-Disciplinary Applications

We must go beyond just teaching theory when considering AI literacy in higher education. Students need opportunities to apply AI across many different subjects. This means creating an integrated approach that connects academic departments while carefully balancing technology's capabilities with our educational goals.

The good news is that new no-code platforms are making AI more accessible to everyone. Sundberg and Holmström (2024) found that these platforms allow students from non-technical backgrounds to work meaningfully with machine learning concepts. This democratization of AI education is essential now that even traditionally non-technical careers require some understanding of AI technologies.

For AI literacy programs to work effectively, we must think carefully about designing educational experiences. Wang and Li (2024) discovered something fascinating in their study of 721 university students: when students feel confident using AI tools and have the freedom to explore them, their learning improves significantly. This reminds us that we need to focus not just on teaching technical skills but also on building students' confidence in using these tools.

We must also reconsider how we think about knowledge acquisition when integrating AI into education. Kramm and McKenna (2023) make a compelling case against the "police-catch-punish" approach many universities have adopted in response to tools like ChatGPT. Instead, they suggest that higher education should focus on "nurturing transformative relationships with knowledge" (p. 2174). This perspective connects with Reiss's (2021) observation that AI has tremendous potential to break down traditional boundaries between different learning environments, creating learning opportunities that transcend physical limitations.

One of AI's most exciting capabilities is personalization. AI can create learning environments where "students can put theory into practice" (Reiss, 2021, p. 6), helping them develop deeper understanding across diverse contexts. This ability to customize learning experiences is particularly valuable in addressing the varying needs of students from different disciplines and backgrounds, providing tailored support that enhances engagement and comprehension.

Despite these promising possibilities, we face significant challenges in implementing AI in higher education. Munawar et al. (2024) highlight critical concerns universities must address, particularly regarding ethics and equitable access. Their research emphasizes that "several issues and concerns with using AI tools in the schooling sector" exist (p. 122). Finding this balance between innovation and protection requires institutional commitment to developing comprehensive strategies that ensure all students can access and benefit from AI tools, regardless of their background (p. 126)

Academic integrity and ethical AI usage present additional implementation challenges. Zhang (2022) notes that AI-driven educational systems can overcome "traditional subjective approaches to educational design" (p. 5), while improving assessment validity. However, Popenici (2022) criticizes the expansion of monitoring technologies in higher education, arguing that excessive surveillance systems can potentially inhibit the innovative thinking and intellectual inquiry that universities aim to cultivate (p. 120)

How do we measure AI literacy? We need assessment frameworks that evaluate technical skills and critical thinking related to AI applications. Ibrahim et al. (2023) explored the complex implications of AI tools across 32 university courses, revealing significant challenges and potential opportunities for integrating technological innovations into educational assessment methods (p. 9). Their research highlights the importance of developing assessment methods that measure students' ability to use AI tools and their understanding of when and how to apply these technologies appropriately.

Developing standardized assessment approaches benefits collaboration between educational institutions and industry partners. Su and Yang (2023) propose a framework for applying generative AI in education that aligns educational strategies with workplace requirements. Their approach shows how assessment methodologies must evolve to reflect the changing landscape of AI applications in professional settings, ensuring graduates develop the specific competencies employers need.

AI's ability to cross boundaries creates continuous learning opportunities beyond traditional educational environments. As Reiss (2021) observes, "AI should increasingly enable such traditional divides as 'school versus home' to be straddled with learning" (p. 7). This integration allows students to develop AI competencies they can apply in both academic and professional contexts.

Effective AI literacy programs bridge the gap between education and workplace requirements through thoughtful design and implementation. Bearman et al.'s (2023, pp. 381-382) emphasize the importance of developing critical perspectives on AI that prepare students to navigate the complex technological landscapes they will encounter in professional environments. Their critical literature review shows how higher education institutions can foster the analytical skills students need to evaluate AI applications in diverse contexts.

UNIVERSITIES AS AI KNOWLEDGE HUBS: CONNECTING ACADEMIA, INDUSTRY, AND SOCIETY

Universities also take the lead in developing comprehensive assessment frameworks for AI competencies. Munawar et al.'s (2024) research on university-level AI implementation shows that institutions are creating evaluation methods that measure technical proficiency and critical thinking skills related to AI applications. These assessment tools help graduates and undergraduates understand and apply AI technology effectively and ethically in professional contexts. This dual focus on technical and analytical skills reflects higher education's commitment to developing well-rounded professionals capable of navigating AI-enhanced work environments.

Collaboration between universities and industry partners has become increasingly important in shaping Artificial intelligence in education. Higher education institutions collaborate with businesses to create real-world learning scenarios reflecting workplace challenges. These partnerships help ensure academic programs remain relevant and students develop the specific AI competencies employers seek. Universities can continuously update their curricula through industry feedback to address emerging technological trends and workplace requirements, creating a dynamic learning environment that evolves with industry needs.

Universities are not just focusing on their regular students - they are reaching out to help people already in their careers learn about AI, too. Think of it like going back to school part-time, but specifically to understand how AI can make you better at your job. Many schools have set up special programs where working professionals can learn AI skills directly applicable to daily work. For example, a marketing manager might learn how AI can help analyze customer data, while a healthcare worker might learn how AI assists in patient care. It is like having the best of both worlds - learning from academic experts while practicing with real-world examples from your industry. This way, universities are helping everyone keep learning and growing throughout their careers, not just traditional students.

In the public sphere, universities are crucial intermediaries between advanced AI technology and community needs. Through public outreach programs and partnerships with local organizations, higher education institutions help make AI literacy accessible to broader populations. These efforts often include workshops, seminars, and demonstration projects that help community members understand and engage with AI technology. Universities also collaborate with public agencies to develop AI-enhanced services that benefit local communities, applying academic research to solve real-world challenges.

The development of public AI literacy programs requires careful attention to accessibility and inclusion. Following Munawar et al.'s (2024) recommendations, universities create educational resources that accommodate diverse learning needs and backgrounds. This includes offering materials in multiple languages, developing adaptive learning tools, and ensuring accessibility for individuals with disabilities. Through these efforts, higher education institutions help ensure that AI literacy becomes available to all members of society, not just traditional students.

Universities also play a critical role in addressing ethical considerations surrounding AI implementation. They serve as platforms for essential discussions about AI's impact on society, helping develop guidelines for responsible AI use in both professional and public contexts. Through research, teaching, and public discourse, higher education institutions help shape policies and practices that promote ethical AI development and implementation.

Looking toward the future, university leadership in AI education becomes increasingly vital. As Wang and Li (2024) emphasize, successful AI integration requires attention not just to technical competencies but also to develop students' confidence and autonomy in using AI tools. Universities must continue evolving their teaching approaches while maintaining their commitment to academic excellence and ethical considerations. This evolution includes expanding interdisciplinary programs, strengthening industry partnerships, and developing new pedagogical methods that effectively integrate AI technology.

The transformation of higher education through AI creates opportunities for innovation in teaching and learning methods. Universities are exploring ways to use AI to enhance educational experiences while preserving the valuable aspects of traditional academic instruction. This includes developing hybrid learning environments that combine AI-powered tools with human guidance, ensuring that technology augments rather than replaces effective teaching practices. By thoughtfully implementing AI tools and maintaining a focus on student learning outcomes, universities can create innovative and meaningful educational experiences that prepare graduates for success in an AI-enhanced world.

Figure 1 presents a comprehensive framework that organizes AI-enhanced digital literacy into three interconnected components: academic integration, industry requirements, and collaborative framework. This model is not just a structure but a shared mission that unites educational institutions and workplace needs in developing AI literacy, inviting all stakeholders to be part of this transformative journey.

The framework illustrates how these three domains must work together to prepare students for an AI-integrated future. Rather than treating educational preparation and workplace demands as separate concerns, the model shows how they interconnect through collaborative elements, represented by the dotted lines between components.

Figure 1. AI-enhanced digital literacy framework illustrating the interconnected components of academic integration, industry requirements, and collaborative frameworks

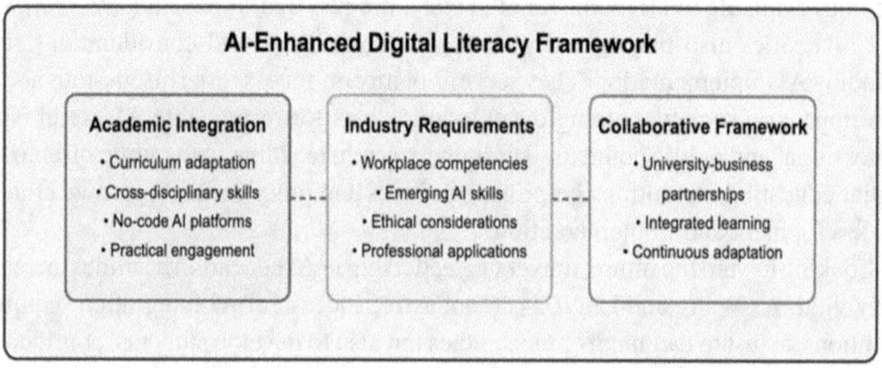

Academic Integration

The first component of our framework focuses on how universities adapt their educational approaches to incorporate AI literacy in their curriculum and requirements. This includes curriculum adaptation across disciplines, developing cross-disciplinary skills, implementing low-code or no-code AI platforms, and creating opportunities for practical engagement from non-science academic areas. These practical implications of AI literacy in education and industry underscore the real-world application of the academic integration component.

Curriculum Adaptation

- Systematically redesigning course content to incorporate AI concepts
- Ensuring AI literacy is integrated across all academic disciplines
- Developing flexible learning modules that can adapt to rapidly changing AI technologies

Cross-Disciplinary Skills

- Fostering skills that transcend traditional academic boundaries
- Encouraging critical thinking and problem-solving in AI contexts
- Developing adaptability and interdisciplinary collaboration capabilities

No-Code AI Platforms

- Providing accessible tools that lower the technical barrier to AI learning
- Enabling students from non-technical backgrounds to engage with AI concepts
- Democratizing AI education through user-friendly interfaces

Practical Engagement

- Creating hands-on learning experiences with real-world AI applications
- Developing project-based learning opportunities
- Encouraging experimental and experiential learning approaches

Sundberg and Holmström (2024) highlight the value of no-code platforms in this integration. Their research demonstrates how these platforms allow students without technical backgrounds to meaningfully engage with machine learning concepts, democratizing access to AI education. As one student in their study remarked, "With the no-code approach, I got the opportunity to try experiments and thus got a 'black-boxed' grasp of how it works" (p. 61). The authors note that "access to user-friendly, low-code AI could democratize the adoption of these systems and stimulate their multidisciplinary use" (p. 57), showing how these tools can make AI education accessible to students from diverse academic backgrounds.

The cross-disciplinary skills aspect aligns with Wang and Li's (2024) research with 721 university students, which found that "when students feel confident using AI tools and are given the freedom to explore them, their learning improves significantly." This underscores the importance of creating learning environments that build student confidence across various disciplines.

Ibrahim et al.'s (2023) research across 32 university courses highlighted the potential for AI tools in education, suggesting they could be "potentially utilized as an assistive tool that can facilitate both teaching and learning" (p. 9). The researchers proposed that "teachers could use large language models as a pedagogical tool to generate multiple examples and explanations when teaching" and "students could use them as a tutor that is available at their disposal to answer questions and provide explanations" (Ibrahim et al., 2023, p. 9).

However, the study also emphasized the critical need to examine both the challenges and opportunities of AI technologies. The researchers called for future work that would "examine both the issues such technology presents from the perspective of plagiarism as well as the opportunity this technology provides for students and educators" (Ibrahim et al., 2023, p. 9).

Industry Requirements

The vital component addresses the competencies and skills workplaces demand in an AI-enhanced environment. This includes workplace competencies, emerging AI skills, ethical considerations, and professional applications.

Workplace Competencies

- Identifying and developing skills directly applicable to AI-enhanced work environments
- Understanding how AI transforms traditional job roles
- Preparing students for flexible and adaptive professional landscapes

Emerging AI Skills

- Tracking and integrating the latest AI technological developments
- Developing predictive and analytical capabilities
- Understanding machine learning and artificial intelligence fundamentals

Ethical Considerations

- Addressing privacy and data protection concerns
- Developing critical thinking about AI's societal implications
- Creating frameworks for responsible AI use
- Understanding potential biases in AI systems

Professional Applications

- Connecting AI skills to specific industry needs
- Developing case studies and real-world problem-solving scenarios
- Bridging theoretical knowledge with practical implementation

Su and Yang (2023) emphasize the need for educational institutions to prepare students who can effectively utilize AI technologies while developing distinctly human capabilities. They argue that when implementing AI in education, "it is important to consider the role of human teachers" and recognize that teachers play a "crucial role in ensuring that students receive high-quality education and foster positive learning experiences" (p. 10). The authors suggest that AI should support rather than replace human capabilities, noting that "ChatGPT should not replace the important role of human coaches in providing support and guidance" (p. 6). This balance between technological proficiency and human skills is central to their IDEE framework for effective AI integration in education.

The ethical considerations element connects with Popenici (2022) caution against the "significantly broadening role of surveillance and data collection in education," highlighting the importance of preparing students to navigate ethical complexities in professional settings. Similarly, Kramm and McKenna (2023, p. 2173) argue for approaches that focus on " a space for nurturing transformative relationships with knowledge " rather than restrictive policies.

Professional applications align with Zhang (2022) insights that correctly implemented AI-driven systems can move beyond traditional subjective approaches in professional contexts. This component focuses on preparing students for the transformative impact of AI across various industries and professional practices.

Collaborative Framework

The right component outlines how educational institutions and industry partners can work together to create cohesive approaches to AI literacy. This includes university-business partnerships, integrated learning opportunities, and mechanisms for continuous adaptation to evolving technologies. The collaborative framework plays a crucial role in fostering this shared responsibility between educational institutions and industry partners.

University-Business Partnerships

- Creating structured connections between academic institutions and industries
- Developing internship and collaborative research opportunities
- Ensuring curriculum alignment with workforce requirements

Integrated Learning Opportunities

- Designing programs that combine academic study with professional experience
- Creating mentorship and knowledge-transfer mechanisms
- Developing flexible learning pathways

Continuous Adaptation

- Establishing mechanisms for ongoing curriculum review
- Creating feedback loops between educational institutions and industries
- Developing agile learning frameworks that can quickly respond to technological changes

Bearman et al. (2023, p. 381) stress that "effective frameworks must be comprehensive yet adaptable to remain relevant amid rapid technological change". This adaptability is not just a feature but a reassurance that our framework is designed to evolve alongside technological developments, ensuring its continued relevance

The university-business partnerships element creates structured connections between academic learning and workplace applications. These partnerships provide avenues for industry input into curriculum development and opportunities for students to engage with real-world AI applications before entering the workforce.

Munawar et al. (2024) point out that numerous sectors face "ethical issues about the exploitation of AI technology and data protection" (p. 122). This balance is a goal, and a commitment facilitated through the collaborative framework, ensuring that ethical and practical concerns are carefully managed. The authors emphasize that universities should approach AI implementation by "employing artificial intelligence, with explicit ethical principles for AI development that cover bias mitigation, student data protection, and responsible development" (p. 126).

Interconnected Implementation

The dotted lines connecting the three components represent knowledge, skills, and feedback flow between academic settings and industry contexts. This interconnectedness is essential for ensuring that what students learn aligns with emerging workplace requirements and that academic research informs professional practice.

Students who can train their models and use AI properly, including through no-code AI platforms, demonstrate consistently high satisfaction, regardless of their technical background. This suggests that systematic approaches to AI literacy yield significantly better outcomes than ad-hoc methods.

This framework visualizes our central argument: preparing individuals for an AI-integrated future requires collaborative approaches that bridge traditional divides between education and industry. As Reiss (2021) observes, AI has the potential to enable learning that transcends conventional boundaries, creating opportunities for "traditional divides as 'school versus home' to be straddled about learning"(p. 7).

By structuring AI literacy development around these three interconnected components, educational institutions can create comprehensive approaches that prepare students to use AI tools and thrive in professional environments where AI is increasingly central to everyday practice.

NAVIGATING THE COMPLEX LANDSCAPE OF AI INTEGRATION IN HIGHER EDUCATION

The following chapter explores the multifaceted challenges depicted in the conceptual framework in Figure 2, "Challenges in AI Integration in Higher Education." This visual representation organizes the obstacles into four interconnected domains: technical, ethical, social, pedagogical, and implementation challenges. As Figure 2 illustrates, successful AI integration requires addressing these challenges holistically rather than in isolation.

The Technological Landscape of Modern Higher Education

Imagine walking through a university campus, where the whispers of technological transformation echo through classrooms, laboratories, and faculty lounges. In the rapidly evolving world of higher education, technological integration represents more than just a trend—it is a profoundly human story of reimagining how knowledge is created, shared, and experienced. The challenge of implementing Artificial Intelligence (AI) extends far beyond simple technological upgrades; it demands a holistic transformation of educational ecosystems that touches the very heart of human learning.

Figure 2. Challenges in AI integration in higher education: A comprehensive overview of technical, ethical and social, pedagogical, and implementation challenges

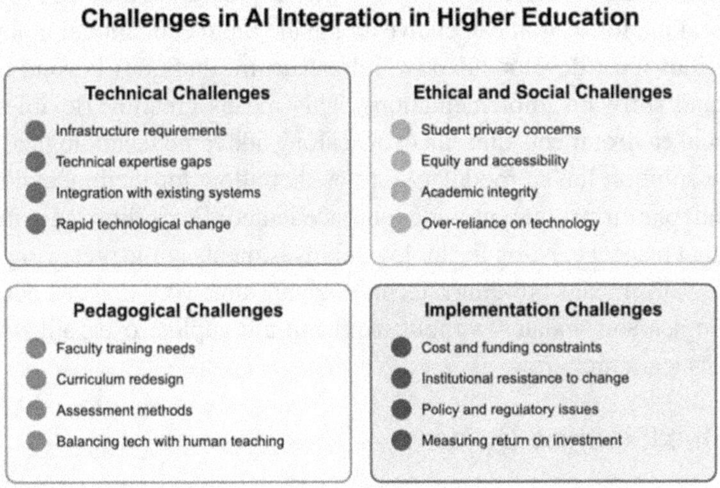

This transformation, far from being cold or mechanical, promises a more efficient, effective, and engaging educational experience. It instills a sense of hope and optimism about the future of education. Behind every algorithm and technological innovation are human stories of curiosity, adaptation, and potential, fostering a sense of connection and engagement with the AI transformation.

Recent scholarship underscores the transformative potential of this technological shift. Munawar et al. (2024) highlight the profound implications of AI integration in higher education, emphasizing that this is not merely a technological upgrade but a comprehensive reimagining of educational methodologies. Similarly, Wang and Li (2024) argue that AI represents a fundamental restructuring of how educational institutions conceptualize learning and knowledge creation, inspiring a hopeful vision of the future of education.

Technological Infrastructure: Beyond Simple Upgrades

The journey begins with infrastructure—modern universities' complex technological nervous system. Picture an aging institution, its hallways lined with decades of academic history, now attempting to integrate innovative AI technologies into networks and systems designed in a pre-digital era. This is a technical challenge and a profoundly human story of adaptation and resilience.

Technological infrastructure research provides critical insights into this transformation. Zhang (2022) demonstrates that successful AI integration requires more than hardware upgrades; it demands a strategic approach to technological ecosystems. Sundberg and Holmström (2024) further elaborate on the need for adaptive technological platforms that can evolve alongside rapid educational innovations.

Universities must develop adaptive infrastructure that goes beyond traditional hardware and software implementations. This means creating flexible, scalable technological environments that can evolve alongside rapid technological advancements. The solution lies in modular systems that allow for incremental upgrades, cloud-based platforms that provide unprecedented flexibility, and integration strategies that respect existing technological investments while preparing for future innovations. This means building a technological framework that can adapt to new AI technologies and updates without requiring a complete overhaul—much like how humans learn and grow.

Bridging the Expertise Divide

The most significant human challenge is the expertise gap. Experienced educators navigate a new landscape of machine learning, algorithmic thinking, and AI-enhanced pedagogies. This is not about replacing human expertise but about augmenting and expanding the incredible capabilities of passionate educators.

The literature reveals the critical nature of faculty adaptation. Ibrahim et al. (2023) emphasize that the expertise gap represents a fundamental challenge in technological transformation. Su and Yang (2023) argue that comprehensive professional development is key to bridging this divide, transforming technological uncertainty into intellectual opportunity, and highlighting the integral role of educators in the AI integration process.

Comprehensive professional development becomes crucial. It empowers educators to understand AI technologies and reimagine their pedagogical approaches. This involves creating mentorship programs, providing ongoing support, and developing a culture of continuous learning that transforms technological uncertainty into intellectual curiosity. We must embark on this journey, and we promise to keep our profession vibrant and relevant, fostering a sense of motivation and commitment to the AI integration process.

Ethical Considerations: Preserving Human Dignity in a Digital Age

The ethical dimensions of AI integration represent the most critical challenge. At its core, this is a human story about privacy, equity, and the fundamental purpose of education—a deeply personal narrative that goes beyond mere technological implementation.

Scholarly examination of AI ethics provides crucial context. Reiss (2021) offers a comprehensive analysis of ethical considerations in educational technology, emphasizing the importance of maintaining human dignity in technological integration. Kramm and McKenna (2023, p. 2173) argue for a nuanced approach that prioritizes ethical considerations over technological capabilities, reassuring policymakers about the ethical considerations in AI integration.

Protecting Student Privacy and Ensuring Equity

Data becomes the new currency of education, raising profound questions about student privacy and technological access. Universities must develop transparent, student-centered approaches that prioritize individual rights and experiences. This means creating robust consent frameworks, implementing anonymous data collection methods, and developing comprehensive policies that protect student information.

Privacy and equity emerge as critical concerns. Munawar et al. (2024) highlight the paramount importance of student privacy in AI integration. Ilieva et al. (2023, p. 11) provide additional context on potential risks and necessary safeguards in technological educational approaches.

Equity emerges as a critical concern. If not carefully managed, AI technologies risk creating new forms of educational inequality. The solution requires a multifaceted approach: providing universal access to AI tools, developing adaptive learning technologies to support diverse learning needs, and creating support systems that ensure no student is left behind in the technological transformation.

Reimagining Academic Integrity

The rise of generative AI tools challenges traditional notions of original work and academic honesty. Universities must move beyond punitive approaches and develop nuanced assessment methods that recognize AI as a collaborative tool rather than a threat to academic integrity.

Scholarly research provides important insights into this challenge. Shuliar et al. (2023) examine the complex landscape of academic integrity in AI-enhanced education. Bearman et al.'s (2023, pp. 379-382) critically review AI's impact on academic practices, emphasizing the need for nuanced approaches.

This involves redesigning assessment approaches emphasizing critical thinking, creative problem-solving, and the unique human capacities that AI cannot replicate. The goal is not to prevent AI use but to teach students how to use these tools ethically, critically, and creatively.

Pedagogical Transformation: Learning in the Age of AI

The pedagogical challenges represent a fundamental reimagining of knowledge creation and sharing. Traditional disciplinary boundaries dissolve as AI demonstrates its capacity to connect and synthesize knowledge across domains.

Su and Yang (2023) explore AI's transformative potential in educational approaches, highlighting the need to rethink pedagogical methodologies radically. Their research suggests that AI can fundamentally reshape how we conceptualize learning and knowledge transfer.

Curriculum as a Living, Adaptive Ecosystem

Curriculum design must become a dynamic, flexible process. Education can no longer be a static transfer of information. Instead, universities must develop interdisciplinary frameworks that allow for rapid adaptation, cross-departmental collaboration, and learning experiences that mirror real-world challenges' complex, interconnected nature.

Bearman et al. (2023, pp. 381-382) critically examine curriculum transformation in the age of AI, emphasizing the need for adaptive, interdisciplinary approaches. Their research suggests that traditional disciplinary boundaries are becoming increasingly porous in an AI-enhanced educational landscape.

Faculty training becomes central to this transformation. Educators must be supported in developing skills beyond traditional disciplinary expertise. This means creating robust professional development programs, peer learning communities, and institutional cultures that value continuous learning and technological adaptation.

Practical Implementation: Bridging Vision and Reality

Implementing AI integration challenges organizational change, resource allocation, and strategic vision. Ilieva et al. (2023, pp. 22-23) offer critical perspectives on the practical challenges of AI integration in educational settings, highlighting the complex interplay between technological innovation and institutional culture.

Navigating Financial and Institutional Constraints

Financial constraints often emerge as the most immediate barrier. Universities must develop creative approaches to funding technological transformation, including public-private partnerships, strategic grant applications, and phased implementation strategies demonstrating clear value and return on investment.

Institutional resistance represents another significant challenge. Academic institutions are traditionally conservative and often deeply skeptical of radical transformations. Overcoming this requires leadership that can articulate a compelling vision, demonstrate tangible benefits, and create cultural change from within.

A Holistic Approach to Technological Integration

Successfully integrating AI in higher education is not about technological replacement but about creating more powerful, human-centered learning experiences. It requires a delicate balance between technological innovation and core educational values. This balanced approach ensures that while we embrace AI's potential, we also preserve the essence of education that has been our guiding light for centuries.

Popenici (2022) provides a critical narrative on the balance between technological innovation and core educational values, emphasizing the need for a humanistic approach to technological integration.

Universities must become adaptive learning organisms—institutions that can evolve, experiment, and continuously reimagine themselves. This means developing:

- Flexible technological infrastructures
- Comprehensive ethical frameworks
- Adaptive pedagogical approaches
- Supportive organizational cultures

The goal is not technological sophistication but enhanced human potential. AI should be a tool that expands our capacity to learn, create, and understand—a collaborative partner in the ongoing human journey of knowledge creation.

ACADEMIC INTEGRATION - THE ADAPTATION OF UNIVERSITY CURRICULA TO INCORPORATE DIGITAL SKILLS

Academic integration requires a comprehensive restructuring of university curricula to embed digital skills across all disciplines rather than isolating them in technical departments. Students who use AI and can train their models consistently report high satisfaction regardless of their technical background, demonstrating the importance of structured approaches to artificial intelligence in education. Wang and Li's (2024) research with 721 university students confirms this pattern, showing that when students develop confidence in using AI tools, they become more effective learners. This integration must focus on technical proficiency and critical thinking, enabling students to understand how to use digital tools and when and why to apply them.

Curriculum adaptation benefits from the emergence of no-code platforms that have made AI education accessible to students from all academic backgrounds, as highlighted by Sundberg and Holmström (2024). These platforms enable every department to incorporate AI learning into various courses, ensuring all graduates possess fundamental AI literacy regardless of specialization. This reflects the framework illustrated in the colored squares diagram, which maps relationships between implementation components across various institutional contexts. Ibrahim et al.'s (2023) study across 32 university courses revealed complex challenges in AI integration, highlighting the need for nuanced approaches to technological engagement in educational settings. The researchers noted potential opportunities for AI as an assistive tool, while also emphasizing the critical importance of examining both the "issues such technology presents from the perspective of plagiarism as well as the opportunity this technology provides for students and educators" (p. 9).

Bringing AI into higher education is not as simple as installing new software. It is not easy, but the rewards can be tremendous. Figure 3 shows this journey as a strategic roadmap, turning abstract tech possibilities into meaningful learning experiences that prepare students for tomorrow's workforce. This framework recognizes that integrating AI is not about checking boxes—it is a dynamic, interconnected transformation that requires collaboration and thoughtful navigation.

Figure 3. AI integration process in higher education: A systematic approach depicting sequential stages from assessment and planning to evaluation and refinement

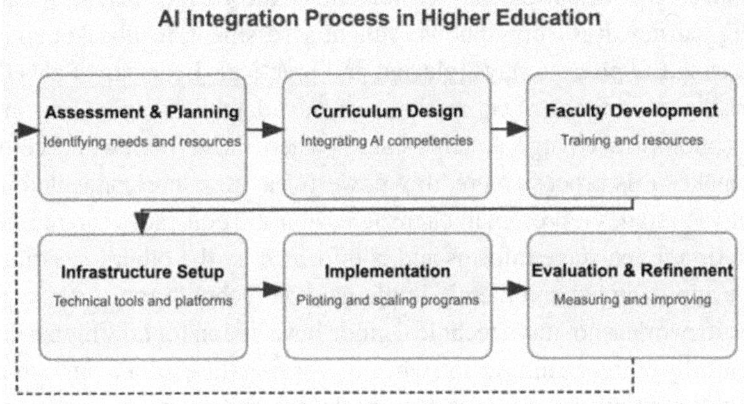

The journey begins with assessment and planning. This goes beyond taking inventory of your tech. Universities must dive deep into their unique institutional landscape, mapping existing capabilities, spotting potential roadblocks, and aligning AI with their educational mission. Munawar et al. (2024) point out that this is not just about whether your technology is ready but about understanding your institution's entire ecosystem. next comes curriculum design, where abstract AI potential becomes concrete learning opportunities. This is not about tackling isolated tech courses. It is about reimagining how AI can enrich learning across all disciplines. Sundberg and Holmström (2024) emphasize making AI education accessible to everyone—ensuring students from all backgrounds can meaningfully engage with these technologies, regardless of their technical knowledge.

Faculty development represents the human heart of this transformation. Technology is only as powerful as the educators implementing it. The challenge is significant—Lérias et al. (2024) found that many educators still struggle with AI literacy, with only 62.4% demonstrating intermediate to advanced competencies. This stage is not just about training but about fostering a culture of continuous learning and technological empowerment.

Infrastructure setup goes beyond buying new tech. It is about creating flexible, secure, innovative technological ecosystems that support advanced learning approaches. Ibrahim et al. (2023) highlight the importance of building platforms that are not just technologically sophisticated but pedagogically meaningful.

Implementation is where strategy meets reality. This stage involves careful piloting, strategic scaling, and a willingness to adapt. It is not about wholesale replacement of existing educational methods but thoughtful integration that enhances learning experiences. Su and Yang (2023) remind us that the goal is to develop graduates who can confidently use AI while maintaining critical human capabilities like creative thinking and ethical reasoning.

The final stage, evaluation, and refinement, acknowledges that AI integration is an ongoing journey. It is a continuous cycle of assessment, feedback, and improvement, ensuring the process stays relevant and practical. Bearman et al.'s (2023, p. 381) stress the importance of comprehensive and adaptable frameworks in the face of rapid technological change, and this stage is where those frameworks come to life.

What makes this process incredibly powerful is how interconnected it is. The arrows between stages represent linear progression and constant dialogue, feedback, and adaptation. Each stage informs and is informed by the others, creating a comprehensive approach beyond merely implementing technology.

This framework is not just a technical guide but a vision for how higher education can thoughtfully embrace innovation while preserving the essential human elements of learning. It recognizes that AI is not a replacement for human intelligence but a powerful tool that can enhance our educational capabilities.

As Zhang (2022) eloquently notes, this is about augmenting educational experiences, not replacing them. It is a delicate balance of technological innovation and pedagogical wisdom, preparing students for a future where AI is not just a tool but a collaborative partner in learning and discovery.

Organizations Require Personnel Capable of Navigating AI-Enhanced Environments

Modern organizations increasingly require personnel who can effectively navigate AI-enhanced work environments. Su and Yang (2023) emphasize that organizations need employees who can leverage AI capabilities while maintaining critical thinking, creativity, and ethical judgment skills that complement automated systems.

The Figure 2 challenges diagram identifies key obstacles in AI integration, including technical infrastructure limitations, faculty resistance, and ethical considerations. Addressing these challenges is crucial for preparing students for professional environments where AI augmentation has become standard practice. Ibrahim et al.'s (2023) research demonstrates that optimal productivity occurs when workers understand the capabilities and limitations of AI tools in their specific professional context. This aligns with the Figure 3 implementation process diagram, which outlines steps for systematically incorporating AI tools into educational settings, focusing on developing practical competencies applicable to workplace requirements. Munawar et al. (2024) further highlight that successful AI integration requires careful attention to student privacy and equal access while developing the collaborative skills necessary for an AI-integrated workforce.

Educational Institutions and Industry Must Establish Standardized Digital Literacy Frameworks

The lack of standardized digital literacy frameworks creates significant challenges for educational institutions and industry, as illustrated in Figure 2. Munawar et al. (2024) identify significant concerns universities must address, particularly ethics and equal access while ensuring that frameworks prepare students for workforce needs. Structured approaches to AI education, particularly those involving model training capabilities, correlate strongly with high satisfaction across technical and non-technical students. As Sundberg and Holmström (2024) demonstrate, when students from diverse academic backgrounds engage with AI through accessible platforms, they develop practical competencies that bridge theoretical understanding with applied skills. This suggests that established frameworks for AI competency development yield measurable improvements in learning outcomes, providing a foundation for standardized approaches that bridge academic and industry requirements.

Bearman et al.'s (2023, pp. 381-382) critical literature review emphasizes that effective frameworks must be comprehensive yet adaptable to remain relevant amid rapid technological change. Figure 1 AI-enhanced digital literacy framework provides a structured approach to implementation that can evolve with technological advancements while maintaining core educational values. Wang and Li's (2024) research with 721 university students demonstrates that students who develop confidence with AI tools, particularly those who can effectively use and customize these systems, report significantly higher learning satisfaction and outcomes. Similarly, Sundberg and Holmström (2024) found that when students could meaningfully engage with machine learning concepts through hands-on model interaction, their educational experience improved regardless of technical background. Su and Yang (2023) reinforce this through their framework for applying generative AI in education, demonstrating how educational strategies must align with workplace requirements to produce graduates capable of thriving in increasingly AI-integrated professional settings. The Figure 3 implementation process diagram further illustrates how systematic framework adoption leads to improved outcomes, creating an optimistic continuous feedback loop between educational approaches and workplace requirements.

CONCLUSION

Integrating AI into higher education is not just about adding innovative technology—it is about reimagining how we teach, learn, and create knowledge for a future where AI is everywhere. We have seen some exciting developments in this space. Wang and Li (2024) showed us that when students feel comfortable with AI tools, they learn better. Sundberg and Holmström (2024) discovered that no-code platforms are making AI accessible to students from all backgrounds, not just tech majors. Moreover, Ibrahim and colleagues (2023) demonstrated across 32 university courses that AI can enhance learning while keeping academic standards high. These successes should reassure anyone worried about maintaining educational integrity while embracing innovative technologies, instilling confidence in the future of education.

Students who received structured AI training, especially those who learned to train AI models or use chatbots effectively, experienced a remarkable transformation in their learning journey. This structured approach facilitated comprehension of complex concepts and improved practical application skills. A notable shift in understanding was evident as students, regardless of academic background, realized they could successfully implement sophisticated technologies. This inclusive approach to AI education valued all students, fostering similar enthusiasm in technical and non-technical students. This was true whether they came from technical or non-technical backgrounds. As Kramm and McKenna (2023, p. 2173) beautifully put it, higher education should be "a space for nurturing transformative relationships with knowledge." AI can enhance those relationships rather than replace them.

Making this work takes teamwork. It is a collaborative effort where universities, businesses, and government agencies must work closely together. Our framework has three main parts that work together: Academic Integration puts AI into coursework across disciplines; Industry Requirements ensure students learn skills employers need; and Collaborative Frameworks create partnerships that benefit everyone involved. As Munawar and colleagues (2024) remind us, this is not just about teaching technical skills—universities must also address ethical questions and make sure everyone has equal access to these powerful learning tools. It is a shared mission of which we are all part.

Universities are becoming bridges between innovative technology and community needs. Through public programs, industry partnerships, and thoughtful curriculum changes, they are preparing students for success while helping the broader public understand AI's impact. The University of Florida's "AI Across the Curriculum" initiative, highlighted by Southworth and colleagues (2023), shows how this can work—they are weaving AI throughout different subjects and connecting advanced technology with real community needs (Southworth et al., 2023). When used responsibly, AI can be a powerful tool for addressing societal challenges and improving people's lives.

Schools cannot stand still in any case. They need to keep evolving while staying true to their educational mission. This means creating teaching methods that cross traditional subject boundaries, building stronger ties with industry, and using AI to enhance rather than replace good teaching. Educators play a crucial role in this process; as AI advances, universities must help faculty develop new skills and create learning environments that work for all students. The need for this evolution becomes more urgent every day.

By following the systematic approach, we have outlined—from assessing needs through planning, implementation, and ongoing refinement—educational institutions can navigate AI's challenges while harnessing its incredible potential. With continued innovation, ethical vigilance, and strong partnerships, higher education can help create an AI-literate society ready for tomorrow's technological advances. Through it all, we must remember that meaningful education remains deeply human at its core—AI is our tool, not our replacement.

REFERENCES

Atchley, P., Pannell, H., Woford, K., Hopkins, M., & Atchley, R. A. (2024). Human and AI collaboration in the higher education environment: Opportunities and concerns. *Cognitive Research: Principles and Implications*, *9*(20), 20. Advance online publication. DOI: 10.1186/s41235-024-00547-9 PMID: 38589710

Bearman, M., Ryan, J., & Ajjawi, R. (2023). Discourses of artificial intelligence in higher education: A critical literature review. *Higher Education*, *86*(2), 369–385. DOI: 10.1007/s10734-022-00937-2

Chen, X., Xie, H., & Hwang, G. J. (2020). A multi-perspective study on Artificial Intelligence in Education: Grants, conferences, journals, software tools, institutions, and researchers. *Computers and Education: Artificial Intelligence*, *1*, 100005. DOI: 10.1016/j.caeai.2020.100005

Evans, N., Miklosik, A., & Du, J. T. (2023). University-industry collaboration as a driver of digital transformation: Types, benefits, and enablers. *Heliyon*, *9*(10), e21017. DOI: 10.1016/j.heliyon.2023.e21017 PMID: 37867890

Ibrahim, H., Liu, F., Asim, R., Battu, B., Benabderrahmane, S., Alhafni, B., & Zhang, Y. (2023). Perception, performance, and detectability of conversational artificial intelligence across 32 university courses. DOI: 10.1038/s41598-023-38964-3

Ilieva, G., Yankova, T., Klisarova-Belcheva, S., Dimitrov, A., Bratkov, M., & Angelov, D. (2023). Effects of Generative Chatbots in Higher Education. *Information (Basel)*, *14*(9), 492. DOI: 10.3390/info14090492

Kramm, N., & McKenna, S. (2023). AI amplifies the tough question: What is higher education really for? *Teaching in Higher Education*, *28*(8), 2173–2178. DOI: 10.1080/13562517.2023.2263839

Lérias, E., Guerra, C., & Ferreira, P. (2024). Literacy in artificial intelligence as a challenge for teaching in higher education: A case study at Portalegre Polytechnic University. *Information (Basel)*, *15*(4), 205. DOI: 10.3390/info15040205

Munawar, D. S., Ghouri, J., & Jahanzeb, F. (2024). Challenges of Using Artificial Intelligence at the University Level. *Journal of Arts & Social Sciences*, *11*(1), 122–126. DOI: 10.46662/jass.v11i1.463

National Security Commission on Artificial Intelligence. (2021). Final report (NSCAI Final Report, 2021). https://www.dwt.com/-/media/files/blogs/artificial-intelligence-law-advisor/2021/03/nscai-final-report--2021.pdf

Popenici, S. (2022). *Artificial Intelligence and Learning Futures: Critical Narratives of Technology and Imagination in Higher Education*. Routledge., DOI: 10.4324/9781003266563

Reiss, M. J. (2021). The use of AI in education: Practicalities and ethical considerations. *London Review of Education, 19*(1), 1–14. DOI: 10.14324/LRE.19.1.05

Shao, Z., Yuan, S., & Wang, Y. (2020). Institutional collaboration and competition in Artificial Intelligence. *IEEE Access : Practical Innovations, Open Solutions, 8*, 1–10. DOI: 10.1109/ACCESS.2020.2986383

Shuliar, V., Shkurko, V., Polukhtovych, T., Semeniako, Y., Shanaieva-Tsymbal, L., & Koltok, L. (2023). Using Artificial Intelligence in Education. BRAIN. *Broad Research in Artificial Intelligence and Neuroscience, 14*(3), 516–529. DOI: 10.18662/brain/14.3/488

Southworth, J., Migliaccio, K., Glover, J., Glover, J., Reed, D., McCarty, C., Brendemuhl, J., & Thomas, A. (2023). Developing a model for AI Across the curriculum: Transforming the higher education landscape via innovation in AI literacy. *Computers and Education: Artificial Intelligence, 4*, 100127. DOI: 10.1016/j.caeai.2023.100127

Su, J., & Yang, W. (2023). *Unlocking the Power of ChatGPT: A Framework for Applying Generative AI in Education*. ECNU Review of Education., DOI: 10.1177/20965311231168423

Sundberg, L., & Holmström, J. (2024). Teaching Tip: Using No-Code AI to Teach Machine Learning in Higher Education. *Journal of Information Systems Education, 35*(1), 56–66. DOI: 10.62273/CYPL2902

Tas, E. (2023). Data literacy education through university-industry collaboration. *Information and Learning Science, 124*(11/12). Advance online publication. DOI: 10.1108/ILS-06-2023-0077

Wang, L., & Li, W. (2024). The Impact of AI Usage on University Students' Willingness for Autonomous Learning. *Behavioral Sciences (Basel, Switzerland), 14*(10), 956. DOI: 10.3390/bs14100956 PMID: 39457827

Yang, T.-C. (2023). Application of Artificial Intelligence techniques in analysis and assessment of digital competence in university courses. *Journal of Educational Technology & Society, 26*(1), 232–243. DOI: 10.30191/ETS.202301_26(1).0017

Zhang, F. (2022). Design and Application of Artificial Intelligence Technology-Driven Education and Teaching System in Universities. *Computational and Mathematical Methods in Medicine, 2022*, 1–10. Advance online publication. DOI: 10.1155/2022/8503239 PMID: 36124170

APPENDIX

Table 1. Key terms and definitions in AI-enhanced digital literacy

Term	Definition
AI Literacy	The knowledge, skills, and abilities required to critically evaluate, effectively use, and ethically implement artificial intelligence technologies in educational and professional contexts.
Digital Competence	The confident, critical, and responsible use of digital technologies for learning, work, and participation in society, including information literacy, communication, content creation, safety, and problem-solving.
No-Code AI Platforms	Software tools that allow users without programming experience to design, develop, and implement AI models through graphical user interfaces rather than writing code.
Model Training	The process of teaching a machine learning algorithm to make predictions or decisions based on data involves feeding the algorithm with labeled examples from which it can learn patterns.
AI Integration	The systematic incorporation of AI tools and technologies into educational curricula, teaching methodologies, and learning environments.
Cross-Disciplinary Applications	The implementation of AI technologies and methodologies across different academic fields, allowing for knowledge transfer and innovative problem-solving approaches.
Learning Satisfaction	The degree to which students feel their educational needs, expectations, and desires have been fulfilled through specific learning experiences.
University-Industry Collaboration	Formal partnerships between higher education institutions and businesses aimed at knowledge transfer, innovation development, and workforce preparation.
Academic Integrity	The moral code or ethical policy in educational settings includes values such as avoidance of cheating, maintaining academic standards, and rigor in research and academic publishing.
Metacognition	Awareness and understanding of one's own thought processes, particularly regarding learning strategies, including the ability to self-reflect on and regulate one's learning.

Note: These definitions are derived from the synthesis of literature reviewed in this paper and represent current understanding within the field of AI-enhanced digital literacy in higher education.

Chapter 8
University Libraries are Supporters of Digital Literacy in Universities:
An Analysis Study Through University Rankings

Canan Ergün
https://orcid.org/0000-0002-6687-3870
Istanbul Medeniyet University, Turkey

ABSTRACT

Developments in information technology and internet technology are also shaping the educational needs and expectations of new generations. Therefore, digital literacy, defined as "the ability to understand and use information from various sources in multiple formats" (Gilster, 1997), has become a fundamental part of higher education. This is because higher education institutions have the responsibility to teach, present, ensure understanding, and promote the use of information. In this regard, digital literacy has facilitated a transition to a new model based on computers and technology in universities, leading to a transformation of traditional education (Mavutha & Mabotja, 2024). Digital literacy in universities has positive effects on education, research, and employment. University libraries have the capacity and leadership strength to best support digital literacy in collaboration with other units through their available resources. Therefore, in this section, the impact of university libraries on digital literacy is examined through THE World University Rankings.

DOI: 10.4018/979-8-3373-0004-7.ch008

INTRODUCTION

The rapid advancement of technology encourages universities to adopt new teaching methods and to facilitate learning through modern technological means. In this context, digital competencies have made it mandatory to know DL, defined as the ability to find, understand, use, manage, evaluate, and communicate information in digital formats across all fields in today's world (Levine-Clark & Dean, 2013). DL encompasses not only finding, understanding, and using computer-based resources but also enables individuals to benefit from the new opportunities offered by the Internet while simultaneously protecting their privacy, security, and autonomy (Greene & Crompton, 2024; Kammer, Cherner & Hays, 2021). Supporting this, Buckingham (2015) states that DL includes a specific set of skills. This skill set allows individuals to work effectively with software tools or to perform basic information-gathering tasks, extending beyond effectively using a computer or conducting online searches; it encompasses the searching, finding, transforming, disseminating, and using information in digital environments in an effective, efficient, and ethically compliant manner (Green, 2020; Koltay, 2011)

Bond et al. (2020) suggest that DL is a skill that comprises a combination of technologies, attitudes, and capabilities. As can be understood from all definitions, DL has three fundamental dimensions: using, understanding, and creating. When these three fundamental dimensions of DL are elaborated, it is observed that they also include skills such as understanding the relationships between digital information, establishing connections between information, testing the reliability of information, evaluating its validity and purpose, as well as digital competence (Martínez-Bravo, Chalezquer & Serrano-Puche, 2022). Curtarelli et al. (2016) identify three main categories of digital skills for assessing or developing digital competence: basic DL skills, workplace IT skills including ICT applications, and advanced ICT professions requiring innovative and creative digital skills.

Due to advancements in telecommunications and informatics, the transition from the electronic age to the digital age was completed in the late 1980s (Odubiyi, Aigbavboa & Thwala, 2021). Consequently, since then, the global utilization of Information and Communication Technologies (ICT) has significantly increased, with computers assuming an integral role in various aspects of life.

Today, they are intensively present in educational institutions, workplaces, public service areas, and homes. This situation has led individuals to realize that knowing how to use computers and other digital tools is an important life skill necessary for effectively benefiting from and providing digital services as a worker (Asamoah–Hassan, 2022). With the proliferation of the internet in the 1990s, the importance of digital skills has increased. Meridha (2024) noted in his research that 14.58% of the seven articles he examined highlighted that deficiencies in DL directly affect career, personal life, and development skills. Indeed, today, DL has become a vital skill in education, access to information, effective use of knowledge, and professional life.

The development and increasing importance of DL can be attributed to the role of digitization becoming a transformative force in many areas (Arnaud, Mamede & Branco, 2024). Digitization and digital transformation are compelling universities to change their core functions – knowledge production, dissemination, research, and teaching. It can have a profound impact, especially on learning processes and forms. Universities are increasingly incorporating technology and digitization, both of which shape them. The concept of learning has been redefined through this impact (Littlejohn, Beetham & McGill, 2012). In the field of education, DL is suggested to consist of seven factors related to digital information, communication skills, collaboration skills, ICT infrastructure, social environment, social media, and learning activity (Nagari, Sahid & Hussin, 2023). These seven factors impact education. The incorporation of DL into university curriculums may positively affect learning processes, promote success, and shift the educational approach from passive to active (Mokhtari, 2023).

Digital literacy (DL) is an essential skill for students to effectively utilize and comprehend e-learning resources. DL is important in university education as it contributes to academic success, supports technology usage, facilitates access to information, enhances life skills, increases global awareness, and aids in career development (Jaya & Sucipto, 2023; Chaudhary et al., 2024). High levels of DL improve e-learning design, service quality, student experience, and satisfaction (Lu & Khan, 2024). Thus, developing DL among faculty, students, staff, and support personnel is crucial for finding, creating, and sharing information, improving academic performance, accessing digital technologies, integrating into digital culture, and bridging communication gaps (Rodríguez et al., 2021).

Universities need to create an environment where students can use tools and interactions from both the digital and real worlds effectively and safely (Masterman & Shuyska, 2011; Anthony et al, 2020). They must plan, organize, and offer supportive services for technology use. Some countries are investing in new educational systems and digital infrastructure at universities to enhance DL levels through technology integration in education (Novak, Rabiee & Tjoa, 2018; Nguyen, 2024; Westberg & Mickevičius, 2021).

University libraries, with their technological facilities, amenities, and skilled personnel, can provide training, create educational materials, and develop digital learning platforms, thereby effectively supporting DL (IFLA, 2020). For instance, Migliorino (2011) highlights the importance of utilizing libraries to promote participation in the digital society and to eliminate barriers that lead to exclusion.

Paul and Crowe (2023) argue that in this context, libraries prominently offer personal training, face-to-face private lessons, workshops, YouTube training videos, consultancy services, help desk applications, and teaching supports. Additionally, libraries can contribute to enhancing their users' DL skills through practical workshops, seminars, and other courses. Furthermore, Manu and Gala (2023) and Ng et al. (2024) suggest that libraries can be successful in improving DL by implementing gamification. University libraries should create digital strategies and frameworks that align with their institutional mission and vision. They need support in areas such as staffing, budget allocation for training, technical assistance, consultancy, and technological infrastructure setup. Moreover, steps should be taken to integrate libraries' DL services (training, workshops, subject guides, videos, technology labs, etc.) into the curriculum at universities, to establish collaborative environments within the institution (Barak & Levenberg, 2016; Breen, Waters & O'Shea, 2023; Oliver & de St Jorre, 2018), and to keep.

The reason for choosing this topic in the research is that the role of university libraries in supporting DL has not been sufficiently examined within the expanding scope of digital life. In this book chapter, a model will be proposed that demonstrates the role of libraries in DL based on university rankings. Additionally, the chapter will focus on two main questions:

- Is there a benefit for universities in how libraries support DL?
- Do libraries' DL services have an effect and contribution to universities' success in rankings such as THE (Times Higher Education)?

DIGITAL LITERACY IN UNIVERSITIES

Education at all levels is rapidly adopting a technology-focused structure. This has led to DL (Coiro, 2003; Dresang & McClelland, 1999; Leu & Kinzer, 2000)—which includes the ability to understand, use, and modify texts in digital environments—becoming a fundamental building block that allows students to solve various problems encountered in education and daily life. Additionally, the increasing demand for online courses has highlighted the importance of skills such as navigating digital content, conducting research, and analyzing the reliability and accuracy of information. DL is crucial for young people to navigate the digital world comfortably and keep themselves safe (Obeidat, 2017). Universities must improve digital skills for their students and faculty. Digital literacy should be developed during university studies, as it is harder to learn after joining the workforce. Universities can address technological inequalities and overcome barriers related to DL, offering equal opportunities for all learners (Mavutha & Mabotja, 2024). Students should acquire core competencies at universities, such as accessing digital information, navigating digital environments safely and critically, using digital information effectively, paying attention to details, and creating new digital content using the acquired information (Wells, 2011). The DL acquired in university helps students to gain and develop new digital, cognitive, and technical skills even after graduating from university (Techataweewan & Prasertsin, 2018; Tiernan & Farren, 2017; Lo Presti, 2023). The establishment of a DL ecosystem at the university level (Sanka et al., 2024) necessitates its association with the curriculum, teaching it (Tuamsuk, Subramaniam, 2017; Coldwell-Neilson et al., 2019; Sharpe & Benfield, 2012), and determining ways of conveying it (Kelly, 2019). In particular, when designing the curriculum and supplementary educational resources, the digital competency needs of students must be taken into account (Alonso García et al., 2024). Miliou & Angeli (2023) suggest that project-based learning enhances academic performance and develops DL skills.

The literature review categorizes DL research in universities under five main headings. The first heading is the impact of DL on academic achievement, which includes students' ability to reach educational goals, gain knowledge, and show competence in various disciplines. There are studies suggesting a positive effect of DL on this process (Li & Chen, 2024; Feng & Liu, 2024; Lopez, 2013; Naz et al., 2022; Pascarella & Terenzini, 2005; Schmidt & DeSchryver, 2022; Tekin, 2024). Another study, the European Commission's (2019) publication titled "Key Competences For Lifelong Learning," states that DL is one of the fundamental elements in engaging in a knowledge-based society, achieving academic excellence, and advancing career opportunities. The effects of DL on academic achievement can be listed as facilitating student learning (Morachat & Seechaliao, 2024), ensuring student engagement (Bond, 2020; Junco, 2012; Salaber, 2014), and promoting knowledge acquisition (Zhao et al., 2005). Secondly, digital learning (DL) enhances student satisfaction. DL improves the student experience in digital learning environments, positively increases student motivation and sense of belonging, and enhances overall learning satisfaction (Lu & Khan, 2024). Research highlights the need for faculty to have digital literacy skills. To meet student demands and facilitate information transfer through technology, instructors must enhance their expertise in this area (Vuorikari et al., 2016). Additionally, Adetimirin (2011) suggests that university faculty should encourage students to use information and communication technologies (ICT) in their learning to develop their DL skills. This is because faculty members' possession of DL skills will positively impact the quality and success of education (Maxwell, 2020; Montenegro-Rueda & Fernández-Batanero, 2022; Platonova et al., 2020). For this purpose, studies aimed at increasing faculty members' digital competency are recommended (Maguire & Pauli, 2020). DL training courses can be organized to encourage faculty to comprehensively utilize digital information resources (Abdel-

Al, H & Abdel-Al, A., 2022). The ability to create educational content presented in university courses in a digital environment using digital technologies will enhance the quality and efficiency of education. At this point, the importance of raising the DL levels of faculty members becomes evident again. Ip (2024) proposes that educators could provide courses on online learning platforms such as Coursera and YouTube to help students gain knowledge about digital business operations.

Another important aspect of the issue is ensuring the effective use of digital resources and content by both faculty members and students in education. Here, Ikenwe and Aiyebelehin (2024) argue for the necessity of librarians providing training in digital skills to university faculty to improve their use of digital resources. Similarly, Soltovets, Chigisheva, and Dmitrova (2020) indicate that today, librarians are valuable as mentors for enhancing students' DL.

Fourthly, there are studies in the literature regarding the acquisition of DL competencies in the educational process for career and employment life. Cham et al. (2022) found in their research that 81% of students determined that gaining competence in digital skills would enhance their careers and professional development. This is because DL equips students with the necessary skills to succeed in the modern workforce and navigate the digital environment adeptly. DL also has a significant impact on graduates' ability to find jobs, as it increases the employability of their qualifications (Ferrari, 2013; Epifanova & Polozkov, 2020; Folorunso & Momoh, 2022; Ferreira, Coetzee & Potgieter, 2024; NMC, 2017; McLeod & Torres, 2020; Murray, Pérez & Fluker, 2022; Muzaki, Kaddu & Haumba, 2022; Ruddy & Ponte, 2019; Xiong & Yu, 2024) and is stated to be a necessary and advantageous competency (ECDL Foundation, 2014). Therefore, it is communicated in various studies that including DL training in university curricula and the training received in the curriculum is critically important for employability (Cham et al., 2022; González, 2023). The World Bank's Future of Work Report (2019) highlights that technology has changed the skills required for work. The report predicts increased demand for advanced cognitive, socio-behavioral, and adaptive skills, and notes that technology enables online work and participation in the gig economy. Studies show that lacking digital skills can result in reduced productivity, higher labor costs, slower growth, and difficulty adapting to new technologies (Curtarelli et al., 2016). It is important for governments, educational institutions and employers to develop new assessment tools to measure digital competencies so that institutions can evaluate and develop the digital behaviors and skills of their workforce (Canina & Orero-Blat, 2021). With these efforts, institutions can compete and survive in the labor market. To achieve this, additional programs need to be designed and implemented (Bejaković & Mrnjavac, 2020; Institute (European Information Technologies Certification Institute [EITCI], 2017; Rahmat & Apriliani, 2024). A study on this subject suggests that the graduates with the highest employment potential are those possessing DL skills (Tuamsuk & Subramaniam, 2017). Furthermore, there are studies indicating that students with DL competencies are more successful in their career choices and are able to find quality jobs (Blayone, 2018; Vuorikari et al., 2016). Digital technologies are increasingly being integrated into business strategies and operations. This integration of digital technologies in the business environment not only saves time, personnel, and money but also enhances efficiency (Zahra et al., 2006; Sousa-Zomer et al., 2020). Folorunso and Momoh (2022) indicate that DL is important for reducing unemployment and increasing workplace productivity. There is a strong demand for digital skills in every sector, in almost every occupation, including entry-level and senior positions. The DL skills gap has been found to disproportionately impact low-income individuals and rural residents due to inequalities (National Skills Coalition, 2023).

The fifth most studied topic is the increase in self-confidence for entrepreneurship due to DL. It is well known that the presence of entrepreneurs is a significant factor in winning in a competitive environment, ensuring economic growth, and sustaining it (Rakib et al., 2024). Therefore, it is one of the main responsibilities of universities to raise all young people, especially university students, as individuals with a sufficient level of self-confidence and behavioral approaches for entrepreneurship (Mudasih, Subroto & Susanti, 2021). Bayrakdaroğlu, F. and Bayrakdaroğlu A. (2017) state that it is essential for young entrepreneur candidates to possess DL in order to engage in business entrepreneurship in the digital environment (online) and that DL is a significant component of internet entrepreneurship. Similar studies have found that DL positively affects the self-confidence of university students for entrepreneurship, enables them to actively contribute to the national economy, and encourages them to actively participate in society and the economy (Ganefri et al., 2024; Vodă et al., 2022; Liza & Andriyanti, 2020; Prabawati, 2019; Salsabila, 2019). Chandra and Hendayana (2024) similarly state that entrepreneurship education and DL play a very important role in developing entrepreneurial competencies in individuals. Ip (2024), examining the direct effects of DL on social entrepreneurial intentions, has shown the positive effects of DL and social entrepreneurial intentions on social entrepreneurial behaviors. This research found that digital literacy is crucial for fostering social entrepreneurial intentions and behaviors. Kang et al. (2024) mention in their research that financial literacy, digital skills, and entrepreneurship are very important competencies for adapting to the changing work environment, especially after the COVID-19 pandemic, and for supporting new ventures. Therefore, they suggest that students need more training in these areas. In research conducted in Serbia, Šević et al. (2021) emphasized the importance of developing digital skills in general DL. The authors have emphasized the necessity of DL for young people to easily integrate into the workforce or participate in entrepreneurship. Additionally, it is known that young people possess a higher level of DL compared to other age groups, which is an important factor for entrepreneurship (Hannemann, Henn & Schäfer, 2023). The positive impact of digital literacy (DL) on future learning, research, development, and employment in universities is significant. However, obstacles such as limited access to digital materials, weak internet infrastructure, and inadequate curricula hinder achieving DL. These barriers negatively affect future job prospects (Meridha, 2024). Planning and allocating resources to teach DL at all educational levels are essential for effectively using technology in higher education.

University Libraries and Digital Literacy

University libraries have been positively influenced by technological advancements. With technology, libraries have incorporated advanced configurations of computers, browsers, self-check machines, kiosks, 3D printers, robots, AI-supported services, and various digital tools. They strive to provide resources and services to support, enhance, and further improve teaching and research in universities (Tenya, Maina, Awuor, 2024). With their technological infrastructure, university libraries can help ensure that university students possess 21st-century skills in their education and subsequent work life, and assist in further developing these skills. Among the 21st-century skills listed are collaboration and communication, critical thinking, creativity, and digital and information literacy. These skills are also important for conducting scientific research and scientific writing (Cintamulya, Murtini & Warli, 2024). The listed 21st-century skills are essential for faculty members, students, and other individuals to face complex problems in the global age. University libraries have a mission and duty to support the development of students' DL, which is considered one of the 21st-century skills (Hagel, 2015; Hallam, Amberyn & Beach, 2018; Huber & Shalavin, 2018; Martzoukou, 2021). Rafi et al. (2019) similarly state that among the responsibilities of academic libraries are ensuring the use of digital technology, developing technology skills, and increasing students' levels of DL. It is quite normal and essential for the university library to lead in DL due to the necessity of a more complex, integrated, and globalized information infrastructure for education and research (Kight, 2021). As an institution, digital technologies and DL directly influence libraries' modes of service and their personnel. For instance, the American Library Association Office for Information Technology Policy's Digital Literacy Task Force (Task Force) (2013, p. 14) report states that libraries' success in DL directly affects many of their services, such as information literacy.

In the literature review conducted on the effects of university libraries on DL, studies have been identified that emphasize the importance of utilizing library resources, facilities, and services for students' success and continuity in the university, as well as the supportive roles of librarians (Ahmed & Roche, 2021; Kot & Jones, 2015; Maxwell, 2020; New Media Consortium [NMC], 2016; Popescu, 2019; Soria et al., 2017; Thorpe et al., 2016). Another prominent topic in the literature review is the support for research competence by libraries. There is a significant correlation between research competence and DL (Indah et al., 2022). Consequently, it has become essential for university libraries to enhance digital research skills, solve access issues related to digital resources, plan technology-supported training with rich content on this subject, and finally take on an important role in the educational development processes at the university. Cham et al. (2022) have highlighted the importance of libraries increasing their support in this area in their research. They found that only 11% of students participating in the study could receive support in learning digital skills through library services and resources, attending workshops, and completing course assignments. This result indicates an urgent need to increase the support provided by libraries for DL. Farooq et al. (2022) reports that, similarly, the most significant issue in providing online library services during the COVID-19 pandemic has been the insufficient DL skills among library users, and they have stated that they are attempting to address this by offering services.

During this research, studies suggesting methods for libraries to build DL in universities were found. One of these methods is micro-credentialed courses created by libraries. Through these courses, libraries can enhance students' DL skills and help in understanding digital trends (Collins & Crowe, 2021; Musa, Hamid & Ishak, 2021; Ruddy & Ponte, 2019). Another is arranging DL workshops. Users can be given the opportunity to develop and improve their DL through technology-based face-to-face workshops held in libraries (Canuel et al., 2017; Soltovets, Chigisheva & Dmitrova, 2020; Breen, Waters & O'Shea, 2023). One of the first examples in this regard is a study conducted by Yeste et al. (2016), which provides information about various workshops organized by the library on academic and DL. Another example is the workshop held at Singapore Management University Library (Zhenyan, 2023). This workshop covers critical interaction with digital information, problem-based learning, and hands-on group activities. It aims to help users identify their information needs, access digital resources, evaluate digital information, and understand its reliability. Breen, Aters, and O'Shea (2023) provide information about a similar workshop in Ireland. The authors state that the reason for starting the workshop was the results of Ireland's first National Digital Experience Survey (INDEX) at the end of 2019. This survey revealed that 38% of students in Ireland had the opportunity to review and update their digital skills, prompting consideration of whether the DL skills of the other 62% of students could be developed through the library's workshops. The research shows that 97% found the workshop beneficial. Students prefer YouTube or online resources, with digital learning materials aiding self-directed learning. Live workshops are regarded as dynamic and effective. Participants often seek technical advice from friends or peers, and library workshops enhance their skills and confidence.

Thirdly, research in the literature review has suggested that libraries could organize training sessions to be effective in DL. In fact, libraries conduct a variety of training activities to introduce their services and digital resources to users. Libraries promote their services and enhance users' digital literacy skills through orientation programs, content provider talks, demonstrations, training sessions, announcements, workshops, and focus group studies (Manu & Gala, 2023). However, the factors affecting the success of DL training initiatives must be carefully addressed both before and after the training. Organizing staff for training, training staff, providing sustainable funding for training, reaching users in need of training, scheduling training sessions, developing content, sharing content (identifying best practices), and collecting and evaluating training data are important issues (Detlor & Julien, 2020; Sharpe & Benfield, 2012).

The fourth method is the creation of DL training modules by libraries. For this purpose, libraries can conduct a survey to identify their DL needs, expectations, and the elements that should be included in the training module. This can facilitate the development of an effective training module (Johnston, 2020; Sato, Smeaton & Palmer, 2019). The fifth method is the establishment of digital technology areas within the library. University libraries can create digital technology centers within their own buildings, support functional literacy through these centers, provide access to digital design technologies to enable university users to interact with technology, and offer consultancy for rhetorical and critical literacy to their users (Collins & Crowe, 2021). It helps to reduce digital inequalities by providing all users with access to these facilities and promoting a consistent level of digital literacy within the university. To achieve this, there is a great need among librarians for digital competencies to develop and manage digital content and to stay current in the 21st century information environment (McMahon, 2021; Okeji, Tralagba & Obi, 2019). In this sense, there is a need to train librarians in library schools to take on roles in DL and Open Educational Resources (OER) (Martzoukou, 2021; Popescu, 2019), and to increase and strengthen their self-efficacy in digital changes in the academic community (Deja, Rak & Bell, 2021). Popescu (2019) adds that librarians also need to be knowledgeable about digital publishing, data management, and the availability of high-quality open access resources. Addressing this issue, Kenney (2008) states that librarians are the people who are expected to know the most about technological developments and applications. Kenney (2008) goes on to point out that it is important for librarians to develop competencies in new technological applications in order to be able to teach them to students. For example, Kashif Ali (2022), in his study of library professionals in Pakistan, found that the majority of respondents learned DL skills either on their own or through conferences, workshops, friends and colleagues. Kashif Ali (2022), in his research, lists lack of funding, outdated LIS curricula, challenging working conditions, and lack of support from senior officials as barriers to acquiring digital information literacy skills. Similar studies have been conducted by other authors (Ghosh, & McCoy, 2024; Mulat & Natarajan, 2020; Muzaki, Kaddu & Haumba, 2022).

Studies show that incorporating library use into academic courses is crucial for success in distance learning. These studies examined in detail the importance of libraries integrating information literacy and DL training into the curriculum and how digital learning tools are experienced in these trainings (Kelly, 2019; Skov et al, 2022). With this integration, libraries can add library materials that improve DL and the quality of students' learning outcomes can be positively affected (Killick, 2023). At this point, libraries can take the initiative and include DL in the curriculum together with academic and administrative staff. Thus, they can offer approaches to DL at the level of each scientific education program for learning and teaching at the university and contribute to the university's strategies and standards (Archambault & Masunaga, 2015; Hallam, Amberyn & Beach, 2018; Maharaj et al., 2021). In these collaborative efforts, librarians and lecturers can take a collaborative approach to embed information literacy and other emerging literacies such as DL and artificial intelligence literacy into the university's curriculum for the benefit of the university. Including, planning, and implementing library instruction in all courses to develop DL can be accomplished by librarians in a collaborative approach with faculty (Ford et al., 2015). Yadav and Sharma (2023) reported that 16.28% of the faculty members who participated in their survey agreed that DL programs organized by the library helped them improve their ICT skills.

Academic libraries are in the best position to organize, plan and deliver a university's DL training and should take advantage of it (Breen, Waters & O'Shea, 2023). Libraries have the capability to collaborate with other departments and utilize their available resources to support student engagement. University libraries are well-positioned to lead initiatives in DL at universities and foster the development of digital skills on campus. However, how active are libraries in this regard and are they recognized as a primary resource by their users? For example, a study conducted in the UK found that a low 7% of responses to the question "Where do students go for help with online learning?" were "library staff" (Joint Information Systems Committee [JISC], 2021). Folorunso and Momoh (2022) argue that strategic plans should be developed that include libraries instilling digital skills at all levels of education and for those already in the workforce as a way to reduce unemployment and underemployment and to increase economic self-management and reduce workplace inconvenience. Furthermore, libraries should focus on advocacy (Sato et al., 2019) and promotional activities to persuade decision-makers to include DL training in the curriculum.

In summary, university libraries must be integrated into the curriculum, properly funded and staffed, and actively promote their role in DL to fully support the university's DL and well-being.

The University Rankings and Libraries

The Academic Ranking of World Universities (ARWU), also referred to as the Shanghai Ranking, was initiated in 2003. In 2004, Times Higher Education and Quacquarelli Symonds created the QS-THE Ranking. In 2009, they split and began publishing separate rankings: Times Higher Education World University Rankings and QS (Stack, 2021). These rankings assist parents, students, politicians, investors, and funders in assessing universities and their programs.

In this research, THE World University Rankings was selected due to its status as a widely recognized international ranking. University rankings evaluate institutions based on research quality, graduate employment rates, international reputation, and education standards. These indicators and their ratios are as follows:

- The evaluation rate of the Quality of Scientific Research is 60%,
- The evaluation rate of the graduates' employment rate is 10%,
- International Reputation's evaluation rate 10%
- The evaluation rate of Education Quality is 20% (Saka & Yaman, 2011).

Strong 21st century skills have a great impact on increasing the quality of research, which is the first of these. DL, directly affects scientific research performances by increasing participation in online and face-to-face education (Jaya & Sucipto, 2023). Hannemann, Henn & Schäfer (2023). As discussed extensively in the section on DL in universities, it increases the employment rates of graduates and positively affects the quality of education (Platonova, 2020; Yazıcıoğlu, Yaylak & Genç, 2020). The six components of university reputation are social contributions, physical environments, leadership, funding, research and development, and student guidance (Khoi, 2020). Almost all of THE's criteria are directly affected by university libraries and services. Upon analysis, it can be noted that THE's evaluation ratios influence the use of digital technologies in various teaching and learning areas and students' acquisition of these skills. Furthermore, in a rapidly changing digital environment, university libraries provide a platform for faculty and students to interact with information and communication technologies.

In the research section of this book chapter, the libraries of the top fifty universities in THE World University Rankings 2025 (THE, 2024) - there are 51 universities in the top fifty - were examined between November 15 and December 15, 2024 through DL activities on their websites, technology labs that support DL, subject guides on DL, and DL videos on Youtube. The main challenge of the research was that explicit information was sometimes not identifiable in the collected data.

This data explores the connection between libraries and DL skills at universities. It aims to show how libraries support the university community in developing these skills and presents a model based on successful universities' libraries, highlighting their role in university success.

Table 1 presents the distribution of universities examined in this research, categorized by country.

Table 1. Number of universities by country

Country	n	%
Australia	1	2
Belgium	1	2
Canada	3	5,9
China	4	7,8
France	1	2
Germany	3	5,9
Hong Kong	2	3,9
Japan	1	2
Singapore	2	3,9
Sweden	1	2
Switzerland	2	3
United Kingdom	7	13
United States	23	45
TOTAL	**51**	**100**

Analysis of Table 1 reveals that 45% of the universities in the top fifty rankings are from the United States, followed by the United Kingdom with 13% and China with 7.8%.

Table 2 shares the results regarding whether libraries organize DL workshops or events.

Table 2. Digital literacy workshops & events in the libraries

Country	Number of universities	Yes	No
Australia	1	1	0
Belgium	1	0	1
Canada	3	2	1
China	4	3	1
France	1	0	1
Germany	3	1	2
Hong Kong	2	2	0
Japan	1	0	1
Singapore	2	2	0
Sweden	1	0	1
Switzerland	2	2	0
United Kingdom	7	4	3
United States	23	17	6
TOTAL	**51**	**34**	**17**

Table 2 lists DL workshops and events hosted by libraries. These workshops help users enhance their knowledge and directly engage with universities. Aligning library workshops with student needs can maximize their benefits. Table 2 data indicates that U.S. universities actively promote DL through these activities.

Table 3 shares data on whether libraries have technology laboratories within their own structure.

Table 3. Technology lab in the libraries

Country	n	Yes	No
Australia	1	0	1
Belgium	1	1	0
Canada	3	2	1
China	4	1	3
France	1	0	1
Germany	3	1	2
Hong Kong	2	2	0
Japan	1	0	1
Singapore	2	1	1
Sweden	1	1	0
Switzerland	2	1	1
United Kingdom	7	3	4
United States	23	22	1
TOTAL	**51**	**35**	**16**

Digital literacy is crucial in universities, yet access to technology remains a challenge. University libraries should provide accessible technology and offer training sessions with expert staff to ensure effective use. Table 3 shows that the

United States has the most university library technology laboratories (n=22). Some universities also place technology laboratories outside their libraries.

Table 4 aims to show whether libraries organize training related to DL.

Table 4. Digital literacy related trainings in the library

Country	n	Yes	No
Australia	1	0	1
Belgium	1	0	1
Canada	3	3	0
China	4	3	1
France	1	1	0
Germany	3	1	2
Hong Kong	2	2	0
Japan	1	0	1
Singapore	2	1	1
Sweden	1	0	1
Switzerland	2	1	1
United Kingdom	7	4	3
United States	23	18	5
TOTAL	**51**	**34**	**17**

Universities train students, faculty, and staff on technology tools, with libraries playing a key role. Libraries offer training on technology, tools, and applications to support their university's mission. They help users develop digital literacy skills, teach ethical use of information resources, and demonstrate effective working skills using technology. As seen in Table 4, the majority (n=34) of the (n=51) university libraries (n=34) organized trainings on these topics.

Table 5 shows whether the libraries have videos related to DL.

Table 5. Number of library subject guides on digital literacy

Country	n	Yes	No
Australia	1	1	0
Belgium	1	1	0
Canada	3	3	0
China	4	2	2
France	1	1	0
Germany	3	1	2
Hong Kong	2	2	0
Japan	1	0	1
Singapore	2	2	0
Sweden	1	1	0
Switzerland	2	2	0
United Kingdom	7	5	2
United States	23	19	4
TOTAL	**51**	**40**	**11**

Libraries create subject guides on their websites to help users find the relevant resources quickly. This allows users to efficiently access information related to their interests in a rapidly changing environment. Such guides can help users easily find the information, resources and tools necessary for their research in a simple and visual layout. This reduces users' cognitive load, time loss, and encourages them to use library resources (Liu, 2020). Table 5 shows that the vast majority of libraries (n=40) include subject guides that directly or indirectly include DL on their websites.

Table 6 presents data on the availability of YouTube videos related to DL in libraries.

Table 6. Digital literacy YouTube videos prepared by university library

Country	n	Yes	No
Australia	1	0	1
Belgium	1	0	1
Canada	3	1	2
China	4	0	4
France	1	0	1
Germany	3	2	1
Hong Kong	2	1	1
Japan	1	0	1
Singapore	2	2	0
Sweden	1	0	1
Switzerland	2	1	1
United Kingdom	7	1	6
United States	23	16	7
TOTAL	**51**	**24**	**27**

Since its launch in 2005, YouTube offers a range of educational and entertainment videos. Universities use YouTube to help students engage with course material, improve comprehension, access diverse resources, enhance education through visuals, increase focus and information retention, boost student engagement, develop skills, cater to various learning needs, and provide varied educational content (Fleck et al., 2014). Kristiawan et al. (2023) state that YouTube can be used to improve technological skills. Libraries utilize YouTube as an educational tool due to its various benefits. This study found that the rates of YouTube use (n=24) and non-use (n=27) for developing digital literacies in libraries were similar. Table 6 presents the data.

University libraries enhance digital literacy through activities, training programs, subject guides, YouTube videos, and technology labs. Figure 1 shows that these efforts support digital literacy, positively impacting student academic achievement, career prospects, satisfaction, confidence for entrepreneurship, and overall university success.

Figure 1. The model showing that university libraries support digital literacy in universities

CONCLUSION

Technology, computers and the internet have become a central part of daily life in all areas, especially in education. This means that DL has become a necessity for everyone to learn in order to keep up with the ever-changing world. Digital technology and DL are changing and transforming the educational environment, resources and employees, who are increasingly moving from there to digital (Okoye et al., 2023).

Universities are enhancing DL skills for students and faculty. DL is crucial for university students, positively influencing academic success, satisfaction, career prospects, self-confidence in entrepreneurship, and intentions towards digital or internet entrepreneurship.

In universities, teaching DL improves students' ability to conduct research, collaborate and interact with various multimedia resources (Chaudhary et al., 2024). The research highlighted the need to develop DL skills among university faculty members. Enhancing these skills can make learning more effective and efficient for educators. Research shows that integrating DL into university programs is essential. Adding it to teaching practices will enhance its effective use in academia. In the integration of DL trainings into curriculum activities; it would be appropriate to address it in different ways such as determining common learning objectives, preparing common digital courses, workshops, subject librarians and including it in assignments to develop DL skills. Otherwise, it will be difficult to ensure the quality of education and academic success (Berber, Deveciyan, & Alay, 2023).

University libraries can contribute to the development of DL through their co-operation with other units, accessibility, technological infrastructure, and trained staff. Libraries can enhance DL by offering workshops, events, training sessions, credit courses, DL subject guides, YouTube instructional videos, and technology labs within their facilities. Moreover, incorporating innovative methods such as game-based learning can effectively improve DL, supplementing traditional educational approaches. For example, Kasperski and Ben-Yehudah (2024) report that in their study comparing traditional print-based education with digital-based education, they found that survey participant students in the digital group had better performance in both reading and writing. These will increase interest in libraries' services for DL and research. In addition, digital technologies in the field of education enable traditional learning to be strengthened and education to be personalized (Platonova et al., 2020).

This research highlights the need for universities to enhance DL, not just for students but also for faculty, library staff, and other employees. In universities, it has been revealed that basic studies and research to improve DL identification of needs, and a planned DL education will be more effective. University libraries are ideal for DL training and services. They can address DL gaps by being involved in all processes, including curricula. University libraries should effectively support students' learning and help them gain digital skills. This involves evolving DL to equip the next generation with necessary competences. In particular, in the context of DL education, the constant evolution of digital learning tools makes it imperative to keep a close eye on their future state and design. University libraries adapt to students' changing learning and research methods. They aim to meet the digital skills needs of the university community but need financial, human, and technical support. Libraries must ensure librarians receive training to effectively manage DL programs.

This study explores how university libraries can support digital technologies and literacy amidst evolving missions. It emphasizes the importance for students and service providers to embrace DL despite challenges. This book chapter aims to assist those interested in the role of university libraries in DL.

REFERENCES

Abdel-Al, H. A.-Z., & Abdel-Al, A. B. (2022). Scientific research skills in the digital environment: A case study of faculty members at King Khalid University and Northern Border University (Kingdom of Saudi Arabia). *REMAH Journal*, *71*, 317–346.

Adetimirin, A. E. (2011). ICT Literacy among Undergraduates in Nigerian Universities. *Education and Information Technologies*, *17*(4), 381–397. DOI: 10.1007/s10639-011-9163-y

Ahmed, S. T., & Roche, T. (2021). Making the connection: Examining the relationship between undergraduate students' digital literacy and academic success in an English medium instruction (EMI) university. *Education and Information Technologies*, *26*(4), 4601–4620. DOI: 10.1007/s10639-021-10443-0

Ali, K. (2022). Digital Information Literacy Skills among Library and Information Science Professionals in University Libraries of Sindh Pakistan. *Journal of Information Management and Practices*, *2*(1), 41–61. DOI: 10.52461/jimp.v2i1.1035

Alonso García, S., Victoria Maldonado, J., Martínez Domingo, J., & Berral Ortiz, B. (2024). Analysis of self-perceived digital competences in future educators: A study at the university of Granada. *Journal of Technology and Science Education*, *14*(1), 4–15. DOI: 10.3926/jotse.2521

American Library Association Office for Information Technology Policy. Digital Literacy Task Force (2013). *Digital literacy, libraries, and public policy: Report of the Office for Information Technology Policy's Digital Literacy Task Force*. https://alair.ala.org/server/api/core/bitstreams/db72e923-1e14-45b8-ab0e-b113241c0e4c/content

Anthony, W., Levine-Brown, P., Fynn, N., Gadzekpo, P., & Spinks, M. (2020). Technology Considerations and Opportunities in Higher Education. *Journal Of College Academic Support Programs*, *3*(1), 31–42. DOI: 10.36896/3.1sppfa1

Archambault, G. S., & Masunaga, J. (2015). Curriculum mapping as a strategic planning tool. *Journal of Library Administration*, *55*(6), 503–519. DOI: 10.1080/01930826.2015.1054770

Arnaud, J., Mamede, H. S., & Branco, F. (2024). The relationship between digital transformation and digital literacy - an explanatory model: Systematic literature review. *F1000 Research*, *13*, 252–285. DOI: 10.12688/f1000research.146991.1

Barak, M., & Levenberg, A. (2016). Flexible thinking in learning: An individual differences measure for learning in technologyenhanced environments. *Computers & Education*, *99*, 39–52. DOI: 10.1016/j.compedu.2016.04.003

Bayrakdaroğlu, F., & Bayrakdaroğlu, A. (2017). A Comparative Analysis Regarding The Effect of Financial Literacy and Digital Literay on Internet Entrepreneurship Intention. *Journal of Entrepreneurship and Development.*, *12*(2), 27–38.

Bejaković, P., & Mrnjavac, Ž. (2020). The importance of digital literacy on the labour market. *Employee Relations*, *42*(4), 921–932. DOI: 10.1108/ER-07-2019-0274

Berber, Ş., Devecíyan, M. T., & Alay, H. K. (2023). Digital Literacy Level and Career Satisfaction of Academics. *Itobiad: Journal of the Human & Social Science Researches / İnsan ve Toplum Bilimleri Araştırmaları Dergisi, 12*(4), 2363–2387. https://doi.org/DOI: 10.15869/itobiad.1343893

Blayone, T. (2018). Reexamining digital-learning readiness in higher education: Positioning digital competencies as key factors and a profile application as a readiness tool. *International Journal on E-Learning*, *17*(4), 425–451.

Bond, M., Buntins, K., Bedenlier, S., Zawacki-Richter, 0. & Kerres, M. (2020). Mapping research in student engagement and educational technology in higher education: A systematic evidence map. *International Journal of Technology in Higher Education, 17*(2). https://doi.org/ 9-0176-8DOI: 10. 1 186/s41239-01

Breen, M., Waters, J., & O'Shea, L. (2023). Taking a Lead on Digital Literacy for Students—A Case Study from the Library at the University of Limerick. *New Review of Academic Librarianship*, *29*(1), 11–32. DOI: 10.1080/13614533.2022.2039243

Buckingham, D. (2015). Defining digital literacy - What do young people need to know about digital media? *Nordic Journal of Digital Literacy*, *10*(Jubileumsnummer), 21–35. DOI: 10.18261/ISSN1891-943X-2015-Jubileumsnummer-03

Canina, L., & Orero-Blat, M. (2021). A practical tool to measure digital competences: Teamschamp. *International Journal of Services Operations and Informatics*, *11*(1), 1–12. DOI: 10.1504/IJSOI.2021.114107

Canuel, R., MacKenzie, E., Senior, A., & Torabi, N. (2017). Apps for academic success: Developing digital literacy and awareness to increase usage. *Education for Information*, *33*(3), 135–152. DOI: 10.3233/EFI-160085

Cham, K. M., Edwards, M.-L., Kruesi, L., Celeste, T., & Hennessey, T. (2022). Digital Preferences and Perceptions of Students in Health Professional Courses at a Leading Australian University: A Baseline for Improving Digital Skills and Competencies in Health Graduates. *Australasian Journal of Educational Technology*, *38*(1), 69–86.

Chandra, J., & Hendayana, Y. (2024). The Influence of Entrepreneurship Education and Digital Literacy in Forming Entrepreneurial Competence. [DIJMS]. *Dinasti International Journal of Management Science*, *5*(6), 1154–1161. DOI: 10.38035/dijms.v5i6.2802

Chaudhary, K. K., Kishore, A., Soni, K., Singh, A. K., & Singh, A. (2024). Assessing The Digital Literacy Skills of Postgraduate Students: A Case Study of Bra Bihar University, Muzaffarpur, Bihar. *Library of Progress-Library Science. Information Technology & Computer*, *44*(3), 20449–20458.

Cintamulya, I., Murtini, I., & Warli, W. (2024). Optimizing Collaboration and Communication Skills of Pre-Service Biology Teachers Based on Cognitive Styles through Scientific Paper Tasks. *Participatory Educational Research*, *11*(6), 262–279. DOI: 10.17275/per.24.89.11.6

Coldwell-Neilson, J., Armitage, J. A., Wood-Bradley, R. J., Kelly, B., & Gentle, A. (2019). Implications of updating digital literacy: A case study in an optometric curriculum. Issues in Informing Science & Information Technology, 16, 33–49 Available at http://iisit.org/Vol16/IISITv16p033-049Coldwell5567. pdf. Accessed 7 Jul 2020.

Collins, A. R., & Crowe, K. (2021). Where do we grow from here? Assessing the perceived impact of a digital media commons on student success. *Performance Measurement and Metrics*, *22*(3), 174–186. DOI: 10.1108/PMM-09-2020-0049

Curtarelli, M., Gualtieri, V., Shater Jannati, M., & Donlevy, V. (2016*). ICT for Work: Digital Skills in the Workplace*, European Commission, Brussels https://op.europa.eu/en/publication-detail/-/publication/7a51fb41-92ad-11e7-b92d-01aa75ed71a1

Deja, M., Rak, D., & Bell, B. (2021). Digital transformation readiness: Perspectives on academia and library outcomes in information literacy. *Journal of Academic Librarianship*, *47*(5), 102403. Advance online publication. DOI: 10.1016/j.acalib.2021.102403

Detlor, B., & Julien, H. (2020). Success factors affecting digital literacy training initiatives led by local community organizations. *Proceedings of the Association for Information Science and Technology*, *57*(1), e331. Advance online publication. DOI: 10.1002/pra2.331

ECDL Foundation. (2014). The Fallacy of the 'Digital Native': Why Young People Need to Develop their Digital Skills. https://ec.europa.eu/futurium/en/system/files/ged/the_fallacy_of_the_digitalnative_-_ecdl_foundation.pdf

EITCI Institute (European Information Technologies Certification Institute). (2017). Digitalskills and jobs coalition. https://eitci.org/digital-skills-and-jobs-coalition

Epifanova, N. S., & Polozkov, M. (2020). Digital literacy as a prerequisite for transforming the modern russian education system. *Public Administration*, *22*(5), 62–66. DOI: 10.22394/2070-8378-2020-22-5-62-66

European Commission. (2019). *Key Competences For Lifelong Learning*. https://op.europa.eu/en/publication-detail/-/publication/297a33c8-a1f3-11e9-9d01-01aa75ed71a1

Farooq, M. U., Ghafoor, A., & Bajwa, M. A. (2022). UAF Library services in VUCA environment: Best practices and lessons learned during COVID-19 pandemic. *Pakistan Library & Information Science Journal*, *53*(2), 5–10.

Ferrari, A. (2013). *DIGCOMP: A Framework for Developing and Understanding Digital Competence in Europe. European Commission, Joint Research Centre and Institute for Prospective Technological Studies*. Publications Office of the European Union.

Ferreira, N., Coetzee, M., & Potgieter, I. L. (2024). Predicting Students' Work World Awareness through Their Readiness and Competency for the Digital World. *Journal of Teaching and Learning for Graduate Employability*, *15*(1), 53–65. DOI: 10.21153/jtlge2024vol15no1art1788

Fitra, J. (2023). Digital Literacy, Academic Self-Efficacy, and Student Engagement: Its Impact on Student Academic Performance in Hybrid Learning. *Journal of Innovation in Educational and Cultural Research*, *4*(3), 458–470. DOI: 10.46843/jiecr.v4i3.719

Fleck, B. K. B., Beckman, L. M., & Sterns, J. L. (2014). YouTube in the Classroom: Helpful Tips and Student Perceptions. *The Journal of Effective Teaching*, *14*(3), 21–37.

Folorunso, L. A., & Momoh, E. O. (2022). Underscoring the Value of Digital Literacy as a Tool for Reducing Unemployment and Enhancing Workplace Productivity. In Asamoah–Hassan, H. (Ed.), *Digital Literacy, Inclusivity and Sustainable Development in Africa* (pp. 146–156). Facet Publishing. DOI: 10.29085/9781783305131.013

Ford, E., Izumi, B., Lottes, J., & Richardson, D. (2015). Badge it!: A collaborative learning outcomes based approach to integrating information literacy badges within disciplinary curriculum. *RSR. Reference Services Review*, *43*(1), 31–44. DOI: 10.1108/RSR-07-2014-0026

Ganefri, W. K., Makky, M., Hidayat, H. & Rahmawati, Y. (2024). Entrepreneurship Education and Entrepreneurial Intention among University Students: The Roles of Entrepreneurial Mindset, Digital Literacy, and Self-Efficacy. *Journal of Social Studies Education Research / Sosyal Bilgiler Eğitimi Araştırmaları Dergisi, 15*(4), 85–134.

Ghosh, S., & McCoy, D. (2024). Looking Ahead: Incorporating AI in MLIS Competencies. [SRJ]. *Student Research Journal, 14*(2), 28–42.

González, P. A. (2023). Digital Literacy in Employability of Graduates during COVID-19: A Qualitative Phenomenological Study. In *ProQuest LLC*.

Green, C. (2020). Digital literacies and the skills of the digital age. In Tutaleni I. Asino (Ed.), *Learning in the Digital Age*. Oklahoma State University Libraries. https://open.library.okstate.edu/learninginthedigitalage/

Greene, J. A., & Crompton, H. (2024). Synthesizing Definitions of Digital Literacy for the Web 3.0. *TechTrends: Linking Research and Practice to Improve LearningA Publication of the Association for Educational Communications & Technology*, 1–17. DOI: 10.1007/s11528-024-01015-3

Hagel, P. (2015). What is good practice in the development, assessment and evaluation of digital literacy for graduate employability? discourse: *Deakin University Library Research And Practice*, No. 2, http://hdl.handle.net/10536/DRO/DU:30073199

Hallam, G., Thomas, A., & Beach, B. (2018). Creating a Connected Future Through Information and Digital Literacy: Strategic Directions at The University of Queensland Library. *Journal of the Australian Library & Information Association, 67*(1), 42–54. DOI: 10.1080/24750158.2018.1426365

Hannemann, M., Henn, S., & Schäfer, S. (2023). Participation in Online Research: Towards a Typology of Research Subjects with Regard to Digital Access and Literacy. *International Journal of Qualitative Methods, 22*, 1–10. DOI: 10.1177/16094069231205188

Huber, E., & Shalavin, C. A. (2018). Surveying the digital literacy landscape for academic and professional staff in higher education. *Senior Deputy Vice-Chancellor and Deputy Vice-Chancellor (Education) - Papers*.

IFLA. (2020, December, 9). Libraries in digital skills policies. https://www.ifla.org/wp-content/uploads/2019/05/assets/hq/topics/info-society/documents/libraries_in_digital_skills_policies.pdf

Ikenwe, I. J., & Aiyebelehin, A. J. (2024). Information Literacy Skills as Predictors of the Use of Digital Library Resources by Academics in Selected Federal Universities in Nigeria. *International Journal of Education and Development Using Information and Communication Technology*, *20*(1), 25–38.

Indah, R. N., Toyyibah, , Budhiningrum, A. S., & Afifi, N. (2022). The Research Competence, Critical Thinking Skills and Digital Literacy of Indonesian EFL Students. *Journal of Language Teaching & Research*, *13*(2), 315–324. DOI: 10.17507/jltr.1302.11

Ip, C. Y. (2024). Effect of digital literacy on social entrepreneurial intentions and nascent behaviours among students and practitioners in mass communication. *Humanities & Social Sciences Communications*, *11*(1), 34. Advance online publication. DOI: 10.1057/s41599-023-02587-w

Jaya, F., & Sucipto, S. (2023). Digital Literacy, Academic Self-Efficacy, and Student Engagement: Its Impact on Student Academic Performance in Hybrid Learning. *Journal of Innovation in Educational and Cultural Research*, *4*(3), 458–470. DOI: 10.46843/jiecr.v4i3.719

JISC. (2021).Student digital experience insights survey 2020/21: UK higher education find-ings.https://repository.jisc.ac.uk/8318/1/DEI-P1-HE-student-briefing-2021-FINAL.pdf

Johnston, N. (2020). The Shift towards Digital Literacy in Australian University Libraries: Developing a Digital Literacy Framework. *Journal of the Australian Library & Information Association*, *69*(1), 93–101. DOI: 10.1080/24750158.2020.1712638

Junco, R. (2012). The relationship between frequency of Facebook use, participation in Facebook activities, and student engagement. *Computers & Education*, *58*(1), 162–171. DOI: 10.1016/j.compedu.2011.08.004

Kammer, J., Cherner, T., & Hays, L. (2021). Digital literacy in the academy. In Hays, L., & Kammer, J. (Eds.), *Integrating Digital Literacy in the Disciplines* (pp. 7–14). Routledge.

Kang, G.-L., Park, C.-W., & Jang, S.-H. (2024). A Study on the Impact of Financial Literacy and Digital Capabilities on Entrepreneurial Intention: Mediating Effect of Entrepreneurship. *Behavioral Sciences (2076-328X)*, *14*(2), 121. DOI: 10.3390/bs14020121

Kasperski, R., & Ben-Yehudah, G. (2024). Developing digital academic skills in preservice teachers: Performance and metacognitive perspectives. *Journal of Education for Teaching*, *50*(4), 613–626. DOI: 10.1080/02607476.2024.2323583

Kelly, B. (2019). Uncovering Digital Literacy and Supporting the Implicit: A Case Study of Library-Faculty Collaboration. *IATUL Annual Conference Proceedings*, 328–336.

Kenney, B. (2008). Leaping into technology. *School Library Journal*, *54*, 11.

Khoi, B. H. (2021). Factors Influencing on University Reputation: Model Selection by AIC. In Ngoc Thach, N., Kreinovich, V., & Trung, N. D. (Eds.), *Data Science for Financial Econometrics. Studies in Computational Intelligence* (Vol. 898). Springer., DOI: 10.1007/978-3-030-48853-6_13

Kight, D. (2021, September 1). Taking the Lead in Digital Literacy Initiatives. *Computers in Libraries*, *41*(7), 14.

Killick, S. (2023). The library's influence and impact on learning: A case study from The Open University (UK). *Asian Association of Open Universities Journal*, *18*(3), 279–291. DOI: 10.1108/AAOUJ-04-2023-0051

Koltay, T. (2011). The media and the literacies: Media literacy, information literacy, digital literacy. *Media Culture & Society*, *33*(2), 211–221. DOI: 10.1177/0163443710393382

Kot, F. C., & Jones, J. L. (2015). The Impact of Library Resource Utilization on Undergraduate Students' Academic Performance: A Propensity Score Matching Design. *College & Research Libraries*, *76*(5), 566–586. DOI: 10.5860/crl.76.5.566

Kristiawan, M., Oka, I. G. A. A. M., Haenilah, E. Y., Wachidi, W., Ediansyah, E., Aprianto, I., Zulinto, A., Perrodin, D. D., & Utama, H. B. (2023). Youtube For Developing Technological Skill. [JAETS]. *Journal of Applied Engineering and Technological Science*, *4*(2), 868–982. DOI: 10.37385/jaets.v4i2.1539

Levine-Clark, M. & Dean, Toni Carter. (2013). *ALA Glossary of Library and Information Science*. ALA Editions.

Li, C., & Chen, F. (2024). Impacts of ICT-related factors on students' digital reading literacy: Evidence from high-performing Asian countries and regions. *Education and Information Technologies*, *29*(13), 16717–16747. DOI: 10.1007/s10639-024-12501-9

Littlejohn, A., Beetham, H., & McGill, L. (2012). Learning at the digital frontier: A review of digital literacies in theory and practice. *Journal of Computer Assisted Learning*, *28*(6), 547–556. DOI: 10.1111/j.1365-2729.2011.00474.x

Liu, W. (2020). Knowledge map: A creative visual path to library guides and resources. *The Electronic Library*, *38*(5/6), 943–962. DOI: 10.1108/EL-03-2020-0055

Liza, K., & Andriyanti, E. (2020). Digital literacy scale of English pre-service teachers and their perceived readiness toward the application of digital technologies. [EduLearn]. *J.Educ Learn, 14*(1), 74–79. DOI: 10.11591/edulearn.v14i1.13925

Lo Presti, V. (2023). The social impact of distance learning in Roman schools: "Success," social innovation, teaching practices. *Frontiers in Sociology, 8*, 1141435. Advance online publication. DOI: 10.3389/fsoc.2023.1141435 PMID: 37091726

Lopez, J. R. (2013). *Digital literacy and academic success in online education for underprivileged communities: The prep@ net case* [Phd Dissertations]. The University of Texas at Austin.

Lu, Y., & Khan, M. S. (2024). Influence of Higher Education E-Service Quality on E-Learning Student Satisfaction; as Moderated by Digital Literacy: A Mixed Method Research Approach. *Revista de Gestao Social e Ambiental, 18*(1), e06077. Advance online publication. DOI: 10.24857/rgsa.v18n1-112

Maguire, D., Dale, L., & Pauli, M. (2020). Learning and teaching reimagined: a new dawn for higher education? Bristol: JISC. Retrieved 21 February, 2021, from https://repository.jisc.ac.uk/8150/1/learning-and-teaching-reimagined-a-new-dawn-for-higher-education.pdf

Maharaj, N. G. M., Kanadia, P. K., Dr., & Tandel, R. J., Dr. (2021). Digital Information Literacy among the Faculty Members of Gujarat Adani Institute of Medical Sciences. *Library Philosophy and Practice (e-Journal).*

Manu, T. R., & Gala, B. (2023). Gamification for Digital Humanities in Libraries: A Survey of the Web-based Games on Digital Literacy. *DESIDOC Journal of Library and Information Technology, 43*(4), 241–248. DOI: 10.14429/djlit.43.04.19259

Martínez-Bravo, M. C., Chalezquer, C. S., & Serrano-Puche, J. (2022). Dimensions of digital literacy in the 21st century competency frameworks. *Sustainability (Basel), 14*(3), 1867–1880. DOI: 10.3390/su14031867

Martzoukou, K. (2021). Academic libraries in COVID-19: A renewed mission for digital lit-eracy. *Library Management, 42*(4/5), 266–276. DOI: 10.1108/LM-09-2020-0131

Masterman, E., & Shuyska, J. A. (2011). Digitally mastered? Technology and transition in the experience of taught postgraduate students. *Learning, Media and Technology, 37*(4), 335–354. DOI: 10.1080/17439884.2011.608361

Mavutha, W., & Mabotja, T. (2024). Digital literacy: A foreign language for students from rural areas in South Africa. *International Journal of Research in Business & Social Science, 13*(5), 784–793. DOI: 10.20525/ijrbs.v13i5.3315

Maxwell, L. (2020). Digital Literacy and Digital Legacy. *Library Technology Reports*, *56*(5), 7–11.

McLeod, A., & Torres, L. (2020). Enhancing first year university students'digital skills withthe Digital Skill Development (DSD) framework. In D. Schmidt-Crawford (Ed.),*Proceeding of society for information technology and teacher education international con-ference*(pp. 373–379). Waynesville, NC: Association for the Advancement of Computingin Education (AACE). https://researchmgt.monash.edu/ws/portalfiles/portal/332253378/329859476.pdf

McMahon, M. (2021). *Social Aspects of Technology in Education*. Salem Press Encyclopedia.

Meridha, J. M. (2024). The causes of poor digital literacy in educational practice, and possible solutions among the stakeholders: A systematic literature review. *SN Social Sciences*, *4*(11), 210. Advance online publication. DOI: 10.1007/s43545-024-01010-8

Migliorino, P. (2011). Digital technologies can unite but also divide: CALD communities in the digital age. *Australasian Public Libraries and Information Services*, *24*(3), 107–110.

Miliou, O., & Angeli, C. (2023). *The Impact of a Project-Based Learning Environment on the Development of Undergraduate Students' Digital Literacy Skills*. https://www.learntechlib.org/primary/p/224350/

Mokhtari, F. (2023). Fostering Digital Literacy in Higher Education: Benefits, Challenges and Implications. *International Journal of Linguistics. Literature and Translation*, *6*(10), 160–167. DOI: 10.32996/ijllt.2023.6.10.19

Montenegro-Rueda, M., & Fernández-Batanero, J. M. (2022). Digital Competence of Special Education Teachers: Impact, Challenges and Opportunities. *Australasian Journal of Special and Inclusive Education*, *46*(2), 178–192. DOI: 10.1017/jsi.2022.8

Mudasih, I., & Subroto, W. T., & Susanti. (2021). The Effect of Financial Literacy, Digital Literacy, and Entrepreneurial Learning Outcome on Entrepreneur Behavior of Students at SMK Negeri 1 Surabaya. *Technium Social Sciences Journal*, *15*, 303–320.

Mulat, T., & Natarajan, M. (2020). Digital Literacy Skills among Library Professionals in Jimma University Libraries. *Library Philosophy and Practice (e-Journal)*.

Murray, M., Pérez, J., & Fluker, J. (2022). Digital Literacy in the Core: The Emerging Higher Education Landscape. *Issues in Informing Science & Information Technology*, *19*, 1–13. DOI: 10.28945/4957

Musa, N., Hamid, N. A., & Ishak, M. S. (2021). Understanding the Trends of Digital Literacy Among Islamic Students (Positive Internet Analysis Study). *DAYAH: Journal of Islamic Education*, *4*(2), 141–158. DOI: 10.22373/jie.v4i2.10360

Muzaki, F., Kaddu, S., & Haumba, E. N. (2022). Digital Literacy Skills Investigation among Third-Year Bachelor of Library and Information Science Students of Makerere University. In Asamoah–Hassan, H. (Ed.), *Digital Literacy, Inclusivity and Sustainable Development in Africa* (pp. 106–119). Facet Publishing. DOI: 10.29085/9781783305131.009

Nagari, P. M., Sahid, S., & Hussin, M. (2023). Critical Success Factors for Enhancing Digital Literacy Among Undergraduate Students. *Pegem Journal of Education & Instruction / Pegem. Egitim ve Ögretim*, *13*(4), 249–259. DOI: 10.47750/pegegog.13.04.30

National Skill Coalition. (2023, February 6). *New Report: 92% of Jobs Require Digital Skills, One-Third of Workers Have Low or No Digital Skills Due to Historic Underinvestment, Structural Inequities.* https://nationalskillscoalition.org/news/press-releases/new-report-92-of-jobs-require-digital-skills-one-third-of-workers-have-low-or-no-digital-skills-due-to-historic-underinvestment-structural-inequities/

Naz, F. L., Raheem, A., Khan, F. U., & Muhammad, W. (2022). An effect of digital literacy on the academic performance of University-Level students. *Journal of Positive School Psychology*, *6*(8), 10720–10732.

New Media Consortium. (2016). *Digital Literacy in Higher Education, Part II: An NMC Horizon Project Strategic Brief*https://www.nmc.org/publication/digital-literacy-an-nmc-horizon-project-strategic-brief/

New Media Consortium (NMC). (2017). 2017 Digital Literacy Impact Study. *An NMC Horizon Project Strategic Brief.*, *3*, 5.

Ng, D. T. K., Xinyu, C., Leung, J. K. L., & Chu, S. K. W. (2024). Fostering students' AI literacy development through educational games: AI knowledge, affective and cognitive engagement. *Journal of Computer Assisted Learning*, *40*(5), 2049–2064. DOI: 10.1111/jcal.13009

Novak, N., Rabiee, M., & Tjoa, A. (2018). Head in the Clouds: An Initiative for Digital Learning among Roma Communities in Europe, *Proceedings of the 10th International Conference on Computer Supported Education*, https://doi.org/DOI: 10.5220/0006806803840390

Obeidat, O. A. (2017). The Role of Knowledge Stations in Bridging the Digital Information Literacy in Jordan. *Dirasat: Educational Sciences*, *44*(1), 339–358. DOI: 10.12816/0039833

Odubiyi, T. B., Aigbavboa, C. O., & Thwala, W. D. (2021). A Concise Review of the Evolution of Information and Communication Technologies For Engineering Innovations. *IOP Conf. Series: Materials Science and Engineering, 1107*, https://doi:DOI: 10.1088/1757-899X/1107/1/012231

Okeji, C. C., Tralagba, E. C., & Obi, I. C. (2020). An investigation of the digital literacy skills and knowledge-based competencies among librarians working in university libraries in Nigeria. *Global Knowledge, Memory and Communication*, *69*(4/5), 311–330. DOI: 10.1108/GKMC-05-2019-0054

Okoye, K., Hussein, H., Arrona-Palacios, A., Quintero, H. N., Ortega, L. O. P., Sanchez, A. L., Ortiz, E. A., Escamilla, J., & Hosseini, S. (2023). Impact of digital technologies upon teaching and learning in higher education in Latin America: An outlook on the reach, barriers, and bottlenecks. *Education and Information Technologies*, *28*(2), 2291–2360. DOI: 10.1007/s10639-022-11214-1 PMID: 35992366

Oliver, B., & Jorre de St Jorre, T. (2018). Graduate attributes for 2020 and beyond: Recommendations for Australian higher education providers. *Higher Education Research & Development*, *37*(4), 1–16. DOI: 10.1080/07294360.2018.1446415

Pascarella, E. T., & Terenzini, P. T. (2005). *How college affects students: a third decade of research* (Vol. 2). Jossey-Bass.

Paul, H. W., & Crowe, M. M. (2023). Digital Literacy Inequities, Higher Education, and the New Digital Divide. *International Journal of Intelligent Computing Research*, *14*(1), 1177–1180. DOI: 10.20533/ijicr.2042.4655.2023.0144

Platonova, R. I., Gabarova, K. V., Olesova, M. M., Platonova, A. Z., Storozheva, N. N., & Evseeva, M. M. (2020). Digital technologies in educational environment. *EurAsian Journal of Biosciences*, *14*(2), 5441–5444.

Popescu, E. (2019). Accessibility of the Digital Scientific Literature – A Study on Researchers' Perspective. *ELearning & Software for Education, 2*, 479–486. https://doi.org/DOI: 10.12753/2066-026X-19-136

Prabawati, S. (2019). Pengaruh efikasi diri, pendidikan kewirausahaan, literasi keuangan dan literasi digital terhadap perilaku berwirausaha siswa SMK Negeri 10 Surabaya. *Jurnal pendidikan akuntansi,* [The influence of self-efficacy, entrepreneurship education, financial literacy and digital literacy on entrepreneurial behavior of students of SMK Negeri 10 Surabaya. Journal of accounting education]. 7(1), 64-76

Rafi, M., JianMing, Z., & Ahmad, K. (2019). Technology integration for students' information and digital literacy education in academic libraries. *Information Discovery and Delivery, 47*(4), 203–217. DOI: 10.1108/IDD-07-2019-0049

Rakib, M., Azis, M., Najib, M., & Isma, A. (2024). Impact of Digital Literacy, Business Innovation, Competitive Advantage on the Existence of SMEs: A quantitative study in Makassar City, Indonesia. *Quality - Access to Success, 25*(198), 277–283. DOI: 10.47750/QAS/25.198.30

Rodríguez, U.; Cantabrana, L. & Gisbert, J. (2021). Validation of a tool for self-evaluating teacher digital competence. Educación XX1, 24(1), 353-373. https://doi.org/DOI: 10.5944/educxx1.27080

Ruddy, C., & Ponte, F. (2019). Preparing students for university studies and beyond: A micro-credential trial that delivers academic integrity awareness. *Journal of the Australian Library & Information Association, 68*(1), 56–67. DOI: 10.1080/24750158.2018.1562520

Saka, Y., & Yaman, S. (2011). Üniversite sıralama sistemleri; kriterler ve yapılan eleştiriler. *Yükseköğretim ve Bilim Dergisi*, [University ranking systems; criteria and criticisms. Higher Education and Science Journal]. *1*(2), 72–79.

Salaber, J. (2014). Facilitating student engagement and collaboration in a large post-graduate course using wiki-based activities. *International Journal of Management Education, 12*(2), 115–126. DOI: 10.1016/j.ijme.2014.03.006

Salsabila, F. (2019). Pengaruh Literasi Ekonomi dan Literasi Digital terhadap Perilaku Berwirausaha Sektor Kuliner yang terdaftar pada aplikasi Go-Food Di Pasar Segar Kota Makassar. *Eprints Universitas Negeri Makassar.* Diunduh dari. [The Influence of Economic Literacy and Digital Literacy on Entrepreneurial Behavior in the Culinary Sector Registered on the Go-Food Application at Pasar Segar, Makassar City. Eprints, Makassar State University. Downloaded from]. https://eprints.unm.ac.id/id/eprint/14271

Sanka, A. I., Wong, J., Liu, C., Hung, P., & Cheung, R. C. C. (2024). *Building a Learner-Centric Citywide Digital Literacy Ecosystem: Train-the-Trainer, Community-Based Learning, and Gifted Education : A Guide for Educators, Policymakers, and Stakeholders* (Vol. 14797). Springer Nature Singapore., DOI: 10.1007/978-981-97-4442-8_1

Sato, M., Smeaton, K., & Palmer, T. (2019). What's Up, Doc?: Selling Digital Literacy to Academics. *IATUL Annual Conference Proceedings*, 162–177.

Schmidt, L. J., & DeSchryver, M. (2022). The role of digital application literacy in online assessment. *Journal of Educational Technology Systems, 50*(3), 356–378. DOI: 10.1177/00472395211052644

Šević, N. P., & Dobrilović, M., P., M. I., & Ranković, M. (2021). Serbian Rural Neet Youth Inclusion through the Development of Digital Entrepreneurial Competences and Digital Entrepreneurship. *Proceedings of the International May Conference on Strategic Management, 17*(1), 75–84.

Sharpe, R., & Benfield, G. (2012). Institutional strategies for supporting learners in a digital age. *Enhancing Learning in the Social Sciences, 4*(2), 1–17. DOI: 10.11120/elss.2012.04020004

Skov, M., Svarre, T., & Lykke, M. (2022). *Student experience of digital learning tools: information literacy training in higher education*. https://doi.org/DOI: 10.18452/25257

Soltovets, E., Chigisheva, O., & Dmitrova, A. (2020). The Role of Mentoring in Digital Literacy Development of Doctoral Students at British Universities. *Eurasia Journal of Mathematics, Science and Technology Education, 16*(4). Advance online publication. DOI: 10.29333/ejmste/117782

Soria, K. M., Fransen, J., & Nackerud, S. (2017). The Impact of Academic Library Resources on Undergraduates' Degree Completion. *College & Research Libraries, 78*(6), 812–823. DOI: 10.5860/crl.78.6.812

Sousa-Zomer, T. T., Neely, A., & Martinez, V.Sousa-Zomer. (2020). Neely, & Martinez, V. (2020). Digital transforming capability and performance: A microfoundational perspective. *International Journal of Operations & Production Management, 40*(7/8), 1095–1128. DOI: 10.1108/IJOPM-06-2019-0444

Stack, M. (2021). *Global University Rankings and the Politics of Knowledge*. University of Toronto Press. DOI: 10.3138/9781487545154

Techataweewan, W., & Prasertsin, U. (2018). Development of digital literacy indicators for Thai undergraduate students using mixed method research. *Kasetsart Journal of Social Sciences, 39*(2), 215–221. DOI: 10.1016/j.kjss.2017.07.001

Tekin, E. (2024). E-Öğrenmeye Yatkınlığın Akademik Performansa Etkisinde Dijital Okuryazarlığın Düzenleyici Rolü: Geleceğin Öğretmenleri Üzerine Bir Araştırma. *Itobiad: Journal of the Human & Social Science Researches / İnsan ve Toplum Bilimleri Araştırmaları Dergisi, [The Moderating Role of Digital Literacy in the Effect of E-Learning Approach on Academic Performance: A Study on Future Teachers. Itobiad: Journal of the Human & Social Science Researches]. 13*(4), 54–77. https://doi.org/DOI: 10.15869/itobiad.1522652

Tenya, A. N., Maina, J. C., & Awuor, F. M. (2024). *Digital literacy as a tool for enhancing access and utilization of information in digital resource platforms among academic staff in uiiversity libraries.*

THE. (2024). *World University Rankings 2025*. THE. Retrieved December 15, 2024, from https://www.timeshighereducation.com/world-university-rankings/latest/world-ranking

Thorpe, A., Lukes, R., Bever, D. J., & He, Y. (2016). The Impact of the Academic Library on Student Success: Connecting the Dots. *Portal (Baltimore, Md.)*, *16*(2), 373–392. DOI: 10.1353/pla.2016.0027

Tuamsuk, K., & Subramaniam, M. (2017). The current state and influential factors in the development of digital literacy in Thailand's higher education. *Information and Learning Science*, *118*(5/6), 235–251. DOI: 10.1108/ILS-11-2016-0076

Vodă, A. I., Cautisanu, C., Grădinaru, C., Tănăsescu, C., & de Moraes, G. H. S. M. (2022). Exploring Digital Literacy Skills in Economics and Social Sciences and Humanities Students. *Sustainability (Basel)*, *14*(5), 1–31. DOI: 10.3390/su14052483

Vuorikari, R. Punie, Y., Carretero Gomez S., & Van den Brande, G. (2016). *DigComp 2.0: The digital competence framework for citi:ens. Update phase 1: The conceptual reference model* (EUR 27948EN). *European Union*. Advance online publication. DOI: 10.2791/11517

Wells, K. (2011). Social media in medical school education. *Surgery*, *150*(1), 2–4. DOI: 10.1016/j.surg.2011.05.023 PMID: 21683853

Westberg, D., & Mickevičius, G. (2021). *Clearing the fog from the definition of Digital Literacy : A study investigating what it means to be digitally literate and if students at Jönköping University meet these requirements* (Dissertation). Retrieved from https://urn.kb.se/resolve?urn=urn:nbn:se:hj:diva-53252

World Bank. (2019) The Changing Nature of Work, https://www.worldbank.org/en/publication/wdr2019

Xiong, Y., & Yu, J. (2024). Research on Strategies to Improve Digital Literacy of College Students to Enhance Employment Quality in the Intelligent Era. *Applied Mathematics and* Yadav, S., & Sharma, S. (2023). Digital Literacy Awareness among Research Scholars of Maharishi Dayanand University, Rohtak: A Study. *International Journal of Information Dissemination & Technology*, *13*(2), 60–64. DOI: 10.5958/2249-5576.2023.00012.2

Yazıcıoğlu, A., Yaylak, E., & Genç, G. (2020). Okulöncesi ve Sınıf Öğretmen Adaylarının Dijital Okuryazarlık Düzeyleri. *Journal of Social Sciences Research / Sosyal Bilimler Araştırmaları Dergisi, 10*(2), 274–286.

Yeste, M. G., Pettersson, K., & Svensson, A. (2016). Integrating Reference Practices and Information Literacy in Academic Writing: A Collaboration Between Faculty and Library. *Nordic Journal of Information Literacy in Higher Education*, *8*(1). Advance online publication. DOI: 10.15845/noril.v8i1.245

Zahra, S., Sapienza, H. J., & Davidsson, P. (2006). H. J. & Davidsson, P., (2006). Entrepreneurship and dynamic capabilities: A review, model and research agenda. *Journal of Management Studies*, *43*(4), 917–955. DOI: 10.1111/j.1467-6486.2006.00616.x

Zhao, Y., Lei, J., Yan, B., Lai, C., & Tan, H. S. (2005). What makes the difference? A practical analysis of research on the effectiveness of distance education. *Teachers College Record, 107*(8), 1836–1884. . 1467- 9620. 2005. 00544.DOI: 10. 1111/j

Zhenyan, L. (2023). Keep Calm and Read Laterally! A Bite-sized Information Literacy Programme at Singapore Management University (SMU) Libraries. *Singapore Journal of Library & Information Management*, *49*, 26–31.

Chapter 9
The Role of Massive Open Online Courses (MOOCs) in Bridging Digital Literacy Gaps in Higher Education and Workforce Readiness in India

Swapna Rose
https://orcid.org/0000-0003-0443-2065
St. Aloysius University, India

B. Nakhatra
St. Aloysius University, India

ABSTRACT

The chapter explores the pivotal role of Massive Open Online Courses (MOOCs) in addressing the digital literacy gap in India, focusing on their potential to enhance both higher education and workforce readiness. Despite India's strides toward becoming a digital economy, disparities between urban and rural digital literacy rates remain significant, with MOOCs providing a scalable and flexible solution to bridge this gap. The chapter highlights how MOOCs, with their open-access model, can democratize education, offering cost-effective and accessible learning options to students from diverse backgrounds. Furthermore, MOOCs align with industry needs by offering up-to-date training in high-demand fields, making them a key tool in preparing students for a rapidly evolving job market. However, the chapter also acknowledges the challenges of MOOC adoption, such as infrastructure limitations

DOI: 10.4018/979-8-3373-0004-7.ch009

and language barriers, and calls for further investment in digital infrastructure and the inclusion of regional languages to maximize their impact.

INTRODUCTION

India is on the cusp of a digital transformation that holds the promise of accelerating its growth as a global economic powerhouse. The country's ambitious goal of becoming a $1 trillion digital economy by 2025 has sparked numerous initiatives to harness the potential of technology across various sectors (Press Information Bureau, 2019). However, this journey is fraught with challenges, particularly in addressing the significant digital literacy gap that exists between urban and rural areas. According to recent reports, urban regions in India report a digital literacy rate of 61%, a stark contrast to the 25% reported in rural areas (Chakravorty & Bedi, 2020). This divide presents a formidable obstacle to the nation's goal of widespread economic growth and inclusion. In an era where technology permeates every aspect of life, from education to healthcare to employment, this gap poses a serious risk to equitable progress. For India to truly become a digital economy, it is imperative to create inclusive strategies that bridge the divide and equip all segments of society with the skills needed to thrive in a digital world.

One of the most effective tools to address this challenge is the growing prominence of Massive Open Online Courses (MOOC). MOOCs have emerged as a powerful means of democratizing education, especially in a country like India, where access to quality education is often limited by geographical, economic, and infrastructural constraints. The transformative potential of MOOCs lies not only in their ability to address the digital literacy gap but also in their capacity to offer a scalable, flexible, and cost-effective alternative to traditional education. In a rapidly changing world, the flexibility of online education allows students from all walks of life to access resources that were once out of reach. With internet access becoming more widespread, particularly through affordable mobile data plans, MOOCs are poised to revolutionize education by making learning opportunities available to anyone, anywhere, at any time.

The traditional education system in India faces several limitations that hinder its ability to cater to the diverse needs of the population. While the country boasts one of the largest higher education systems in the world, it is also affected by challenges such as inadequate infrastructure, high student-to-teacher ratios, and limited access to specialized knowledge (Child Rights and You [CRY], n.d.). Rural areas, in particular, are disproportionately affected by these issues, as educational institutions in these regions often lack the resources necessary to provide a high-quality learning experience. MOOCs, by offering online courses from prestigious global institutions, can bypass these barriers, bringing world-class education directly to students, regardless of their location. This creates a unique opportunity to bridge the rural-urban divide, ensuring that students in underserved regions are not left behind in the race for knowledge and skills that are critical for success in a digital economy.

In addition to providing academic knowledge, MOOCs also play a crucial role in fostering a culture of lifelong learning. In a world where the pace of technological advancement is accelerating, the ability to continuously learn and adapt is becoming increasingly important. MOOCs offer a flexible, accessible way for individuals of all ages and backgrounds to continue their education throughout their lives. Whether it's a student looking to enhance their degree with additional skills, a working professional seeking to stay current in their field, or an individual exploring a completely new area of interest, MOOCs provide an ideal platform for continuous skill development. This flexibility is especially important in India, where many learners have varying schedules, commitments, and access to resources (BSSS Publications, n.d.). With MOOCs, they can tailor their learning experience to fit their individual needs and circumstances.

Moreover, MOOCs can cater to a wide range of learners, including working professionals, who are increasingly seeking opportunities to up skill and reskill, themselves to stay competitive in a fast-evolving job market. In India, where the workforce is rapidly shifting toward technology-driven sectors, there is a growing demand for skilled workers in fields such as artificial intelligence, data science, and cyber security. Unfortunately, traditional educational institutions often struggle to keep pace with the rapidly changing needs of the workforce, leaving many workers without the necessary skills to succeed in the professional fields. (WorldatWork, 2019).MOOCs can fill this gap by providing up-to-date, industry-relevant courses that prepare individuals for the demands of the modern job market. One such initiative is Infosys Springboard, a digital learning platform designed to equip students with essential digital and life skills (Infosys, n.d.). Infosys Springboard has actively collaborated with higher education institutions across India to enhance students' job readiness by integrating industry-aligned digital learning resources into university curricula. For instance, in March 2024, Alliance University signed a Memorandum of Understanding (MoU) with Infosys Springboard to provide students access to a range of digital courses and training programs designed to bridge the gap between academic learning and industry requirements (Alliance University, 2024). Similarly, the Sandip Group of Institutions has partnered with Infosys to utilize the Springboard platform, enabling students to acquire skills essential for their professional careers (Sandip Foundation, 2023). Through such collaborations, universities can integrate industry-driven learning platforms into their academic programs, ensuring that graduates are equipped with practical knowledge. This not only enhances employability but also enables higher education institutions to stay relevant in a rapidly evolving workforce landscape.

The potential for MOOCs to transform education in India is enormous, especially when it comes to enhancing digital literacy. As the government continues to invest in expanding internet access, the country is seeing an increase in the number of people who can engage with online learning (Press Information Bureau, 2023). This presents a golden opportunity to address the digital literacy gap that exists between urban and rural populations. MOOCs can equip learners with the digital skills needed to navigate the online world, from basic computer literacy to more advanced skills such as coding and data analysis. In doing so, they can help ensure that all citizens are able to participate in the digital economy, regardless of their background or location.

RELEVANCE OF MOOCS IN DIGITAL LITERACY

The rapid digital transformation of economies worldwide has amplified the importance of digital literacy, particularly in countries like India, where access to quality education remains a significant barrier for a vast portion of the population. The rise of Massive Open Online Courses (MOOCs) offers a potential solution to these challenges, providing accessible, flexible, and often free educational content. India faces a growing demand for digital literacy across sectors, from education to workplace (Dasss, 2021; Singh & Sha2022). According to UNESCO Institute for Statistics (n.d.), "Digital literacy involves the confident and critical use of a full range of digital technologies for information, communication, and basic problem-solving in all aspects of life." Yet, for many students in India, particularly those in rural areas or from lower socio-economic backgrounds, acquiring these essential skills remains difficult. The disparity in digital literacy rates between urban and rural areas is stark, with reports indicating that while 61% of urban Indians possess digital literacy, this figure drops to just 25% in rural regions (Khanna, 2023). MOOCs, with their open-access model, can play a transformative role in addressing this gap. One of the key advantages of MOOCs is that they eliminate many traditional barriers to education, such as physical infrastructure limitations and high costs. Unlike traditional education systems that require students to be physically present at a school or university, MOOCs can be accessed from anywhere, provided there is an internet connection. This makes MOOCs particularly valuable in rural or remote regions of India, where access to high-quality educational institutions may be limited. Thus MOOCs have the potential to ensure inclusive education in India, offering opportunities to millions of students.

Moreover, the flexibility that MOOCs offer is a crucial factor in their relevance for improving digital literacy. Traditional education often follows rigid schedules, which can be difficult for students who must balance other commitments, such as work or family responsibilities. This is especially true in rural India, where many students are expected to contribute to household income or agricultural work (Austin Career Institute, n.d.; CRY, n.d.). MOOCs, on the other hand, allow learners to study at their own pace and choose courses that align with their interests and career goals. This flexibility not only makes learning more accessible but also increases the likelihood that students will engage with the material and acquire the digital skills they need.

MOOCs also cater to diverse learning needs, offering a broad range of subjects that can help students enhance their digital literacy. Digital skills are not limited to basic computing or internet usage; they encompass a wide range of competencies, including data analysis, coding, artificial intelligence, and cyber security, all of which are critical for success in the modern workforce. Many MOOC platforms, such as Coursera, edX, and SWAYAM (SWAYAM, n.d.), offer courses specifically designed to build digital competencies (Coursera, n.d.; edX, n.d.; SWAYAM (SWAYAM, n.d.). By engaging with these courses, students can develop skills that are in high demand across industries, improving their employability and ability to compete in a global job market (Nair, 2023).

The affordability of MOOCs is another factor that makes them relevant to India's digital literacy challenges. Higher education in India, particularly in specialized fields like engineering or information technology, can be excessively expensive for many students. MOOCs provide a cost-effective alternative, offering access to courses from leading universities and institutions at little to no cost. This low barrier to entry makes MOOCs an attractive option for students from low-income backgrounds, who may otherwise be unable to afford quality education. As mentioned by Mishra (2022), the cost-efficiency of MOOCs is particularly beneficial in a country like India, where economic disparities often limit educational opportunities. Furthermore, MOOCs contribute to digital literacy not only by teaching technical skills but also by providing a platform for students to practice and apply these skills in real-world contexts. The National Academy of Agricultural Research Management (NAARM, 2024) has successfully implemented MOOCs, significantly impacting individual learners and organizations within the agricultural and educational sectors. These initiatives have fostered continuous learning and innovation, contributing to improved teaching quality, skill development, and the advancement of higher education infrastructure in India. Many MOOCs include interactive components such as discussion forums, peer assessments, and hands-on projects, allowing students to collaborate and engage with digital tools in a meaningful way (Siemens, 2020). However, a key concern regarding the scalability of MOOCs is faculty compensation. While many MOOCs are free to access, universities often integrate them into degree programs through a freemium model, where basic content remains free, but students pay for certification, graded assignments, or instructor-led support (Hollands & Tirthali, 2014). This revenue can be used to compensate faculty, along with funding from government initiatives and partnerships with private organizations investing in workforce development (Yuan & Powell, 2013).This type of experiential learning is essential for developing digital fluency, as it helps students move beyond theoretical knowledge to practical application. According to Kumar (2023), experiential learning through MOOCs is an effective way to build confidence and competence in digital skills, preparing students for the demands of a technology-driven world.

Another important consideration in the relevance of MOOCs is their ability to reach marginalized populations. In India, women and other marginalized groups often face significant barriers to accessing education due to social, cultural, and economic factors. Massive Open Online Courses (MOOCs) offer flexible and remote learning options that can help these groups overcome such barriers. Additionally, e-learning platforms, virtual classrooms, and MOOCs enable students from marginalized communities to enroll in courses that were previously inaccessible, thus empowering them through education (Sociology Institute, n.d.).Women in rural areas, for example, who may be restricted by societal norms or family obligations, can still engage in learning through MOOCs without having to leave their homes. In this way, MOOCs have the potential to promote greater gender equity in digital literacy and workforce participation (Sinha, 2022).

Despite these advantages, the effectiveness of MOOCs in improving digital literacy in India is not without challenges. One of the main obstacles is the digital divide (Singh, 2010) itself—the very issue MOOCs seek to address. Access to the internet and digital devices is still limited in many parts of India, particularly in rural areas. Without reliable internet connectivity or access to smartphones, tablets, or computers, many students are unable to benefit from MOOCs. As Agarwal (2022) points out, while MOOCs offer an innovative solution to educational disparities, their success in India is contingent upon continued investment in digital infrastructure, particularly in underserved regions.

Another challenge is the language barrier. Although many MOOCs are offered in English, a significant portion of India's population is not proficient in the language, which creates barriers to access (UNESCO, 2019; Ministry of Education, 2022). To maximize the impact of MOOCs on digital literacy, it is essential that courses be offered in regional languages and tailored to the cultural and linguistic diversity of India. The Indian government's SWAYAM (SWAYAM, n.d.) platform has made strides in this regard, offering courses in multiple Indian languages (Economic Times,

2020). However, further efforts are needed to ensure that MOOCs are accessible to all learners, regardless of their language proficiency (Mishra, 2022).

MOOCs hold significant potential in addressing the digital literacy needs of India's population, particularly in the context of higher education and workforce development. By providing accessible, flexible, and affordable educational content, MOOCs can help students enhance their digital literacy skills, making them more competitive in the global workforce. However, for MOOCs to fully realize their potential in India, it is crucial to address challenges related to digital infrastructure, internet access, and language barriers. With the right support from government, educational institutions, and private organizations, MOOCs can play a transformative role in bridging the digital literacy gap and ensuring that all students, regardless of their background or location, have the opportunity to succeed in the digital age.

IHE AND WORKPLACE COLLABORATION

The collaboration between Institutes of Higher Education (IHE) and the workforce is vital in preparing students to meet the evolving demands of the global job market, particularly in an era marked by rapid technological advancement. The integration of Massive Open Online Courses (MOOCs) within traditional educational systems offers a scalable and innovative approach to enhance digital literacy and bridge the gap between academic learning and workforce needs (Sangrà et al., 2017).By forging partnerships with industries and leveraging MOOCs, higher education institutions (IHEs) can ensure that students acquire the technical skills, critical thinking, and adaptability required for employability in a digital-first economy.

One of the most pressing issues in today's job market is the mismatch between the skills that graduates possess and those that employers require. The World Economic Forum's Future of Jobs 2023 report emphasizes that 85 million jobs are expected to be displaced by automation by 2025, while 97 million new roles will emerge in industries such as artificial intelligence (AI), data analysis, and cloud computing (World Economic Forum, 2023). This shift underscores the need for students to develop a robust skillsets that prepares them for these rapidly transforming industries. By collaborating with the workforce, Indian higher education institutions (IHEs) can align their curricula with industry needs, ensuring that students are equipped with relevant, job-ready competencies. For instance, IIT Kanpur's collaboration with the Indian aerospace industry has contributed to advancements in space technology, highlighting the role of academic-industry alliances in driving innovation (Sharma & Verma, 2024). By integrating MOOCs into traditional academic programs, IHEs can offer students opportunities to supplement their learning with courses tailored to the specific demands of the workforce.

One of the most significant advantages of MOOCs is their ability to provide targeted and modular learning experiences. Industry partnerships can contribute to the design of MOOC courses that meet specific skill needs, such as programming languages, cyber security, or project management. For instance, Coursera's partnerships with leading technology companies like Google and IBM allow students to earn professional certificates that are recognized and valued by employers (Coursera, 2023). By integrating such programs into their curricula, IHEs can ensure that students are exposed to relevant technologies and industry standards while still studying. Through collaboration with IHEs, industries can encourage employees to up skill by enrolling in MOOCs, enabling them to keep pace with technological advancements while also fostering a culture of continuous learning (Mishra, 2022).

In addition to technical skills, MOOCs also provide platforms for developing soft skills such as critical thinking, problem-solving, and adaptability, which are increasingly valued in the workforce (Harvard Business Review, 2019). These skills are essential in today's complex, fast-paced business environment, where employees are often required to navigate ambiguity and solve problems creatively. A study by Kumar (2023) highlights how MOOCs that incorporate problem-based learning and interactive elements, such as peer feedback and real-world case studies; enhance students' critical thinking and problem-solving abilities. Collaboration between IHEs and industry can help integrate these competencies into MOOC offerings, ensuring that students are well-rounded and prepared for the challenges of modern workplaces. However, successful collaboration between IHEs and industry requires more than just content integration; it also demands a strong focus on adaptability and responsiveness to changing industry needs. Traditional academic curricula are often slow to adapt to new developments in technology and industry standards, creating a gap between what is taught in universities and what is needed in the workforce (World Economic Forum, 2020). By integrating MOOCs into their programs, IHEs can offer a more agile and responsive educational model that keeps pace with industry trends. Agarwal (2022) notes that MOOCs are updated more frequently than traditional courses, and their modular structure allows for the addition of new content without overhauling entire curricula. This adaptability ensures that students are always learning the latest technologies and practices, keeping them competitive in the job market. However, some argue that MOOCs are not always updated as frequently as claimed, depending on the platform and course provider. The collaboration between IHEs and industry through MOOCs also holds significant potential for fostering innovation and entrepreneurship. By exposing students to industry-led challenges and real-world problems through MOOCs, IHEs can encourage innovation and entrepreneurial thinking. Many MOOC platforms offer courses on entrepreneurship, business development, and innovation, providing students with the tools to launch their ventures or bring innovative solutions to their workplaces. Industry partnerships can also facilitate mentorship programs, where students work with industry experts to develop their business ideas and bring them to fruition (Nair, 2023).

Collaboration between Institutes of Higher Education (IHEs) and industry through MOOCs not only addresses the evolving skill needs of the workforce but also fosters robust networks between academia and employers. This partnership enhances the relevance of educational offerings and aligns them with industry demands. A study by Hamonic et al. (2023) demonstrates that such collaborations, especially those involving blended learning models combining MOOCs and on-site workshops, can effectively bridge the gap between theoretical knowledge and practical application, thereby strengthening ties between educational institutions and industry partners. This network can facilitate better access to job opportunities for graduates, internships for students, and professional growth for employees. By building strong ties with industry partners, IHEs can help students transition from academia to professional environments more seamlessly, ensuring that their skills align with the needs of employers' right from the start. For example, in February 2024, the Government of India launched the SWAYAM(SWAYAM CENTRAL,N.D) Plus platform in Delhi, developed in collaboration with industry leaders such as Larsen & Toubro, Microsoft, and CISCO. This platform focuses on enhancing employability and professional skills among students. The Indian Institute of Technology Madras oversees its operations, leveraging its experience with the SWAYAM (Swayam Central,n.d)-NPTEL platform. By integrating industry-relevant content into the curriculum, SWAYAM (SWAYAM CENTRAL, N.D) Plus ensures that learners acquire the latest knowledge and skills demanded by employers, thereby improving their job prospects (Mordor Intelligence, 2024).

Industry collaboration through Massive Open Online Courses (MOOCs) can help mitigate the rising costs of education. By integrating industry-sponsored certifications and online courses into their programs, IHEs can offer students access to high-quality, globally recognized learning experiences without the need for substantial financial investment in developing proprietary courses. These industry-sponsored MOOCs often provide a wealth of resources, including video lectures, assessments, and practical exercises that would otherwise be unavailable in traditional university settings. This approach allows students to gain a world-class education without incurring significant debt, making higher education more affordable and accessible (The Hindu, 2024).

In addition to providing students with technical and soft skills, MOOCs can also help foster a culture of self-directed learning. Through self-paced courses, students are empowered to take control of their learning journeys, choosing topics and skills that align with their career goals and personal interests. This independence in learning not only builds confidence but also enhances students' ability to manage their careers effectively. In today's fast-paced job market, employees are increasingly expected to be proactive about up skilling and adapting to new challenges. By embracing MOOCs and the self-directed learning model, students can develop the continuous learning mind-set necessary for success in their careers. For example, a study by Milligan & Littlejohn (2017) found that MOOCs support self-regulated learning by helping learners set goals, monitor progress, and reflect on their learning. Similarly, a report by the World Economic Forum (2020) emphasized the role of online learning platforms in fostering continuous skill development and career adaptability.

Moreover, integrating MOOCs into higher education can also encourage a culture of global citizenship. With MOOCs offering access to international expertise and resources, students can interact with peers and instructors from across the world, gaining exposure to different cultures, perspectives, and ways of thinking (De Waard et al., 2014). This cross-cultural exposure is particularly valuable in today's globalized workforce, where companies are increasingly operating on a global scale. Research suggests that students who participate in international MOOCs develop a global mind-set, enhancing their ability to work in diverse teams and understand the complexities of operating in global markets (Joksimović et al., 2015).

While MOOCs offer valuable learning experiences, the lack of standardization in course quality and certification can create challenges for students and employers. This issue affects credibility, employability, and academic recognition, necessitating clearer guidelines, quality benchmarks, reliable accreditation, and fair and consistent evaluation methods to ensure equitable learning opportunities (Stracke, 2017). Research highlights that without standardized frameworks, MOOCs may not always be recognized by employers and academic institutions, limiting their effectiveness in career advancement and formal education (Yuan & Powell, 2013).

Thus, the collaboration between institutes of higher education and the workforce is essential for ensuring that digital literacy education remains aligned with the needs of the modern job market. By integrating MOOCs into traditional curricula and building partnerships with industry, IHEs can equip students with the technical skills, critical thinking, and adaptability needed to thrive in a rapidly evolving digital landscape. Through such collaboration, MOOCs can serve as a powerful tool for bridging the skills gap, fostering innovation, and preparing students for the future of work.

In an era defined by rapid technological advancements, the need for continuous education has never been more critical (Schmidt & Cohen, 2013). The dynamic nature of the modern job market, driven by developments in artificial intelligence, machine learning, and automation, requires workers to constantly adapt to new technologies and methods. This is where the concept of lifelong learning becomes essential—a philosophy deeply rooted in the belief that education is not confined to childhood or the traditional academic setting but is an on-going process throughout one's life (UNESCO, 2016). Lifelong learning embraces the idea that individuals must continually seek knowledge and skills to thrive personally, professionally, and socially. Massive Open Online Courses have emerged as a powerful enabler of this philosophy, providing a scalable and flexible means for individuals to up skill or reskill in order to maintain their relevance in an ever-changing job market.

MOOCs, by their nature, expand educational equity, removing barriers of geography, time, and financial resources that often limit access to quality learning. This open access resonates with the philosophical underpinnings of perpetual learning, as espoused by educational theorists like John Dewey and Paulo Freire. Dewey's progressive education theory emphasizes the importance of experience and continuous learning for personal growth and societal contribution (Dewey, 1938). Freire's notion of education as a practice of freedom also aligns with the MOOC model, as it allows learners from diverse backgrounds to engage in self-directed learning at their own pace and according to their own needs (Freire, 1970). The flexibility of MOOCs enables individuals, particularly working professionals, to pursue new learning without the constraints of a traditional classroom environment, making it a key tool in promoting on-going skill enhancement.

One of the most compelling aspects of MOOCs as a tool for continuous education is their adaptability to the evolving needs of the workforce. In today's knowledge-driven economy, the half-life of skills is shrinking rapidly. According to the Future of Jobs Report 2025 by the World Economic Forum, an estimated 39% of core skills among workers will change or become obsolete between 2025 and 2030, emphasizing the urgent need for on-going reskilling (World Economic Forum, 2025). This highlights the adaptability of MOOCs in equipping individuals with relevant skills to stay competitive in the evolving job market. This shift highlights the importance of continuous learning as a mechanism for individuals to keep pace with the demands of their professions. By enabling professionals to acquire new skills in these high-demand areas, MOOCs serve as a bridge between the existing workforce and the future job market.

The role of MOOCs in fostering digital literacy, a core component of sustained knowledge development, cannot be overstated. In today's digital economy, digital literacy is as fundamental as traditional literacy. Traditional literacy refers to the ability to read, write, and comprehend written language, enabling individuals to communicate effectively and engage with information in a meaningful way. Digital literacy, on the other hand, involves not only the ability to use digital tools but also the capacity to critically evaluate information, engage in online collaboration, and understand the ethical implications of technology use (UNESCO, 2023). As the digital landscape evolves, so too must the skills of those who navigate it. MOOCs provide continuous opportunities for learners to enhance their digital literacy by offering courses on emerging technologies such as cloud computing and block chain (UNESCO, 2023). For working professionals, staying current with these technological advancements are crucial for maintaining competitiveness in their respective fields (World Economic Forum, 2020). MOOCs enable individuals to re-enter the learning environment and acquire the skills necessary to improve their employability and socio-economic status (Yuan & Powell, 2013). This open-access model aligns with the philosophical foundations of education as a human right, emphasizing equity and access for all (United Nations, 2015). By transcending barriers of class, geography, and socio-economic status, MOOCs serve as a key enabler of a more inclusive, lifelong learning ecosystem (Daniel, 2012).

According to the University Grants Commission and recent estimates from Wikipedia (2023), India has over 1,100 universities and more than 40,000 colleges, making it one of the largest education systems in the world. The government has made significant strides in recent years to expand access to higher education, recognizing its importance for national development and individual opportunity. For example, the Gross Enrolment Ratio in higher education has steadily risen, reaching 28.4% in the 18-23 age groups during the 2021-22 academic year, up from 23.7% in 2014-15 (Economic Survey, 2025, Times of India, 2024). The Indian government has set an ambitious target to increase the Gross Enrolment Ratio to 50% by 2035, aiming to expand access to higher education and foster national development (National Education Policy 2020, Government of India). Despite expansion efforts, the Indian higher education system struggles to accommodate the increasing demand for university places, particularly in popular fields of study. According to the All India Survey on Higher Education (AISHE, 2021), approximately 3.9 million students were awarded undergraduate degrees in 2022. However, premier institutions like the Indian Institutes of Technology (IITs) have an acceptance rate of less than 1%, leading to intense competition (Wired, 2023). Moreover, dropout rates in higher education institutions remain a concern, with over 34,000 students dropping out from central universities, IITs, National Institutes of Technology (NITs), and Indian Institutes of Management (IIMs) between 2019 and 2023 due to academic pressures and lack of support systems (Hindustan Times, 2023).

These challenges highlight the need for systemic reforms to enhance capacity and support mechanisms in India's higher education sector. Many universities, especially in rural areas, lack adequate infrastructure and resources, impacting the quality of education students receive. According to the AISHE (2021), about 50% of Indian universities report a shortage of faculty members, and many institutions lack modern classrooms, libraries, and laboratories. This issue is compounded by the scarcity of technological resources and digital literacy, particularly in rural areas, which further limits students' ability to access high-quality education (AISHE, 2021).

Some argue that traditional curriculum design in Indian universities is inflexible and does not adequately prepare graduates for the demands of the modern workforce. The curriculum in many institutions has not evolved to keep pace with the rapidly changing needs of industries. A report by the National Association of Software and Service Companies highlights that around 40% of Indian engineering graduates are considered unemployable due to outdated curricula that do not equip them with the necessary skills for the job market.

While government investment in higher education has increased, the cost remains a significant barrier for many students, particularly those from disadvantaged backgrounds. A report by the National Sample Survey Office (NSSO, 2020) revealed that average education expenses nearly doubled over the previous decade, with annual per-student costs rising from 5,856 in 2008 to 12,345 in 2018 in rural areas and from 12,000 to 28,000 in urban areas. This escalation has led to concerns over affordability and equitable access to education (Ministry of Education, n.d.).

CHALLENGES AND SOLUTIONS IN MOOC ADOPTION

In response to these challenges, the Indian government has introduced financial assistance schemes to support students pursuing higher education. The Central Sector Interest Subsidy Scheme provides interest subsidies on education loans for economically weaker sections, while the Credit Guarantee Fund Scheme for Education Loans offers guarantees for loans up to 7.5 lakh without collateral (Ministry of Education, n.d.). Despite these initiatives, the rising cost of higher education remains a significant barrier, limiting access for many students (Agarwal, 2021; Gupta & Sharma, 2020).

Amidst these financial constraints, MOOCs have emerged as a potential solution to promote educational inclusivity and enhance digital literacy (Liyanagunawardena, Adams, & Williams, 2013). However, their effectiveness is hindered by challenges such as low student engagement, high dropout rates, variability in course quality, and limited recognition by traditional academic institutions (Jordan, 2014; Reich & Ruipérez-Valiente, 2019). To fully leverage the benefits of MOOCs, these challenges must be addressed through innovative strategies, including blended learning models, university collaborations, and the establishment of supportive learning communities (Kizilcec, Pérez-Sanagustín, & Maldonado, 2017). Furthermore, government policies and educational frameworks play a crucial role in integrating MOOCs into mainstream education, ensuring their sustainability and effectiveness (Laurillard, 2016).

The lack of personalized attention and support is a significant issue in MOOCs. Students can feel isolated without the immediate feedback or guidance that they would receive in a classroom or even in smaller online courses (Hew & Cheung, 2014; Kizilcec, Pérez-Sanagustín, & Maldonado, 2017). In traditional learning environments, instructors can tailor their teaching to the needs of their students and offer one-on-one support when required. In contrast, the massive scale of MOOCs makes this kind of individualized attention impossible. While discussion forums and peer review systems attempt to replicate this engagement, they are often insufficient substitutes for direct interaction with instructors. The impersonal nature of MOOCs can make it difficult for students to clarify doubts, seek feedback, or feel motivated to persist through challenges.

To overcome these challenges, one effective solution lies in adopting blended learning models, which combine the flexibility of MOOCs with the support and structure of traditional classroom settings. In a blended learning approach, students can use MOOCs as supplementary resources that complement their in-person coursework (Garrison & Kanuka, 2004). This allows for the scalability and accessibility of MOOCs while providing students with the guidance, feedback, and peer interaction they need to stay engaged (Means, Toyama, Murphy, & Baki, 2013).

Studies have shown that when MOOCs are integrated into a blended learning environment, completion rates significantly improve (Holotescu, Grosseck, Cretu, & Naaji, 2014). Universities adopting this model have reported better student retention, improved comprehension, and enhanced problem-solving skills compared to purely online or traditional formats (Bernard et al., 2014). Additionally, students in blended learning settings benefit from active discussions, group activities, and real-time assessments, which reinforce MOOC content and reduce feelings of isolation (Bonk & Graham, 2012).

Additionally, building robust learning communities is essential for enhancing student engagement in MOOCs. Learning communities, whether online or in-person, provide a social aspect to the learning process, allowing students to discuss ideas, ask questions, and motivate each other to complete the course. This can take the form of virtual study groups, discussion forums moderated by teaching assistants, or even in-person meetups where MOOC participants can collaborate on projects. By fostering a sense of community, MOOCs can better mimic the interactive and collaborative aspects of traditional education, which are crucial for deep learning and retention.

Another solution is the formal integration of MOOCs into university and workforce training programs. Many universities have started recognizing MOOC certificates as valid credits toward a degree, which increases the perceived value of MOOCs and encourages students to complete courses (University Grants Commission [UGC], 2022). Such integration also addresses concerns about the inconsistent quality of MOOCs, as universities can curate and recommend specific MOOCs that align with their academic standards. For example, universities can partner with MOOC platforms to co-create courses that are designed to meet the specific needs of their students while maintaining academic rigor. This not only improves the quality of MOOCs but also ensures that students see clear pathways between their MOOC learning and formal academic progression.

The role of government policy and educational frameworks is crucial in promoting MOOCs as a legitimate and valuable tool for education and workforce development. Governments can create incentives for institutions to adopt and integrate MOOCs, such as funding for the development of high-quality online courses or creating accreditation frameworks that recognize MOOC credentials. Educational frameworks must also evolve to incorporate digital learning as a core component of lifelong education, rather than viewing it as a peripheral or supplementary option. For instance, national accreditation bodies could develop standards for MOOCs that ensure consistency in course quality, assessment, and learning outcomes, thereby increasing the credibility and acceptance of MOOCs in both academic and professional contexts.

Furthermore, public-private partnerships between governments, universities, and industry stakeholders can help ensure that MOOCs address the actual needs of the workforce. By collaborating with industries, higher education institutions can ensure that MOOC curricula are aligned with the skills that are in demand, particularly in sectors such as information technology, data science, and digital marketing. This alignment helps to close the skills gap that currently exists between graduates and the evolving needs of the job market. Industries can also play a role by offering internships, job placements, or mentorship opportunities to students who successfully complete MOOC programs, further incentivizing learners to stay engaged and complete their courses.

While MOOCs present significant challenges in terms of high dropout rates, lack of personalized attention, and variable course quality, these obstacles are not insurmountable. Solutions such as blended learning models, stronger learning communities, and partnerships between universities and industries offer ways to enhance student engagement and ensure that MOOCs remain relevant and valuable. Government policies and educational frameworks must also evolve to support the integration of MOOCs into the mainstream educational ecosystem, recognizing their potential as a powerful tool for lifelong learning and workforce development. By addressing these challenges, MOOCs can play a pivotal role in expanding access to education, fostering digital literacy, and preparing individuals for the demands of the future workforce.

THE IMPACT OF MOOCS ON STUDENT AND WORKFORCE READINESS

The impact of MOOCs on student and workforce readiness is profound, particularly in equipping learners with the digital literacy and soft skills essential for navigating the modern job market. Various factors contribute to the successful adoption of MOOCs, including perceived ease of use, attitudes toward the platform, and the ability to observe tangible benefits. Understanding these factors helps explain how MOOCs can bridge the gap between educational outcomes and workforce needs, promoting digital literacy and preparing students for real-world challenges.

Perceived ease of use is a critical determinant in the adoption of any new technology, including MOOCs. Studies show that learners are more likely to adopt MOOCs if they find the platform easy to navigate and understand (Davis, 1989). A user-friendly interface, accessible learning materials, and a clear structure enhance the learning experience and encourage continued participation. In the context of India, where digital literacy varies widely, particularly between urban and rural areas, ease of use becomes even more crucial. A well-designed MOOC platform can help students from diverse backgrounds engage with digital tools, enhancing their confidence and digital literacy skills (Alraimi, Zo, & Ciganek, 2015).

Attitudes toward MOOCs also play a vital role in student adoption. Positive attitudes are often driven by the perceived benefits of MOOCs, such as flexibility, cost-effectiveness, and the opportunity to learn at one's own pace. Research by Alraimi et al. (2015) suggests that learners with a favorable attitude towards MOOCs are more likely to engage fully with the content and complete their courses. In India, where higher education is often limited by infrastructure and financial constraints, MOOCs offer a scalable solution that can overcome these barriers. By fostering a positive attitude towards online learning, MOOCs can increase digital literacy and prepare students for the demands of a technology-driven workforce (Jung & Lee, 2018).

Tangible benefits, such as the acquisition of marketable skills, are a powerful motivator for students to adopt MOOCs. Many learners seek out MOOCs to develop specific technical and soft skills that align with workforce requirements. For example, MOOCs in areas like data science, programming, and digital marketing have gained popularity because of their direct relevance to high-demand job markets (Cheng et al., 2019). By equipping students with these skills, MOOCs help them meet the expectations of employers who increasingly seek digitally literate and adaptable workers. Moreover, MOOCs often provide certificates that validate the learner's achievements, further motivating students to pursue these courses and boosting their employability.

The alignment between MOOCs and workforce requirements is essential for ensuring that students gain the skills they need to thrive in a digitally transformed workplace. Employers today are not only looking for candidates with technical competencies but also for individuals who possess critical thinking, problem-solving, and communication skills. MOOCs, particularly those that encourage collaboration, peer interaction, and project-based learning, can help students develop these soft skills alongside technical expertise (Hollands & Tirthali, 2014).

In addition to digital literacy, MOOCs also contribute to the development of self-regulated learning skills, which are essential for career advancement (Kop, Fournier, & Mak, 2011). The flexibility of MOOCs requires students to take ownership of their learning, set goals, and manage their time effectively. These self-regulation skills are highly valued in the workplace, where employees must be able to adapt to changing conditions and independently acquire new knowledge as needed. By fostering these skills, MOOCs prepare students to be proactive, adaptable, and capable of continuous learning.

Research has demonstrated that MOOCs have a significant impact on workforce readiness. A study by Milligan and Littlejohn (2014) found that MOOCs positively influenced participants' career development, with many reporting that the skills and knowledge gained from MOOCs helped them secure new job opportunities or advance in their current roles. Similarly, the World Economic Forum's Future of Jobs Report (2020) highlights the increasing demand for digital skills in the workforce and the role of online learning platforms like MOOCs in meeting this demand.

CONCLUSION

The role of Massive Open Online Courses in bridging digital literacy gaps and enhancing workforce readiness in India has been extensively explored in this chapter. Theoretical insights suggest that MOOCs have the potential to equalize learning opportunities by making high-quality learning accessible to diverse populations, particularly those in rural and underserved communities. MOOCs contribute to digital literacy by offering learners exposure to essential technological skills, such as data analysis, artificial intelligence, and coding, which are integral to today's job market. By providing open-access educational resources, MOOCs help bridge the urban-rural divide, enabling students from different socio-economic backgrounds to gain knowledge and skills that were previously out of reach. The affordability and flexibility of these courses allow learners to tailor their educational journeys based on individual needs, schedules, and career aspirations.

The integration of MOOCs into higher education institutions has also been identified as a transformative approach to enhancing digital competencies. By complementing traditional curricula, MOOCs offer students opportunities to engage with global experts, access industry-relevant content, and develop critical thinking and problem-solving abilities. Furthermore, partnerships between IHEs and industries have played a crucial role in aligning MOOCs with workforce demands. Employers increasingly recognize MOOC certifications as valid credentials, thereby improving graduates' employability and ensuring that they possess skills relevant to modern industries.

Workforce readiness is another critical area where MOOCs have shown remarkable potential. In an era where technological advancements continuously reshape industries, traditional education models struggle to keep pace with the evolving job market. MOOCs provide a timely, cost-effective solution to up skilling and reskilling workers, enabling them to stay relevant in a highly competitive environment. From IT professionals seeking advanced technical expertise to business leaders exploring digital transformation strategies, MOOCs cater to a wide spectrum of learners across various domains.

Despite their numerous advantages, MOOCs face certain challenges that must be addressed to maximize their impact. The digital divide (Singh, 2010)—stemming from unequal access to the internet, computers, and digital literacy skills—remains a significant barrier in India. While MOOCs offer free or low-cost education, their effectiveness is contingent upon learners' ability to navigate online platforms and engage with digital content. Therefore, strengthening digital infrastructure and expanding internet connectivity in rural and remote areas are imperative steps toward making MOOCs truly inclusive.

Another challenge lies in MOOC completion rates. Research indicates that while enrollment numbers for MOOCs are high, completion rates tend to be low due to a lack of motivation, engagement, and structured support. Self-paced learning, though flexible, may not be suitable for all students, particularly those accustomed to traditional classroom settings. To address this, blended learning models—combining online courses with in-person mentorship and collaborative learning experiences—can enhance student engagement and improve completion rates.

The language barrier is another factor that affects MOOC adoption in India. Since many MOOCs are offered in English, students with limited proficiency in the language may struggle to benefit from them. Initiatives such as the Indian government's SWAYAM platform, which offers courses in multiple regional languages, are steps in the right direction. Expanding multilingual content and incorporating culturally relevant examples in MOOCs can further increase their accessibility and impact.

The effectiveness of MOOCs also depends on the development of a robust accreditation and certification system. While some employers recognize MOOC certifications, widespread acceptance is still evolving. Government policies and industry collaborations can play a pivotal role in standardizing MOOC credentials, ensuring their credibility, and integrating them into formal education and professional development frameworks. Universities and corporate entities should work together to establish MOOC-based degree programs, micro-credentials, and skill certification pathways that align with industry needs.

The rise of MOOCs has also facilitated lifelong learning—a key component of professional and personal growth in the digital era. As job roles evolve and industries undergo digital transformation, continuous learning becomes indispensable.

MOOCs support lifelong learning by enabling individuals to up skill at any stage of their careers, providing them with the tools to adapt to shifting market trends and technological advancements. Employers, too, can leverage MOOCs as part of corporate training programs to enhance workforce productivity and innovation.

The COVID-19 pandemic has further underscored the significance of MOOCs in ensuring uninterrupted learning. As educational institutions and businesses worldwide transitioned to remote operations, the demand for online learning surged. MOOCs emerged as a reliable alternative to conventional classroom-based education, proving their resilience and effectiveness in times of crisis. Moving forward, integrating MOOCs into mainstream education systems and workforce training programs will be crucial for fostering resilience and adaptability in the face of future disruptions.

Governments, academic institutions, and private organizations must collaborate to optimize the potential of MOOCs in India. Strategic investments in digital infrastructure, awareness campaigns to promote digital literacy, and financial incentives for MOOC development can drive widespread adoption. Public-private partnerships can also facilitate MOOC expansion, ensuring that courses remain relevant, up-to-date, and aligned with industry demands.

In conclusion, MOOCs represent a transformative force in bridging digital literacy gaps and enhancing workforce readiness in India. By providing accessible, flexible, and high-quality education, MOOCs empower learners with the skills necessary for academic success and career advancement. However, for MOOCs to reach their full potential, concerted efforts must be made to address challenges related to digital accessibility, language barriers, engagement, and accreditation. As India moves toward a knowledge-driven economy, the integration of MOOCs into education and workforce development strategies will be instrumental in shaping a digitally literate, skilled, and competitive workforce. By leveraging the power of MOOCs, India can create an inclusive, future-ready education system that caters to the diverse needs of its learners and propels the nation toward sustained economic and social growth.

REFERENCES

Agarwal, P. (2021). *Higher education in India: The need for change. Oxford University Press. Gupta, R., & Sharma, P. (2020). Financing higher education in India: Policies and perspectives*. Springer.

Agarwal, P. (2022). Democratizing education through MOOCs: The Indian perspective. *Journal of Educational Technology & Society*, *25*(3), 12–18. DOI: 10.1016/j.edusoc.2022.09.012

Al-Baraa Abdulrahman Al-Mekhlafi, I., Othman, I., & Zamil, A. M. A. (2022). Modeling the impact of massive open online courses (MOOC) implementation factors on continuance intention of students: PLS-SEM approach. *Education and Information Technologies*, *28*(3), 1185–1200. DOI: 10.1007/s10639-022-11519-9

Alliance University. (2024). Alliance University partners with Infosys Springboard to enhance digital learning. https://www.alliance.edu.in/news/alliance-university-and-infosys-springboard-forge-a-new-partnership

Alraimi, K. M., Zo, H., & Ciganek, A. P. (2015). Understanding the MOOCs continuance: The role of openness and reputation. *Computers & Education*, *80*, 28–38. DOI: 10.1016/j.compedu.2014.08.007

Austin Career Institute. (n.d.). Balancing family, work, and school. Retrieved from https://austincareerinstitute.edu/blog/ma/balancing-family-work-school-medical-assistant

Bernard, R. M., Borokhovski, E., Schmid, R. F., Tamim, R. M., & Abrami, P. C. (2014). A meta-analysis of blended learning and technology use in higher education: From the general to the applied. *Journal of Computing in Higher Education*, *26*(1), 87–122. DOI: 10.1007/s12528-013-9077-3

Bishop, J. L., & Verleger, M. A. (2013). The flipped classroom: A survey of the research. *Proceedings of the ASEE Annual Conference & Exposition*, 23, 1–18. DOI: 10.18260/1-2--22585

Bonk, C. J., & Graham, C. R. (2012). *The handbook of blended learning: Global perspectives, local designs*. Wiley.

Bonk, C. J., & Lee, M. M. (2017). Motivation, retention, and dropout in MOOC learning environments. In *Massive open online courses: The MOOC revolution* (pp. 109–134). Springer.

BSSS Publications. (n.d.). Academic flexibilities & opportunities to the learners through MOOCs. Retrieved from https://bssspublications.com/Home/IssueDetailPage?IsNo=647

Chakravorty, S., & Bedi, J. (2020, September 14). The digital dream: Upskilling India for the future. Ideas for India. https://www.ideasforindia.in/topics/governance/the-digital-dream-upskilling-india-for-the-future

Cheng, X., Kaushik, V., & Raheem, A. (2019). Adoption of MOOCs for workforce development in India: A literature review. *International Journal of Educational Technology*, *10*(2), 107–121. DOI: 10.1080/IDLE.2019.090455

Child Rights and You (CRY). (n.d.). Education in rural India: The struggle for a brighter future. Retrieved from https://www.cry.org/blog/education-in-rural-india/

Coursera. (n.d.). Online courses from top universities & institutions. Retrieved from https://www.coursera.org

CRY. (n.d.). Education in rural India: Challenges and solutions. Retrieved from https://www.cry.org/blog/education-in-rural-india

Daniel, J. (2012). Making sense of MOOCs: Musings in a maze of myth, paradox, and possibility. *Journal of Interactive Media in Education*, *2012*(3), 18. DOI: 10.5334/2012-18

Das, S. (2021, December 2). World Computer Literacy Day: The need for digital literacy in India. The CSR Journal. Retrieved from https://thecsrjournal.in/world-computer-literacy-day-digital-literacy-india

Davis, F. D. (1989). Perceived usefulness, perceived ease of use, and user acceptance of information technology. *Management Information Systems Quarterly*, *13*(3), 319–340. DOI: 10.2307/249008

De Waard, I., Gallagher, M. S., Zwart, H., Abajian, S. C., & Hogue, R. J. (2014). Exploring the MOOC format as a pedagogy for global learning. *International Review of Research in Open and Distance Learning*, *15*(2), 1–13. DOI: 10.19173/irrodl.v15i2.1671

Dewey, J. (1938). *Experience and education*. Macmillan.

Economic Times. (2020, May 14). SWAYAM to introduce courses in 8 Indian languages including Hindi and Telugu. The Economic Times. Retrieved from https://government.economictimes.indiatimes.com/news/education/swayam-to-introduce-courses-in-8-indian-languages-including-hindi-and-telugu/75819347 edX. (n.d.). Access 3,000+ online courses from 160 institutions. Retrieved from https://www.edx.org

Freire, P. (1970). *Pedagogy of the oppressed*. Continuum.

Gaebel, M. (2013). *MOOCs: Massive open online courses*. European University Association.

Garrison, D. R., & Kanuka, H. (2004). Blended learning: Uncovering its transformative potential in higher education. *The Internet and Higher Education*, *7*(2), 95–105. DOI: 10.1016/j.iheduc.2004.02.001

Government of India. (2024). Economic Survey 2024-25. Ministry of Finance. https://www.indiabudget.gov.in/economicsurvey/doc/echapter.pdf

Hamonic, A., Boé, L., Jacq, F., & Penilla, J. (2023). Bridging the gap between academia and industry through MOOCs: A blended learning approach. arXiv preprint arXiv:2303.04019. Retrieved from https://arxiv.org/abs/2303.04019

Harvard Business Review. (2019). The soft skills companies need most in 2019. Harvard Business Publishing. Retrieved from https://hbr.org

Hew, K. F., & Cheung, W. S. (2014). Students' and instructors' use of massive open online courses (MOOCs): Motivations and challenges. *Educational Research Review*, *12*, 45–58. DOI: 10.1016/j.edurev.2014.05.001

Hollands, F. M., & Tirthali, D. (2014). *MOOCs: Expectations and reality. Center for Benefit-Cost Studies of Education*. Teachers College, Columbia University.

Hollands, F. M., & Tirthali, D. (2014). MOOCs: Expectations and Reality. Columbia University, Teachers College. Retrieved from https://doi.org/DOI: 10.7916/D8C24W3D

Holotescu, C., Grosseck, G., Cretu, V., & Naaji, A. (2014). Integrating MOOCs in blended courses. *Proceedings of the International Scientific Conference eLearning and Software for Education*, 1, 243–250. DOI: 10.12753/2066-026X-14-034

Ibrahim, Y. Y. (2023). The impact of massive open online courses (MOOCs) on knowledge management using integrated innovation diffusion theory and the technology acceptance model. *Education Sciences*, *13*(6), 531. DOI: 10.3390/educsci13060531

India Foundation. (n.d.). Role of Massive Open Online Courses (MOOCs) in Achieving Equity in Education and SDG 4. Retrieved from https://indiafoundation.in/articles-and-commentaries/role-of-massive-open-online-courses-moocs-in-achieving-equity-in-education-and-sdg-4/

Infosys. (n.d.). Infosys Springboard: Digital learning platform for lifelong learners. Retrieved from https://www.infosys.com/about/springboard.html

Joksimović, S., Gašević, D., Kovanović, V., Riecke, B. E., & Hatala, M. (2015). Social presence in online discussions as a process predictor of academic performance in MOOCs. *Computers & Education*, *79*, 41–53. DOI: 10.1016/j.compedu.2014.07.002

Jordan, K. (2014). Initial trends in enrollment and completion of massive open online courses. *International Review of Research in Open and Distance Learning*, *15*(1), 133–160. DOI: 10.19173/irrodl.v15i1.1651

Jordan, K. (2014). Initial trends in enrolment and completion of massive open online courses. *International Review of Research in Open and Distance Learning*, *15*(1), 133–160. DOI: 10.19173/irrodl.v15i1.1651

Kizilcec, R. F., Pérez-Sanagustín, M., & Maldonado, J. J. (2017). Self-regulated learning strategies predict learner behavior and goal attainment in massive open online courses. *Computers & Education*, *104*, 18–33. DOI: 10.1016/j.compedu.2016.10.001

Kizilcec, R. F., Pérez-Sanagustín, M., & Maldonado, J. J. (2017). Self-regulated learning strategies predict learner behavior and goal attainment in massive open online courses. *Computers & Education*, *104*, 18–33. DOI: 10.1016/j.compedu.2016.10.001

Kop, R., Fournier, H., & Mak, J. S. F. (2011). A pedagogy of abundance or a pedagogy to support human beings? Participant support on massive open online courses. *International Review of Research in Open and Distance Learning*, *12*(7), 74–93. DOI: 10.19173/irrodl.v12i7.1041

Kumar, A. (2023). Experiential learning in digital education: The role of MOOCs. *International Journal of Digital Learning*, *30*(2), 45–52. DOI: 10.1080/IDLE.2023.091234

Laurillard, D. (2016). The educational problem that MOOCs could solve: Professional development for teachers of disadvantaged students. *Research in Learning Technology*, *24*(1), 29369. Advance online publication. DOI: 10.3402/rlt.v24.29369

Laurillard, D. (2016). *Teaching as a design science: Building pedagogical patterns for learning and technology*. Routledge.

Liyanagunawardena, T. R., Adams, A. A., & Williams, S. A. (2013). MOOCs: A systematic study of the published literature 2008–2012. *International Review of Research in Open and Distance Learning*, *14*(3), 202–227. DOI: 10.19173/irrodl.v14i3.1455

Long, M., & Lee, C. S. (2023). Leveraging MOOCs for learners in economically disadvantaged regions. *Education and Information Technologies, 28*(9), 12243–12268. DOI: 10.1007/s10639-022-11461-2

Means, B., Toyama, Y., Murphy, R., & Baki, M. (2013). The effectiveness of online and blended learning: A meta-analysis of the empirical literature. *Teachers College Record, 115*(3), 1–47. DOI: 10.1177/016146811311500307

Milligan, C., & Littlejohn, A. (2014). Supporting professional learning in a massive open online course. *International Review of Research in Open and Distance Learning, 15*(5), 197–213. DOI: 10.19173/irrodl.v15i5.1855

Milligan, C., & Littlejohn, A. (2017). Why study on a MOOC? The motives of learners and the role of self-regulated learning. *International Review of Research in Open and Distance Learning, 18*(2), 1–18. DOI: 10.19173/irrodl.v18i2.3033

Ministry of Education. (2022). SWAYAM: Expanding access through multilingual MOOCs. Retrieved from https://swayam.gov.in

Ministry of Education. (n.d.). Rising cost of higher education in India and its impact on accessibility. Government of India. Retrieved from https://www.education.gov.in

Ministry of Education. (n.d.). Education loan schemes in India. Government of India. Retrieved from https://www.education.gov.in

Mishra, A. (2022). Economic Implications of MOOCs in Higher Education: An Indian Perspective. World Economics Association. Retrieved from https://www.worldeconomicsassociation.org/newsletterarticles/moocs-india/

Mordor Intelligence. (2024). *Massive Open Online Course (MOOC) Market Report.* Retrieved from https://www.mordorintelligence.com/industry-reports/massive-open-online-course-mooc-market.

Nair, P. (2023). Digital competency and workforce readiness: MOOCs in the Indian context. In *Advancements in Digital Literacy* (pp. 74–90). Springer., DOI: 10.1007/978-3-030-90760-2_5

National Academy of Agricultural Research Management (NAARM). (2024). MOOCs for Digital Education and Capacity Building – A Success Story. Retrieved from https://naarm.org.in/wp-content/uploads/2024/10/MOOCs-a-Success-Story.pdf

National Sample Survey Office (NSSO). (2020). Household social consumption on education in India. Ministry of Statistics and Programme Implementation. Retrieved from https://mospi.gov.in

Press Information Bureau. (2019, February 20). Report on India's trillion-dollar digital opportunity released. https://pib.gov.in/PressReleasePage.aspx?PRID=1565669

Press Information Bureau. (2023, September 15). BharatNet: Bridging the Digital divide (Singh, 2010). Retrieved from https://pib.gov.in/PressReleaseIframePage.aspx?PRID=2086701

Reich, J., & Ruipérez-Valiente, J. A. (2019). The MOOC pivot. *Science*, *363*(6423), 130–131. DOI: 10.1126/science.aav7958 PMID: 30630920

Sandip Foundation. (2023). Sandip Group of Institutions collaborates with Infosys Springboard for digital skill development. Retrieved from https://www.sandipfoundation.org/placement/infosys.php

Sangrà, A., Raffaghelli, J. E., Veletsianos, G., & Zheng, R. (2017). Massive open online courses (MOOCs): A blended learning approach to enhance digital literacy. *International Journal of Educational Technology in Higher Education*, *14*(8). Advance online publication. DOI: 10.1186/s41239-017-0085-7

Schmidt, E., & Cohen, J. (2013). *The new digital age: Reshaping the future of people, nations and business*. Alfred A. Knopf.

Siemens, G. (2020). Connectivism: A Learning Theory for the Digital Age. *International Journal of Instructional Technology and Distance Learning*, *2*(1), 3–10.

Sillak-Riesinger, B. (2017). The potential of massive open online courses in the context of corporate training and development. *Journal of Corporate Education*, *28*(4), 111–126. DOI: 10.1007/978-3-658-16649-6

Singh, R., & Sharma, P. (2022). MOOCs: A revolution in education for the digital era. Turkish Online Journal of Qualitative Inquiry, 13(4), 1234-1245. Retrieved from https://www.tojqi.net/index.php/journal/article/download/8057/5727/8639

Singh, S. (2010). Digital divide (Singh, 2010) in India: Measurement, determinants, and policy for addressing the challenges in bridging the digital divide (Singh, 2010). *International Journal of Innovation in the Digital Economy*, *1*(2), 1–24. DOI: 10.4018/jide.2010040101

Sinha, M. (2022). MOOCs as a tool for gender equity in digital literacy: Challenges and opportunities. *Gender and Education Review*, *18*(4), 205–218. DOI: 10.1177/GE2022.04.31212

Sociology Institute. (n.d.). ICTs and Their Potential to Empower India's Marginalized in Higher Education. Retrieved from https://sociology.institute/sociology-of-education/icts-empower-marginalized-higher-education-india/

Stracke, C. M. (2017). The quality of MOOCs: How to improve the design of open education and online courses for learners? In *Proceedings of the 2017 IEEE Global Engineering Education Conference (EDUCON)* (pp. 1639-1643). IEEE. DOI: 10.1007/978-3-319-58509-3_23

SWAYAM. (n.d.). Study Webs of Active Learning for Young Aspiring Minds. Retrieved from https://swayam.gov.in

The Hindu. (2024). IIT-M signs MoUs with industry partners for online courses. Retrieved from https://www.thehindu.com/news/national/tamil-nadu/iit-m-signs-mous-with-industry-partners-for-online-courses/article68366759.ece

Times of India. (2024, February 5). Economic Survey 2024-25: Higher education institutions grow by 13.8%, gross enrollment ratio rises to 28.4%. The Times of India. https://timesofindia.indiatimes.com

UNESCO. (2016). Learning to be: A holistic and integrated approach to values education for human development. United Nations Educational, Scientific and Cultural Organization. Retrieved from https://unesdoc.unesco.org/ark:/48223/pf0000245990

UNESCO. (2019). *Digital learning and MOOCs: Overcoming language barriers in online education*. United Nations Educational, Scientific and Cultural Organization.

UNESCO. (2023). Global education monitoring report: Technology in education. United Nations Educational, Scientific and Cultural Organization. Retrieved from https://www.unesco.org/reports/

UNESCO-UNEVOC. (n.d.). Digital literacy. TVETipedia Glossary. Retrieved from https://unevoc.unesco.org/home/TVETipedia%2BGlossary/lang%3Den/show%3Dterm/term%3Ddigital%2Bliteracy

United Nations. (2015). Transforming our world: The 2030 Agenda for Sustainable Development. https://sdgs.un.org/2030agenda

University Grants Commission. (2022). Credit framework for online learning courses through SWAYAM. UGC. Retrieved from https://www.ugc.gov.in/pdfnews/3501421_Step-by-step-procedure-involved-in-adoption-of-MOOCs.pdf

University Grants Commission. (n.d.). Welcome to UGC, New Delhi, India. Retrieved from https://www.ugc.gov.in/ • https://en.wikipedia.org/wiki/List_of_universities_in_India

Veletsianos, G., & Shepherdson, P. (2016). A systematic analysis and synthesis of the empirical MOOC literature published in 2013–2015. *International Review of Research in Open and Distance Learning*, *17*(2). Advance online publication. DOI: 10.19173/irrodl.v17i2.2448

Wikipedia. (2024). National Programme on Technology Enhanced Learning (NPTEL). Retrieved from https://en.wikipedia.org/wiki/National_Programme_on_Technology_Enhanced_Learning

World Economic Forum. (2020). The future of jobs report 2020. Retrieved from https://www.weforum.org/reports/the-future-of-jobs-report-2020

World Economic Forum. (2023). Future of Jobs 2023 Report. https://www.weforum.org/reports

World Economic Forum. (2025). The future of jobs report 2025. Retrieved from https://www.weforum.org/publications/the-future-of-jobs-report-2025/digest

WorldatWork. (2019). Cutting ties with traditional higher education. Retrieved from https://worldatwork.org/publications/evolve-magazine/cutting-ties-with-traditional-higher-education

Yuan, L., & Powell, S. (2013). MOOCs and Open Education: Implications for Higher Education. JISC. Retrieved from https://publications.cetis.org.uk/2013/667

Yuan, L., & Powell, S. (2013). MOOCs and open education: Implications for higher education. JISC Centre for Educational Technology & Interoperability Standards. Retrieved from https://publications.cetis.org.uk/2013/667

Yuan, L., & Powell, S. (2013). *MOOCs and open education: Implications for higher education*. JISC CETIS.

Zhu, M., & Doo, M. Y. (2022). The relationship among motivation, self-monitoring, self-management, and learning strategies of MOOC learners. *Journal of Computing in Higher Education*, *34*(4), 713–732. DOI: 10.1007/s12528-021-09301-2 PMID: 34744400

Chapter 10
Strategies for Utilizing Generative AI in Educational Environments:
Looking Towards the Workforce

Wyatt Porter Jones
https://orcid.org/0009-0008-5361-2867
Belmont University, USA

Stiles B. Logan
Belmont University, USA

ABSTRACT

The development of widely accessible generative AI tools, such as ChatGPT, has significantly impacted education and the workforce. Users have the capability to synthesize information from across the whole internet in seconds, which gives rise to new methods of learning, teaching, and optimizing workflows. The ways in which educators choose to handle this development greatly affects the quality and equity of instruction and learning available to their students, and their preparedness for life after education. This chapter will share research regarding generative AI and educational strategies. This research will be used as the basis for a list of strategies to help implement generative AI tools into the classroom effectively to prepare students for their futures.

DOI: 10.4018/979-8-3373-0004-7.ch010

BACKGROUND

Generative AI is a rapidly evolving technology that has already had an impact on a wide variety of fields. In order to utilize generative AI effectively, it is important to understand its most common forms, how they function, and how they can be utilized effectively.

AI, or artificial intelligence, is "technology that enables computers and machines to simulate human learning, comprehension, problem solving, decision making, creativity and autonomy" (Stryker & Kavlakoglu, 2024, para. 1). While discussions around AI have spiked recently, the technology is not new. It was first envisioned in 1950 by Alan Turing, who published the first paper questioning whether machines can imitate human intelligence (Turing, 1950). Since then, AI has developed rapidly, been implemented into a number of technologies (Muthukrishnan et al., 2020), and seen a huge surge in popularity and development.

This is largely due to recent advancements in the field of "generative" artificial intelligence technology. (Kılınç & Keçecioğlu, 2024). The term "generative AI" refers to "computational techniques that are capable of generating seemingly new, meaningful content such as text, images, or audio from training data" (Feuerriegel et al., 2023, p. 1). Not all of the newly created generative AI tools are the same, and it is important to recognize the differences in model types to properly utilize each tool. In this chapter we will discuss three major model types: the Generative Adversarial Network, the Diffusion Model, and the Generative Pre-trained Transformer.

Generative Adversarial Network

The first model type is called a Generative Adversarial Network, or GAN. Proposed by Ian Goodfellow and his colleagues at Université de Montréal in 2014, Generative Adversarial Network model AIs use two "networks" and a "discriminator" to operate. One network attempts to generate a synthetic response (for example, a picture of an apple), while the other network displays real images and videos from the software's training data. The discriminator then chooses which image it believes to be real. As this process is repeated, the generating network learns to produce images that become continually more accurate to the training data. When the discriminator can no longer decipher between the images and identifies the synthetic image as "real," then the verification process is completed, and the synthetic image is returned to the user. (Baidoo-Anu & Owusu, 2023)

The main use of this type of model is digital image/content generation. The model has seen heavy use in digital media and fashion, for things like creating renders for video games (Amazon, 2024), designing shoes (Wei, 2019), and even creating "the world's first digital supermodel" (Wong, 2019, para. 3). While this model is primarily used for image generation, it also shows promise in science and medicine and has been used for things like visualizing the future effects of climate change (Knight, 2022), detecting glaucoma (Bisneto et al., 2020), and modeling jet formations for physics experiments (De Oliveira et al., 2017).

Diffusion Model

The second type of generative AI model is the diffusion model, invented in 2015 by Dr. Jascha Sohl-Dickstein of Stanford University (Stanford University, 2025). This model functions relatively similarly to the first. The model is used almost exclusively for image generation and utilizes a two-step process. First, the model trains by progressively adding noise, essentially TV static, to images from a training dataset, then learning to reverse the noise. Then, when given a text prompt by a user, the model creates an image entirely composed of noise and uses its training to denoise it into outputs related to the user's prompt (Chen, 2024).

These diffusion models were a great step forward from GANs in several ways, surpassing prior models in both fidelity and diversity of images generated (Generative AI Lab, 2024). Perhaps the most important result of the development of diffusion models, however, was that they opened the door for the creation of revolutionary user-facing image generation platforms.

Stable Diffusion

In August 2022, Stability AI released their text-to-image model Stable Diffusion, the first publicly released image generation model based on a diffusion model. While Stable Diffusion's model is fairly similar to the one originally created by Dr. Sohl-Dickstein, a few key differences exist. Most notably, Stable Diffusion's model uses "reduced-definition latent space" in place of the pixel space of the original image (Amazon, 2024). This simply means that the model compresses the image into a smaller size before processing it. This allows the software to be run on a desktop with a consumer-grade graphics card (Amazon, 2024). Despite Stable Diffusion's image compression and low technical barriers, Aurora Solar (2025) found that "diffusion models can… produce realistic images that match and even outperform GAN-generated images". By creating powerful image generation software that could be run on a fairly modest computer and releasing it publicly for users to experiment with, Stability AI grabbed the public's attention and sparked new discussions around AI.

Beyond image generation, we have also seen diffusion models widely adopted in fields like computer and audio generation, text generation, and even life science (Chen, 2024). In the coming years, it will not be surprising to see diffusion models develop rapidly, especially in the fields of digital media, science, and medicine.

Generative Pre-trained Transformer

The third type of model, which is the most applicable of the three to our discussion, is called a Generative Pre-trained Transformer, or GPT. These GPTs are a type of Autoregressive language model, meaning that they are trained simply to "predict the next component in a sequence by taking measurements from previous inputs" (Amazon Web Services, 2024, para. 1). GPTs are not acquiring their information directly from a source; rather, they are searching through their databases for words related to the prompt and guessing what word to put next.

These models are trained using a process called Reinforcement Learning from Human Feedback, or RLHF (OpenAI, 2022). RLHF uses reinforcement learning techniques to train software to make decisions that maximize rewards. This reinforcement is combined with the incorporation of human feedback to allow the model to "perform tasks more aligned with human goals, wants, and needs." (Amazon Web Services, 2024, para. 1). While training a program by hand and having it guess answers word by word may sound primitive, it is quite effective when the database that the GPT has access to makes up essentially the entire internet.

Open AI and Chat GPT

Their effectiveness has been shown by OpenAI, the company behind the GPT model of AI. In 2018, the company publicly released their first GPT model, and an accompanying paper detailing how the model operates (Radford et al., 2018). After a few more years of improving the software and model, the company launched their AI chatbot "ChatGPT" in 2022. Within just five days, the public model reached one million users (Hu, 2023), fully propelling discussion of generative AI into the mainstream. Since then, ChatGPT and the field of generative AI as a whole have both continued to grow and gain traction rapidly, especially in the realm of education. Due to this growth, it is critical that educators understand artificial intelligence and be able to use it to their and their students' advantages.

INDEPENDENT STUDENT USE OF GENERATIVE A.I.

The release of ChatGPT in 2022 revolutionized user-facing generative AI tools. The software has already had several effects on a wide array of different fields. Modern companies are increasingly focused on improving efficiency through automation, machinery, and new technologies (Rashid & Kausik, 2024), leading to a 270% increase in enterprise adoption of generative AI tools from 2020 to 2024. The tools are being used across many different industries, from IT and cybersecurity to HR and PR, and even agriculture (Deloitte, 2024; Muck Rack, 2023).

Specifically, Generative AI tools have greatly affected the field of education. Students are now able to generate coherent and contextually appropriate responses to almost any question on command. While this new technology raises some questions regarding misinformation and cheating, it is a very powerful tool that could be considered necessary for entrance into some modern industries and can provide a variety of benefits to students (Mollick & Mollick, 2023).

Individualized Learning Experiences

One of the most valuable developments that modern generative AI tools have brought to students is the ability to receive fully individualized, one-on-one instruction on any topic almost instantly (Yuskovych-Zhukovska et al., 2022). Students are now able to generate content that helps them learn new concepts in ways that are most effective for them from home. If a student is a visual learner, for example, AI can prepare charts and graphs to aid its explanations, and if the student is an auditory learner, AI can create a podcast for the student to listen to that discusses the topics at hand. If one explanation doesn't make sense to a student, ChatGPT can create practically infinite examples and analogies to ensure that the student is able to grasp the concepts. Whatever specific question or issue a student has, AI is able to adapt uniquely to each student, allowing for a level of personalization in instruction that teachers, professors, and tutors cannot meet (Mollick & Mollick, 2023).

These generative AI tools can also provide students with lessons that are adjusted based on their progress and current understanding, "ranging from whether they need extra practice on certain topics or are ready to advance to more challenging material" (Neuenschwander, 2024, p. 3). For example, students can input the problems they got wrong on their last test to the AI, and the AI can develop personalized problems to help the student better understand the content they struggled with. This level of personalization helps students to learn at their own pace while also receiving the extra support needed to overcome challenges or gaps in learning, enhancing autonomy and independent learning (Yuskovych-Zhukovska et al., 2022).

These educational capabilities of generative AI for students have led to significant recent development in AI-powered adaptive learning platforms like DreamBox, Smart Sparrow, and Classavo. These platforms are unique in that they can adjust the difficulty and type of questions based on student responses, while also providing educators with feedback on class performance. They can also "provide instant feedback on student answers and questions, reinforcing the learning process by correcting mistakes in real-time" (Neuenschwander, 2024, p. 4).

Writing and Editing Assistance

Over the last few years, these models have developed significantly in their writing and editing abilities. In 2022 Meredith Ringel Morris interviewed twenty PhD scientists at Google Research, "interviewees noted that… language models that assisted in writing would improve writing quality for a large number of students" (pp. 6-7). In 2023, researchers at the University of Passau in Germany conducted a large-scale comparison of human-written and ChatGPT-generated essays and found that "ChatGPT generates essays that are rated higher regarding quality than human-written essays" (Herbold, 2023, para. 1). This writing ability, combined with the program's access to the entire internet, makes it an extremely valuable and multifaceted tool in student research and writing. By utilizing generative AI tools in their writing and research processes, students can save time, produce a higher-quality output, and ultimately learn how to become better writers.

One way students can utilize generative AI models in their writing is by treating them as a brainstorming partner. For example, if a student must write a social media marketing plan for a new e-commerce platform, they could ask ChatGPT to generate a list of five potential marketing strategies (Atlas, 2023). This can allow students to focus fully on their writing and help keep them from hitting a wall and getting stuck at the start of an assignment.

Similarly, students can also use ChatGPT to create outlines for writing projects. This can be very helpful for students, as it allows them to "pick relevant information or quotes from sources early on, and [have] a steady foundation and groundwork when beginning the writing process" (Rutgers, 2025, para. 1). This process can help students come up with new ideas and stay organized and on-topic in their writing.

Probably the most effective use we have seen of generative AI for writing so far, though, is in editing. While editing tools like autocorrect and Grammarly have existed for years now, generative AI tools present multiple advantages over this traditional editing software and offer features that can be extremely valuable for students.

First, this generative AI editing software can resolve more complex issues and provide more in-depth, contextual suggestions than prior software. ChatGPT seems to be especially effective at this, with research finding that the software is "particularly good at understanding context and generating text that is coherent and well-formed" (Atlas, 2023, p. 11). ChatGPT has since found use in the editing of medical and scientific papers. In an article about this use, researchers from the Universiti Sains Malaysia found that "[ChatGPT-4]'s ability to provide context-sensitive guidance and a degree of flexibility surpassing that of traditional software tools has been instrumental in helping researchers enhance the quality of their academic writing" (Alyasiri et al., 2023, Section 4.1, Para. 6). By using ChatGPT to assist with proof-reading and editing, students can "improve the clarity, concision, and narrative flow of [their] written work." (Atlas, 2023, p. 54).

New generative AI tools also hold an advantage over traditional editing software in terms of customizability. While other software will simply analyze a document and present any "errors" back to the user, generative AI tools can be used much more intensively than this. For example, a student could upload a history paper and ask the AI to edit only for content and historical accuracy, or they could upload a scientific paper and ask the AI to make sure that it's written in proper APA style. This gives students feedback on their writing in a way that allows for much more focused and thoughtful editing than traditional software.

One of the greatest advantages of generative AI is the constructive feedback that the models can provide to users. In addition to correcting the student's spelling, grammar, and structure, these generative AI software can analyze the student's mistakes, determine the best way to help them learn, and provide immediate feed-back to help the student practice proper writing habits. This feedback is especially valuable because students often lack sufficient opportunities to practice writing and incorporate feedback to improve their writing experience (Aldabbus & Almansouri, 2022; Gupta et al., 2022). This practice "can help students identify and correct their own errors, improving their writing skills over time" (Atlas, 2023, p. 54).

Research Assistance

In addition to writing and editing assistance, AI tools can also offer valuable help to students who struggle with research. One of the valuable utilizations of ChatGPT we have seen in student research is to help find access to quality sources. The 2023 Universiti Sains Malaysia study found that Chat GPT-4, "despite its inability to access external databases, … effectively guided users toward specific databases and provided useful search terms for literature exploration, demonstrating its utility in facilitating research endeavors" (Alyasiri et al., 2023). Further research by Duke University Libraries demonstrated that ChatGPT is effective for suggesting relevant databases for student research, as well as generating ideas for related concepts and terms (Duke University, 2023). This tool can be very helpful for students researching a topic they are unfamiliar with or just starting out in research. In addition to saving time for students, this utilization of generative AI ensures that students are accessing databases with high quality academic articles that are applicable to their research.

Similarly, generative AI tools can be used by students to find individual sources. This has been a point of contention in the past, as up until recently, services like ChatGPT were unable to provide the sources from which they derived the information in their answers. This raised questions of accuracy and misinformation, with many users having trouble fact-checking the information that they received from these platforms (Gewirtz, 2024). However, over the last couple of years in particular, these technologies have undergone significant developments that have made them much more valuable for finding sources.

This has been demonstrated by comparing studies looking at the two most recent GPT models. In a study of ChatGPT's GPT-3 model, Gravel et al. (2023) provided the model with 20 medical questions derived from research publications and asked for the corresponding citation. Of the 59 distinct citations contained in ChatGPT's response, reviewers found that only 31% of the citations were real. Compare this to a 2024 Georgetown University study of the improved GPT-4 model, though. This study asked the new model to accurately identify 1,326 scientific facts and link them to sources and found GPT-4 improved to 78% accuracy in citations (Toney-Wails, 2024). This has been a major development over one year, and while the software is not perfect, it can serve as a valuable tool to help students save time and find applicable, high-quality academic sources.

These tools also have several applications as time-saving tools for students trying to conduct research quickly. Students can ask a generative AI tool to turn a list of links into a list of APA citations; or a student who is trying to find applicable references could ask the tool to summarize different articles to figure out which best applies to their subject matter. While this doesn't directly translate to improved quality in student writing, it gets students writing sooner.

Learning Towards Industry

All the generative AI strategies previously mentioned have the potential to positively impact a student's industry readiness. Using generative AI to help individualize learning, to draft and edit pieces of writing, and to automate the process of searching for information are all ways that students transitioning into the workforce can quickly improve their workplace practices and optimize and professionalize their workflow. Students should be encouraged to practice these strategies in preparation for their future roles in industry.

GENERATIVE AI FOR EDUCATORS

Generative AI provides several potential benefits for educators, their students, and their classroom. While the tools do present technical issues and ethical questions, when used effectively, generative AI has the power to make educators' teaching more effective and their preparatory work more efficient. To create the most effective learning environment possible, educators should attempt to understand the capabilities of modern AI, as well as strategies that use it to their advantage.

Lesson Planning and Content Creation

Creating meaningful lesson plans and class content is time-consuming for educators but serves a critical role in ensuring that their students learn effectively. By using generative AI tools to assist with lesson planning and content creation, educators can reallocate this preparation time towards other tasks throughout their day.

As an educator, developing effective lesson plans is essential to ensuring that the class is conducted in an organized manner and all necessary content is covered (Van den Berg & Du Plessis, 2023). While generative AI tools are not yet capable of generating fully polished lesson plans, they can be very effective for generating a rough draft or starting point, which educators can then modify to meet the needs of their class and their students. This can save educators a significant amount of time to spend elsewhere. Additionally, a study from researchers at the University of South Africa found that this practice is valuable for the educator's development as well (Van den Berg & Du Plessis, 2023, p.10). Educators still need to refine the generated output into a full lesson plan, requiring critical thinking, particularly when ensuring the plan's appropriateness for their classroom environment. Using a generative AI tool to create drafts and then personally editing them is a very effective strategy for creating lesson plans that can be applied to several other tasks as well, including the creation of assignments and exams. By testing the efficiency of ChatGPT, certain professors have found that, through automation of certain tasks and processes, they are able to save time for other important activities like spending more time with students (Alshater, 2022; Terwiesch, 2023).

AI can also be utilized to create unique and relevant class content that helps students stay engaged and understand difficult concepts. Research has found that "reflecting on activities created by ChatGPT can help to broaden teachers' perspectives and inspire creativity by offering a range of potential activities and approaches to teaching a particular topic. [Encouraging] teachers to think outside the box and consider new and innovative ways to engage their learners in the learning process." (Van den Berg & Du Plessis, 2023, Section 5, Para. 2). For example, a middle school English teacher might say to ChatGPT: "I'm a 7th grade English teacher and my students seem bored with learning grammatical devices. Could you give me some content or examples that would be relevant to them?" We posed this question to ChatGPT, which responded with several unique ideas, including having students create "profiles" for inanimate objects to learn personification and turning alliteration into a game where students try to come up with a sentence or short paragraph in which every word starts with the same letter.

Similarly, generative AI can assist with creating examples. It has been shown that students perform better when learning complicated concepts if they are given many examples, as they can better generalize the ideas and improve their overall understanding (Kirschner & Heal, 2022; Mollick & Mollick, 2023). Creating the necessary diverse examples can be a time-consuming and challenging task for educators, though, as they should involve some form of student engagement and be balanced between detail and clarity. By using generative AI to create examples, educators can save time, while also helping students stay engaged and better grasp difficult concepts.

Low-Stakes Tests

One classroom strategy that was extremely difficult to incorporate pre-AI is the utilization of frequent, low-stakes tests for students. Frequent low-stakes testing has been shown to be an effective teaching strategy across educational levels and settings (Mollick & Mollick, 2023). These tests are not meant to measure knowledge, rather, they are a learning strategy, intended to exercise students' knowledge retention and retrieval.

The repeated retrieval practice provided by low-stakes testing has been shown to be extremely beneficial for students. A 2008 study by researchers at Purdue demonstrated that, "practicing retrieval during tests produces more learning than additional encoding or study…" (Karpicke & Roediger, 2008, Para. 12). Additionally, it has been shown that low-stakes tests provide active retrieval practice, which helps students remember and retrieve information in the future (Kirschner & Heal, 2022; Mollick & Mollick, 2023)

While it was known that repeated testing and retrieval practice are beneficial to students, these strategies have been very difficult to implement because they are so time-consuming. Creating daily or weekly quizzes for students, and then returning all of them with graded feedback, can be too much work for one educator. Generative AI makes implementing this strategy into the classroom significantly more feasible. Mollick & Mollick (2023) provide a short guide for the implementation of generative AI as a quiz creator:

1. Let the AI know its role. In this case, the role assigned to the AI is quiz creator of diagnostic quizzes.
2. Inform the AI of the topic you want to teach and the teaching strategy you want to pursue (low-stakes test to assess student knowledge).
3. If you're using Bing and there is a publicly available document or online article you have assigned as a reading, write the article(s) into the prompt.
4. You can also give it directions about the types of multiple-choice questions it should produce; for instance, *multiple choice questions should include plausible, competitive alternate responses and should not include an "all of the above option."*
5. Check its output; you may need to work with it to develop factual and higher-order questions. (pp. 12-13)

This strategy lets educators quickly create assessments for their students, making low-stakes frequent testing much easier. Educators can then choose to take the time to grade some or all of these assessments by hand or with the assistance of AI, helping them to evaluate student proficiency, utilizing repeated retrieval practice to enhance student knowledge retention, and clearing up confusions before higher-stakes assessment or more difficult concepts (Mollick & Mollick, 2023).

AI Tools for Monitoring Student Learning and Assessing Knowledge Gaps

There are several valuable ways that educators can utilize generative AI to monitor and assess student learning. While possible to assess student learning pre-AI, these new tools instantly provide feedback about student knowledge and points of confusion (Mollick & Mollick, 2023). This feedback allows educators to keep tabs on their students' progress, and students to immediately see where they went wrong and try to correct their thought process.

AI tools can also be used by educators to gain a much deeper insight into the feedback provided by these assignments. For example, AI systems like IBM's Watson Education can analyze student assessments and not only grade them, but also create personalized learning profiles for students (Pan et al., 2023). These profiles identify which areas each student struggles with, and which teaching strategies are most effective for them. Based on these profiles, the system can offer proactive insights based on student performance trends, which helps with informing both short-term lesson plans and long-term educational strategies (Yuskovych- Zhukovska et al., 2022). These tools can be extremely valuable for educators, and open the door to a bright future of much more effective and efficient student assessments. By making use of AI-powered assessments, educators can much more easily assess and plan around student progress, while also allowing students to learn more effectively by immediately seeing and understanding their mistakes.

CONCERNS WITH GENERATIVE AI

Generative AI tools have the capability of revolutionizing modern education and industry, however, proper utilization of the tools requires understanding some of the major drawbacks with the technology.

Model Bias

Generative AI model bias, much like human bias, can be the result of both conscious and subconscious prejudice (Chapman, 2024). "Garbage in, garbage out" is a computing concept that details how incorrect or poor input results in an output of similar quality. Because generative AI trains on data created by humans, generative models adopt human biases. The biases of the training data selected by the model creators and the creators' decisions to include or exclude certain training data directly impacts the biases exhibited by the model.

An early example of Ai bias comes from Microsoft's Twitter (now X) chatbot Tay.AI (Microsoft, 2016). Tay utilized machine learning techniques (the building blocks of generative AI creation) to "learn" from the users who interacted with it. Malicious users who interacted with Tay introduced the model to massive amounts of racist and anti-semetic rhetoric. Despite Microsoft's attempts to ensure positive user interactions, the model learned many of the offensive ideas it was exposed to and began to respond to users with them. Microsoft was then forced to turn off Tay. AI the day after its implementation.

Lots of research has been conducted showing human biases also being present in the output of image generating tools like Midjourney and Dall-E. For example, a 2023 study found that across five different image generating software prompted with "face of a doctor in the United States", "face of a physician in the United States", "photo of a doctor in the United States", and "photo of a physician in the United States" resulted in 82% white doctors (compared to only 63% white doctors as found in an Association of American Medical Colleges survey) and 93% male doctors (compared to 62% male doctors) (Lee et al., 2024). Another similar effort found Midjourney responding to the prompt "An Indian Person" with almost all older bearded men wearing a headscarf or turban, creating a homogenized and prejudicial view of a diverse nation (Aaron et al., 2024).

Attempts to address these issues have been made, but not without controversy. Google quickly removed the image generating aspect of their generative AI model Google Gemini after its attempts to increase the diversity of images resulted in images containing obviously erroneous subject matter, infamously including depictions of black nazi soldiers (Raghavan, 2024).

Because generative AI is created by and trained on humans and human made data, there will likely never be a fully unbiased model. This means the end users of generative AI tools and viewers of the generated content must be aware of the potential for biased results, and will need to develop skills to critically engage with the content generated by the AI tool.

Hallucinations/Factual Errors

Another issue with today's generative AI tools is that they sometimes "hallucinate," or make up, responses, resulting in inaccurate information being passed on to end users (IBM, 2023). This primarily occurs because generative AI "learns" is only capable of learning the relationships between pieces of data, not actual information about that data. These tools are also limited by the data used in their training. The AI is unable to learn new information after it finishes its training period, and therefore cannot accurately respond to questions related to anything from outside of that scope (Welborn, 2023). Today, some of the newest models do have internet search capabilities, like ChatGPT Search, but as this technology is new, errors still occur. Consequently, generative AI can produce false information that it cannot warn the end user about.

Similarly, these tools generally struggle to accurately cite information, especially when the topic is more obscure and therefore less data exists within the AI's training data. For example, in 2023 lawyers from the Law Offices of Levidow and Oberman submitted a filing for their client's personal injury case (Mata v. Avianca, 2023). When it was later discovered that six of the cases cited did not exist or were falsified, one of the lawyers came forward and revealed they used ChatGPT for their research, leading to the hallucinated cases cited. The judge presiding over the case placed sanctions on the legal group "for, among other things, misrepresenting facts or making frivolous legal arguments," arguing that the responsibility for ensuring the integrity of their sources laid squarely on the lawyers who failed to do so (Mata v. Avianca, 2023).

Image generation software can also cause false information to be spread. Users are able to create images of almost anyone anywhere, giving bad actors the capability of generating false narratives from faked images. For instance, in 2023 the French President Macron pushed for reform to the retirement system in France, wanting to raise the legal age of retirement (Armstrong, 2023). Protests broke out in response, but AI generated images of the president taking part in the protests began circulating on social media (Mouriquand, 2023). This caused confusion for some protestors and French citizens who were unable to recognize that the images were fake. This story became news internationally, helping to combat early confusion, but with the ease of access to image generation software and social media platforms, it has never been easier to create and spread falsified images.

With generative AI, users have the responsibility to ensure the accuracy of any information generated, or else they risk unintentionally spreading misinformation created by AI hallucination. Users of image generation software should also consider the ethical ramifications of the images they create.

Job Security

Regardless of the performance of generative AI tools, concerns exist around the impact of generative AI on job security across all parts of the workforce. Many industries already see its effect on the workplace, as shown by the reported 270% increase in enterprise adoption of these tools (Rashid & Kausik, 2024). Many workers within these industries are worried about the effect these tools will have in reducing the worker's role or potentially even outright replacement. This section will directly discuss the concerns held by those in creative fields, but note that they can apply to many other parts of the workforce as well.

On May 2, 2023 The Writers Guild of America (WGA) went on strike over concerns of unfair payment on successful streaming service shows and movies, poor job security, and small writer's rooms (Coyle, 2023). Late night shows quickly stopped production and other productions followed suit. As the strike continued, another concern grew louder amongst the guild and eventually became one of the most vocal talking points of the picketing writers, generative AI's role in the script-writing process. Generative AI became seen as an existential threat to the value of the writer. Their immediate concern was not total replacement by AI, but rather of a diminishment of their role in the writing process, and therefore a diminishment of pay and job safety (Coyle, 2023). The strike would end on September 27, 2023, with writers receiving increased control over the ways AI could be implemented in writer's rooms and preventing production leads from forcing writers to use generative AI tools.

The Screen Actors Guild – American Federation of Television and Radio Artists went on strike July 9, 2023, overlapping with the WGA's strike. On their list of concerns, studio use of generative AI to replace/enhance actors voices, attempts at using generative AI to alter physical performances, and use generative AI to create entirely digital performances (sometimes posthumously) (Dalton, 2023). The strike ended November 9, 2023, with similar control over AI use within the industry, but

SAG-AFTRA would return to strike on July 26, 2024, over AI use in the video game industry, continuing their efforts to improve their job security.

Beyond questions of job security, creative fields and the public also question the merit behind the use of generative AI tools and the question of ownership of generated works.

Public conversation arose when one Colorado man's Midjourney based art won the Colorado State Fair's digital art competition in 2022. The self-described "author" of the piece broke no rules in submitting an AI generated piece, and the competition judges stated they still would have awarded the piece first place if they knew the piece was made using AI thanks to the "spirit" of the work (Winfrey, 2022). Online discourse, however, viewed the piece's victory as a sign of devaluation to man-made art, and an omen of job losses to come, something the author themself acknowledged as a potential cause for fear.

While the public remained divided on the creative merit of the piece, legally, the piece is considered uncopyrightable according to recent copyright office filings. The courts found AI generated pieces to lack the "human authorship necessary to support a copyright claim" (Thaler, 2023). The author of the piece was rejected by the US Copyright Court for the third and final time, rendering the piece free for public use (Appel, 2025). This is not exclusive to visual AI art, but extends to any work primarily created by AI, including music, voice recordings, video, and writing. This means that users of generative AI tools seeking the copyright for the work will need to ensure the human element demonstrably outweighs the AI element, and has potentially wide-reaching implications for any company choosing to use generative AI tools in their workflow.

Ethical Concerns

It takes a lot of data to train powerful generative AI models. ChatGPT 3.0, the version of the model that was first released to the public, trained on 570 GB of filtered text data sourced from 45 TB of compressed plain text from the internet (Brown et al., 2020). That data was taken from databases like Common Crawl, internet-based book corpora, Wikipedia, and an internal corpus of data scraped specifically by OpenAI for its quality. This data is what powers the capabilities of generative AI, but the creators of the content used for the training data likely did so with no expectation of their work being used by generative AI tools. They had no opportunity to opt-in or opt-out of data training. The databases OpenAI used are supposed to only contain open-source content, but the novelty of generative AI tools gives rise to conversation about if the original content authors were given proper opportunity to consent to this new use. Controversially, OpenAI and ChatGPT were found to be potentially bypassing paywalls in 2023, resulting in the New York

Times' lawsuit against OpenAI and Microsoft (Roth, 2023). The New York Times alleges that ChatGPT could produce almost word for word reproductions of their paywalled articles when prompted.

In the classroom, generative AI tools offer students an easy path towards cheating. If the student is motivated to use the tool, they will often be rewarded with results that are just as good and sometimes better than the results of the average student for a fraction of the effort (Ibrahim et al., 2023). Students who grow reliant on generative AI risk missing out on developing their critical thinking skills and creativity (Ali, 2023). Initial efforts by universities to detect AI usage with AI detection software such as GPTZero and Turnitin's detection functionality were also found to inaccurately classify human work, causing leading universities like Vanderbilt to turn away from using the tools entirely. The detection software, built with the same technology as the generative AI they try to detect, inherited human biases, often over classifying non-native English speakers as AI generated and they can easily be circumvented through running the words through other AI generated tools. This leads to difficulty when trying to prevent AI based cheating, particularly when using traditional teaching methods.

STRATEGIES FOR GENERATIVE AI IN EDUCATION

Modern generative AI technology poses unique benefits and challenges in its educational implementation. These tools offer substantial benefits to productivity and development for both educators and students and allow educators to use new and effective teaching strategies that were too time consuming to implement before. When misused, however, these tools have the potential to significantly damage the learning and teaching environment of the classroom. The use of these tools in education is made particularly complex by the fact that generative AI tools are constantly evolving, and their capabilities are always changing. Below, we recommend a number of strategies based on our background research that educators can use to effectively implement generative AI into their classroom.

Explore How Generative AI Can Benefit Teaching Practices

Generative AI can be utilized by educators to make their lives easier, their teaching more effective, and their preparatory work more efficient. While these tools have been a point of contention in teaching since their public release, the tool has shown that it can be extremely valuable for educators in a number of ways. To create the most effective learning environment possible, educators must try to understand the power and capabilities of modern AI, as well as strategies to use it to their advantage.

By utilizing AI, educators can save time on content that requires a lot of monotonous work, like lesson plans and tests. The use of AI can also help to ensure this content is relevant and engaging to students. Additionally, the use of AI allows for the use of new teaching strategies that were impractical before, such as the use of frequent, low-stakes tests to exercise students' knowledge retention. By taking advantage of the potential benefits of ChatGPT, educators can save time and make their classroom a more effective learning environment for students.

Create Clear Guidelines for Student Use of Generative AI

To create a functioning work environment for both students and educators, it is imperative that all guidelines related to student use of generative AI are clear and that the reasons behind the guidelines are explained. Students have likely already formed their own opinions on the correct use cases for generative AI within the classroom, transparency behind the decision-making process can help alleviate any conflicting viewpoints and any tension that may cause. Clear expectations lead to less frustration amongst students and can help reduce the temptations for irresponsible generative AI use (Byrne, 2024). These expectations should be supported by generative AI's benefits and issues as outlined in this chapter and elsewhere. Research should also be done into how related industry fields are utilizing generative AI before committing to guidelines. Students in a creative writing class should have different generative AI standards than those in a public relations course.

Educators must also clearly explain their methodology for classifying work as cheated. Generative AI detection software is oftentimes ineffective and exhibits similar biases to the generative AI tools they attempt to address, meaning there is no true shortcut to determining what was and was not created using only generative AI. Instead, educators will likely need to return to more personal methods of cheating detection, with the chance for student appeal. Educators must recognize that they will occasionally incorrectly determine that an assignment utilized generative AI in a manner that was outside of specified guidelines, and as such they cannot approach potential issues of intentional academic dishonesty with a mindset of guilty until proven innocent at the risk of alienating the students they misclassified.

Encourage Responsible Student Use of Generative AI

Encouraging responsible student use of generative AI to further learning and is extremely important for creating an effective classroom environment today. By encouraging their students to responsibly experiment with generative AI and showing them strategies to use it effectively, educators open their classroom up to a number of benefits.

Generative AI can allow students to have much more effective and individualized learning experiences outside of class. AI tools can create explanations tailored uniquely for each student, influenced not only by learning styles and preferences, but also progress and current understanding. They can help to keep students engaged, as well as develop their skills more efficiently. They can also "provide instant feedback on student answers and questions, reinforcing the learning process by correcting mistakes in real-time" (Pan et al., 2023; Neuenschwander, 2024, p. 4).

Generative AI is also a powerful tool for writing, editing, and research. These tools can provide immediate feedback on student writing and suggest edits based on specific prompts, helping students improve the quality of the piece they are working on as well as develop their writing abilities. Generative AI can help with monotonous or frustration-inducing research tasks, like finding scholarly sources and combing through long articles. By utilizing generative AI tools in these processes, students are able to save time, better engage with the course content, and ultimately learn more effectively.

By encouraging their students to use this new technology, educators open their students up to the benefits that they offer, in addition to the idea that it is valuable to experiment with new technologies. This encourages a curious mindset that can help keep students engaged and invested in academic pursuits in the long run. Additionally, this can encourage students to explore more around the class content, helping them become genuinely interested in the material.

To responsibly engage with generative AI tools, students must be made aware of the tools' shortcomings, including the bias inherent to the models, the capacity for generative AI hallucinations/factual errors, and the potential for misuse and overreliance on the tools. Students using generative AI tools must ensure that the information they are told is accurate and fair before using it in their own work.

CONCLUSION

Generative AI quickly left its mark on the world. The revolutionary technology opened possibilities for automation and optimization of tasks that were previously very time-consuming and created new avenues for expression and creation through tools like ChatGPT and Midjourney. The launch of these tools did not come without controversy; many became concerned with their potential to be used as cheating software, job replacements, and misinformation spreaders. These concerns are understandable, but when users take the time to properly utilize generative AI, it is a powerful tool that enhances the learning experience, optimizes workflow, and leads to the creation of new knowledge.

REFERENCES

A short history of the internet. National Science and Media Museum. (2020, December 3). https://www.scienceandmediamuseum.org.uk/objects-and-stories/short-history-internet

Aaron, L., Abbate, S., Allain, N. M., Almas, B., Fallon, B., Gavin, D., & Gordon, C. (Barrett), Jadamec, M., Merlino, A., Pierie, L., Solano, G., & Wolf, D. (2024). AI Bias Concerns. In *Optimizing AI in Higher Education: SUNY FACT² Guide, Second Edition* (pp. 5–9). State University of New York Press. https://doi.org/DOI: 10.2307/jj.20522984.11

Aldabbus, S., & Almansouri, E. (2022). Academic writing difficulties encountered by university EFL learners. *British Journal of English Linguistics*, *10*(3), 1–11. DOI: 10.37745/bjel.2013/vol10n3111

Ali, F., Open, A. I., & Inc, C. (2023). Let the devil speak for itself: Should ChatGPT be allowed or banned in hospitality and tourism schools? *Journal of Global Hospitality and Tourism*, *2*(1), 1–6. https://www.doi.org/10.5038/2771-5957.2.1.1016. DOI: 10.5038/2771-5957.2.1.1016

Alshater, M. (2022). Exploring the Role of Artificial Intelligence in Enhancing Academic Performance: A Case Study of ChatGPT. SSRN Electronic Journal. https://doi.org/DOI: 10.2139/ssrn.4312358

Alyasiri, O., Salisu, S., Younis, H., Salman, A. M., Sahib, T. M., Akhtom, D., & Hayder, I. M. (2023). ChatGPT Revisited: Using ChatGPT-4 for Finding References and Editing Language in Medical Scientific Articles. *Journal of Stomatology, Oral and Maxillofacial Surgery*, •••, 125. PMID: 38521243

Amazon Web Services. (2024). What are Autoregressive Models? Amazon. https://aws.amazon.com/what-is/autoregressive-models/

Amazon Web Services. (2024). What is AGI (Artificial General Intelligence)? Amazon. https://aws.amazon.com/what-is/artificial-general-intelligence/

Amazon Web Services. (2024). What is a GAN? Amazon. https://aws.amazon.com/what-is/gan/

Amazon Web Services. (2024). What is RHLF? Amazon. https://aws.amazon.com/what-is/reinforcement-learning-from-human-feedback/

Amazon Web Services. (2024). What is Stable Diffusion? Amazon. https://aws.amazon.com/what-is/stable-diffusion/

Appel, G., Neelbauer, J., & Schweidel, D. A. (2025, January 13). *Generative AI has an intellectual property problem.* Harvard Business Review. https://hbr.org/2023/04/generative-ai-has-an-intellectual-property-problem

Armstrong, K. (2023, April 15). France pension reforms: Macron signs pension age rise to 64 into law. BBC News. https://www.bbc.com/news/world-europe-65279818

Atlas, S. (2023, January). ChatGPT for Higher Education and Professional Development. University of Rhode Island College of Business Faculty Publications.

Baidoo-Anu, D., & Owusu Ansah, L. (2023, December 31). Education in the Era of Generative Artificial Intelligence (AI): Understanding the Potential Benefits of CHATGPT in Promoting Teaching and Learning. *Journal of AI, 7*(1), 52–62. DOI: 10.61969/jai.1337500

Bisneto, T. R., de Carvalho Filho, A. O., & Magalhães, D. M. (2020). Generative Adversarial Network and Texture Features Applied to Automatic Glaucoma Detection. [DOI]. *Applied Soft Computing, 90*, 90. DOI: 10.1016/j.asoc.2020.106165

Brown, T. B. Benjamin Mann, Nick Ryder, Melanie Subbiah, Jared Kaplan, Prafulla Dhariwal, Arvind Neelakantan, Pranav Shyam, Girish Sastry, Amanda Askell, Sandhini Agarwal, Ariel Herbert-Voss, Gretchen Krueger, Tom Henighan, Rewon Child, Aditya Ramesh, Daniel M. Ziegler, Jeffrey Wu, Clemens Winter, Christopher Hesse, Mark Chen, Eric Sigler, Mateusz Litwin, Scott Gray, Benjamin Chess, Jack Clark, Christopher Berner, Sam McCandlish, Alec Radford, Ilya Sutskever, and Dario Amodei. 2020. Language models are few-shot learners. In Proceedings of the 34th International Conference on Neural Information Processing Systems (NIPS '20). Curran Associates Inc., Red Hook, NY, USA, Article 159, 1877–1901. https://arxiv.org/pdf/2005.14165

Byrne, M. D. (2024). CHATGPT without a safety net. *Nursing Education Perspectives, 45*(1), 63–65. DOI: 10.1097/01.NEP.0000000000001225 PMID: 38117603

Chapman University. (2024). Bias in Ai. Bias in AI | Chapman University. https://www.chapman.edu/ai/bias-in-ai.aspx

Chen, M., Mei, S., Fan, J., & Wang, M. (2024). Opportunities and Challenges of Diffusion Models for Generative AI. *National Science Review, 11*(12), nwae348. DOI: 10.1093/nsr/nwae348 PMID: 39554240

Cisco Systems. (January 25, 2024). Companies' concerns related to the use of generative artificial intelligence (GenAI) in 2023 [Graph]. In Statista. Retrieved November 13, 2024, from https://www.statista.com/statistics/1455833/gen-ai-users-concerns

Coley, M. (2023, August 16). Guidance on AI detection and why we're disabling Turnitin's AI detector. Vanderbilt University. https://www.vanderbilt.edu/brightspace/2023/08/16/guidance-on-ai-detection-and-why-were-disabling-turnitins-ai-detector/

Coyle, J. (2023, May 2). *Late-night TV shows go dark as writers strike for better pay*. AP News. https://apnews.com/article/writers-strike-hollywood-wga-926179281803e10b1d501dcab93e30d

Coyle, J. (2023, May 5). *Could Ai Pen "casablanca"? screenwriters take aim at chatgpt*. AP News. https://apnews.com/article/ai-hollywood-writers-strike-artificial-intelligence-dc71c4cabcca0ee1b1afe0050d392a36

Dalton, A. (2023, July 21). *Ai is the wild card in Hollywood's strikes. here's an explanation of its unsettling role*. AP News. https://apnews.com/article/artificial-intelligence-hollywood-strikes-explained-writers-actors-e872bd63ab52c3ea9f7d6e825240a202

De Oliveira, L., Paganini, M., & Nachman, B. (2017, September 29). Learning Particle Physics by Example: Location-Aware Generative Adversarial Networks for Physics Synthesis. *Computing and Software for Big Science*, *1*(1), 4. DOI: 10.1007/s41781-017-0004-6

Deloitte. (January 15, 2024). Share of Professionals Using generative Artificial Intelligence (AI)

Duke University. (2024, October 9). Artificial Intelligence Policies: Guidelines and considerations. Duke Learning Innovation & Lifetime Education. https://lile.duke.edu/ai-and-teaching-at-duke-2/artificial-intelligence-policies-in-syllabi-guidelines-and-considerations/

Feuerriegel, S., Hartmann, J., Janiesch, C., & Zschech, P. (2023, August 7). Generative AI. SSRN Electronic Journal, 66, 111–126. DOI: 10.2139/ssrn.4443189

Generative, A. I. Lab. (2024, August 19). *Comparing Diffusion, GAN, and VAE Techniques*. Generative AI Lab. https://generativeailab.org/l/generative-ai/a-tale-of-three-generative-models- comparing-diffusion-gan-and-vae-techniques/569/

Gewirtz, D. (2024, June 28). *How to Make ChatGPT Provide Sources and Citations*. ZDNET. https://www.zdnet.com/article/how-to-make-chatgpt-provide-sources-and-citations/

Goodfellow, I. J., Pouget-Abadie, J., Mirza, M., Xu, B., Warde-Farley, D., Ozair, S., Courville, A., & Benign, Y. (2014). *Generative Adversarial Nets*. Université de Montréal.

Gravel, J., D'Amours-Gravel, M., & Osmanlliu, E. (2023). Learning to Fake it: Limited Responses and Fabricated References Provided by ChatGPT for Medical Questions. *Mayo Clinic Proceedings. Digital Health, 1*(3), 226–234. DOI: 10.1016/j.mcpdig.2023.05.004

Gupta, S., Jaiswal, A., Paramasivam, A., & Kotecha, J. (2022). Academic writing challenges and supports: Perspectives of international doctoral Students and their supervisors. *Frontiers in Education, 7*, 891534. DOI: 10.3389/feduc.2022.891534

Herbold, S., Hautli-Janisz, A., Heuer, U., Kikteva, Z., & Trautsch, A. (2023). A Large-Scale Comparison of Human-Written Versus ChatGPT-Generated Essays. *Scientific Reports, 13*(1), 18617. DOI: 10.1038/s41598-023-45644-9 PMID: 37903836

IBM. (2023, September 1). *What are ai hallucinations?* IBM. https://www.ibm.com/think/topics/ai-hallucinations#:~:text=Use%20data%20templates,and%20refine%20the%20system%20continually

Ibrahim, H., Liu, F., Asim, R., Battu, B., Benabderrahmane, S., Alhafni, B., Adnan, W., Alhanai, T., AlShebli, B., Baghdadi, R., Bélanger, J. J., Beretta, E., Celik, K., Chaqfeh, M., Daqaq, M. F., Bernoussi, Z. E., Fougnie, D., Garcia de Soto, B., Gandolfi, A., & Zaki, Y. (2023). Perception, performance, and detectability of conversational artificial intelligence across 32 university courses. *Scientific Reports, 13*(1), 12187. DOI: 10.1038/s41598-023-38964-3 PMID: 37620342

In Organizations Worldwide as of. 2024, by Function [Graph] Statista. https://www.statista.com/statistics/1451298/genai-adoption-by-function-worldwide

Karpicke, J. D., & Roediger, H. L.III. (2008). The critical importance of retrieval for learning. *Science, 319*(5865), 966–968. DOI: 10.1126/science.1152408 PMID: 18276894

Kılınç, H. K., & Keçecioğlu, F. (2024, May 31). Generative Artificial Intelligence: A Historical and Future Perspective. *Academic Platform Journal of Engineering and Smart Systems, 12*(2), 47–58. DOI: 10.21541/apjess.1398155

Kirschner, P. A., Hendrick, C., & Heal, J. (2022). *How Teaching Happens: Seminal Works in Teaching and Teacher Effectiveness and What They Mean in Practice*. Routledge. DOI: 10.4324/9781003228165

Knight, W. (2022, May 17). AI can show us the ravages of climate change. MIT Technology Review. https://www.technologyreview.com/2019/05/16/135323/ai-can-show-us-the-ravages-of-climate-change

Lee, P. (2016, March 25). *Learning from Tay's introduction*. The Official Microsoft Blog. https://blogs.microsoft.com/blog/2016/03/25/learning-tays-introduction/

Lee, S. W., Morcos, M., Lee, D. W., & Young, J. (2024). Demographic Representation of Generative Artificial Intelligence Images of Physicians. *JAMA Network Open*, *7*(8), e2425993. DOI: 10.1001/jamanetworkopen.2024.25993 PMID: 39106070

Mata v. Avianca, Inc., JUSTIA Dockets & Filings (United States District Court Southern District of New York June 6, 2023). Retrieved January 24, 2025, from https://docs.justia.com/cases/federal/district-courts/new-york/nysdce/1:2022cv01461/575368/45

Mollick, E. R., & Mollick, L. (2023). Using AI to Implement Effective Teaching Strategies in Classrooms: Five Strategies, Including Prompts. *Wharton School of the University of Pennsylvania & Wharton Interactive*. https://doi.org/DOI: 10.2139/ssrn.4391243

Morris, M. R. (2023, April 4). *Scientists' Perspectives on the Potential for Generative AI in their Fields*. Google Research.

Mouriquand, D. (2023, March 23). How ai is putting president macron at the heart of the French pension protests | euronews. euronews. https://www.euronews.com/culture/2023/03/23/how-ai-is-putting-president-macron-at-the-heart-of-the-french-pension-protests

Muck Rack. (January 3, 2024). *Leading ways public relations (PR) professionals used generative artificial intelligence (AI) in their workflow as of December 2023 [Graph]*. Statista. https://www.statista.com/statistics/1440861/ways-prs-used-generative-ai-work

Muthukrishnan, N., Maleki, F., Ovens, K., Reinhold, C., Forghani, B., & Forghani, R. (2020, November). Brief History of Artificial Intelligence. *Neuroimaging Clinics of North America*, *30*(4), 393–399. DOI: 10.1016/j.nic.2020.07.004 PMID: 33038991

Myers, A. (2023, May 15). Ai-detectors biased against Non-Native English writers. Stanford HAI. https://hai.stanford.edu/news/ai-detectors-biased-against-non-native-english-writers

Neuenschwander, B.E. (2024, September 27). *Benefits of Artificial Intelligence in Education: Personalized Learning and Enhanced Classroom Management*. Florida State University.

Northern Illinois University. (2024). *Class policies for AI Tools: Center for Innovative Teaching and learning*. Northern Illinois University. https://www.niu.edu/citl/resources/guides/class-policies-for-ai-tools.shtml

Open, A. I. (2022, November 30). *Introducing ChatGPT*. https://openai.com/index/chatgpt

Pan, L., Saxon, M., Xu, W., Nathani, D., Wang, X., & Wang, W. Y. (2023, August 30). Automatically Correcting Large Language Models: Surveying the landscape of diverse self-correction strategies. arXiv.org. https://arxiv.org/abs/2308.03188

Qian, S., & Feng, Q. (2020). Research on the Integration of Artificial Intelligence and Education. *Journal of Physics: Conference Series*, *1570*(1), 012063. DOI: 10.1088/1742-6596/1570/1/012063

Radford, A., Narasimhan, K., Salimans, T., & Sutskever, I. (2018, June). *Improving Language Understanding by Generative Pre-Training*. OpenAI. https://openai.com/index/chatgpt

Raghavan, P. (2024, February 23). *Gemini image generation got it wrong. we'll do better*. Google. https://blog.google/products/gemini/gemini-image-generation-issue

Rashid, A. B., & Kausik, A. K. (2024b). AI Revolutionizing Industries Worldwide: A Comprehensive Overview of its Diverse Applications. *Hybrid Advances*, *7*, 100277. Advance online publication. DOI: 10.1016/j.hybadv.2024.100277

Ross, S. M. (2020). Technology infusion in K-12 classrooms: A retrospective look at three decades of challenges and advancements in research and practice. *Educational Technology Research and Development*, *68*(5), 2003–2020. DOI: 10.1007/s11423-020-09756-7

Roth, E. (2023, December 27). The New York Times is suing OpenAI and Microsoft for copyright infringement. The Verge. https://www.theverge.com/2023/12/27/24016212/new-york-times-openai-microsoft-lawsuit-copyright-infringement

Rutgers Learning Centers. The Importance of Outlining. (2025). https://learningcenters.rutgers.edu/resources/importance-outlining

Silvernail, D. L., Pinkham, C. A., Wintle, S. E., Walker, L. C., & Bartlett, C. L. (2011). *A Middle*

Stanford University. (2025). *Surya Ganguli's Work on Diffusion Models Powers Modern AI Tools like DALL-E*. Stanford University. https://appliedphysics.stanford.edu/news/surya-gangulis-work-diffusion-models-powers-modern-ai-tools-dall-e

Stryker, C., & Kavlakoglu, E. (2024, December 19). *What is Artificial Intelligence (AI)?* IBM. https://www.ibm.com/think/topics/artificial-intelligence

Tamim, R. M., Bernard, R. M., Borokhovski, E., Abrami, P. C., & Schmid, R. F. (2011). What Forty Years of Research Says About the Impact of Technology on Learning. *Review of Educational Research*, *81*(1), 4–28. DOI: 10.3102/0034654310393361

Tamim, R. M., Borokhovski, E., Bernard, R. M., Schmid, R. F., Abrami, P. C., & Pickup, D. I. (2021). A study of meta-analyses reporting quality in the large and expanding literature of educational technology. *Australasian Journal of Educational Technology, 37*(4), 100–115. DOI: 10.14742/ajet.6322

Terwiesch, C. (2023). Would Chat GPT3 Get a Wharton MBA? A Prediction Based on Its Performance in the Operations Management Course. *Mack Institute for Innovation Management at the Wharton School*, University of Pennsylvania, 2023.

Thaler v. Perlmutter, uscourts.gov (United States District Court for the District of Columbia August 18, 2023). Retrieved January 24, 2025, from https://ecf.dcd.uscourts.gov/cgi-bin/show_public_doc?2022cv1564-24

Toney-Wails, A. (2024). What Kind of Sourcery is This? Evaluating GPT-4's Performance on Linking Scientific Fact to Citations. *Proceedings of the 1st Workshop on Customizable NLP: Progress and Challenges in Customizing NLP for a Domain, Application, Group, or Individual (CustomNLP4U)*, 257–268. https://doi.org/DOI: 10.18653/v1/2024.customnlp4u-1.19

Turing, A. M. (1950). Computing Machinery and Intelligence. *Mind, 49*(236), 433–460. DOI: 10.1093/mind/LIX.236.433

Van den Berg, G., & Du Plessis, E. (2023). ChatGPT and Generative AI: Possibilities for Its Contribution to Lesson Planning, Critical Thinking and Openness in Teacher Education. *Education Sciences, 13*(10), 998. Advance online publication. DOI: 10.3390/educsci13100998

Vanderbilt University. (2024). *Syllabus AI policies*. Vanderbilt University. https://as.vanderbilt.edu/gci-ai/syllabus-ai-policies/

Wei, J. (2019, July 3). *Generating Shoe Designs with Machine Learning*. Medium. https://towardsdatascience.com/generating-shoe-designs-with-deep-learning-5dde432a23b8

Welborn, A. (2023, March 9). *ChatGPT and fake citations*. Duke University Libraries Blogs. https://blogs.library.duke.edu/blog/2023/03/09/chatgpt-and-fake-citations/#:~:text=ChatGPT%20is%20based%20on%20a,or%20write%20your%20literature%20review

Winfrey, A. L. (2022, September 2). *"someone had to be first": Pueblo artist criticized after Ai painting wins at Colorado State Fair*. Pueblo Chieftain. https://www.chieftain.com/story/news/2022/08/31/ai-painting-wins-at-colorado-state-fair-pueblo-artist-explains-jason-allen/65466872007/

Wong, C. (2019, May 27). *The Rise of AI Supermodels*. CDOTrends. https://www.cdotrends.com/story/14300/rise-ai-supermodels

Yuskovych-Zhukovska, V., Poplavska, T., Diachenko, O., Mishenina, T., Topolnyk, Y., & Gurevych, R. (2022). Application of Artificial Intelligence in Education. Problems and Opportunities for Sustainable Development. *BRAIN -. Broad Research in Artificial Intelligence and Neuroscience*, *13*(1), 339–356. DOI: 10.18662/brain/13.1Sup1/322

KEY TERMS AND DEFINITIONS

Artificial Intelligence: Computer software that can mimic aspects of human intelligence when given tasks.

Diffusion: The application of noise to existing data that is then removed in a pre-trained process to create an output.

Generative: Computer software output that is created through the blending of data sources, rather than the repetition of original data.

Generative Adversarial Network: A type of generative AI model that improves its performance by training two models in opposition.

Generative AI Model: The computer software that produces human-like generated responses.

Generative Pre-trained Transformer: A type of generative AI model that performs natural language processing and outputs natural language responses.

Hallucination: Generative AI output that contains false information, caused by a lack of relevant training data and the training process.

Model Bias: Purposeful or accidental oversights in the training of a model that lead to prejudiced output.

Compilation of References

Aaron, L., Abbate, S., Allain, N. M., Almas, B., Fallon, B., Gavin, D., & Gordon, C. (Barrett), Jadamec, M., Merlino, A., Pierie, L., Solano, G., & Wolf, D. (2024). AI Bias Concerns. In *Optimizing AI in Higher Education: SUNY FACT^2 Guide, Second Edition* (pp. 5–9). State University of New York Press. https://doi.org/DOI: 10.2307/jj.20522984.11

Abdel-Al, H. A.-Z., & Abdel-Al, A. B. (2022). Scientific research skills in the digital environment: A case study of faculty members at King Khalid University and Northern Border University (Kingdom of Saudi Arabia). *REMAH Journal, 71*, 317–346.

Acuña, F., & Fernández Ugalde, R. (2024). Dissenting from what? the rupture of Chilean teachers with the long-term consensus on teacher professional development. *Globalisation, Societies and Education, 23*(1), 63–78. https://doi.org/10.1080/14767724.2023.2294133

Adetimirin, A. E. (2011). ICT Literacy among Undergraduates in Nigerian Universities. *Education and Information Technologies, 17*(4), 381–397. DOI: 10.1007/s10639-011-9163-y

Adhikari, D. R., & Shrestha, P. (2023). Knowledge management initiatives for achieving sustainable development goal 4.7: Higher education institutions' stakeholder perspectives. *Journal of Knowledge Management, 27*(4), 1109–1139. DOI: 10.1108/JKM-03-2022-0172

Afzal, A., Khan, S., Daud, S., Ahmad, Z., & Butt, A. (2023). Addressing the digital divide: Access and use of technology in education. *Journal of Social Sciences Review, 3*(2), 883–895. DOI: 10.54183/jssr.v3i2.326

Agarwal, P. (2021). *Higher education in India: The need for change. Oxford University Press. Gupta, R., & Sharma, P. (2020). Financing higher education in India: Policies and perspectives*. Springer.

Agarwal, P. (2022). Democratizing education through MOOCs: The Indian perspective. *Journal of Educational Technology & Society*, *25*(3), 12–18. DOI: 10.1016/j.edusoc.2022.09.012

Agovino, T. (2019). Bridging the Gender Divide. HRMagazine. https://www.researchgate.net/publication/361772157. Accessed: 03/09/ 2024.

Ahmad, N.S., Ismail, A. and Yaakob, M.N., (2024). A decade of progress: A bibliometric analysis of research trends in professional development for middle leaders in education (2014-2023). *Journal of Contemporary Social Science and Education Studies (JOCSSES) E-ISSN-2785-8774, 4*(2), pp.225-247.

Ahmed, M., & Rahman, M. (2020). Teacher recruitment and retention challenges in Bangladesh's educational system: A critical review. *The Journal of Educational Research, 15*(2), 115–130.

Ahmed, S. T., & Roche, T. (2021). Making the connection: Examining the relationship between undergraduate students' digital literacy and academic success in an English medium instruction (EMI) university. *Education and Information Technologies, 26*(4), 4601–4620. DOI: 10.1007/s10639-021-10443-0

Akiba, M., Byun, S. Y., Jiang, X., Kim, K., & Moran, A. J. (2023). Do teachers feel valued in society? Occupational value of the teaching profession in OECD countries. *AERA Open, 9*, 23328584231179184. DOI: 10.1177/23328584231179184

Akinlabi, O. O. (2023). *Understanding the Impact of the Digital Divide and New Methods of Learning on Humanities Students at UKZN during the Coronavirus Pandemic. Master of Arts Media and Cultural Studies*. University of KwaZulu-Natal.

Alam, A., & Kabir, M. (2021). Teacher recruitment and retention issues in rural Bangladesh. *Asian Journal of Education, 44*(1), 13–27.

Alangari, H. (2024). Transforming Learning: The Rise of Micro-Credentials in Higher Education. In *Digital Transformation in Higher Education, Part A* (pp. 83-100). Emerald Publishing Limited.

Al-Baraa Abdulrahman Al-Mekhlafi, I., Othman, I., & Zamil, A. M. A. (2022). Modeling the impact of massive open online courses (MOOC) implementation factors on continuance intention of students: PLS-SEM approach. *Education and Information Technologies, 28*(3), 1185–1200. DOI: 10.1007/s10639-022-11519-9

Aldabbus, S., & Almansouri, E. (2022). Academic writing difficulties encountered by university EFL learners. *British Journal of English Linguistics, 10*(3), 1–11. DOI: 10.37745/bjel.2013/vol10n3111

Aldamen, H., Alkhateeb, H., Kercher, K., Duncan, K., & Hollindale, J. (2021). Core competencies for the global workplace: A cross-cultural and skill-based simulation project in accounting. *Accounting Education, 30*(4), 385–412. DOI: 10.1080/09639284.2021.1906719

Alderete, M. V., Di Meglio, G., & Formichella, M. M. (2017). Access to ICT and educational performance: Is there a relationship enhanced by its use? An analysis for Spain. *Journal of Education, 377*, 54–81.

Ali, A. (2022). Corruption and inefficiency in the teacher recruitment system of Bangladesh. *Journal of Education Policy, 39*(2), 145–163.

Ali, F., Open, A. I., & Inc, C. (2023). Let the devil speak for itself: Should ChatGPT be allowed or banned in hospitality and tourism schools? *Journal of Global Hospitality and Tourism, 2*(1), 1–6. https://www.doi.org/10.5038/2771-5957.2.1.1016. DOI: 10.5038/2771-5957.2.1.1016

Ali, K. (2022). Digital Information Literacy Skills among Library and Information Science Professionals in University Libraries of Sindh Pakistan. *Journal of Information Management and Practices, 2*(1), 41–61. DOI: 10.52461/jimp.v2i1.1035

Allen, M., & Joseph, B. (2019). Strategies for effective stakeholder engagement in educational partnerships. *Education + Training, 61*(4), 482–497.

Alliance University. (2024). Alliance University partners with Infosys Springboard to enhance digital learning. https://www.alliance.edu.in/news/alliance-university-and-infosys-springboard-forge-a-new-partnership

Alonso García, S., Victoria Maldonado, J., Martínez Domingo, J., & Berral Ortiz, B. (2024). Analysis of self-perceived digital competences in future educators: A study at the university of Granada. *Journal of Technology and Science Education, 14*(1), 4–15. DOI: 10.3926/jotse.2521

Alraimi, K. M., Zo, H., & Ciganek, A. P. (2015). Understanding the MOOCs continuance: The role of openness and reputation. *Computers & Education, 80*, 28–38. DOI: 10.1016/j.compedu.2014.08.007

Alshater, M. (2022). Exploring the Role of Artificial Intelligence in Enhancing Academic Performance: A Case Study of ChatGPT. SSRN Electronic Journal. https://doi.org/DOI: 10.2139/ssrn.4312358

Altan-Olcay, Ö., & Bergeron, S. (2024). Care in times of the pandemic: Rethinking meanings of work in the university. *Gender, Work and Organization, 31*(4), 1544–1559. DOI: 10.1111/gwao.12871 PMID: 35942417

Alyasiri, O., Salisu, S., Younis, H., Salman, A. M., Sahib, T. M., Akhtom, D., & Hayder, I. M. (2023). ChatGPT Revisited: Using ChatGPT-4 for Finding References and Editing Language in Medical Scientific Articles. *Journal of Stomatology, Oral and Maxillofacial Surgery*, •••, 125. PMID: 38521243

Amazon Web Services. (2024). What are Autoregressive Models? Amazon. https://aws.amazon.com/what-is/autoregressive-models/

Amazon Web Services. (2024). What is a GAN? Amazon. https://aws.amazon.com/what-is/gan/

Amazon Web Services. (2024). What is AGI (Artificial General Intelligence)? Amazon. https://aws.amazon.com/what-is/artificial-general-intelligence/

Amazon Web Services. (2024). What is RHLF? Amazon. https://aws.amazon.com/what-is/reinforcement-learning-from-human-feedback/

Amazon Web Services. (2024). What is Stable Diffusion? Amazon. https://aws.amazon.com/what-is/stable-diffusion/

American Library Association Office for Information Technology Policy. Digital Literacy Task Force (2013). *Digital literacy, libraries, and public policy: Report of the Office for Information Technology Policy's Digital Literacy Task Force*. https://alair.ala.org/server/api/core/bitstreams/db72e923-1e14-45b8-ab0e-b113241c0e4c/content

Anapey, G. M. (2024). Achieving Education for Sustainable Education Learning Outcomes: An Integrated Model for Higher Education in the Global South. *International Journal of Educational Reform*. 10567879241270503. DOI: 10.1177/10567879241270503

Ankrah, S., & AL-Tabbaa, O. (2015). Universities–industry collaboration: A systematic review. *Scandinavian Journal of Management*, *31*(3), 387–408. DOI: 10.1016/j.scaman.2015.02.003

Anthony, W., Levine-Brown, P., Fynn, N., Gadzekpo, P., & Spinks, M. (2020). Technology Considerations and Opportunities in Higher Education. *Journal Of College Academic Support Programs*, *3*(1), 31–42. DOI: 10.36896/3.1sppfa1

Appel, G., Neelbauer, J., & Schweidel, D. A. (2025, January 13). *Generative AI has an intellectual property problem*. Harvard Business Review. https://hbr.org/2023/04/generative-ai-has-an-intellectual-property-problem

Archambault, G. S., & Masunaga, J. (2015). Curriculum mapping as a strategic planning tool. *Journal of Library Administration*, *55*(6), 503–519. DOI: 10.1080/01930826.2015.1054770

Archer, D. (2023). Transforming the financing of education at the mid-point of the sustainable development goals. *International Journal of Educational Development*, *103*, 102931. DOI: 10.1016/j.ijedudev.2023.102931

Armstrong, K. (2023, April 15). France pension reforms: Macron signs pension age rise to 64 into law. BBC News. https://www.bbc.com/news/world-europe-65279818

Arnaud, J., Mamede, H. S., & Branco, F. (2024). The relationship between digital transformation and digital literacy - an explanatory model: Systematic literature review. *F1000 Research*, *13*, 252–285. DOI: 10.12688/f1000research.146991.1

Ata, R., & Alpaslan, M. M. (2024). The role of digital literacy, epistemological belief and reading motivation and engagement in teaching 21st century skills. *International Journal of Information and Learning Technology*, *41*(3), 304–317. DOI: 10.1108/IJILT-08-2023-0142

Atchley, P., Pannell, H., Woford, K., Hopkins, M., & Atchley, R. A. (2024). Human and AI collaboration in the higher education environment: Opportunities and concerns. *Cognitive Research: Principles and Implications*, *9*(20), 20. Advance online publication. DOI: 10.1186/s41235-024-00547-9 PMID: 38589710

Atlas, S. (2023, January). ChatGPT for Higher Education and Professional Development. University of Rhode Island College of Business Faculty Publications.

Austin Career Institute. (n.d.). Balancing family, work, and school. Retrieved from https://austincareerinstitute.edu/blog/ma/balancing-family-work-school-medical-assistant

Baena-Morales, S., Prieto-Ayuso, A., Merma-Molina, G., & González-Víllora, S. (2024). Exploring physical education teachers' perceptions of sustainable development goals and education for sustainable development. *Sport Education and Society*, *29*(2), 162–179. DOI: 10.1080/13573322.2022.2121275

Baidoo-Anu, D., & Owusu Ansah, L. (2023, December 31). Education in the Era of Generative Artificial Intelligence (AI): Understanding the Potential Benefits of CHATGPT in Promoting Teaching and Learning. *Journal of AI*, *7*(1), 52–62. DOI: 10.61969/jai.1337500

Bailey, P. M. (2017). Thank you for being late: An Optimist's Guide to Thriving in the Age of Accelerations. *Perspectives on Science and Christian Faith*, *69*(4), 250–252.

Baker, V. L., & Baldwin, R. G. (2015). A case study of liberal arts colleges in the 21st century: Understanding organizational change and evolution in higher education. *Innovative Higher Education, 40*(3), 247–261. DOI: 10.1007/s10755-014-9311-6

Baker, V. L., & Baldwin, R. G. (2015). *Leading academic change: Vision, strategy, transformation*. Johns Hopkins University Press.

Balderas-Mireles, M. A., Mata-Mata, R., Lujano-Gutiérrez, L., Rodríguez Sánchez, J. L., & Pérez López, J. J. (2021). The use of ICTs in teaching at the normal superior school "Profr. Moisés Sáenz Garza": An exploratory study. *Journal of Higher Education Theory and Practice, 22*(3), 90–99.

Baldwin, K. E. (2020). *Preservice Teacher Engagement in Science and Mathematics Practices within Research Settings*. Illinois State University.

Baldwin, R. G., & Chang, D. A. (2020). Collaborative spaces in higher education: The role of physical and digital environments in facilitating teamwork. *Journal of Higher Education Policy and Management, 42*(3), 345–360.

Barak, M., & Levenberg, A. (2016). Flexible thinking in learning: An individual differences measure for learning in technologyenhanced environments. *Computers & Education, 99*, 39–52. DOI: 10.1016/j.compedu.2016.04.003

Barreto, I. B., & Córdova, R. A. S. (2022). Discussion on Digital Inclusion Good Practices at Europe's Libraries. In *Handbook of Research on Comparative Approaches to the Digital Age Revolution in Europe and the Americas. E-book.* IGI Global.

Barrett, P., & Barrett, L. (2020). Modern higher education: Technology and collaboration challenges.

Barrett, P., Chigona, W., & Chigona, A. (2021). *Digital ecosystems in higher education: Opportunities and challenges*. IGI Global.

Barton, A. M. (2021). Teaching Lawyers to Think Like Leaders: The Next Big Shift in Legal Education. *Baylor Law Review, 73*, 115.

Barton, M., & Hart, M. (2018). Soft skills for success in the digital workplace: Bridging the gap between education and employment. *Journal of Educational Technology, 29*(3), 125–137.

Bates, A. T. (2020). *Teaching in a digital age: Guidelines for designing teaching and learning*. Tony Bates Associates Ltd.

Bates, T. (2022). Teacher retention in Canada: Challenges and solutions. *Canadian Journal of Education, 35*(1), 77–89.

Bawden, D. (2008). Origins and concepts of digital literacy. In Lankshear, C., & Knobel, M. (Eds.), *Digital literacies: Concepts, policies and practices* (pp. 17–32). Peter Lang Publishing.

Bayrakdaroğlu, F., & Bayrakdaroğlu, A. (2017). A Comparative Analysis Regarding The Effect of Financial Literacy and Digital Literay on Internet Entrepreneurship Intention. *Journal of Entrepreneurship and Development.*, *12*(2), 27–38.

Bearman, M., Ryan, J., & Ajjawi, R. (2023). Discourses of artificial intelligence in higher education: A critical literature review. *Higher Education, 86*(2), 369–385. DOI: 10.1007/s10734-022-00937-2

Becker, G. S. (2009). *Human capital: A theoretical and empirical analysis, with special reference to education*. University of Chicago Press.

Behera, A., Mahakhud, S., & Panda, R. B. (2024). Transformative Role of Artificial Intelligence in Education. *Redshine Archive*, *9*(10). Advance online publication. DOI: 10.25215/9358798181.01

Bejaković, P., & Mrnjavac, Ž. (2020). The importance of digital literacy on the labour market. *Employee Relations*, *42*(4), 921–932. DOI: 10.1108/ER-07-2019-0274

Bennett, D., Lemoine, J., & McDonald, C. (2020). Fostering professional development in higher education: Supporting faculty, staff, and administrators through continuous learning. *Journal of Educational Leadership*, *32*(2), 112–126.

Bennett, N. J., Katz, L., Yadao-Evans, W., Ahmadia, G. N., Atkinson, S., Ban, N. C., Dawson, N. M., de Vos, A., Fitzpatrick, J., Gill, D., Imirizaldu, M., Lewis, N., Mangubhai, S., Meth, L., Muhl, E.-K., Obura, D., Spalding, A. K., Villagomez, A., Wagner, D., & Wilhelm, A. (2021). Advancing social equity in and through marine conservation. *Frontiers in Marine Science*, *8*, 711538. DOI: 10.3389/fmars.2021.711538

Berber, Ş., Deveciyan, M. T., & Alay, H. K. (2023). Digital Literacy Level and Career Satisfaction of Academics. *Itobiad: Journal of the Human & Social Science Researches / İnsan ve Toplum Bilimleri Araştırmaları Dergisi, 12*(4), 2363–2387. https://doi.org/DOI: 10.15869/itobiad.1343893

Bernard, R. M., Borokhovski, E., Schmid, R. F., Tamim, R. M., & Abrami, P. C. (2014). A meta-analysis of blended learning and technology use in higher education: From the general to the applied. *Journal of Computing in Higher Education*, *26*(1), 87–122. DOI: 10.1007/s12528-013-9077-3

Berry, J. (2014). Y in the workplace: Comparative analysis of values, skills and perceptions of government communication amongst university students and government staff. *Foresight*, *16*(5), 432–447. DOI: 10.1108/FS-03-2013-0010

Billett, S. (2011). *Vocational education: Purposes, traditions and prospects*. Springer Science & Business Media. DOI: 10.1007/978-94-007-1954-5

Bishop, J. L., & Verleger, M. A. (2013). The flipped classroom: A survey of the research. *Proceedings of the ASEE Annual Conference & Exposition*, 23, 1–18. DOI: 10.18260/1-2--22585

Bisneto, T. R., de Carvalho Filho, A. O., & Magalhães, D. M. (2020). Generative Adversarial Network and Texture Features Applied to Automatic Glaucoma Detection. [DOI]. *Applied Soft Computing*, *90*, 90. DOI: 10.1016/j.asoc.2020.106165

Björk, L. (2021). Collaborative technologies for higher education: Bridging departments and silos. *International Journal of Educational Technology*, *17*(3), 290–306.

Björk, M., Eklund, A., Skyvell Nilsson, M., & Nyman, V. (2024). The collaborative and professional boundary challenges from a bottom-up perspective: An insider action research study on a hospital ward. *Journal of Health Organization and Management*, *38*(9), 389–406. DOI: 10.1108/JHOM-03-2023-0093 PMID: 39620901

Blackmore, J., Hobbs, L., & Rowlands, J. (2024). Aspiring teachers, financial incentives, and principals' recruitment practices in hard-to-staff schools. *Journal of Education Policy*, *39*(2), 233–252. DOI: 10.1080/02680939.2023.2193170

Blagodarny, E. V., Vedyakhin, A., & Raygorodsky, A. M. (2018). Development of Educational Projects on the Basis of Technological Platforms with Artificial Intelligence: The Experience of MIPT on the Use of High Vox-Platform. *International Conference on Artificial Intelligence Applications and Innovations (IC-AIAI)*. Nicosia, Cyprus. DOI: 10.1109/IC-AIAI.2018.8674452

Blank, G., & Groselj, D. (2014). Dimensions of Internet use: Amount, variety, and types. *Information Communication and Society*, *17*(4), 417–435. DOI: 10.1080/1369118X.2014.889189

Blayone, T. (2018). Reexamining digital-learning readiness in higher education: Positioning digital competencies as key factors and a profile application as a readiness tool. *International Journal on E-Learning*, *17*(4), 425–451.

Bohm, A., & Smith, C. (2019). Collaborative problem-solving in higher education: Insights and strategies for cross-functional teams. *Journal of Higher Education Collaboration*, *25*(3), 201–213.

Boland, R. J., & Phillips, N. (2019). *Managing as designing*. Stanford University Press.

Bolliger, D. U., & Wasilik, O. (2020). The role of technology in supporting student engagement and learning: An overview of best practices. *Journal of Educational Technology, 17*(1), 24–35.

Bolman, L. G., & Deal, T. E. (2017). *Reframing organizations: Artistry, choice, and leadership* (6th ed.). Jossey-Bass. DOI: 10.1002/9781119281856

Bond, M., Buntins, K., Bedenlier, S., Zawacki-Richter, 0. & Kerres, M. (2020). Mapping research in student engagement and educational technology in higher education: A systematic evidence map. *International Journal of Technology in Higher Education, 17*(2). https://doi.org/ 9-0176-8DOI: 10. 1 186/s41239-01

Bonk, C. J., & Graham, C. R. (2012). *The handbook of blended learning: Global perspectives, local designs*. Wiley.

Bonk, C. J., & Lee, M. M. (2017). Motivation, retention, and dropout in MOOC learning environments. In *Massive open online courses: The MOOC revolution* (pp. 109–134). Springer.

Borg, J., Borg, N., Scott-Young, C. M., & Naderpajouh, N. (2021). The work readiness–career resilience linkage: Implications for project talent management. *International Journal of Managing Projects in Business, 14*(4), 917–935. DOI: 10.1108/IJMPB-04-2020-0129

Brand, J. E. (2023). *Overcoming the odds: The benefits of completing college for unlikely graduates*. Russell Sage Foundation.

Braun, V., & Clarke, V. (2006). Using thematic analysis in psychology. *Qualitative Research in Psychology, 3*(2), 77–101. DOI: 10.1191/1478088706qp063oa

Breen, M., Waters, J., & O'Shea, L. (2023). Taking a Lead on Digital Literacy for Students—A Case Study from the Library at the University of Limerick. *New Review of Academic Librarianship, 29*(1), 11–32. DOI: 10.1080/13614533.2022.2039243

Brown, T. B. Benjamin Mann, Nick Ryder, Melanie Subbiah, Jared Kaplan, Prafulla Dhariwal, Arvind Neelakantan, Pranav Shyam, Girish Sastry, Amanda Askell, Sandhini Agarwal, Ariel Herbert-Voss, Gretchen Krueger, Tom Henighan, Rewon Child, Aditya Ramesh, Daniel M. Ziegler, Jeffrey Wu, Clemens Winter, Christopher Hesse, Mark Chen, Eric Sigler, Mateusz Litwin, Scott Gray, Benjamin Chess, Jack Clark, Christopher Berner, Sam McCandlish, Alec Radford, Ilya Sutskever, and Dario Amodei. 2020. Language models are few-shot learners. In Proceedings of the 34th International Conference on Neural Information Processing Systems (NIPS '20). Curran Associates Inc., Red Hook, NY, USA, Article 159, 1877–1901. https://arxiv.org/pdf/2005.14165

Brown, A. (2022). Industry-academic partnerships in higher education: Bridging the gap for future workforce development. *Journal of Higher Education Collaboration, 15*(3), 123–137.

Brown, A., & Green, T. D. (2019). The necessity of digital literacy in the modern workforce. *The Journal of Technology Studies, 45*(2), 96–109.

Brunetti, A., Büchel, K., Jakob, M., Jann, B., & Steffen, D. (2024). Inadequate teacher content knowledge and what could be done about it: Evidence from El Salvador. *Journal of Development Effectiveness, 16*(2), 206–229. DOI: 10.1080/19439342.2023.2213681

Brynjolfsson, E., & McAfee, A. (2014). *The second machine age: Work, progress, and prosperity in a time of brilliant technologies*. W. W. Norton & Company.

Brynjolfsson, E., & McAfee, A. (2014). *The second Machine Age: Work, progress, and prosperity in a time of brilliant technologies*. WW Norton & Company.

Bryson, J. M., Crosby, B. C., & Bloomberg, L. (2019). *Public administration: The state of the art*. Routledge.

Bryson, J. M., Crosby, B. C., & Stone, M. M. (2015). Designing and implementing cross-sector collaborations: Needed and challenging. *Public Administration Review, 75*(5), 647–663. DOI: 10.1111/puar.12432

Bryson, J. M., Crosby, B. C., & Stone, M. M. (2017). Designing and implementing cross-sector collaborations: Needed and operational guidelines. *Public Administration Review, 77*(5), 673–684.

BSSS Publications. (n.d.). Academic flexibilities & opportunities to the learners through MOOCs. Retrieved from https://bssspublications.com/Home/IssueDetailPage?IsNo=647

Buckingham, D. (2015). Defining digital literacy - What do young people need to know about digital media? *Nordic Journal of Digital Literacy*, *10*(Jubileumsnummer), 21–35. DOI: 10.18261/ISSN1891-943X-2015-Jubileumsnummer-03

Byrne, M. D. (2024). CHATGPT without a safety net. *Nursing Education Perspectives*, *45*(1), 63–65. DOI: 10.1097/01.NEP.0000000000001225 PMID: 38117603

Cable. (2022). Worldwide Mobile Data Pricing 2022. https://www.cable.co.uk/mobiles/worldwide-data-pricing/. Accessed: 04/10/2024.

Cai, Y., Kenderdine, T., & Long, B. (2019). Evaluating the effectiveness of university-industry partnerships in providing digital literacy skills. *Higher Education*, *78*(4), 639–655.

Calero, M., Pina, T., Mayoral, O., Cantó, J., Ull, M. Á., & Vilches, A. (2024). A study about pre-service teachers' knowledge of the Sustainable Development Goals. *International Journal of Sustainability in Higher Education.*

Cambridge University. (2023). *University of Cambridge and Microsoft partnership in data science and AI.* Retrieved from https://www.cam.ac.uk/partnerships

Canina, L., & Orero-Blat, M. (2021). A practical tool to measure digital competences: Teamschamp. *International Journal of Services Operations and Informatics*, *11*(1), 1–12. DOI: 10.1504/IJSOI.2021.114107

Canuel, R., MacKenzie, E., Senior, A., & Torabi, N. (2017). Apps for academic success: Developing digital literacy and awareness to increase usage. *Education for Information*, *33*(3), 135–152. DOI: 10.3233/EFI-160085

Cappelli, P. (2012). Why good people can't get jobs: The skills gap and what companies can do about it. In *Why Good People Can't Get Jobs.* University of Pennsylvania Press.

Carayannis, E. G., & Morawska, J. (2023). Digital and green twins of Industry & Society 5.0: the role of universities. In *The Elgar Companion to Digital Transformation, Artificial Intelligence and Innovation in the Economy, Society and Democracy* (pp. 166-202). Edward Elgar Publishing.

Castaneda, G. 2024. *Considerations for Clinicians Working With Bisexual Military Populations in Mental Health Settings* (Doctoral dissertation, Alliant International University).

Chakravorty, S., & Bedi, J. (2020, September 14). The digital dream: Upskilling India for the future. Ideas for India. https://www.ideasforindia.in/topics/governance/the-digital-dream-upskilling-india-for-the-future

Cham, K. M., Edwards, M.-L., Kruesi, L., Celeste, T., & Hennessey, T. (2022). Digital Preferences and Perceptions of Students in Health Professional Courses at a Leading Australian University: A Baseline for Improving Digital Skills and Competencies in Health Graduates. *Australasian Journal of Educational Technology*, *38*(1), 69–86.

Chan, A. J., Hooi, L. W., & Ngui, K. S. (2021). Do digital literacies matter in employee engagement in digitalised workplace? *Journal of Asia Business Studies*, *15*(3), 523–540. DOI: 10.1108/JABS-08-2020-0318

Chandra, J., & Hendayana, Y. (2024). The Influence of Entrepreneurship Education and Digital Literacy in Forming Entrepreneurial Competence. [DIJMS]. *Dinasti International Journal of Management Science*, *5*(6), 1154–1161. DOI: 10.38035/dijms.v5i6.2802

Chan, G. H. (2024). Enhancing digital literacy in education: Educational directions. *Education + Training*, *66*(1), 127–142. DOI: 10.1108/ET-09-2022-0390

Change, E. (2001). Leading in a Culture of Change.

Chapman University. (2024). Bias in Ai. Bias in AI | Chapman University. https://www.chapman.edu/ai/bias-in-ai.aspx

Chaudhary, K. K., Kishore, A., Soni, K., Singh, A. K., & Singh, A. (2024). Assessing The Digital Literacy Skills of Postgraduate Students: A Case Study of Bra Bihar University, Muzaffarpur, Bihar. *Library of Progress-Library Science. Information Technology & Computer*, *44*(3), 20449–20458.

Cheng, H. (2023). Mentorship programs and professional development for teachers in Singapore. *International Journal of Educational Management*, *37*(1), 112–125.

Cheng, X., Kaushik, V., & Raheem, A. (2019). Adoption of MOOCs for workforce development in India: A literature review. *International Journal of Educational Technology*, *10*(2), 107–121. DOI: 10.1080/IDLE.2019.090455

Chen, M., Mei, S., Fan, J., & Wang, M. (2024). Opportunities and Challenges of Diffusion Models for Generative AI. *National Science Review*, *11*(12), nwae348. DOI: 10.1093/nsr/nwae348 PMID: 39554240

Chen, X., Xie, H., & Hwang, G. J. (2020). A multi-perspective study on Artificial Intelligence in Education: Grants, conferences, journals, software tools, institutions, and researchers. *Computers and Education: Artificial Intelligence*, *1*, 100005. DOI: 10.1016/j.caeai.2020.100005

Chesbrough, H. (2003). *Open Innovation: The New Imperative for Creating and Profiting from Technology*. Harvard Business Review Press.

Chesbrough, H. (2020). *Open innovation: The new imperative for creating and profiting from technology*. Harvard Business Press.

Chetty, K., Aneja, U., Mishra, V., Gcora, N. & Josie, J. (2017). *Bridging the digital divide: Skills for the new age*. Germany: G20.

Chew, E., & Majeed, A. P. A. (Eds.). (2024). *Fostering Women's Engagement in STEM Through Education: A Cross-cultural Academic-industry Journey*. CRC Press. DOI: 10.1201/9781003514626

Chigona, A., & Sosibo, L. (2024). Research and postgraduate supervision during the coronavirus-19 pandemic: Lessons learned. *South African Journal of Higher Education, 38*(1), 42–61. DOI: 10.20853/38-1-6281

Chigona, W., & Chigona, A. (2020). Challenges and opportunities of integrating ICT in African universities. *The African Journal of Information Systems, 12*(2), 101–121.

Chigumira, E. (2021). *Interdisciplinary approaches to technology in higher education in Zimbabwe*. University of Zimbabwe Press.

Chikwature, W., Munodawafa, D., & Maphosa, C. (2019). Integration of ICT in teaching and learning in Zimbabwean universities. *Zimbabwe Journal of Educational Research, 31*(1), 55–69.

Child Rights and You (CRY). (n.d.). Education in rural India: The struggle for a brighter future. Retrieved from https://www.cry.org/blog/education-in-rural-india/

Chintala, S. R. 2024. *Embedded in Informality: Political Economy of Platform Work in India* (Doctoral dissertation, New York University).

Chiwaridzo, O. T. 2024. Energizing the future: Unleashing the potential of innovative waste-to-energy technologies for energy development and sustainability within Zimbabwe's tourism sector. *Waste Management & Research*, p.0734242X241291939.

Chiweshe, M. K. (2022). *Transforming institutional cultures: A case for collaboration in Zimbabwean higher education.* Bulawayo: Mambo Press.

Choudhary, H., & Bansal, N. (2022). Addressing Digital Divide through Digital Literacy Training Programs: A Systematic Literature Review. *Digital Education Review, 41*(1), 224–248. DOI: 10.1344/der.2022.41.224-248

Chowdhury, N. (2022). Education reform in Bangladesh: Challenges in teacher professional development. *South Asian Journal of Education, 28*(3), 97–111.

Chowdhury, N., & Rahman, M. (2023). Teacher compensation in Bangladesh: A comparative study. *International Journal of Educational Development, 50*(3), 129–140.

Christensen, C. M., Horn, M. B., & Johnson, C. W. (2020). *Disrupting class: How disruptive innovation will change the way the world learns*. McGraw-Hill Education.

Cintamulya, I., Murtini, I., & Warli, W. (2024). Optimizing Collaboration and Communication Skills of Pre-Service Biology Teachers Based on Cognitive Styles through Scientific Paper Tasks. *Participatory Educational Research, 11*(6), 262–279. DOI: 10.17275/per.24.89.11.6

Cisco Systems. (January 25, 2024). Companies' concerns related to the use of generative artificial intelligence (GenAI) in 2023 [Graph]. In Statista. Retrieved November 13, 2024, from https://www.statista.com/statistics/1455833/gen-ai-users-concerns

Coldwell-Neilson, J., Armitage, J. A., Wood-Bradley, R. J., Kelly, B., & Gentle, A. (2019). Implications of updating digital literacy: A case study in an optometric curriculum. Issues in Informing Science & Information Technology, 16, 33–49 Available at http://iisit.org/Vol16/IISITv16p033-049Coldwell5567. pdf. Accessed 7 Jul 2020.

Coley, M. (2023, August 16). Guidance on AI detection and why we're disabling Turnitin's AI detector. Vanderbilt University. https://www.vanderbilt.edu/brightspace/2023/08/16/guidance-on-ai-detection-and-why-were-disabling-turnitins-ai-detector/

Collins, A. R., & Crowe, K. (2021). Where do we grow from here? Assessing the perceived impact of a digital media commons on student success. *Performance Measurement and Metrics, 22*(3), 174–186. DOI: 10.1108/PMM-09-2020-0049

Coursera. (n.d.). Online courses from top universities & institutions. Retrieved from https://www.coursera.org

Cox, K., & Sims, J. (2022). Industry-university collaborations for curriculum co-design: Bridging the gap between academia and the workforce. *The Journal of Higher Education, 47*(2), 125–142.

Coyle, J. (2023, May 2). *Late-night TV shows go dark as writers strike for better pay*. AP News. https://apnews.com/article/writers-strike-hollywood-wga-92617928180 3e10b1d501dcab93e30d

Coyle, J. (2023, May 5). *Could Ai Pen "casablanca"? screenwriters take aim at chatgpt*. AP News. https://apnews.com/article/ai-hollywood-writers-strike-artificial -intelligence-dc71c4cabcca0ee1b1afe0050d392a36

Creswell, J. W. (2014). *Research design: Qualitative, quantitative, and mixed methods approaches* (4th ed.). SAGE Publications.

CRY. (n.d.). Education in rural India: Challenges and solutions. Retrieved from https://www.cry.org/blog/education-in-rural-india

Curtarelli, M., Gualtieri, V., Shater Jannati, M., & Donlevy, V. (2016). *ICT for Work: Digital Skills in the Workplace*, European Commission, Brussels https://op.europa.eu/en/publication-detail/-/publication/7a51fb41-92ad-11e7-b92d-01aa75ed71a1

Dalton, A. (2023, July 21). *Ai is the wild card in Hollywood's strikes. here's an explanation of its unsettling role*. AP News. https://apnews.com/article/artificial-intelligence-hollywood-strikes-explained-writers-actors-e872bd63ab52c3ea9f7d6e825240a202

Damek, S., Söbke, H., Weise, F., & Reichelt, M. (2022). (Meta) Competences for Digital Practice: Educational Scenarios for the Workplace of the Future Exemplified by Building Information Modeling Work Processes. *arXiv preprint arXiv:2207.01498*.

Dandaya, V. (2022). Importance of vocational training and technical skills. *Global Science Research Journals*, *10*(3), 1–2.

Daniel, J. (2012). Making sense of MOOCs: Musings in a maze of myth, paradox, and possibility. *Journal of Interactive Media in Education*, *2012*(3), 18. DOI: 10.5334/2012-18

Darling-Hammond, L. (2020). The right to learn: A framework for teachers and policy makers. *Education Policy Analysis Archives*, *28*(65), 1–25.

Das, S. (2021, December 2). World Computer Literacy Day: The need for digital literacy in India. The CSR Journal. Retrieved from https://thecsrjournal.in/world-computer-literacy-day-digital-literacy-india

Davis, F. D. (1989). Perceived usefulness, perceived ease of use, and user acceptance of information technology. *Management Information Systems Quarterly*, *13*(3), 319–340. DOI: 10.2307/249008

De Oliveira, L., Paganini, M., & Nachman, B. (2017, September 29). Learning Particle Physics by Example: Location-Aware Generative Adversarial Networks for Physics Synthesis. *Computing and Software for Big Science*, *1*(1), 4. DOI: 10.1007/s41781-017-0004-6

De Waard, I., Gallagher, M. S., Zwart, H., Abajian, S. C., & Hogue, R. J. (2014). Exploring the MOOC format as a pedagogy for global learning. *International Review of Research in Open and Distance Learning*, *15*(2), 1–13. DOI: 10.19173/irrodl.v15i2.1671

Deja, M., Rak, D., & Bell, B. (2021). Digital transformation readiness: Perspectives on academia and library outcomes in information literacy. *Journal of Academic Librarianship*, *47*(5), 102403. Advance online publication. DOI: 10.1016/j.acalib.2021.102403

Delcker, J., & Ifenthaler, D. (2021). Teachers' Perspective on School Development at German Vocational Schools During the Covid-19 Pandemic. *Technology, Pedagogy and Education*, *30*(1), 125–139. DOI: 10.1080/1475939X.2020.1857826

Deloitte. (January 15, 2024). Share of Professionals Using generative Artificial Intelligence (AI)

Department of Higher Education and Training [DHET]. (2013). *White Paper for Post-School Education and Training: Building an Expanded, Effective and Integrated Post-School System.* Pretoria, South Africa.

Detlor, B., & Julien, H. (2020). Success factors affecting digital literacy training initiatives led by local community organizations. *Proceedings of the Association for Information Science and Technology*, *57*(1), e331. Advance online publication. DOI: 10.1002/pra2.331

Devisakti, A., & Muftahu, M. (2023). Digitalization in higher education: Does personal innovativeness matter in digital learning? *Interactive Technology and Smart Education*, *20*(2), 257–270. DOI: 10.1108/ITSE-10-2021-0182

Dewey, J. (1938). *Experience and education*. Macmillan.

Dewey, J. (1986, September). Experience and education. []. Taylor & Francis Group.]. *The Educational Forum*, *50*(3), 241–252. DOI: 10.1080/00131728609335764

Dewey, J. (2001). *Democracy and education: An introduction to the philosophy of education*. The Pennsylvania State University.

Di Battista, A., Grayling, S., Hasselaar, E., Leopold, T., Li, R., Rayner, M., & Zahidi, S. (2023). Future of jobs report 2023. In *World Economic Forum, Geneva, Switzerland.*https://www. weforum. org/reports/the-future-of-jobs-report-2023

Dubois, D., & Prade, H. (2023). Possibility theory. In *The Palgrave Encyclopedia of the Possible* (pp. 1064–1073). Springer International Publishing.

Duke University. (2024, October 9). Artificial Intelligence Policies: Guidelines and considerations. Duke Learning Innovation & Lifetime Education. https://lile.duke.edu/ai-and-teaching-at-duke-2/artificial-intelligence-policies-in-syllabi-guidelines-and-considerations/

Duma, N. M., Mlambo, S., Mbambo-Mkwanazi, S., & Morgan, W. (2021). Digital Inequalities in rural Schools in South Africa. *Ocean Science Journal*, *6*(3), 1–15.

Dyer, S., & Ward, C. (2020). Collaborating with industry partners to enhance workforce readiness: A guide for higher education institutions. *Journal of Higher Education and Industry Partnerships*, *12*(4), 227–245.

ECDL Foundation. (2014). The Fallacy of the 'Digital Native': Why Young People Need to Develop their Digital Skills. https://ec.europa.eu/futurium/en/system/files/ged/the_fallacy_of_the_digitalnative_-_ecdl_foundation.pdf

Economic Times. (2020, May 14). SWAYAM to introduce courses in 8 Indian languages including Hindi and Telugu. The Economic Times. Retrieved from https://government.economictimes.indiatimes.com/news/education/swayam-to-introduce-courses-in-8-indian-languages-including-hindi-and-telugu/75819347

Edmondson, A. C. (2018). *The fearless organization: Creating psychological safety in the workplace for learning, innovation, and growth.* Wiley.

edX. (n.d.). Access 3,000+ online courses from 160 institutions. Retrieved from https://www.edx.org

EITCI Institute (European Information Technologies Certification Institute). (2017). Digitalskills and jobs coalition. https://eitci.org/digital-skills-and-jobs-coalition

Eliyawati, W., Widodo, A., Kaniawati, I., & Fujii, H. (2023). The Development and Validation of an Instrument for Assessing Science Teacher Competency to Teach ESD. *Sustainability (Basel)*, *15*(4), 3276. DOI: 10.3390/su15043276

Epifanova, N. S., & Polozkov, M. (2020). Digital literacy as a prerequisite for transforming the modern russian education system. *Public Administration*, *22*(5), 62–66. DOI: 10.22394/2070-8378-2020-22-5-62-66

Equiss. (2024). Operationalizing the breaking of silos in universities: A step-by-step guide. Equiss. https://www.equiss.org/post/operationalizing-the-breaking-of-silos-in-universities-a-step-by-step-guide

Etzkowitz, H., & Leydesdorff, L. (2000). The dynamics of innovation: From National Systems and "Mode 2" to a Triple Helix of university–industry–government relations. *Research Policy*, *29*(2), 109–123. DOI: 10.1016/S0048-7333(99)00055-4

European Commission. (2019). *Key Competences For Lifelong Learning*. https://op.europa.eu/en/publication-detail/-/publication/297a33c8-a1f3-11e9-9d01-01aa75ed71a1

Evans, N., Miklosik, A., & Du, J. T. (2023). University-industry collaboration as a driver of digital transformation: Types, benefits, and enablers. *Heliyon*, *9*(10), e21017. DOI: 10.1016/j.heliyon.2023.e21017 PMID: 37867890

Falck, O., Mang, C., & Woessmann, L. (2018). Virtually no effect? Different uses of classroom computers and their effect on student achievement. *Oxford Bulletin of Economics and Statistics*, *80*(1), 1–38. DOI: 10.1111/obes.12192

Faloye, S.T., Ajayi, N. & Raghavjee, R. (2020). Managing the Challenges of the Digital Divide among First Year Students: A Case of UKZN." 2020 IST-Africa Conference (IST-Africa), 18–22 May 2020.

Faloye, S. T., & Ajayi, N. (2021). Understanding the impact of the digital divide on South African students in higher educational institutions. *African Journal of Science, Technology, Innovation and Development*, *14*(7), 1734–1744. DOI: 10.1080/20421338.2021.1983118

Farooq, M. U., Ghafoor, A., & Bajwa, M. A. (2022). UAF Library services in VUCA environment: Best practices and lessons learned during COVID-19 pandemic. *Pakistan Library & Information Science Journal*, *53*(2), 5–10.

Feerrar, J. (2019). Development of a framework for digital literacy. *RSR. Reference Services Review*, *47*(2), 91–105. DOI: 10.1108/RSR-01-2019-0002

Feldman, M. (2022). Building sustainable industry-academic partnerships: A guide to effective collaborations. *Journal of Higher Education Partnerships*, *33*(2), 210–224.

Fernández-Gutiérrez, M., Gimenez, G., & Calero, J. (2020). Is the use of ICT in education leading tohigher student outcomes? Analysis from the Spanish autonomous communities. *Computers & Education*, *157*, 1–15. DOI: 10.1016/j.compedu.2020.103969

Ferrari, A. (2013). *DIGCOMP: A Framework for Developing and Understanding Digital Competence in Europe. European Commission, Joint Research Centre and Institute for Prospective Technological Studies*. Publications Office of the European Union.

Ferreira, N., Coetzee, M., & Potgieter, I. L. (2024). Predicting Students' Work World Awareness through Their Readiness and Competency for the Digital World. *Journal of Teaching and Learning for Graduate Employability*, *15*(1), 53–65. DOI: 10.21153/jtlge2024vol15no1art1788

Ferrero, V. (2023). Equity and Excellence in Education: SDG 4 of the 2030 Agenda in the Italian Context–Public Education Policies and Their Impact. In *Public Policy's Role in Achieving Sustainable Development Goals* (pp. 206-235). IGI Global.

Feuerriegel, S., Hartmann, J., Janiesch, C., & Zschech, P. (2023, August 7). Generative AI. SSRN Electronic Journal, 66, 111–126. DOI: 10.2139/ssrn.4443189

Finnish Ministry of Education and Culture. (2019). *Education Policy Outlook*. Ministry of Education and Culture.

Fisher, A., Garrison, D. R., & Vaughan, N. D. (2021). The role of technology in supporting blended learning: A review of best practices. *Journal of Educational Technology Systems*, *50*(1), 88–106.

Fitra, J. (2023). Digital Literacy, Academic Self-Efficacy, and Student Engagement: Its Impact on Student Academic Performance in Hybrid Learning. *Journal of Innovation in Educational and Cultural Research*, *4*(3), 458–470. DOI: 10.46843/jiecr.v4i3.719

Fleaca, , BFleaca, , EMaiduc, , S. (2022). Digital transformation and current challenges of higher education. *TEM Journal*, *11*(3), 1235.

Fleck, B. K. B., Beckman, L. M., & Sterns, J. L. (2014). YouTube in the Classroom: Helpful Tips and Student Perceptions. *The Journal of Effective Teaching*, *14*(3), 21–37.

Fleming, J. (2014). *Exploring stakeholders perspectives of cooperative education in sport tertiary education* (Doctoral dissertation, Deakin University).

Folorunso, L. A., & Momoh, E. O. (2022). Underscoring the Value of Digital Literacy as a Tool for Reducing Unemployment and Enhancing Workplace Productivity. In Asamoah–Hassan, H. (Ed.), *Digital Literacy, Inclusivity and Sustainable Development in Africa* (pp. 146–156). Facet Publishing. DOI: 10.29085/9781783305131.013

Ford, E., Izumi, B., Lottes, J., & Richardson, D. (2015). Badge it!: A collaborative learning outcomes based approach to integrating information literacy badges within disciplinary curriculum. *RSR. Reference Services Review*, *43*(1), 31–44. DOI: 10.1108/RSR-07-2014-0026

Frandell, A. (2023). *Knowledge Flows from Invention to Public Value: the Impacts of Academic-industry Collaborations* (Doctoral dissertation, Arizona State University).

Freire, P. (1970). *Pedagogy of the oppressed*. Continuum.

Fresen, J. W. (2020). *Embracing distance education in a blended learning model: Challenges and prospects*. Exploring Dual and Mixed Mode Provision of Distance Education. DOI: 10.4324/9780429287473-8

Friedman, A., & O'Brien, D. (2022). Teachers as moral guides: The role of educators in shaping ethical societies. *The Journal of Educational Research*, *98*(3), 45–56.

Friedman, T. L. (2021). *Thank you for being late: An optimist's guide to thriving in the age of accelerations*. Farrar, Straus and Giroux.

Frost, J., Brockmann, E., & Huggett, K. (2020). Interdisciplinary collaboration in higher education: A case study of effective curriculum integration. *Journal of Interdisciplinary Studies in Education*, *9*(2), 58–73.

Fubah, C. N., & Moos, M. (2025). Exploring network typology and their role in immigrant entrepreneurship: Insights from South Africa. *Journal of Enterprising Communities: People and Places in the Global Economy*, *19*(2), 202–224. DOI: 10.1108/JEC-07-2023-0138

Fullan, M. (2016). *The new meaning of educational change* (5th ed.). Routledge.

Fullan, M. (2020). *Leading in a culture of change: A handbook for educators*. Jossey-Bass.

Fuller, A. (2015). Vocational Education. *International Encyclopedia of the Social & Behavioral Sciences*, 25: 232–238.

Gaebel, M. (2013). *MOOCs: Massive open online courses*. European University Association.

Gaftandzhieva, S., Hussain, S., Hilcenko, S., Doneva, R., & Boykova, K. (2023). Data-driven decision making in higher education institutions: State-of-play. *International Journal of Advanced Computer Science and Applications*, *14*(6). Advance online publication. DOI: 10.14569/IJACSA.2023.0140642

Ganefri, W. K., Makky, M., Hidayat, H. & Rahmawati, Y. (2024). Entrepreneurship Education and Entrepreneurial Intention among University Students: The Roles of Entrepreneurial Mindset, Digital Literacy, and Self-Efficacy. *Journal of Social Studies Education Research / Sosyal Bilgiler Eğitimi Araştırmaları Dergisi, 15*(4), 85–134.

Gann, D., Montresor, F., & Eisenberg, J. (2018, November). 3 ways to nurture collaboration between universities and industry. In *World Economic Forum: Education, Skills and Learning,[online]*. Retrieved from: https://www.weforum.org/stories/2018/11/3-ways-to-nurture-collaboration-between-universities-and-industry/

García-Feijoo, M., Eizaguirre, A., & Rica-Aspiunza, A. (2020). Systematic review of sustainable-development-goal deployment in business schools. *Sustainability (Basel)*, *12*(1), 440. DOI: 10.3390/su12010440

Garcia, R. (2021). Digital literacy and social inclusion. *Information Communication and Society*, *24*(7), 985–1002.

Garrison, D. R., & Kanuka, H. (2004). Blended learning: Uncovering its transformative potential in higher education. *The Internet and Higher Education*, *7*(2), 95–105. DOI: 10.1016/j.iheduc.2004.02.001

Garrison, D. R., & Kanuka, H. (2020). *Blended learning in higher education: Framework, principles, and guidelines*. Wiley.

Gautam, S., Jain, A., Chaudhary, J., Gautam, M., Gaur, M., & Grover, S. (2024). Concept of mental health and mental well-being, it's determinants and coping strategies. *Indian Journal of Psychiatry*, *66*(Suppl 2), S231–S244. DOI: 10.4103/indianjpsychiatry.indianjpsychiatry_707_23 PMID: 38445271

Generative, A. I. Lab. (2024, August 19). *Comparing Diffusion, GAN, and VAE Techniques*. Generative AI Lab. https://generativeailab.org/l/generative-ai/a-tale-of-three-generative-models- comparing-diffusion-gan-and-vae-techniques/569/

Gewirtz, D. (2024, June 28). *How to Make ChatGPT Provide Sources and Citations*. ZDNET. https://www.zdnet.com/article/how-to-make-chatgpt-provide-sources-and-citations/

Ghamrawi, N. (2023). Toward agenda 2030 in education: Policies and practices for effective school leadership. *Educational Research for Policy and Practice*, *22*(2), 325–347. DOI: 10.1007/s10671-023-09341-8 PMID: 38625155

Ghamrawi, N., Shal, T., & Ghamrawi, N. A. (2024). Cultivating teacher leadership: Evidence form a transformative professional development model. *School Leadership & Management*, *44*(4), 1–29. DOI: 10.1080/13632434.2024.2328056

Ghosh, A., & Khan, S. (2023). Teacher participation in policy-making: A global perspective. *Education Policy Review*, *34*(4), 202–215.

Ghosh, A., & Khan, S. (2023). Teachers' voices in policy reform: The case of South Asia. *Education Review*, *29*(4), 85–100.

Ghosh, S., & McCoy, D. (2024). Looking Ahead: Incorporating AI in MLIS Competencies. [SRJ]. *Student Research Journal*, *14*(2), 28–42.

Gibson, P. F., & Smith, S. (2018). Digital literacies: Preparing pupils and students for their information journey in the twenty-first century. *Information and Learning Science*, *119*(12), 733–742. DOI: 10.1108/ILS-07-2018-0059

Gilmour, A. F., Theobald, R., & Nathan, D. J. (2023). Economic interventions as policy levers for attracting and retaining special education teachers. *Handbook of Research on Special Education Teacher Preparation*, 190-212.

Gilster, P. (1997). *Digital literacy*. Wiley Computer Publishing.

Gómez-Trigueros, I. M. (2020). Digital teaching competence and space competence with TPACK in social sciences. *International Journal of Emerging Technologies in Learning*, *15*(19), 37–52. DOI: 10.3991/ijet.v15i19.14923

González, P. A. (2023). Digital Literacy in Employability of Graduates during COVID-19: A Qualitative Phenomenological Study. In *ProQuest LLC*.

Goodfellow, I. J., Pouget-Abadie, J., Mirza, M., Xu, B., Warde-Farley, D., Ozair, S., Courville, A., & Benign, Y. (2014). *Generative Adversarial Nets*. Université de Montréal.

Gooding, P., Crook, R., Westwood, M., & Peters, S. (2024), "Ways to wellbeing in postgraduate research students: interactions with positive perceptions of relationships with university staff", *Studies in Graduate and Postdoctoral Education*, Vol. ahead-of-print No. ahead-of-print. DOI: 10.1108/SGPE-07-2023-0063

Government of India. (2024). Economic Survey 2024-25. Ministry of Finance. https://www.indiabudget.gov.in/economicsurvey/doc/echapter.pdf

Goyal, A., Kumar, P., & Shalini. (2024). Quality Education: A Key Component of the United Nations Sustainable Development Goals (SDGs). In *Digital Technologies to Implement the UN Sustainable Development Goals* (pp. 127-151). Cham: Springer Nature Switzerland.

Gravel, J., D'Amours-Gravel, M., & Osmanlliu, E. (2023). Learning to Fake it: Limited Responses and Fabricated References Provided by ChatGPT for Medical Questions. *Mayo Clinic Proceedings. Digital Health*, *1*(3), 226–234. DOI: 10.1016/j.mcpdig.2023.05.004

Green, C. (2020). Digital literacies and the skills of the digital age. In Tutaleni I. Asino (Ed.), *Learning in the Digital Age*. Oklahoma State University Libraries. https://open.library.okstate.edu/learninginthedigitalage/

Greene, J. A., & Crompton, H. (2024). Synthesizing Definitions of Digital Literacy for the Web 3.0. *TechTrends: Linking Research and Practice to Improve LearningA Publication of the Association for Educational Communications & Technology*, 1–17. DOI: 10.1007/s11528-024-01015-3

Green, S., & Harris, R. (2023). Collaborative training programs in academia and industry: A model for success. *Educational Innovations*, *29*(4), 45–61.

Grew, R. (2024). Breaking down silos: Enhancing collaboration and innovation in higher education. Vygo. https://blog.vygoapp.com/silos

Grobler, S., & Dittrich, A. K. (2024). Envisioning quality education for sustainability transformation in teacher education: Perspectives from an international dialogue on Sustainable Development Goal 4. *International Journal of Comparative Education and Development*, *26*(3), 270–285. DOI: 10.1108/IJCED-06-2023-0048

Gumaste, S. V., Paweloszek, I., & Kumar, N. (2024). Sustainable Management in Higher Technical Education—Need for Internationalism. In *Sustainable Innovations in Management in the Digital Transformation Era* (pp. 281–288). Routledge. DOI: 10.4324/9781003450238-28

Güngör, G. (2020). Problems and solution suggestions encountered in vocational skill training in vocational high schools: Teachers' views. *European Journal of Education Studies*, *7*(4), 233–253.

Gupta, S., Jaiswal, A., Paramasivam, A., & Kotecha, J. (2022). Academic writing challenges and supports: Perspectives of international doctoral Students and their supervisors. *Frontiers in Education*, *7*, 891534. DOI: 10.3389/feduc.2022.891534

Gusha, I. S. (2022). *Paul's ethics of reconciliation in dialogue with Ndebele and Shona ethnic cohesion*. University of Bamberg Press. DOI: 10.20378/irb-54882

Guthery, S., & Bailes, L. P. (2023). Unintended Consequences of Expanding Teacher Preparation Pathways: Does alternative licensure attenuate new teacher pay? *AERA Open*, *9*, 23328584231159900. DOI: 10.1177/23328584231159900

Habibi, A., Sofyan, S., & Mukminin, A. (2023). Factors affecting digital technology access in vocational education. *Scientific Reports*, *13*(1), 1–12. DOI: 10.1038/s41598-023-32755-6 PMID: 37029180

Hagel, P. (2015). What is good practice in the development, assessment and evaluation of digital literacy for graduate employability? discourse: *Deakin University Library Research And Practice*, No. 2, http://hdl.handle.net/10536/DRO/DU:30073199

Hakan, K. Ö. (2020). Digital transformation in higher education: A case study on strategic plans. *Высшее образование в России*, (3), 9-23.

Hallam, G., Thomas, A., & Beach, B. (2018). Creating a Connected Future Through Information and Digital Literacy: Strategic Directions at The University of Queensland Library. *Journal of the Australian Library & Information Association*, *67*(1), 42–54. DOI: 10.1080/24750158.2018.1426365

Hamonic, A., Boé, L., Jacq, F., & Penilla, J. (2023). Bridging the gap between academia and industry through MOOCs: A blended learning approach. arXiv preprint arXiv:2303.04019. Retrieved from https://arxiv.org/abs/2303.04019

Handal, B., Watson, K., Petocz, P., & Maher, M. (2018). Choosing to teach in rural and remote schools: The zone of free movement. *Education Research and Perspectives, 45*, 1–32. DOI: 10.70953/ERPv45.18001

Hannemann, M., Henn, S., & Schäfer, S. (2023). Participation in Online Research: Towards a Typology of Research Subjects with Regard to Digital Access and Literacy. *International Journal of Qualitative Methods, 22*, 1–10. DOI: 10.1177/16094069231205188

Harrison, C., & Brown, L. (2019). Industry-academic collaborations and their impact on curriculum development: A case study approach. *Higher Education Policy Review, 41*(3), 256–275.

Harrison, L. (2024). *Unpacking Micro-Influence within the Australian Creative Sectors.* Springer Nature Singapore. DOI: 10.1007/978-981-97-5914-9

Harrison, R., Hughes, J., & Roll, C. (2019). Building bridges: Partnerships between universities and industries for curriculum development. *Journal of Higher Education Collaboration, 15*(2), 112–125. DOI: 10.1016/j.hec.2019.03.002

Harris, S. G. (1990). The Fifth Discipline: The Art and Practice of the Learning Organization", by Peter M. Senge. *Human Resource Management, 29*(3), 343. DOI: 10.1002/hrm.3930290308

Harvard Business Review. (2019). The soft skills companies need most in 2019. Harvard Business Publishing. Retrieved from https://hbr.org

Hattie, J. (2021). *Visible Learning: A Synthesis of Over 800 Meta-Analyses Relating to Achievement.* Routledge.

Haug, B. S., & Mork, S. M. (2021). Taking 21st century skills from vision to classroom: What teachers highlight as supportive professional development in the light of new demands from educational reforms. *Teaching and Teacher Education, 100*, 103286. DOI: 10.1016/j.tate.2021.103286

Helsper, E. J. (2012). A corresponding fields model for the links between social and digital exclusion. *Communication Theory, 22*(4), 403–426. DOI: 10.1111/j.1468-2885.2012.01416.x

Helsper, E. J., & Eynon, R. (2013). Distinctions in digital literacy: The relationship between the digital literacy gap and social exclusion. *The American Behavioral Scientist, 57*(7), 963–986.

Herbold, S., Hautli-Janisz, A., Heuer, U., Kikteva, Z., & Trautsch, A. (2023). A Large-Scale Comparison of Human-Written Versus ChatGPT-Generated Essays. *Scientific Reports, 13*(1), 18617. DOI: 10.1038/s41598-023-45644-9 PMID: 37903836

Herridge, C., 2024. The Patterns and Structures of Information Technology Departments in Higher Education.

Herring, R., Dyer, K., Howkins, P. and Ward, C., 2020. Characterisation of the offshore precipitation environment to help combat leading edge erosion of wind turbine blades. *Wind energy science, 5*(4), pp.1399-1409.

Hew, K. F., & Cheung, W. S. (2014). Students' and instructors' use of massive open online courses (MOOCs): Motivations and challenges. *Educational Research Review, 12*, 45–58. DOI: 10.1016/j.edurev.2014.05.001

Hill, C., & Lawton, A. (2018). Universities, the digital divide and global inequality. *Journal of Higher Education Policy and Management, 40*(6), 598–610. DOI: 10.1080/1360080X.2018.1531211

Hollands, F. M., & Tirthali, D. (2014). *MOOCs: Expectations and reality. Center for Benefit-Cost Studies of Education.* Teachers College, Columbia University.

Hollands, F. M., & Tirthali, D. (2014). MOOCs: Expectations and Reality. Columbia University, Teachers College. Retrieved from https://doi.org/DOI: 10.7916/D8C24W3D

Holotescu, C., Grosseck, G., Cretu, V., & Naaji, A. (2014). Integrating MOOCs in blended courses. *Proceedings of the International Scientific Conference eLearning and Software for Education*, 1, 243–250. DOI: 10.12753/2066-026X-14-034

Hong, J., & Thakuriah, P. V. (2018). Examining the relationship between different urbanization settings, smartphone use to access the internet and trip frequencies. *Journal of Transport Geography, 69*, 11–18. DOI: 10.1016/j.jtrangeo.2018.04.006

Hossain, M., Rahman, M., & Islam, S. (2022). Regional disparities in teacher quality in Bangladesh: A review of the rural-urban divide. *Educational Review, 21*(4), 103–118.

Huan, Y., Liang, T., Li, H., & Zhang, C. (2021). A systematic method for assessing progress of achieving sustainable development goals: A case study of 15 countries. *The Science of the Total Environment, 752*, 141875. DOI: 10.1016/j.scitotenv.2020.141875 PMID: 33207501

Huber, E., & Shalavin, C. A. (2018). Surveying the digital literacy landscape for academic and professional staff in higher education. *Senior Deputy Vice-Chancellor and Deputy Vice-Chancellor (Education) - Papers*.

Hughes, M., Ginnett, R. C., & Curphy, G. J. (2019). *Leadership: Enhancing the lessons of experience* (9th ed.). McGraw-Hill Education.

IBM. (2023, September 1). *What are ai hallucinations?* IBM. https://www.ibm.com/think/topics/ai-hallucinations#:~:text=Use%20data%20templates,and%20refine%20the%20system%20continually

Ibrahim, H., Liu, F., Asim, R., Battu, B., Benabderrahmane, S., Alhafni, B., & Zhang, Y. (2023). Perception, performance, and detectability of conversational artificial intelligence across 32 university courses. DOI: 10.1038/s41598-023-38964-3

Ibrahim, Y. Y. (2023). The impact of massive open online courses (MOOCs) on knowledge management using integrated innovation diffusion theory and the technology acceptance model. *Education Sciences*, *13*(6), 531. DOI: 10.3390/educsci13060531

IEEE. (2024). 2024 IEEE/ACM Workshop on Gender Equality, Diversity, and Inclusion in Software Engineering. Lisbon: GE@ICSE.

IFLA. (2020, December, 9). Libraries in digital skills policies. https://www.ifla.org/wp-content/uploads/2019/05/assets/hq/topics/info-society/documents/libraries_in_digital_skills_policies.pdf

Ikenwe, I. J., & Aiyebelehin, A. J. (2024). Information Literacy Skills as Predictors of the Use of Digital Library Resources by Academics in Selected Federal Universities in Nigeria. *International Journal of Education and Development Using Information and Communication Technology*, *20*(1), 25–38.

Ilieva, G., Yankova, T., Klisarova-Belcheva, S., Dimitrov, A., Bratkov, M., & Angelov, D. (2023). Effects of Generative Chatbots in Higher Education. *Information (Basel)*, *14*(9), 492. DOI: 10.3390/info14090492

In Organizations Worldwide as of. 2024, by Function [Graph] Statista. https://www.statista.com/statistics/1451298/genai-adoption-by-function-worldwide

Indah, R. N., Toyyibah, , Budhiningrum, A. S., & Afifi, N. (2022). The Research Competence, Critical Thinking Skills and Digital Literacy of Indonesian EFL Students. *Journal of Language Teaching & Research*, *13*(2), 315–324. DOI: 10.17507/jltr.1302.11

India Foundation. (n.d.). Role of Massive Open Online Courses (MOOCs) in Achieving Equity in Education and SDG 4. Retrieved from https://indiafoundation.in/articles-and-commentaries/role-of-massive-open-online-courses-moocs-in-achieving-equity-in-education-and-sdg-4/

Infosys. (n.d.). Infosys Springboard: Digital learning platform for lifelong learners. Retrieved from https://www.infosys.com/about/springboard.html

Inusah, Y., Kazaz, A., & Ulubeyli, S. (2025). Barriers to E-Tendering Implementation in the Construction Industry: A Comprehensive Review and Analysis of a Decade and Beyond. *Sustainability (Basel)*, *17*(5), 2052. DOI: 10.3390/su17052052

Ip, C. Y. (2024). Effect of digital literacy on social entrepreneurial intentions and nascent behaviours among students and practitioners in mass communication. *Humanities & Social Sciences Communications*, *11*(1), 34. Advance online publication. DOI: 10.1057/s41599-023-02587-w

Islam, M. R., & Rahman, M. M. (2023). Bridging the digital divide: Teacher training and development in Bangladesh's education sector. *Journal of Educational Technology*, *30*(1), 74–91.

Jackson, D. (2013). Student perceptions of the importance of employability skill provision in business undergraduate programs. *Journal of Education for Business*, *88*(5), 271–279. DOI: 10.1080/08832323.2012.697928

Jackson, D. (2017). Enhancing industry engagement in engineering education: The potentials of integrated work-study programs. *Journal of Professional Issues in Engineering Education and Practice*, *143*(4), 04017005.

Jackson, D. (2019). Student perceptions of the importance of employability skill provision in business undergraduate programs. *Journal of Education and Work*, *32*(2), 77–94.

Jantjies, M. (2020). How South Africa can address digital inequalities in e-learning. The Conversation. http://theconversation.com. Accessed: 03/10/2024.

Jatmoko, D., Suyitno, S., Rasul, M. S., Nurtanto, M., Kholifah, N., Masek, A., & Nur, H. R. (2023). The factors influencing digital literacy practice in vocational education: A structural equation modeling approach. *European Journal of Educational Research*, *12*(2), 1109–1121. DOI: 10.12973/eu-jer.12.2.1109

Jena, M., & Sahoo, B. (2024). Perception of students and teachers towards vocational education in secondary schools. [IJHSSI]. *International Journal of Humanities and Social Science Invention*, *13*(3), 139–146.

Jiang, J., & Yip, S. Y. (2024). Teacher shortage: An analysis of the rural teachers living subsidy policy on teacher attraction and retention in rural Western China. *Asia-Pacific Journal of Teacher Education*, *52*(3), 316–331. DOI: 10.1080/1359866X.2024.2328682

Jisc. (2021). *Digital transformation in higher education: Ensuring that universities are ready for the future of work.* Retrieved from https://www.jisc.ac.uk/digital-transformation

JISC. (2021).Student digital experience insights survey 2020/21: UK higher education find-ings.https://repository.jisc.ac.uk/8318/1/DEI-P1-HE-student-briefing-2021-FINAL.pdf

Johnson, M., & Lee, D. (2022). Professional associations and shared professional development: Strengthening connections between academia and industry. *Journal of Professional Development*, *18*(2), 55–69.

Johnston, S. L. (2024). *Addressing Skills Gap: A Systemic Reframe and Redesign of Capstone using Design-Based Research* (Doctoral dissertation, University of Calgary (Canada)).

Johnston, N. (2020). The Shift towards Digital Literacy in Australian University Libraries: Developing a Digital Literacy Framework. *Journal of the Australian Library & Information Association*, *69*(1), 93–101. DOI: 10.1080/24750158.2020.1712638

Joksimović, S., Gašević, D., Kovanović, V., Riecke, B. E., & Hatala, M. (2015). Social presence in online discussions as a process predictor of academic performance in MOOCs. *Computers & Education*, *79*, 41–53. DOI: 10.1016/j.compedu.2014.07.002

Jones, R. (2022). Technological advancements and the changing workforce. *Future of Work Journal*, *3*(1), 34–50.

Jones, S., Lefoe, G., Harvey, M., & Ryland, K. (2012). Distributed leadership: A collaborative framework for academics, executives and professionals in higher education. *Journal of Higher Education Policy and Management*, *34*(1), 67–78. DOI: 10.1080/1360080X.2012.642334

Jordan, K. (2014). Initial trends in enrollment and completion of massive open online courses. *International Review of Research in Open and Distance Learning*, *15*(1), 133–160. DOI: 10.19173/irrodl.v15i1.1651

Junco, R. (2012). The relationship between frequency of Facebook use, participation in Facebook activities, and student engagement. *Computers & Education*, *58*(1), 162–171. DOI: 10.1016/j.compedu.2011.08.004

Kammer, J., Cherner, T., & Hays, L. (2021). Digital literacy in the academy. In Hays, L., & Kammer, J. (Eds.), *Integrating Digital Literacy in the Disciplines* (pp. 7–14). Routledge.

Kang, G.-L., Park, C.-W., & Jang, S.-H. (2024). A Study on the Impact of Financial Literacy and Digital Capabilities on Entrepreneurial Intention: Mediating Effect of Entrepreneurship. *Behavioral Sciences (2076-328X), 14*(2), 121. DOI: 10.3390/bs14020121

Karpicke, J. D., & Roediger, H. L.III. (2008). The critical importance of retrieval for learning. *Science, 319*(5865), 966–968. DOI: 10.1126/science.1152408 PMID: 18276894

Kasperski, R., & Ben-Yehudah, G. (2024). Developing digital academic skills in preservice teachers: Performance and metacognitive perspectives. *Journal of Education for Teaching, 50*(4), 613–626. DOI: 10.1080/02607476.2024.2323583

Katzenbach, J., & Smith, D. (1992). *The wisdom of teams: Creating the high-performance organization*. Harvard Business Press.

Kelly, B. (2019). Uncovering Digital Literacy and Supporting the Implicit: A Case Study of Library-Faculty Collaboration. *IATUL Annual Conference Proceedings*, 328–336.

Kenney, B. (2008). Leaping into technology. *School Library Journal, 54*, 11.

Kezar, A. (2005). Consequences of radical change in governance: A grounded theory approach. *The Journal of Higher Education, 76*(6), 634–668. DOI: 10.1080/00221546.2005.11772303

Kezar, A. (2005). Creating and sustaining a campus-wide culture of innovation: Perceptions of innovation leaders. *The Journal of Higher Education, 76*(4), 425–461.

Kezar, A. (2011). Understanding and facilitating organizational change in the 21st century: Recent research and conceptualizations. *ASHE-ERIC Higher Education Report, 28*(4).

Kezar, A. (2017). *Understanding and facilitating organizational change in the 21st century: Recent research and conceptualizations*. Jossey-Bass.

Kezar, A. (2018). *How colleges change: Understanding, leading, and enacting change*. Routledge. DOI: 10.4324/9781315121178

Kezar, A., & Holcombe, E. (2017). *Shared leadership in higher education: Important lessons from research and practice*. American Council on Education.

Khan, S., & Iqbal, A. (2023). Investing in teacher quality: Addressing rural education challenges in Bangladesh. *Journal of Education and Development*, *32*(2), 77–92.

Khan, Z., & Dam, N. (2020). Resource allocation models in academia and industry collaborations. *Journal of Business Research*, *112*, 216–225.

Khoi, B. H. (2021). Factors Influencing on University Reputation: Model Selection by AIC. In Ngoc Thach, N., Kreinovich, V., & Trung, N. D. (Eds.), *Data Science for Financial Econometrics. Studies in Computational Intelligence* (Vol. 898). Springer., DOI: 10.1007/978-3-030-48853-6_13

Kight, D. (2021, September 1). Taking the Lead in Digital Literacy Initiatives. *Computers in Libraries*, *41*(7), 14.

Kılınç, H. K., & Keçecioğlu, F. (2024, May 31). Generative Artificial Intelligence: A Historical and Future Perspective. *Academic Platform Journal of Engineering and Smart Systems*, *12*(2), 47–58. DOI: 10.21541/apjess.1398155

Killick, S. (2023). The library's influence and impact on learning: A case study from The Open University (UK). *Asian Association of Open Universities Journal*, *18*(3), 279–291. DOI: 10.1108/AAOUJ-04-2023-0051

Kim, J. (2024). Leading teachers' perspective on teacher-AI collaboration in education. *Education and Information Technologies*, *29*(7), 8693–8724. DOI: 10.1007/s10639-023-12109-5

Kirkpatrick, D., & Kirkpatrick, J. (2006). *Evaluating training programs: The four levels*. Berrett-Koehler Publishers.

Kirkwood, A., & Price, L. (2020). *Technology and education: Challenges and opportunities for higher education in the digital age*. Routledge.

Kirschner, P. A., Hendrick, C., & Heal, J. (2022). *How Teaching Happens: Seminal Works in Teaching and Teacher Effectiveness and What They Mean in Practice*. Routledge. DOI: 10.4324/9781003228165

Kizilcec, R. F., Pérez-Sanagustín, M., & Maldonado, J. J. (2017). Self-regulated learning strategies predict learner behavior and goal attainment in massive open online courses. *Computers & Education*, *104*, 18–33. DOI: 10.1016/j.compedu.2016.10.001

Klein, J. T. (2023). Boundary discourse of crossdisciplinary and cross-sector research: Refiguring the landscape of science. *Minerva*, *61*(1), 31–52. DOI: 10.1007/s11024-022-09474-9

Klein, J. T., & Lester, J. (2020). *Promoting interdisciplinary collaboration in higher education: A handbook for leaders and administrators*. Stylus Publishing.

Knight, W. (2022, May 17). AI can show us the ravages of climate change. MIT Technology Review. https://www.technologyreview.com/2019/05/16/135323/ai-can-show-us-the-ravages-of-climate-change

Kolb, D. A. (2014). *Experiential learning: Experience as the source of learning and development*. FT press.

Kolb, D. A. (1984). *Experiential learning: Experience as the source of learning and development*. Prentice-Hall.

Kolesnyk, L., & Biseth, H. (2024). Professional development in teacher education through international collaboration: When education reform hits Ukraine. *Professional Development in Education, 50*(2), 347–359. DOI: 10.1080/19415257.2023.2193197

Koltay, T. (2011). The media and the literacies: Media literacy, information literacy, digital literacy. *Media Culture & Society, 33*(2), 211–221. DOI: 10.1177/0163443710393382

Kop, R., Fournier, H., & Mak, J. S. F. (2011). A pedagogy of abundance or a pedagogy to support human beings? Participant support on massive open online courses. *International Review of Research in Open and Distance Learning, 12*(7), 74–93. DOI: 10.19173/irrodl.v12i7.1041

Kormos, E., & Wisdom, K. (2021). Rural schools and the digital divide: Technology in the learning experience and challenges to integration. *Theory and Practice in Rural Education, 11*(1), 25–39. DOI: 10.3776/tpre.2021.v11n1p25-39

Kot, F. C., & Jones, J. L. (2015). The Impact of Library Resource Utilization on Undergraduate Students' Academic Performance: A Propensity Score Matching Design. *College & Research Libraries, 76*(5), 566–586. DOI: 10.5860/crl.76.5.566

Kotter, J. P. (2012). *Leading Change*. Harvard Business Review Press.

Kotter, J. P. (2014). *Accelerate: Building strategic agility for a faster-moving world*. Harvard Business Review Press.

Kouzes, J., & Posner, B. (2023). *The leadership challenge: How to make extraordinary things happen in organizations*. Wiley.

Kramm, N., & McKenna, S. (2023). AI amplifies the tough question: What is higher education really for? *Teaching in Higher Education, 28*(8), 2173–2178. DOI: 10.1080/13562517.2023.2263839

Kristiawan, M., Oka, I. G. A. A. M., Haenilah, E. Y., Wachidi, W., Ediansyah, E., Aprianto, I., Zulinto, A., Perrodin, D. D., & Utama, H. B. (2023). Youtube For Developing Technological Skill. [JAETS]. *Journal of Applied Engineering and Technological Science*, *4*(2), 868–982. DOI: 10.37385/jaets.v4i2.1539

Kumar, A. (2023). Experiential learning in digital education: The role of MOOCs. *International Journal of Digital Learning*, *30*(2), 45–52. DOI: 10.1080/IDLE.2023.091234

Kumar, S., & Rose, R. C. (2021). Digital literacy in higher education: A case study of student engagement and learning outcomes. *Higher Education*, *81*, 647–665.

Kumar, V., Goodarzian, F., Ghasemi, P., Chan, F. T. S., & Gupta, N. (2025). Artificial intelligence applications in healthcare supply chain networks under disaster conditions. *International Journal of Production Research*, *63*(2), 395–403. DOI: 10.1080/00207543.2024.2444150

Kurebwa, J. (2022). Distance education and the challenge of technology integration at the Zimbabwe Open University. In Global, I. G. I. (Ed.), *Advancing open and distance learning*.

Kurebwa, J. (2022). Urban housing affordability in Zimbabwe: The case of Homelink Housing Mortgage Scheme. *Canadian Social Science*, *18*(5), 43–53.

Kurtoglu, M. (2018). The Dream is Over The Crisis of Clark Kerr's California Idea of Higher Education.

Kuş, Z. (2024). Teachers' and parents' perspectives on citizenship education in Turkey: Consensus and disagreements. *Education, Citizenship and Social Justice*. 17461979241240451. DOI: 10.1177/17461979241240451

Kvon, G., Vaks, V., Kalimullin, A., Bayanova, A., Shaidullina, A., Dolzhikova, A., & Lapidus, N. (2019). Developing the informational and digital environment of a university: Problem analysis and assessment. *Eurasia Journal of Mathematics, Science and Technology Education*, *15*(10), 1–14. DOI: 10.29333/ejmste/109503

Kwihangana, F. (2024). Teacher positioning in educational ICT policies: Implications for digital teacher identity development in under-resourced contexts. *Journal of Education Policy*. 1–24.

Kwok, L. (2022). Labor shortage: A critical reflection and a call for industry-academia collaboration. *International Journal of Contemporary Hospitality Management*, *34*(11), 3929–3943. DOI: 10.1108/IJCHM-01-2022-0103

Laal, M., & Ghodsi, S. M. (2012). Benefits of collaborative learning. *Procedia: Social and Behavioral Sciences, 31*, 486–490. DOI: 10.1016/j.sbspro.2011.12.091

Lang, J. (2023). Workforce upskilling: Can universities meet the challenges of lifelong learning? *International Journal of Information and Learning Technology, 40*(5), 388–400. DOI: 10.1108/IJILT-01-2023-0001

Laurillard, D. (2016). *Teaching as a design science: Building pedagogical patterns for learning and technology*. Routledge.

Laurillard, D. (2016). The educational problem that MOOCs could solve: Professional development for teachers of disadvantaged students. *Research in Learning Technology, 24*(1), 29369. Advance online publication. DOI: 10.3402/rlt.v24.29369

Lavery, M. P. J., Mojtaba, M. A., Bauer, R., Brambilla, G., Cheng, L., Cox, M. A., Dudley, A., Ellis, A. D., Fontaine, N. K., & Kelly, A. E. (2018). Tackling Africa's digital divide. *Nature Photonics, 12*(5), 249–252. DOI: 10.1038/s41566-018-0162-z

Lee, P. (2016, March 25). *Learning from Tay's introduction*. The Official Microsoft Blog. https://blogs.microsoft.com/blog/2016/03/25/learning-tays-introduction/

Lee, S. W., Morcos, M., Lee, D. W., & Young, J. (2024). Demographic Representation of Generative Artificial Intelligence Images of Physicians. *JAMA Network Open, 7*(8), e2425993. DOI: 10.1001/jamanetworkopen.2024.25993 PMID: 39106070

Lei, H., Tang, S., Zhao, Y., & Chen, S. (2024). Enterprise digitalization, employee digital literacy and R&D cooperation: The moderating role of organizational inertia. *Chinese Management Studies, 18*(2), 479–505. DOI: 10.1108/CMS-10-2021-0456

Lembani, R., Mulenga, K., Mwewa, P., Mhango, L., & Chaamwe, N. (2023). Are we leaving students behind? Self-directed learning in an ICT challenged country. *Education and Information Technologies, 28*(3), 3475–3492. DOI: 10.1007/s10639-022-11318-8 PMID: 36189192

Lérias, E., Guerra, C., & Ferreira, P. (2024). Literacy in artificial intelligence as a challenge for teaching in higher education: A case study at Portalegre Polytechnic University. *Information (Basel), 15*(4), 205. DOI: 10.3390/info15040205

Lesser, E. L., & Prusak, L. (2020). *Creating value with knowledge: Insights from the world's leading organizations*. Harvard Business Press.

Lesser, E. L., & Prusak, L. (Eds.). (2004). *Creating value with knowledge: Insights from the IBM Institute for business value*. Oxford University Press. DOI: 10.1093/0195165128.001.0001

Lester, S. E., Dubel, A. K., Hernán, G., McHenry, J., & Rassweiler, A. (2020). Spatial planning principles for marine ecosystem restoration. *Frontiers in Marine Science*, *7*, 328. DOI: 10.3389/fmars.2020.00328

Levine-Clark, M. & Dean, Toni Carter. (2013). *ALA Glossary of Library and Information Science*. ALA Editions.

Li, C., & Chen, F. (2024). Impacts of ICT-related factors on students' digital reading literacy: Evidence from high-performing Asian countries and regions. *Education and Information Technologies*, *29*(13), 16717–16747. DOI: 10.1007/s10639-024-12501-9

Lin, Y., & Yu, Z. (2024). A bibliometric analysis of artificial intelligence chatbots in educational contexts. *Interactive Technology and Smart Education*, *21*(2), 189–213. DOI: 10.1108/ITSE-12-2022-0165

Littlejohn, A., Beetham, H., & McGill, L. (2012). Learning at the digital frontier: A review of digital literacies in theory and practice. *Journal of Computer Assisted Learning*, *28*(6), 547–556. DOI: 10.1111/j.1365-2729.2011.00474.x

Liu, W. (2020). Knowledge map: A creative visual path to library guides and resources. *The Electronic Library*, *38*(5/6), 943–962. DOI: 10.1108/EL-03-2020-0055

Liu, Y., Hu, Y., & Zhang, F. (2021). Finland's teacher recruitment and retention strategies: A global model. *Journal of Education and Teacher Development*, *45*(2), 103–118.

Liyanagunawardena, T. R., Adams, A. A., & Williams, S. A. (2013). MOOCs: A systematic study of the published literature 2008–2012. *International Review of Research in Open and Distance Learning*, *14*(3), 202–227. DOI: 10.19173/irrodl.v14i3.1455

Liza, K., & Andriyanti, E. (2020). Digital literacy scale of English pre-service teachers and their perceived readiness toward the application of digital technologies. [EduLearn]. *J.Educ Learn*, *14*(1), 74–79. DOI: 10.11591/edulearn.v14i1.13925

Lo Presti, V. (2023). The social impact of distance learning in Roman schools: "Success," social innovation, teaching practices. *Frontiers in Sociology*, *8*, 1141435. Advance online publication. DOI: 10.3389/fsoc.2023.1141435 PMID: 37091726

Long, M., & Lee, C. S. (2023). Leveraging MOOCs for learners in economically disadvantaged regions. *Education and Information Technologies*, *28*(9), 12243–12268. DOI: 10.1007/s10639-022-11461-2

Lopez, J. R. (2013). *Digital literacy and academic success in online education for underprivileged communities: The prep@ net case* [Phd Dissertations]. The University of Texas at Austin.

Lukarov, V. (2019). *Scaling up learning analytics in blended learning scenarios* (Doctoral dissertation, Dissertation, RWTH Aachen University, 2019).

Lu, Y., & Khan, M. S. (2024). Influence of Higher Education E-Service Quality on E-Learning Student Satisfaction; as Moderated by Digital Literacy: A Mixed Method Research Approach. *Revista de Gestao Social e Ambiental*, *18*(1), e06077. Advance online publication. DOI: 10.24857/rgsa.v18n1-112

Machingura, F. (2022). *Barriers to technological adoption in Zimbabwean universities: A focus on administrative silos*. Academic Press.

Madsen, S. R. (2023). Leading change in higher education: Overcoming resistance and achieving digital transformation. *Journal of Higher Education Leadership*, *28*(1), 102–115.

Maguire, D., Dale, L., & Pauli, M. (2020). Learning and teaching reimagined: a new dawn for higher education? Bristol: JISC. Retrieved 21 February, 2021, from https://repository.jisc.ac.uk/8150/1/learning-and-teaching-reimagined-a-new-dawn-for-higher-education.pdf

Maharaj, N. G. M., Kanadia, P. K., Dr., & Tandel, R. J., Dr. (2021). Digital Information Literacy among the Faculty Members of Gujarat Adani Institute of Medical Sciences. *Library Philosophy and Practice (e-Journal).*

Mai, N.A., (2019). Policies for higher education development in the People's Republic of China.

Manderino, M., & Castek, J. (2020), Digital Literacies for Disciplinary Learning: Pedagogies Youth Deserve. In Ortlieb, E., Grote-Garcia, S., Cassidy, J. and Cheek, E.H. (Ed.) *What's Hot in Literacy: Exemplar Models of Effective Practice* (*Literacy Research, Practice and Evaluation, Vol. 11*), Emerald Publishing Limited, Leeds, pp. 3-15. DOI: 10.1108/S2048-045820200000011003

Manu, T. R., & Gala, B. (2023). Gamification for Digital Humanities in Libraries: A Survey of the Web-based Games on Digital Literacy. *DESIDOC Journal of Library and Information Technology*, *43*(4), 241–248. DOI: 10.14429/djlit.43.04.19259

Marengo, A., Pagano, A., Pange, J., & Soomro, K. A. (2024). The educational value of artificial intelligence in higher education: A 10-year systematic literature review. *Interactive Technology and Smart Education*, *21*(4), 625–644. DOI: 10.1108/ITSE-11-2023-0218

Marginson, S. (2016). *Higher education and the common good.* Melbourne University Publishing.

Martin, A. (2008). *Digital literacy and the "digital society".* Digital literacies: Concepts, policies and practices, 151-176.

Martínez-Bravo, M. C., Chalezquer, C. S., & Serrano-Puche, J. (2022). Dimensions of digital literacy in the 21st century competency frameworks. *Sustainability (Basel), 14*(3), 1867–1880. DOI: 10.3390/su14031867

Martin, F., & Liao, C. (2020). Learning management systems in higher education: Benefits and barriers to their implementation and use. *Journal of Online Learning and Teaching, 16*(2), 154–167.

Martzoukou, K. (2021). Academic libraries in COVID-19: A renewed mission for digital lit-eracy. *Library Management, 42*(4/5), 266–276. DOI: 10.1108/LM-09-2020-0131

Masterman, E., & Shuyska, J. A. (2011). Digitally mastered? Technology and transition in the experience of taught postgraduate students. *Learning, Media and Technology, 37*(4), 335–354. DOI: 10.1080/17439884.2011.608361

Mata v. Avianca, Inc., JUSTIA Dockets & Filings (United States District Court Southern District of New York June 6, 2023). Retrieved January 24, 2025, from https://docs.justia.com/cases/federal/district-courts/new-york/nysdce/1:2022cv01461/575368/45

Mavutha, W., & Mabotja, T. (2024). Digital literacy: A foreign language for students from rural areas in South Africa. *International Journal of Research in Business & Social Science, 13*(5), 784–793. DOI: 10.20525/ijrbs.v13i5.3315

Maxwell, L. (2020). Digital Literacy and Digital Legacy. *Library Technology Reports, 56*(5), 7–11.

McHenry, M. A., Barrows, J., & White, T. R. (2021). Industry-academic partnerships in technology transfer: Insights from curriculum integration. *Journal of Technology Education, 33*(1), 45–62. DOI: 10.1234/jte.2021.045

McLeod, A., & Torres, L. (2020). Enhancing first year university students'digital skills withthe Digital Skill Development (DSD) framework. In D. Schmidt-Crawford (Ed.),*Proceeding of society for information technology and teacher education international con-ference*(pp. 373–379). Waynesville, NC: Association for the Advancement of Computingin Education (AACE). https://researchmgt.monash.edu/ws/portalfiles/portal/332253378/329859476.pdf

McMahon, M. (2021). *Social Aspects of Technology in Education.* Salem Press Encyclopedia.

Means, B., Toyama, Y., Murphy, R., Bakia, M., & Jones, K. (2009). Evaluation of evidence-based practices in online learning: A meta-analysis and review of online learning studies.

Means, B., Toyama, Y., Murphy, R., & Baki, M. (2013). The effectiveness of online and blended learning: A meta-analysis of the empirical literature. *Teachers College Record, 115*(3), 1–47. DOI: 10.1177/016146811311500307

Menon, S., & Suresh, M. (2022). Assessment framework for workforce agility in higher education institutions. *Higher Education, Skills and Work-Based Learning, 12*(6), 1169–1188. DOI: 10.1108/HESWBL-01-2022-0014

Meridha, J. M. (2024). The causes of poor digital literacy in educational practice, and possible solutions among the stakeholders: A systematic literature review. *SN Social Sciences, 4*(11), 210. Advance online publication. DOI: 10.1007/s43545-024-01010-8

Messaoud, S. B., Ilahi, M., & Cheniti-Belcadhi, L. (2022, March). Towards a personalized micro-credentials approach based on learning analytics for reducing the gap university-industry. In *2022 IEEE Global Engineering Education Conference (EDUCON)* (pp. 1448-1454). IEEE. DOI: 10.1109/EDUCON52537.2022.9766585

Mifsud, D. (2023). Rethinking the concept of teacher education: a problematization and critique of current policies and practices. In *Teacher Education as an Ongoing Professional Trajectory: Implications for Policy and Practice* (pp. 1–23). Springer International Publishing. DOI: 10.1007/978-3-031-28620-9_1

Migliorino, P. (2011). Digital technologies can unite but also divide: CALD communities in the digital age. *Australasian Public Libraries and Information Services, 24*(3), 107–110.

Miliou, O., & Angeli, C. (2023). *The Impact of a Project-Based Learning Environment on the Development of Undergraduate Students' Digital Literacy Skills.* https://www.learntechlib.org/primary/p/224350/

Miller, R., & Luse, A. (2020). Policy recommendations for partnership in digital skills training. *Journal of Policy and Strategy, 31*(2), 204–219.

Milligan, C., & Littlejohn, A. (2014). Supporting professional learning in a massive open online course. *International Review of Research in Open and Distance Learning, 15*(5), 197–213. DOI: 10.19173/irrodl.v15i5.1855

Milligan, C., & Littlejohn, A. (2017). Why study on a MOOC? The motives of learners and the role of self-regulated learning. *International Review of Research in Open and Distance Learning*, *18*(2), 1–18. DOI: 10.19173/irrodl.v18i2.3033

Ministry of Education of the People's Republic of China. (2017). *Double First-Class University Plan.*

Ministry of Education. (2022). SWAYAM: Expanding access through multilingual MOOCs. Retrieved from https://swayam.gov.in

Ministry of Education. (n.d.). Education loan schemes in India. Government of India. Retrieved from https://www.education.gov.in

Ministry of Education. (n.d.). Rising cost of higher education in India and its impact on accessibility. Government of India. Retrieved from https://www.education.gov.in

Ministry of Higher and Tertiary Education. Innovation, Science and Technology Development [MHTEISTD]. (2018). *Education 5.0 Policy.* Government of Zimbabwe.

Mintzberg, H., Ahlstrand, B., & Lampel, J. (2020). *Strategy safari: A guided tour through the wilds of strategic management* (3rd ed.). Pearson.

Mishra, A. (2022). Economic Implications of MOOCs in Higher Education: An Indian Perspective. World Economics Association. Retrieved from https://www .worldeconomicsassociation.org/newsletterarticles/moocs-india/

Mlambo, A. S. (2018). From education for liberation to education for production: Revisiting Zimbabwe's Education 5.0 philosophy. *Journal of Southern African Studies*, *44*(5), 901–915.

Mlambo, V. (2018). An overview of rural-urban migration in South Africa: Its causes and implications. *Archives of Business Research*, *6*(4). Advance online publication. DOI: 10.14738/abr.64.4407

Mokhtari, F. (2023). Fostering Digital Literacy in Higher Education: Benefits, Challenges and Implications. *International Journal of Linguistics. Literature and Translation*, *6*(10), 160–167. DOI: 10.32996/ijllt.2023.6.10.19

Molfenter, T., Heitkamp, T., Murphy, A. A., Tapscott, S., Behlman, S., & Cody, O. J. (2021). Use of Telehealth in Mental Health (MH) Services During and After COVID-19. *Community Mental Health Journal*, *57*(7), 1244–1251. DOI: 10.1007/s10597-021-00861-2 PMID: 34165695

Mollick, E. R., & Mollick, L. (2023). Using AI to Implement Effective Teaching Strategies in Classrooms: Five Strategies, Including Prompts. *Wharton School of the University of Pennsylvania & Wharton Interactive*. https://doi.org/DOI: 10.2139/ssrn.4391243

Montenegro-Rueda, M., & Fernández-Batanero, J. M. (2022). Digital Competence of Special Education Teachers: Impact, Challenges and Opportunities. *Australasian Journal of Special and Inclusive Education*, *46*(2), 178–192. DOI: 10.1017/jsi.2022.8

Moorhouse, B. L., Wong, K. M., & Li, L. (2023). Teaching with technology in the post-pandemic digital age: Technological normalisation and AI-induced disruptions. *RELC Journal*, *54*(2), 311–320. DOI: 10.1177/00336882231176929

Mordor Intelligence. (2024). *Massive Open Online Course (MOOC) Market Report*. Retrieved from https://www.mordorintelligence.com/industry-reports/massive-open-online-course-mooc-market.

Morris, M. R. (2023, April 4). *Scientists' Perspectives on the Potential for Generative AI in their Fields*. Google Research.

Mouriquand, D. (2023, March 23). How ai is putting president macron at the heart of the French pension protests | euronews. euronews. https://www.euronews.com/culture/2023/03/23/how-ai-is-putting-president-macron-at-the-heart-of-the-french-pension-protests

Muchineripi, B., & Moyo, G. (2023). *Resource allocation challenges in higher education: Implications for technology integration*. ZPH Publishers.

Muck Rack. (January 3, 2024). *Leading ways public relations (PR) professionals used generative artificial intelligence (AI) in their workflow as of December 2023 [Graph]*. Statista. https://www.statista.com/statistics/1440861/ways-prs-used-generative-ai-work

Mudasih, I., & Subroto, W. T., & Susanti. (2021). The Effect of Financial Literacy, Digital Literacy, and Entrepreneurial Learning Outcome on Entrepreneur Behavior of Students at SMK Negeri 1 Surabaya. *Technium Social Sciences Journal*, *15*, 303–320.

Mukidi, C. A. (2023). Going against the tide in Uganda's higher education: A brief historical account of Uganda Martyrs University. *African Journal of Rural Development*, *8*(1), 57–72.

Mulat, T., & Natarajan, M. (2020). Digital Literacy Skills among Library Professionals in Jimma University Libraries. *Library Philosophy and Practice (e-Journal)*.

Munawar, D. S., Ghouri, J., & Jahanzeb, F. (2024). Challenges of Using Artificial Intelligence at the University Level. *Journal of Arts & Social Sciences*, *11*(1), 122–126. DOI: 10.46662/jass.v11i1.463

Murphy, L., & Liu, X. (2022). Technology transfer in higher education: The role of industry partnerships in enhancing digital literacy. *Journal of Educational Technology & Society*, *25*(1), 30–44.

Murray, D. D., Williams, C. R., Gaddy, J. A., Rogers, C. D., Kirabo, A., Santisteban, M. M., Wanjalla, C. N., Williams, E. M., Sweetwyne, M. T., Damo, S. M., Murray, S. A., Stokes, D., & Hinton, A.Jr. (2024). The power of junior faculty mentoring committees. *Journal of Cellular Physiology*, *239*(7), e31360. DOI: 10.1002/jcp.31360 PMID: 38962842

Murray, M., Pérez, J., & Fluker, J. (2022). Digital Literacy in the Core: The Emerging Higher Education Landscape. *Issues in Informing Science & Information Technology*, *19*, 1–13. DOI: 10.28945/4957

Musa, S.Z.B.S., (2024). Digital Renaissance: Reinventing Tertiary Language Teaching and Learning Strategies in Evolving Digital Landscape. *Education towards a Global Citizen Generation, 202.*

Musah, M. B., Ali, H. M., Vazhathodi al-Hudawi, S. H., Tahir, L. M., Daud, K. B., Said, H. B., & Kamil, N. M. (2016). Organisational climate as a predictor of workforce performance in the Malaysian higher education institutions. *Quality Assurance in Education*, *24*(3), 416–438. DOI: 10.1108/QAE-10-2014-0048

Musa, N., Hamid, N. A., & Ishak, M. S. (2021). Understanding the Trends of Digital Literacy Among Islamic Students (Positive Internet Analysis Study). *DAYAH: Journal of Islamic Education*, *4*(2), 141–158. DOI: 10.22373/jie.v4i2.10360

Mustafa, F., Nguyen, H. T. M., & Gao, X. A. (2024). The challenges and solutions of technology integration in rural schools: A systematic literature review. *International Journal of Educational Research*, *124*, 1–24. DOI: 10.1016/j.ijer.2024.102380

Musvoto, G., (2021). Household Mobility Dynamics among Young Adults in Established Suburban Council Rental Housing Estates in South African Cities: A Case Study of Kenneth Gardens, Durban. *African Journal of Inter/Multidisciplinary Studies, 3*(1), pp.197-216.

Musvoto, A. (2021). Innovation hubs and technology transfer in Zimbabwe: Challenges and opportunities. *Zimbabwe Economic Review*, *15*(3), 45–58.

Muthukrishnan, N., Maleki, F., Ovens, K., Reinhold, C., Forghani, B., & Forghani, R. (2020, November). Brief History of Artificial Intelligence. *Neuroimaging Clinics of North America, 30*(4), 393–399. DOI: 10.1016/j.nic.2020.07.004 PMID: 33038991

Mwapwele, S. D., Marais, M., Dlamini, S., & van Biljon, J. (2019). Teachers' ICT Adoption in South African Rural Schools: A Study of Technology Readiness and Implications for the South Africa Connect Broadband Policy. *The African Journal of Information and Communication, 24*, 1–24.

Myers, A. (2023, May 15). Ai-detectors biased against Non-Native English writers. Stanford HAI. https://hai.stanford.edu/news/ai-detectors-biased-against-non-native-english-writers

Nagari, P. M., Sahid, S., & Hussin, M. (2023). Critical Success Factors for Enhancing Digital Literacy Among Undergraduate Students. *Pegem Journal of Education & Instruction / Pegem. Egitim ve Ögretim, 13*(4), 249–259. DOI: 10.47750/pegegog.13.04.30

Nair, P. (2023). Digital competency and workforce readiness: MOOCs in the Indian context. In *Advancements in Digital Literacy* (pp. 74–90). Springer., DOI: 10.1007/978-3-030-90760-2_5

Narang, R., & Tiwari, S. (2021). *Antecedents and Consequences of the Growing Popularity of Digital Consumption*. In book "What is Digital Consumption". 5th ed. E-Book: SCOPUS. DOI: 10.4018/978-1-7998-3479-3.ch073

Nash, B., & Allen, M. (2020). *Data-driven decision making in higher education: A guide for institutions and leaders*. Harvard Education Press.

National Academy of Agricultural Research Management (NAARM). (2024). MOOCs for Digital Education and Capacity Building – A Success Story. Retrieved from https://naarm.org.in/wp-content/uploads/2024/10/MOOCs-a-Success-Story.pdf

National Sample Survey Office (NSSO). (2020). Household social consumption on education in India. Ministry of Statistics and Programme Implementation. Retrieved from https://mospi.gov.in

National Security Commission on Artificial Intelligence. (2021). Final report (NSCAI Final Report, 2021). https://www.dwt.com/-/media/files/blogs/artificial-intelligence-law-advisor/2021/03/nscai-final-report--2021.pdf

National Skill Coalition. (2023, February 6). *New Report: 92% of Jobs Require Digital Skills, One-Third of Workers Have Low or No Digital Skills Due to Historic Underinvestment, Structural Inequities.* https://nationalskillscoalition.org/news/press-releases/new-report-92-of-jobs-require-digital-skills-one-third-of-workers-have-low-or-no-digital-skills-due-to-historic-underinvestment-structural-inequities/

Naz, F. L., Raheem, A., Khan, F. U., & Muhammad, W. (2022). An effect of digital literacy on the academic performance of University-Level students. *Journal of Positive School Psychology*, *6*(8), 10720–10732.

Ncube, B., Shekede, M. D., Gwitira, I., & Dube, T. (2020). Spatial modelling the effects of climate change on the distribution of Lantana camara in Southern Zimbabwe. *Applied Geography (Sevenoaks, England)*, *117*, 102172. DOI: 10.1016/j.apgeog.2020.102172

Ncube, N., & Sithole, S. (2023). *Bridging the gap: Strategies for overcoming silos in higher education.* Bulawayo: Mambo Press.

Nedungadi, P. P., Menon, R., Gutjahr, G., Erickson, L., & Raman, R. (2018). Towards an inclusive digital literacy framework for digital India. *Education + Training*, *60*(6), 516–528. DOI: 10.1108/ET-03-2018-0061

Neuenschwander, B.E. (2024, September 27). *Benefits of Artificial Intelligence in Education: Personalized Learning and Enhanced Classroom Management*. Florida State University.

New Media Consortium (NMC). (2017). 2017 Digital Literacy Impact Study. *An NMC Horizon Project Strategic Brief.*, *3*, 5.

New Media Consortium. (2016). *Digital Literacy in Higher Education, Part II: An NMC Horizon Project Strategic Brief*https://www.nmc.org/publication/digital-literacy-an-nmc-horizon-project-strategic-brief/

NewZapp. (2023). Breaking down communication silos in higher education. NewZapp. https://www.newzapp.com/blog/breaking-down-communication-silos-in-higher-education

Ng, D. T. K., Leung, J. K. L., Su, J., Ng, R. C. W., & Chu, S. K. W. (2023). Teachers' AI digital competencies and twenty-first century skills in the post-pandemic world. *Educational Technology Research and Development*, *71*(1), 137–161. DOI: 10.1007/s11423-023-10203-6 PMID: 36844361

Ng, D. T. K., Xinyu, C., Leung, J. K. L., & Chu, S. K. W. (2024). Fostering students' AI literacy development through educational games: AI knowledge, affective and cognitive engagement. *Journal of Computer Assisted Learning*, *40*(5), 2049–2064. DOI: 10.1111/jcal.13009

Ng, P. M. L., Chow, P. K., Wong, P., & Luk, W. M. B. (2024). The impact of digital technology training on developing academics' digital competence in higher education context. *Education + Training*, *66*(9), 1276–1292. DOI: 10.1108/ET-10-2023-0417

Ng, S. (2022). Recruitment and training of teachers in Singapore. *International Journal of Teacher Education*, *49*(1), 55–72.

Nicholls, H., Nicholls, M., Tekin, S., Lamb, D., & Billings, J. (2022). The impact of working in academia on researchers' mental health and well-being: A systematic review and qualitative meta-synthesis. *PLoS One*, *17*(5), e0268890. DOI: 10.1371/journal.pone.0268890 PMID: 35613147

Nikou, S., De Reuver, M., & Mahboob Kanafi, M. (2022). Workplace literacy skills—How information and digital literacy affect adoption of digital technology. *The Journal of Documentation*, *78*(7), 371–391. DOI: 10.1108/JD-12-2021-0241

Noblitt, L., Vance, E., & DeAngelo, L. (2022). Breaking down silos: A collaborative approach to student success initiatives. *Journal of Higher Education Management*, *37*(1), 45–61.

Northern Illinois University. (2024). *Class policies for AI Tools: Center for Innovative Teaching and learning*. Northern Illinois University. https://www.niu.edu/citl/resources/guides/class-policies-for-ai-tools.shtml

Novak, N., Rabiee, M., & Tjoa, A. (2018). Head in the Clouds: An Initiative for Digital Learning among Roma Communities in Europe, *Proceedings of the 10th International Conference on Computer Supported Education*, https://doi.org/DOI: 10.5220/0006806803840390

Nurtanto, M., Sudira, P., & Sofyan, H. (2023). A bibliometric analysis of teacher professional identity (TPI) for vocational education from 2004 to 2021. *AIP Conference Proceedings*, *2671*(1), 050017. DOI: 10.1063/5.0114242

Nyoni, P. (2022). Pedagogies of access and success among South African university students in the extended curriculum programmes amidst COVID-19 disruptions. *South African Journal of Higher Education*, *36*(4), 137–153. DOI: 10.20853/36-4-5206

Nyoni, S. (2022). Decolonizing higher education in Zimbabwe: Towards an Afrocentric curriculum. *Journal of African Studies and Development*, *14*(1), 22–30.

O'Donnell, L., & Turner, T. (2018). Communication strategies for interorganizational cooperation. *Management Communication Quarterly*, *32*(2), 253–280.

O'Neil, H. (2021). Bridging the skills gap: How digital literacy can shape the future workforce. *Economic Analysis Review*, *36*(2), 210–228.

Obeidat, O. A. (2017). The Role of Knowledge Stations in Bridging the Digital Information Literacy in Jordan. *Dirasat: Educational Sciences*, *44*(1), 339–358. DOI: 10.12816/0039833

Oblinger, D. G. (2018). *E-education and digital literacies: Institutional leadership and transformation.*

Ocaña-Fernández, Fernández, Chiparra, Gallarday-Morales & Gallarday-Morales, (2020). Digital Skills and Digital Literacy: New Trends in Vocational Training. *International Journal of Early Childhood Special Education (INT-JECSE)*: 12(1): 370-377.

Odell, V., Molthan-Hill, P., Martin, S., & Sterling, S. (2020). Transformative education to address all sustainable development goals. *Quality education*, 905-916.

Odubiyi, T. B., Aigbavboa, C. O., & Thwala, W. D. (2021). A Concise Review of the Evolution of Information and Communication Technologies For Engineering Innovations. *IOP Conf. Series: Materials Science and Engineering, 1107*, https:// doi:DOI: 10.1088/1757-899X/1107/1/012231

OECD. (2008). *Tertiary education for the knowledge society*. OECD Publishing.

Ojo, O., Alodele, A., Onadokun, I.O. & Akinade, O.A. (2018). Digital literacy assessments in technical and vocational education and training (TVET) sustainability. *SMART-iSTEAMS Multidisciplinary Conference*, 75-86.

Okeji, C. C., Tralagba, E. C., & Obi, I. C. (2020). An investigation of the digital literacy skills and knowledge-based competencies among librarians working in university libraries in Nigeria. *Global Knowledge, Memory and Communication*, *69*(4/5), 311–330. DOI: 10.1108/GKMC-05-2019-0054

Okoye, K., Hussein, H., Arrona-Palacios, A., Quintero, H. N., Ortega, L. O. P., Sanchez, A. L., Ortiz, E. A., Escamilla, J., & Hosseini, S. (2023). Impact of digital technologies upon teaching and learning in higher education in Latin America: An outlook on the reach, barriers, and bottlenecks. *Education and Information Technologies*, *28*(2), 2291–2360. DOI: 10.1007/s10639-022-11214-1 PMID: 35992366

Oliver, B., & Jorre de St Jorre, T. (2018). Graduate attributes for 2020 and beyond: Recommendations for Australian higher education providers. *Higher Education Research & Development*, *37*(4), 1–16. DOI: 10.1080/07294360.2018.1446415

Omilion-Hodges, L. M., Shank, S. E., & Johnson, C. M. (2022). Doubting the connection: Millennials' perceptions of the link between higher education and workplace readiness. *Management Research Review*, *45*(5), 649–663. DOI: 10.1108/MRR-01-2021-0084

Open, A. I. (2022, November 30). *Introducing ChatGPT*. https://openai.com/index/chatgpt

Özdemir, İ. (2023). Atatürk's educational reforms and their impact on modern Turkey. *Educational Review*, *75*(1), 102–115.

Pan, L., Saxon, M., Xu, W., Nathani, D., Wang, X., & Wang, W. Y. (2023, August 30). Automatically Correcting Large Language Models: Surveying the landscape of diverse self-correction strategies. arXiv.org. https://arxiv.org/abs/2308.03188

Parker, A. (2024). *Pride Everyday: Empowering LGBTQ+ Pride in the Workplace and Beyond*. Notion Press.

Parker, M., & Jansen, H. (2021). Celebrating success in higher education: The role of recognition in fostering collaborative cultures. *Higher Education Review*, *44*(2), 135–148.

Park, S. (2011). Digital literacy: A conceptual framework for survival skills in the digital era. *Journal of Multimedia and Hypermedia*, *20*(1), 31–50.

Park, S., & Kim, J. (2022). The role of teachers in South Korea's educational reform process. *Asian Journal of Education*, *46*(2), 200–215.

Pascarella, E. T., & Terenzini, P. T. (2005). *How college affects students: a third decade of research* (Vol. 2). Jossey-Bass.

Patmanthara, S., & Hidayat, W. N. (2018). Improving vocational high school students digital literacy skill throughblended learning model. *Journal of Physics: Conference Series*, *1028*, 012076. DOI: 10.1088/1742-6596/1028/1/012076

Paul, H. W., & Crowe, M. M. (2023). Digital Literacy Inequities, Higher Education, and the New Digital Divide. *International Journal of Intelligent Computing Research*, *14*(1), 1177–1180. DOI: 10.20533/ijicr.2042.4655.2023.0144

Payad, A. (2024). High School Aetas' Course Experience: Benchmark for Streamlining Curricular Program Management. *JPAIR Multidisciplinary Research*, *56*(1), 1–23. DOI: 10.7719/jpair.v56i1.877

Peñate, A. H., Padrón-Robaina, V., & Nieves, J. (2024). The role of technological resources in the reputation of vocational education schools. *Education and Information Technologies*, *29*(3), 1–20. DOI: 10.1007/s10639-023-11919-x

Pierce, J. (2019). Digital Divide. *The International Encyclopedia of Media Literacy*, 1–8.Pooja, M. (2021). Adopting digital technologies in vocational education at the time of crisis. *Advanced Management*, 14: 53–59.

Platonova, R. I., Gabarova, K. V., Olesova, M. M., Platonova, A. Z., Storozheva, N. N., & Evseeva, M. M. (2020). Digital technologies in educational environment. *EurAsian Journal of Biosciences*, *14*(2), 5441–5444.

Pondiwa, S., El Nabahany, U., & Phiri, M. (2022). Integration of ICT into education: Lessons learnt at the State University of Zanzibar and the Midlands State University in Zimbabwe. In *Computer-Mediated Communication*. IntechOpen. DOI: 10.5772/intechopen.98441

Popenici, S. (2022). *Artificial Intelligence and Learning Futures: Critical Narratives of Technology and Imagination in Higher Education*. Routledge., DOI: 10.4324/9781003266563

Popescu, E. (2019). Accessibility of the Digital Scientific Literature – A Study on Researchers' Perspective. *ELearning & Software for Education, 2*, 479–486. https://doi.org/DOI: 10.12753/2066-026X-19-136

Prabawati, S. (2019). Pengaruh efikasi diri, pendidikan kewirausahaan, literasi keuangan dan literasi digital terhadap perilaku berwirausaha siswa SMK Negeri 10 Surabaya. *Jurnal pendidikan akuntansi,* [The influence of self-efficacy, entrepreneurship education, financial literacy and digital literacy on entrepreneurial behavior of students of SMK Negeri 10 Surabaya. Journal of accounting education]. 7(1), 64-76

Press Information Bureau. (2019, February 20). Report on India's trillion-dollar digital opportunity released. https://pib.gov.in/PressReleasePage.aspx?PRID=1565669

Press Information Bureau. (2023, September 15). BharatNet: Bridging the Digital divide (Singh, 2010). Retrieved from https://pib.gov.in/PressReleaseIframePage.aspx?PRID=2086701

Prince, M. J., & Felder, R. M. (2006). Inductive teaching and learning methods: Definitions, comparisons, and research bases. *Journal of Engineering Education*, *95*(2), 123–138. DOI: 10.1002/j.2168-9830.2006.tb00884.x

Qian, S., & Feng, Q. (2020). Research on the Integration of Artificial Intelligence and Education. *Journal of Physics: Conference Series*, *1570*(1), 012063. DOI: 10.1088/1742-6596/1570/1/012063

Queensland University of Technology. (2023). *QUT and IBM: Transforming education through AI and quantum computing partnerships*. Retrieved from https://www.qut.edu.au/partnerships

Rackwitz, M., Breaugh, J., & Hammerschmid, G. (2024). Leadership for intergovernmental collaboration towards digital transformation. In *Collaborating for Digital Transformation* (pp. 124–142). Edward Elgar Publishing. DOI: 10.4337/9781803923895.00016

Radford, A., Narasimhan, K., Salimans, T., & Sutskever, I. (2018, June). *Improving Language Understanding by Generative Pre-Training*. OpenAI. https://openai.com/index/chatgpt

Rafi, M., JianMing, Z. & Ahmad, K. (2019), Technology integration for students' information and digital literacy education in academic libraries. *Information Discovery and Delivery, 47*(4), pp. 203-217. DOI: 10.1108/IDD-07-2019-0049

Raghavan, P. (2024, February 23). *Gemini image generation got it wrong. we'll do better*. Google. https://blog.google/products/gemini/gemini-image-generation-issue

Ragnedda, M., & Muschert, G. W. (2013). *The digital divide: The Internet and social inequality in international perspective*. Routledge. DOI: 10.4324/9780203069769

Rahardjo, T. J. (2020). The role of vocational education on the advancement of human development in Indonesia. *Advances in Social Science, Education and Humanities Research, 443*, 406–410.

Rahman, M. (2022). Teacher shortages and rural education in Bangladesh: A critical review. *International Journal of Educational Development, 34*(3), 120–132.

Rahman, M., & Hossain, S. (2023). Teacher professional development programs in Bangladesh: An evaluation. *Journal of Educational Development, 17*(3), 135–149.

Rahman, M., & Hossain, S. (2023). The significance of teacher development in educational reform. *Journal of Education for Teaching, 45*(1), 71–85.

Rahman, S., & Islam, M. (2021). Political influence in teacher recruitment in Bangladesh: A critical analysis. *Journal of Political Education, 25*(2), 58–73.

Rakib, M., Azis, M., Najib, M., & Isma, A. (2024). Impact of Digital Literacy, Business Innovation, Competitive Advantage on the Existence of SMEs: A quantitative study in Makassar City, Indonesia. *Quality - Access to Success, 25*(198), 277–283. DOI: 10.47750/QAS/25.198.30

Ramaswamy, M., Marciniuk, D. D., Csonka, V., Colò, L., & Saso, L. (2021). Reimagining internationalization in higher education through the United Nations sustainable development goals for the betterment of society. *Journal of Studies in International Education*, *25*(4), 388–406. DOI: 10.1177/10283153211031046

Rashid, A. B., & Kausik, A. K. (2024b). AI Revolutionizing Industries Worldwide: A Comprehensive Overview of its Diverse Applications. *Hybrid Advances*, *7*, 100277. Advance online publication. DOI: 10.1016/j.hybadv.2024.100277

Reich, J., & Ruipérez-Valiente, J. A. (2019). The MOOC pivot. *Science*, *363*(6423), 130–131. DOI: 10.1126/science.aav7958 PMID: 30630920

Reiss, M. J. (2021). The use of AI in education: Practicalities and ethical considerations. *London Review of Education*, *19*(1), 1–14. DOI: 10.14324/LRE.19.1.05

Rodríguez, U.; Cantabrana, L. & Gisbert, J. (2021). Validation of a tool for self-evaluating teacher digital competence. Educación XX1, 24(1), 353-373. https://doi.org/DOI: 10.5944/educxx1.27080

Rogers, E. M. (2003). *Diffusion of Innovations* (5th ed.). Free Press.

Rogers, E. M., Singhal, A., & Quinlan, M. M. (2014). Diffusion of innovations. In *An integrated approach to communication theory and research* (pp. 432–448). Routledge.

Romao, L., Kalinowski, M., Barbosa, C., Araújo, A. A., Barbosa, S. D., & Lopes, H. (2024). Agile Minds, Innovative Solutions, and Industry-Academia Collaboration: Lean R&D Meets Problem-Based Learning in Software Engineering Education. *arXiv preprint arXiv:2407.15982*. DOI: 10.5753/sbes.2024.3456

Ross, S. M. (2020). Technology infusion in K-12 classrooms: A retrospective look at three decades of challenges and advancements in research and practice. *Educational Technology Research and Development*, *68*(5), 2003–2020. DOI: 10.1007/s11423-020-09756-7

Roth, E. (2023, December 27). The New York Times is suing OpenAI and Microsoft for copyright infringement. The Verge. https://www.theverge.com/2023/12/27/24016212/new-york-times-openai-microsoft-lawsuit-copyright-infringement

Rowley, D. J., & Sherman, H. (2004). *From strategy to change: Implementing the plan in higher education*. John Wiley & Sons.

Ruddy, C., & Ponte, F. (2019). Preparing students for university studies and beyond: A micro-credential trial that delivers academic integrity awareness. *Journal of the Australian Library & Information Association, 68*(1), 56–67. DOI: 10.1080/24750158.2018.1562520

Rutgers Learning Centers. The Importance of Outlining. (2025). https://learningcenters.rutgers.edu/resources/importance-outlining

Saddozai, S. K., Hui, P., Akram, U., Khan, M. S., & Memon, S. (2017). Investigation of talent, talent management, its policies and its impact on working environment. *Chinese Management Studies, 11*(3), 538–554. DOI: 10.1108/CMS-10-2016-0206

Saini, M., Sengupta, E., Singh, M., Singh, H., & Singh, J. (2023). Sustainable Development Goal for Quality Education (SDG 4): A study on SDG 4 to extract the pattern of association among the indicators of SDG 4 employing a genetic algorithm. *Education and Information Technologies, 28*(2), 2031–2069. DOI: 10.1007/s10639-022-11265-4 PMID: 35975216

Saka, Y., & Yaman, S. (2011). Üniversite sıralama sistemleri; kriterler ve yapılan eleştiriler. *Yükseköğretim ve Bilim Dergisi*, [University ranking systems; criteria and criticisms. Higher Education and Science Journal]. *1*(2), 72–79.

Salaber, J. (2014). Facilitating student engagement and collaboration in a large postgraduate course using wiki-based activities. *International Journal of Management Education, 12*(2), 115–126. DOI: 10.1016/j.ijme.2014.03.006

Salsabila, F. (2019). Pengaruh Literasi Ekonomi dan Literasi Digital terhadap Perilaku Berwirausaha Sektor Kuliner yang terdaftar pada aplikasi Go-Food Di Pasar Segar Kota Makassar. *Eprints Universitas Negeri Makassar.* Diunduh dari. [The Influence of Economic Literacy and Digital Literacy on Entrepreneurial Behavior in the Culinary Sector Registered on the Go-Food Application at Pasar Segar, Makassar City. Eprints, Makassar State University. Downloaded from]. https://eprints.unm.ac.id/id/eprint/14271

Sanders, C. K., & Scanlon, E. (2021). The Digital Divide Is a Human Rights Issue: Advancing Social Inclusion Through Social Work Advocacy. *Journal of Human Rights and Social Work, 6*(2), 130–143. DOI: 10.1007/s41134-020-00147-9 PMID: 33758780

Sanders, J., Spector, M., & Weber, R. (2021). Faculty-industry partnerships: Enhancing curriculum development and workforce readiness. *Journal of Workforce Development, 22*(4), 48–59.

Sandip Foundation. (2023). Sandip Group of Institutions collaborates with Infosys Springboard for digital skill development. Retrieved from https://www.sandipfoundation.org/placement/infosys.php

Sangrà, A., Raffaghelli, J. E., Veletsianos, G., & Zheng, R. (2017). Massive open online courses (MOOCs): A blended learning approach to enhance digital literacy. *International Journal of Educational Technology in Higher Education*, *14*(8). Advance online publication. DOI: 10.1186/s41239-017-0085-7

Sanka, A. I., Wong, J., Liu, C., Hung, P., & Cheung, R. C. C. (2024). *Building a Learner-Centric Citywide Digital Literacy Ecosystem: Train-the-Trainer, Community-Based Learning, and Gifted Education : A Guide for Educators, Policymakers, and Stakeholders* (Vol. 14797). Springer Nature Singapore., DOI: 10.1007/978-981-97-4442-8_1

Sanyang, B. and Ali, L., (2023). The Power of Cultural Diversity in Project Teams: A Path to Greater Innovation-A qualitative study of how cultural diversity impacts innovation output in project teams.

Sanz Ponce, R., López-Luján, E., & Giménez-Beut, J. A. (2023). Pandemic, poverty and education: A challenge for the sustainable development goals. *Policy Futures in Education*, *21*(8), 886–899. DOI: 10.1177/14782103221112542

Sato, M., Smeaton, K., & Palmer, T. (2019). What's Up, Doc?: Selling Digital Literacy to Academics. *IATUL Annual Conference Proceedings*, 162–177.

Scheerder, A. J., van Deursen, A. J. A. M., & van Dijk, J. A. G. M. (2017). Determinants of Internet skills, uses and outcomes: A systematic review of the second- and third-level digital divide. *Telematics and Informatics*, *34*(8), 1607–1624. DOI: 10.1016/j.tele.2017.07.007

Schmid Mast, M., Kleinlogel, E. P., Tur, B., & Bachmann, M. (2018). The future of interpersonal skills development: Immersive virtual reality training with virtual humans. *Human Resource Development Quarterly*, *29*(2), 125–141. DOI: 10.1002/hrdq.21307

Schmidt, E., & Cohen, J. (2013). *The new digital age: Reshaping the future of people, nations and business*. Alfred A. Knopf.

Schmidt, L. J., & DeSchryver, M. (2022). The role of digital application literacy in online assessment. *Journal of Educational Technology Systems*, *50*(3), 356–378. DOI: 10.1177/00472395211052644

Schwab, K. (2016). *The Fourth Industrial Revolution*.

Schwab, K. (2024). The Fourth Industrial Revolution: what it means, how to respond1. In *Handbook of research on strategic leadership in the Fourth Industrial Revolution* (pp. 29-34). Edward Elgar Publishing. DOI: 10.4337/9781802208818.00008

Selingo, J. J. (2013). *College (Un)Bound: The future of higher education and what it means for students*. Houghton Mifflin Harcourt.

Selwyn, N. (2020). *Education and technology: Key issues and debates*. Routledge.

Senge, P. M. (2006). *The fifth discipline: The art and practice of the learning organization*.

Senthil, B. A., Prema, R. K., & Sharif, L. S. (2025). Industry-Academia Partnerships: Bridging the Gap for R&D Success. In *Evolving Landscapes of Research and Development: Trends, Challenges, and Opportunities* (pp. 191-208). IGI Global Scientific Publishing.

Šević, N. P., & Dobrilović, M., P., M. I., & Ranković, M. (2021). Serbian Rural Neet Youth Inclusion through the Development of Digital Entrepreneurial Competences and Digital Entrepreneurship. *Proceedings of the International May Conference on Strategic Management, 17*(1), 75–84.

Shaji, , G. (2024). The Emergence and Impact of Mental Health Leave Policies on Employee Wellbeing and Productivity. *Partners Universal International Innovation Journal (PUIIJ), 02*(02), 99–120. DOI: 10.5281/zenodo.11002386

Shao, Z., Yuan, S., & Wang, Y. (2020). Institutional collaboration and competition in Artificial Intelligence. *IEEE Access : Practical Innovations, Open Solutions*, *8*, 1–10. DOI: 10.1109/ACCESS.2020.2986383

Sharpe, R., & Benfield, G. (2012). Institutional strategies for supporting learners in a digital age. *Enhancing Learning in the Social Sciences*, *4*(2), 1–17. DOI: 10.11120/elss.2012.04020004

Shelyugina, O., Davydenko, M., & Stepanskaya, A. (2019). Development of digital literacy in vocational education as a condition for regional sustainable development. *International Conference on Sustainable Development of Cross-Border Regions: Economic, Social and Security Challenges (ICSDCBR)*, 364: 140-143. DOI: 10.2991/icsdcbr-19.2019.30

Sheppard, C. and Ntenga, L., (2013). Funding of the South African further education and training sector for an equitable sharing of national revenue. *Technical Report: Submission for the Division of Revenue 2014/2015*.

Shiri, A. (2024). Artificial intelligence literacy: A proposed faceted taxonomy. *Digital Library Perspectives*, *40*(4), 681–699. DOI: 10.1108/DLP-04-2024-0067

Shuliar, V., Shkurko, V., Polukhtovych, T., Semeniako, Y., Shanaieva-Tsymbal, L., & Koltok, L. (2023). Using Artificial Intelligence in Education. BRAIN. *Broad Research in Artificial Intelligence and Neuroscience*, *14*(3), 516–529. DOI: 10.18662/brain/14.3/488

Siddique, A. (2021). Professional development and teacher retention in Bangladesh's primary education sector. *Journal of Educational Development*, *18*(1), 54–69.

Siddique, A. (2022). Teacher professional development in developing countries: Lessons from Bangladesh. *Educational Research Journal*, *38*(2), 90–105.

Siddique, A. (2022). Teachers' voices and their influence on education policy: Lessons from South Asia. *Journal of Educational Management*, *49*(2), 110–124.

Siemens, G. (2004). Elearnspace. Connectivism: A learning theory for the digital age. *Elearnspace. org*, 14-16.

Siemens, G. (2014). Connectivism: A learning theory for the digital age. *International Journal of Instructional Technology and Distance Learning*.

Siemens, G. (2020). Connectivism: A Learning Theory for the Digital Age. *International Journal of Instructional Technology and Distance Learning*, 2(1), 3–10.

Sillak-Riesinger, B. (2017). The potential of massive open online courses in the context of corporate training and development. *Journal of Corporate Education*, *28*(4), 111–126. DOI: 10.1007/978-3-658-16649-6

Silva, L., (2023). An utopian approach to social transformation: the role of urban social movements' fragmentation in Barcelona. *Partecipazione e conflitto-PArticipation and COnflict*.

Silvernail, D. L., Pinkham, C. A., Wintle, S. E., Walker, L. C., & Bartlett, C. L. (2011). *A Middle*

Singh, R., & Sharma, P. (2022). MOOCs: A revolution in education for the digital era. Turkish Online Journal of Qualitative Inquiry, 13(4), 1234-1245. Retrieved from https://www.tojqi.net/index.php/journal/article/download/8057/5727/8639

Singh, A., & Zhan, J. (2021). Government policies for encouraging industry-education collaboration. *Education Policy Analysis Archives*, *29*, 58.

Singh, S. (2010). Digital divide (Singh, 2010) in India: Measurement, determinants, and policy for addressing the challenges in bridging the digital divide (Singh, 2010). *International Journal of Innovation in the Digital Economy, 1*(2), 1–24. DOI: 10.4018/jide.2010040101

Sinha, M. (2022). MOOCs as a tool for gender equity in digital literacy: Challenges and opportunities. *Gender and Education Review, 18*(4), 205–218. DOI: 10.1177/GE2022.04.31212

Sithole, S. (2023). *Benefits of technology: utilisation of blockchain in the South African banking sector amid Industry 4.0*. University of Johannesburg.

Skov, M., Svarre, T., & Lykke, M. (2022). *Student experience of digital learning tools: information literacy training in higher education*. https://doi.org/DOI: 10.18452/25257

Smith, J., & Chang, Z. (2021). Integrating digital literacy in higher education curricula. *Educational Review, 73*(4), 455–472.

Smith, J., & Heyward, P. (2024). Policy efforts to meet UNESCO's Sustainable development Goal 4: A 3-pronged approach. *Journal of Education for Teaching, 50*(2), 266–279. DOI: 10.1080/02607476.2023.2283422

Smith, J., & Jones, P. (2021). Breaking down silos: Collaboration and technology integration in global higher education. In Global, I. G. I. (Ed.), *Trends in educational technology*.

Sobhy, H. (2024). Equity, the transnational and the global learning crisis. *Cogent Social Sciences, 10*(1), 2359268. DOI: 10.1080/23311886.2024.2359268

Sociology Institute. (n.d.). ICTs and Their Potential to Empower India's Marginalized in Higher Education. Retrieved from https://sociology.institute/sociology-of-education/icts-empower-marginalized-higher-education-india/

Soltovets, E., Chigisheva, O., & Dmitrova, A. (2020). The Role of Mentoring in Digital Literacy Development of Doctoral Students at British Universities. *Eurasia Journal of Mathematics, Science and Technology Education, 16*(4). Advance online publication. DOI: 10.29333/ejmste/117782

Soria, K. M., Fransen, J., & Nackerud, S. (2017). The Impact of Academic Library Resources on Undergraduates' Degree Completion. *College & Research Libraries, 78*(6), 812–823. DOI: 10.5860/crl.78.6.812

Sousa-Zomer, T. T., Neely, A., & Martinez, V.Sousa-Zomer. (2020). Neely, & Martinez, V. (2020). Digital transforming capability and performance: A microfoundational perspective. *International Journal of Operations & Production Management, 40*(7/8), 1095–1128. DOI: 10.1108/IJOPM-06-2019-0444

Southworth, J., Migliaccio, K., Glover, J., Glover, J., Reed, D., McCarty, C., Brendemuhl, J., & Thomas, A. (2023). Developing a model for AI Across the curriculum: Transforming the higher education landscape via innovation in AI literacy. *Computers and Education: Artificial Intelligence, 4*, 100127. DOI: 10.1016/j.caeai.2023.100127

Stacey, M., Gavin, M., Fitzgerald, S., McGrath-Champ, S., & Wilson, R. (2024). Reducing teachers' workload or deskilling 'core'work? Analysis of a policy response to teacher workload demands. *Discourse (Abingdon), 45*(2), 187–199. DOI: 10.1080/01596306.2023.2271856

Stack, M. (2021). *Global University Rankings and the Politics of Knowledge*. University of Toronto Press. DOI: 10.3138/9781487545154

Stanford University. (2024). Faculty-Industry Collaborative Research Program. Retrieved from https://www.stanford.edu/faculty-industry-collaboration

Stanford University. (2025). *Surya Ganguli's Work on Diffusion Models Powers Modern AI Tools like DALL-E*. Stanford University. https://appliedphysics.stanford.edu/news/surya-gangulis-work-diffusion-models-powers-modern-ai-tools-dall-e

Stracke, C. M. (2017). The quality of MOOCs: How to improve the design of open education and online courses for learners? In *Proceedings of the 2017 IEEE Global Engineering Education Conference (EDUCON)* (pp. 1639-1643). IEEE. DOI: 10.1007/978-3-319-58509-3_23

Stryker, C., & Kavlakoglu, E. (2024, December 19). *What is Artificial Intelligence (AI)?* IBM. https://www.ibm.com/think/topics/artificial-intelligence

Subramanian, N., & Gunasekaran, A. (2021). Digital transformation in higher education: Challenges and strategies for integration. *Technology Management Journal, 28*(3), 123–145.

Su, J., & Yang, W. (2023). *Unlocking the Power of ChatGPT: A Framework for Applying Generative AI in Education*. ECNU Review of Education., DOI: 10.1177/20965311231168423

Sullivan, H. (2022). *Collaboration and public policy*. Palgrave. DOI: 10.1007/978-3-031-09585-6

Sullivan, P., & Glance, D. (2022). Interdisciplinary approaches to curriculum design in higher education: Fostering collaboration and innovation. *Higher Education Review*, *27*(2), 185–200.

Sundberg, L., & Holmström, J. (2024). Teaching Tip: Using No-Code AI to Teach Machine Learning in Higher Education. *Journal of Information Systems Education*, *35*(1), 56–66. DOI: 10.62273/CYPL2902

SWAYAM. (n.d.). Study Webs of Active Learning for Young Aspiring Minds. Retrieved from https://swayam.gov.in

Swenson, K., & Ghertner, R. (2020). *People in Low-Income Households Have Less Access to Internet Services – 2019 Update.* Office of the Assistant Secretary for Planning & Evaluation. U.S. Department of Health & Human Services.

Tamim, R. M., Bernard, R. M., Borokhovski, E., Abrami, P. C., & Schmid, R. F. (2011). What Forty Years of Research Says About the Impact of Technology on Learning. *Review of Educational Research*, *81*(1), 4–28. DOI: 10.3102/0034654310393361

Tamim, R. M., Borokhovski, E., Bernard, R. M., Schmid, R. F., Abrami, P. C., & Pickup, D. I. (2021). A study of meta-analyses reporting quality in the large and expanding literature of educational technology. *Australasian Journal of Educational Technology*, *37*(4), 100–115. DOI: 10.14742/ajet.6322

Tas, E. (2023). Data literacy education through university-industry collaboration. *Information and Learning Science*, *124*(11/12). Advance online publication. DOI: 10.1108/ILS-06-2023-0077

Taylor, M., Liu, B., & Smith, S. (2020). *Digital literacy disparities among graduates: Implications for workforce development*. Workforce Education Forum, 47(1), 112-130.

Taylor, S., & Hall, D. (2023). Co-designing curricula: Collaborative models between universities and industries. *Journal of Educational Development*, *36*(3), 115–129.

Techataweewan, W., & Prasertsin, U. (2018). Development of digital literacy indicators for Thai undergraduate students using mixed method research. *Kasetsart Journal of Social Sciences*, *39*(2), 215–221. DOI: 10.1016/j.kjss.2017.07.001

Tekin, E. (2024). E-Öğrenmeye Yatkınlığın Akademik Performansa Etkisinde Dijital Okuryazarlığın Düzenleyici Rolü: Geleceğin Öğretmenleri Üzerine Bir Araştırma. *Itobiad: Journal of the Human & Social Science Researches / İnsan ve Toplum Bilimleri Araştırmaları Dergisi, [The Moderating Role of Digital Literacy in the Effect of E-Learning Approach on Academic Performance: A Study on Future Teachers. Itobiad: Journal of the Human & Social Science Researches].* *13*(4), 54–77. https://doi.org/DOI: 10.15869/itobiad.1522652

Tenenbaum, H. R., Crosby, F. J., & Gliner, M. D. (2001). Mentoring relationships in graduate school. *Journal of Vocational Behavior*, *59*(3), 326–341. DOI: 10.1006/jvbe.2001.1804

Tenya, A. N., Maina, J. C., & Awuor, F. M. (2024). *Digital literacy as a tool for enhancing access and utilization of information in digital resource platforms among academic staff in uiiversity libraries.*

Terwiesch, C. (2023). Would Chat GPT3 Get a Wharton MBA? A Prediction Based on Its Performance in the Operations Management Course. *Mack Institute for Innovation Management at the Wharton School*, University of Pennsylvania, 2023.

Thakkar, A., Gupta, A., & De Sousa, A. (2024). Artificial intelligence in positive mental health: A narrative review. *Frontiers in Digital Health*, *6*, 1280235. DOI: 10.3389/fdgth.2024.1280235 PMID: 38562663

Thaler v. Perlmutter, uscourts.gov (United States District Court for the District of Columbia August 18, 2023). Retrieved January 24, 2025, from https://ecf.dcd.uscourts.gov/cgi-bin/show_public_doc?2022cv1564-24

The Hindu. (2024). IIT-M signs MoUs with industry partners for online courses. Retrieved from https://www.thehindu.com/news/national/tamil-nadu/iit-m-signs-mous-with-industry-partners-for-online-courses/article68366759.ece

THE. (2024). *World University Rankings 2025*. THE. Retrieved December 15, 2024, from https://www.timeshighereducation.com/world-university-rankings/latest/world-ranking

Thomas, R. (2019). Accreditation standards and industry collaboration in higher education. *Higher Education Policy*, *32*(3), 401–419.

Thorpe, A., Lukes, R., Bever, D. J., & He, Y. (2016). The Impact of the Academic Library on Student Success: Connecting the Dots. *Portal (Baltimore, Md.)*, *16*(2), 373–392. DOI: 10.1353/pla.2016.0027

Times of India. (2024, February 5). Economic Survey 2024-25: Higher education institutions grow by 13.8%, gross enrollment ratio rises to 28.4%. The Times of India. https://timesofindia.indiatimes.com

Tinmaz, H., Fanea-Ivanovici, M., & Baber, H. (2023). A snapshot of digital literacy. *Library Hi Tech News*, *40*(1), 20–23. DOI: 10.1108/LHTN-12-2021-0095

Toney-Wails, A. (2024). What Kind of Sourcery is This? Evaluating GPT-4's Performance on Linking Scientific Fact to Citations. *Proceedings of the 1st Workshop on Customizable NLP: Progress and Challenges in Customizing NLP for a Domain, Application, Group, or Individual (CustomNLP4U)*, 257–268. https://doi.org/DOI: 10.18653/v1/2024.customnlp4u-1.19

Treviranus, J., & Coombs, N. (2000). Bridging the Digital Divide in Higher Education. For full text: http://www. educause. edu/conference/e2000/proceedings. html. For full text: http://www. educause. edu/asp/doclib/abstract. asp? ID= EDU0028. html.

Tuamsuk, K., & Subramaniam, M. (2017). The current state and influential factors in the development of digital literacy in Thailand's higher education. *Information and Learning Science*, *118*(5/6), 235–251. DOI: 10.1108/ILS-11-2016-0076

Turing, A. M. (1950). Computing Machinery and Intelligence. *Mind*, *49*(236), 433–460. DOI: 10.1093/mind/LIX.236.433

UNESCO. (2016). Learning to be: A holistic and integrated approach to values education for human development. United Nations Educational, Scientific and Cultural Organization. Retrieved from https://unesdoc.unesco.org/ark:/48223/pf0000245990

UNESCO. (2017). Working Group on education: Digital skills for life and work. *Broadband Commission for Sustainable Development*, *9*, 1–128.

UNESCO. (2019). *Digital learning and MOOCs: Overcoming language barriers in online education*. United Nations Educational, Scientific and Cultural Organization.

UNESCO. (2023). Global education monitoring report: Technology in education. United Nations Educational, Scientific and Cultural Organization. Retrieved from https://www.unesco.org/reports/

UNESCO-UNEVOC. (n.d.). Digital literacy. TVETipedia Glossary. Retrieved from https://unevoc.unesco.org/home/TVETipedia%2BGlossary/lang%3Den/show%3Dterm/term%3Ddigital%2Bliteracy

United Nations. (2015). Transforming our world: The 2030 Agenda for Sustainable Development. https://sdgs.un.org/2030agenda

University Grants Commission. (2022). Credit framework for online learning courses through SWAYAM. UGC. Retrieved from https://www.ugc.gov.in/pdfnews/3501421_Step-by-step-procedure-involved-in-adoption-of-MOOCs.pdf

University Grants Commission. (n.d.). Welcome to UGC, New Delhi, India. Retrieved from https://www.ugc.gov.in/ • https://en.wikipedia.org/wiki/List_of_universities_in_India

University of California. (2023). *UC Berkeley and Cisco: Shaping the future of cybersecurity education*. Retrieved from https://www.berkeley.edu/industry-partnerships

University of Melbourne. (2023). *University of Melbourne and PwC: Shaping the future of business consulting education*. Retrieved from https://www.unimelb.edu.au/industry-collaborations

University of Toronto. (2023). Cross-Disciplinary PD Workshops. Retrieved from https://www.utoronto.edu/pd-workshops

Valiente Bermejo, M. A., Eynian, M., Malmsköld, L., & Scotti, A. (2022). University–industry collaboration in curriculum design and delivery: A model and its application in manufacturing engineering courses. *Industry and Higher Education*, *36*(5), 615–622. DOI: 10.1177/09504222211064204

Van den Berg, G., & Du Plessis, E. (2023). ChatGPT and Generative AI: Possibilities for Its Contribution to Lesson Planning, Critical Thinking and Openness in Teacher Education. *Education Sciences*, *13*(10), 998. Advance online publication. DOI: 10.3390/educsci13100998

van der Vlies, R. (2020). Digital strategies in education across OECD countries: Exploring education policies on digital technologies.

Van Deursen, A. J. A. M., & Mossberger, K. (2018). Anything for anyone? A new digital divide in internet-of-things skills. *Policy and Internet*, *10*(2), 122–140. DOI: 10.1002/poi3.171

Van Deursen, A. J. A. M., van der Zeeuw, A., de Boer, P., Jansen, G., & van Rompay, T. (2019). Digital inequalities in the Internet of Things: Differences in attitudes, material access, skills, and usage. *Information Communication and Society*, *24*(2), 258–276. DOI: 10.1080/1369118X.2019.1646777

van Deursen, A. J., & van Dijk, J. A. (2023). IQ and digital inequality: An empirical investigation. *New Media & Society*, *25*(6), 1248–1270. DOI: 10.1177/14614448211024012

Van Dijk, J. (2020). *The digital divide*. Polity.

Van Dijk, J. A. G. M. (2005). *The deepening divide: Inequality in the information society*. John Wiley & Sons, Inc.

Van Dijk, J. A. G. M. (2017). *Digital divide: Impact of access*. University of Twente.

Van Laar, E., van Deursen, A. J. A. M., van Dijk, J. A. G. M., & de Haan, J. (2020). Determinants of 21st-century skills and 21st-century digital skills for workers: A systematic literature review. *SAGE Open*, *10*(1), 1–14. DOI: 10.1177/2158244019900176 van Laar, E., van Deursen, A. J., van Dijk, J. A., & de Haan, J. (2017). The relation between 21st-century skills and digital skills: A systematic literature review. *Computers in Human Behavior*, *72*, 577–588. DOI: 10.1016/j.chb.2017.03.010

Vanderbilt University. (2024). *Syllabus AI policies*. Vanderbilt University. https://as.vanderbilt.edu/gci-ai/syllabus-ai-policies/

Veletsianos, G., & Shepherdson, P. (2016). A systematic analysis and synthesis of the empirical MOOC literature published in 2013–2015. *International Review of Research in Open and Distance Learning*, *17*(2). Advance online publication. DOI: 10.19173/irrodl.v17i2.2448

Vengathattil, S. (2025). Future-Proofing AI Talent in The United States: The Role of Academia in Meeting Industry Demands. *International Journal of Management Science and Information Technology*, *5*(1), 210–217. DOI: 10.35870/ijmsit.v5i1.3837

Viriri, E., Ndimande-Hlongwa, N., & Mufanechiya, A. (2024). Decolonising higher education in Zimbabwe: Prospects and challenges of education 5.0. *Journal of African Education*, *5*(1), 37–56. DOI: 10.31920/2633-2930/2024/v5n1a2

Vivek, V., Gambhir, V., & Gill, A. (2024, September). Understanding the Societal Impacts of Artificial Intelligence and Machine Learning on Employment and Workforce Dynamics. In *2024 International Conference on Advances in Computing Research on Science Engineering and Technology (ACROSET)* (pp. 1-6). IEEE.

Vodă, A. I., Cautisanu, C., Grădinaru, C., Tănăsescu, C., & de Moraes, G. H. S. M. (2022). Exploring Digital Literacy Skills in Economics and Social Sciences and Humanities Students. *Sustainability (Basel)*, *14*(5), 1–31. DOI: 10.3390/su14052483

Vuorikari, R. Punie, Y., Carretero Gomez S., & Van den Brande, G. (2016). *DigComp 2.0: The digital competence framework for citi:ens. Update phase 1: The conceptual reference model* (EUR 27948EN). *European Union*. Advance online publication. DOI: 10.2791/11517

Vygo. (2023). *The impact of silos on higher education institutions*. https://blog.vygoapp.com/silos

Waddock, S. A. (1988). Building successful social partnerships. *MIT Sloan Management Review*, *29*(4), 17.

Wang, F., & Reeves, T. C. (2007). *Why do teachers need to use technology in their classrooms? Issues, challenges, and solutions*. College of Education, University of Georgia.

Wang, H., & Wang, X. (2023). Breaking down silos in higher education: Strategies for effective collaboration. *Journal of Higher Education Policy and Management, 45*(2), 256–273.

Wang, L., & Li, W. (2024). The Impact of AI Usage on University Students' Willingness for Autonomous Learning. *Behavioral Sciences (Basel, Switzerland), 14*(10), 956. DOI: 10.3390/bs14100956 PMID: 39457827

Wei, J. (2019, July 3). *Generating Shoe Designs with Machine Learning*. Medium._https://towardsdatascience.com/generating-shoe-designs-with-deep-learning-5dde432a23b8

Welborn, A. (2023, March 9). *ChatGPT and fake citations*. Duke University Libraries Blogs. https://blogs.library.duke.edu/blog/2023/03/09/chatgpt-and-fake-citations/#:~:text=ChatGPT%20is%20based%20on%20a,or%20write%20your%20literature%20review

Wells, K. (2011). Social media in medical school education. *Surgery, 150*(1), 2–4. DOI: 10.1016/j.surg.2011.05.023 PMID: 21683853

Wenger, E. (1998). *Communities of practice: Learning, meaning, and identity.* Cambridge University Press. DOI: 10.1017/CBO9780511803932

Westberg, D., & Mickevičius, G. (2021). *Clearing the fog from the definition of Digital Literacy : A study investigating what it means to be digitally literate and if students at Jönköping University meet these requirements* (Dissertation). Retrieved from https://urn.kb.se/resolve?urn=urn:nbn:se:hj:diva-53252

Westerman, G., Calméjane, C., Bonnet, D., Ferraris, P., & McAfee, A. (2011). Digital Transformation: A roadmap for billion-dollar organizations. *MIT Center for digital business and capgemini consulting, 1*(1-68).

Westerman, G., Calméjane, C., Ferraris, P., & Bonnet, D. (2014). Digital transformation: A roadmap for billion-dollar organizations. *MIT Sloan Management Review, 55*(2), 36–44.

Wheeler, S. (2018). Innovative models for collaboration between universities and businesses. *TechTrends, 62*(5), 475–483.

White, A. (2009). The corporate university: Meeting the learning needs of a changing workforce. *Strategic HR Review, 8*(4), 11–16. DOI: 10.1108/14754390910963865

Wikipedia. (2024). National Programme on Technology Enhanced Learning (NPTEL). Retrieved from https://en.wikipedia.org/wiki/National_Programme_on_Technology_Enhanced_Learning

Williamson, B. and Hogan, A., (2021). Pandemic privatisation in higher education: Edtech and university reform.

Williams, T. (2024). Mentorship programs and faculty development: Enhancing the academic-industry interface. *Educational Leadership Journal*, *22*(1), 101–115.

Wilson, P., & Walsh, C. (2022). Collaborative models for integrating digital skills in education. *Journal of Education and Work*, *35*(3), 342–359.

Winfrey, A. L. (2022, September 2). *"someone had to be first": Pueblo artist criticized after Ai painting wins at Colorado State Fair*. Pueblo Chieftain. https://www.chieftain.com/story/news/2022/08/31/ai-painting-wins-at-colorado-state-fair-pueblo-artist-explains-jason-allen/65466872007/

Wong, C. (2019, May 27). *The Rise of AI Supermodels*. CDOTrends. https://www.cdotrends.com/story/14300/rise-ai-supermodels

Wong, L. P. (2024). Artificial Intelligence and Job Automation: Challenges for Secondary Students' Career Development and Life Planning. *Merits*, *4*(4), 370–399. DOI: 10.3390/merits4040027

World Bank. (2019) The Changing Nature of Work, https://www.worldbank.org/en/publication/wdr2019

World Bank. (2021). *Digital skills: The why, the what and the how*. The World Bank Group.

World Economic Forum (WEF). (2020). *The future of jobs report*.

World Economic Forum. (2020). The future of jobs report 2020. Retrieved from https://www.weforum.org/reports/the-future-of-jobs-report-2020

World Economic Forum. (2023). Future of Jobs 2023 Report. https://www.weforum.org/reports

World Economic Forum. (2025). The future of jobs report 2025. Retrieved from https://www.weforum.org/publications/the-future-of-jobs-report-2025/digest

WorldatWork. (2019). Cutting ties with traditional higher education. Retrieved from https://worldatwork.org/publications/evolve-magazine/cutting-ties-with-traditional-higher-education

Wu, A., Roemer, E. C., Kent, K. B., Ballard, D. W., & Goetzel, R. Z. (2021). Organizational Best Practices Supporting Mental Health in the Workplace. *Journal of Occupational and Environmental Medicine*, *63*(12), e925–e931. DOI: 10.1097/JOM.0000000000002407 PMID: 34840320

Xiong, Y., & Yu, J. (2024). Research on Strategies to Improve Digital Literacy of College Students to Enhance Employment Quality in the Intelligent Era. *Applied Mathematics and* Yadav, S., & Sharma, S. (2023). Digital Literacy Awareness among Research Scholars of Maharishi Dayanand University, Rohtak: A Study. *International Journal of Information Dissemination & Technology, 13*(2), 60–64. DOI: 10.5958/2249-5576.2023.00012.2

Xu, S. H., Santelli, F. A., Grissom, J. A., Bartanen, B., & Patrick, S. K. (2024). (Dis) connection at Work: Racial Isolation, Teachers' Job Experiences, and Teacher Turnover. *American Educational Research Journal, 61*(6), 00028312241278597. DOI: 10.3102/00028312241278597

Yang, S., & Kwok, D. (2017). A study of students' attitudes towards using ICT in a social constructivist environment. *Australasian Journal of Educational Technology, 33*(5), 50–62.

Yang, T.-C. (2023). Application of Artificial Intelligence techniques in analysis and assessment of digital competence in university courses. *Journal of Educational Technology & Society, 26*(1), 232–243. DOI: 10.30191/ETS.202301_26(1).0017

Yazıcıoğlu, A., Yaylak, E., & Genç, G. (2020). Okulöncesi ve Sınıf Öğretmen Adaylarının Dijital Okuryazarlık Düzeyleri. *Journal of Social Sciences Research / Sosyal Bilimler Araştırmaları Dergisi, 10*(2), 274–286.

Yeste, M. G., Pettersson, K., & Svensson, A. (2016). Integrating Reference Practices and Information Literacy in Academic Writing: A Collaboration Between Faculty and Library. *Nordic Journal of Information Literacy in Higher Education, 8*(1). Advance online publication. DOI: 10.15845/noril.v8i1.245

Yuan, L., & Powell, S. (2013). MOOCs and open education: Implications for higher education. JISC Centre for Educational Technology & Interoperability Standards. Retrieved from https://publications.cetis.org.uk/2013/667

Yuan, L., & Powell, S. (2013). MOOCs and Open Education: Implications for Higher Education. JISC. Retrieved from https://publications.cetis.org.uk/2013/667

Yuan, L., & Powell, S. (2013). *MOOCs and open education: Implications for higher education*. JISC CETIS.

Yuan, Y., & Ma, R. (2019). The role of integrated systems in improving university efficiency: A case study. *Journal of Higher Education Administration, 23*(1), 75–89.

Yuskovych-Zhukovska, V., Poplavska, T., Diachenko, O., Mishenina, T., Topolnyk, Y., & Gurevych, R. (2022). Application of Artificial Intelligence in Education. Problems and Opportunities for Sustainable Development. *BRAIN -. Broad Research in Artificial Intelligence and Neuroscience, 13*(1), 339–356. DOI: 10.18662/brain/13.1Sup1/322

Yu, Z., & Xu, W. (2022). A meta-analysis and systematic review of the effect of virtual reality technology on users' learning outcomes. *Computer Applications in Engineering Education, 30*(5), 1470–1484. DOI: 10.1002/cae.22532

Zahra, S., Sapienza, H. J., & Davidsson, P. (2006). H. J. & Davidsson, P., (2006). Entrepreneurship and dynamic capabilities: A review, model and research agenda. *Journal of Management Studies, 43*(4), 917–955. DOI: 10.1111/j.1467-6486.2006.00616.x

Zaitun, A. B., & Crump, B. (2005). Overcoming the Digital Divide – A Proposal on How Institutions of Higher Education Can Play a Role. *Malaysian Online Journal of Instructional Technology, 2*(1), 1–11.

Zancajo, A., Verger, A., & Bolea, P. (2022). Digitalization and beyond: The efects of Covid-19 on post-pandemic educational policy and delivery in Europe. *Policy and Society, 41*(1), 111–128. DOI: 10.1093/polsoc/puab016

Zhang, F. (2022). Design and Application of Artificial Intelligence Technology-Driven Education and Teaching System in Universities. *Computational and Mathematical Methods in Medicine, 2022*, 1–10. Advance online publication. DOI: 10.1155/2022/8503239 PMID: 36124170

Zhao, Y., Lei, J., Yan, B., Lai, C., & Tan, H. S. (2005). What makes the difference? A practical analysis of research on the effectiveness of distance education. *Teachers College Record, 107*(8), 1836–1884. . 1467- 9620. 2005. 00544.DOI: 10. 1111/j

Zhao, Y. (2019). The role of higher education in closing the digital literacy gap. *The Journal of Higher Education, 90*(3), 424–445.

Zhao, Y., & Bacco, M. (2022). Feedback and evaluation processes in university-industry partnerships. *Educational Evaluation and Policy Analysis, 44*(1), 134–153.

Zheng, L., Wang, X., & Gao, Y. (2020). Bridging the digital divide in higher education: A comprehensive review. *Journal of Educational Technology Research, 38*(4), 567–586.

Zhenyan, L. (2023). Keep Calm and Read Laterally! A Bite-sized Information Literacy Programme at Singapore Management University (SMU) Libraries. *Singapore Journal of Library & Information Management, 49*, 26–31.

Zhuang, T., & Shi, J. (2024). Engagement, determinants and challenges: A multinational systematic review of education-focused university-industry collaborations. *Educational Review*, *76*(5), 1363–1391. DOI: 10.1080/00131911.2022.2149701

Zhu, M., & Doo, M. Y. (2022). The relationship among motivation, self-monitoring, self-management, and learning strategies of MOOC learners. *Journal of Computing in Higher Education*, *34*(4), 713–732. DOI: 10.1007/s12528-021-09301-2 PMID: 34744400

Zickafoose, A., Ilesanmi, O., Diaz-Manrique, M., Adeyemi, A. E., Walumbe, B., Strong, R., Wingenbach, G., Rodriguez, M. T., & Dooley, K. (2024). Barriers and Challenges Affecting Quality Education (Sustainable Development Goal# 4) in Sub-Saharan Africa by 2030. *Sustainability (Basel)*, *16*(7), 2657. DOI: 10.3390/su16072657

Zulfiqar, M., Sony, M., Bhat, S., Antony, J., Salentijn, W., & McDermott, O. (2024). Unlocking the potential: Empirical analysis of enablers, barriers, benefits and technologies for integrating Industry 4.0 and Lean Six Sigma in manufacturing organisations. *The TQM Journal*, *36*(8), 2360–2382. DOI: 10.1108/TQM-05-2023-0130

About the Contributors

Amanda Nelms is an associate professor in the College of Education at Belmont University. She has worked with instructional leaders on national and international projects to provide equitable opportunities for multilingual learners. Dr. Nelms has published articles and book chapters related to effective practices for university online learning, UDL in the higher education setting, and collaboration between university and the community. She has also presented at both national and international conferences on topics related to technology integration in teacher preparation programs, differentiating instruction in blended learning environments, the impact of students' attitudes and beliefs on the college experience, and collaboration among community leaders and universities.

***

Vishal Jain is presently working as Professor at Department of Computer Science and Engineering, School of Engineering and Technology, Sharda University, Greater Noida, U. P. India. Before that, he has worked for several years as an Associate Professor at Bharati Vidyapeeth's Institute of Computer Applications and Management (BVICAM), New Delhi. He has more than 15 years of experience in the academics. He obtained Ph.D (CSE), M.Tech (CSE), MBA (HR), MCA, MCP and CCNA. He has authored more than 100 research papers in reputed conferences and journals, including Web of Science and Scopus. He has authored and edited more than 45 books with various reputed publishers, including Elsevier, Springer, IET, Apple Academic Press, CRC, Taylor and Francis Group, Scrivener, Wiley, Emerald, NOVA Science, IGI-Global and River Publishers. His research areas include information retrieval, semantic web, ontology engineering, data mining, ad hoc networks, and sensor networks. He received a Young Active Member Award for the year 2012–13 from the Computer Society of India, Best Faculty Award for the year 2017 and Best Researcher Award for the year 2019 from BVICAM, New Delhi.

Wyatt Jones is an undergraduate student currently studying Data Science at Belmont University.

Vinay Kambhampati is a Data Analytics graduate student at the Illinois Institute of Technology, Chicago, maintaining a 4.0 GPA. With machine learning and data engineering expertise, he has implemented real-time dashboards and data visualization systems as a Data Engineer at LTIMindtree. His projects include a Crop Yield Prediction System and LinkedIn Data Pipeline platform. Vinay holds a Bachelor's in Electronics and Communication from Chaitanya Bharathi Institute of Technology, where he integrated ML models with embedded systems. He is certified in Python for Data Analytics (IBM) and IoT and Robotics (BITS Pilani), with proficiency in multiple languages, including English, Spanish, Hindi, and Telugu.

Stiles Logan is an undergraduate student currently studying Music Business and Finance at Belmont University.

Archan Mitra is an Assistant Professor at School of Media Studies (SOMS) at Presidency University, Bangalore. He is the author of two book "Cases for Classroom Media and Entertainment Business" and "Multiverse and Media", he also has other several edited books to his credit. He has done his doctorate from Visva-Bharati Santiniketan, West Bengal in the field of "environmental informatics and communication for sustainability". In addition to that he is a certified Science Communicator and Journalism from Indian Science Communication Society (ISCOS), certified Corporate Trainer with Amity Institute of Training and Development, Certified Social Media Network Analyst. He has a strong interest in environmental communication. He was awarded certificate of merit by PRSI, Kolkata Chapter and Medal of Honor by Journalistic Club of Kolkata. He was working as a research assistant with the World Bank's "Environmental Capacity Building in Southeast Asia" project at IIM Kashipur. He was instrumental in launching the World Bank's Green MBA MOOC, he has also assisted in the research project on Uttarakhand disaster mitigation by ICSSR, the leading research on Uttarakhand disaster.

Menard Musendekwa, (PhD) is a distinguished scholar in Theology, specializing in the Old Testament, and a dedicated Minister of Religion. His academic journey spans across multiple disciplines, reflecting his versatile expertise in areas such as Church History, Theology, Gender Studies, Education, and Climate Change, among others. With a rich portfolio of publications in esteemed journals and numerous contributions to book chapters, he has made significant scholarly contributions that resonate across academic circles. Dr. Musendekwa's commitment to academic excellence is further demonstrated through his active engagement in various academic conferences, where he shares insights and collaborates with fellow scholars. Currently serving as the Chair of Theology at Reformed Church University in Zimbabwe and holding the position of Vice-Principal at Murray Theological College, he brings a wealth of experience to his roles. With a profound dedication to university education, Dr. Musendekwa continues to inspire and mentor the next generation of scholars, shaping the future of theological studies and beyond.

JD Ngo Ndjama is a Research Consultant with a strong academic portfolio, having authored over ten research articles in reputable, peer-reviewed journals, as well as contributing to various book chapters. Her scholarly contributions extend to national and international conferences, where she has presented her research findings, and she has also disseminated her work through conference proceedings. Dr. Ngo Ndjama earned her PhD in Business Administration in 2019 from the Vaal University of Technology (VUT), following a commendable academic trajectory that includes a Master's degree in Human Resource Management, which she completed with cum laude honours and received the Vice-Chancellor's award in 2015, also at the Vaal University of Technology. She holds a B. Tech in Human Resource Management in 2011 and an Honours degree in Business Law from the University of Yaoundé 2, awarded in 2008. Throughout her educational journey, she has been recognised with various distinctions, highlighting her commitment to excellence and her ability to excel in a competitive academic environment.

Rahul K. Patel is a seasoned Cyber Security professional with over 25 years of experience defending the Availability, Confidentiality, and Integrity of information assets in the high-tech, banking, and government organizations. Rahul Patel holds a PhD in Management of Information Systems from Northcentral University and many professional cybersecurity certifications.

Swapna Rose is an Assistant Professor in the MBA department at St. Aloysius University, a deemed-to-be university, with a passion for entrepreneurship education and leadership development. She actively mentors students in communication, research, and presentation skills while fostering entrepreneurial thinking. Her research interests include emotional intelligence, employee burnout, and Jesuit-inspired leadership, focusing on integrating values like Magis and Cura Personalis. She is also a PhD guide, exam coordinator, and a proponent of MOOCs and digital literacy in higher education.

Index

I

M

N

O

P

Q

R

S

T

U

W

www.ingramcontent.com/pod-product-compliance
Lightning Source LLC
LaVergne TN
LVHW080602300926
849162LV00005B/1024